Rebel Girl: The Fatherless Daughter

The names in this book have been changed to protect the identities of those written about.

Editor: Bryan Vyhmeister
Cover Design: Susanne Vyhmeister
Cover Hair: Alyssa Jones
Cover Makeup: Ashley Pierce
Cover Photo: Bryan Vyhmeister

ISBN: 0-9993031-1-2
ISBN-13: 978-0-9993031-1-5

http://www.rebelgirlbook.com

Rev 1.5

"And souls that have been degraded into instruments of Satan are still through the power of Christ transformed into messengers of righteousness, and sent forth by the Son of God to tell what 'great things the Lord hath done for thee, and hath had compassion on thee.'"

Desire of Ages 341

This book is dedicated to...

My husband, who loves me deeply in spite of my past and my character deficiencies. You saw and continue to see in me what Christ sees in me.

My children, who I pray will follow Jesus Christ all the days of their lives and know beyond a shadow of a doubt that of our own selves we can do nothing. Christ is our strength and in Him is our victory.

The survivors of trauma, sexual abuse, and sexual assault. Only Christ can give us the power we so desperately need.

Warning

Please be advised that this book may not be suitable for children and teenagers. My husband and I carefully examined the details contained within the chapters of this book to make certain they were not inappropriately graphic; however, they are still sexually explicit. There are many rape scenes described in this book. This book is for individuals who already have a knowledge of sex. We suggest that you may want to read this book first and use wisdom to decide whether your teenager should be reading it. The details that I have included in this book are there for a very specific purpose.

Table of Contents

1. Just Do It 15

2. The School Trip 30

3. Cooler Than I 56

4. Not Today, Kid 81

5. You Promised 96

6. A Loose Screw 112

7. The Shortcut 125

8. At The Beach 135

9. Apple in the Sun 151

10. Hand-in-Hand 169

11. White Trash 184

12. Don't Hit Me 201

13. My Friend Crystal 226

14. Armed to Kill 242

15. The Fence 257

16. Death Warrant 285

17. The Squeeze 297

18.	Rachel Weeping	314
19.	First Blood	326
20.	Tug-of-War	338
21.	"Blow!"	357
22.	Serial Killer	376
23.	Crossroads	394
24.	Crash	414
25.	T-R-O-U-B-L-E	430
26.	Fake	439
27.	Rag Doll	456
28.	Steps Back	469
29.	Crying Out	483
30.	My Desire	501
31.	Worst Case	516
32.	Touched	535
33.	Advocate	547
34.	Soul Suicide	575
35.	Forked Tongue	601
36.	Down to the Jacuzzi	611

Introduction

This is the first book of many. I have many more stories to share that are about the new life that I now lead and I will be writing about the journey to recover from all the trauma I have experienced. Today, I am married to my loving husband of ten years and I have five living children. Marriage has not always been easy, especially with my past, but I am blessed to have a husband like my husband. In fact, my husband edited this book. Not many husbands would be willing to re-live all the past indiscretions of their wife but my husband encouraged me to write this book. I could not have made the contents of this book public without his total support.

I have grown to be thankful for my illness that I mentioned often in this book. I was diagnosed with CVID (Common Variable Immune Deficiency) in 2008 after a lifetime of mysterious illness. Over the years, my illness has become worse and worse. In 2012, I sustained a spinal meningitis infection for which I was hospitalized. Due to several traumatic spinal taps, a hole was left in the dura around my spinal cord that did not heal. I leaked cerebral spinal fluid for a year. I had to spend all day, every day in bed that entire year. This allowed me to become a full time Bible student. Though I am weak in body, I am strong in the Spirit. "My strength is made perfect in weakness. Most gladly therefore will I rather glory in my infirmities, that the power of Christ may rest upon me." 2 Corinthians 12:9.

I spent that year studying the Word of God as if I were a seminary student. Once I developed a taste for the word of God as an all day, every day lifestyle, I never wanted to lose that kind of closeness with the Lord. My walk with God has only deepened since that time. I have had many battles with different sins and temptations. As I get closer to Christ, I see more of the defects in myself that need to change and character weaknesses that need to be strengthened. This is the work of sanctification. This book is in no way a statement of my perfection. It is just the opposite. It is a statement that anyone can get on the path to walk with their Redeemer, anyone. If I can become a full time Bible student then you can too! My favorite time of the day is my 5 AM wake up call to read God's word. The experiences I have had, though dark, have been turned into a blessing because I have had the privilege to counsel and encourage other survivors of sexual abuse and assault.

Why is this book important? I agonized as to whether it was a good idea to detail all my sins. I was finally convicted by the story of Solomon to go ahead and show that anyone can be changed by the power of God and testify to the terrible consequences of a life of sin. I have terrible scars on my heart and on my body to this day from my life in rebellion. It is not a light thing to turn from God toward a life of rebellion. "The true penitent does not put his past sins from his remembrance. He does not, as soon as he has obtained peace, grow unconcerned in regard to the mistakes he has made. He thinks of those who have been led into evil by his course, and tries in every possible way to lead them back into the true path. The clearer the light that he has entered into, the stronger is his desire to set the feet of others in the right way. He does not gloss over his wayward course, making his wrong a light thing, but lifts the danger signal, that others may take warning." *Prophets and King* 78.

Many people are battling the greatest battle, the battle against self, and believe that their sins and the things that have been done to them can never be overcome. These individuals are looking to their sin and circumstances instead of to their Savior. They believe that they have gone too far and are too dirty for God to save them and change them. My story proves otherwise. "If any man sin we have an advocate, Jesus Christ." 1 John 2:1.

Chapter 1

Just Do It

Her face is bright white. It is not so stark when she has her makeup off but no one must ever see her without makeup. Thus, she rises early to spend the majority of her morning applying pounds of synthetic, fleshy-colored material to a beautiful but aging face. When perceived perfection is at last achieved under a mountain of foundation, she is as white as snow. Her face is even whiter against her dark, almost black hair. She primps and plucks at her hair and spends hours getting her hair to perfectly flip in a 1950s style. Perhaps the 1950s were the last time she could remember being truly happy. A white face against such dark hair creates a bold contrast that appears shocking to the human eye. The eyes, her most striking yet dreadful feature to those that know her well, are filled with bitterness. Years of hurts retained and dwelt on for a time when she can return the favor are held behind those lenses. Her eyes change as quickly as her mood. At her job, she is cheerful and pleasing but she arrives home and spouts hate, anger, and misery along with plans to avenge her wounded spirit. She is as eccentric in her appearance as she is in her behavior but she is deceived into thinking that she appears young and happy.

Youth is her primary goal. If she were to discover the Fountain of Youth, she would drown herself to death in it.

Life to her is all about appearing young, successful, and happy. She talks of faith in a world beyond but her life, so full of anxiety over every little moment, proves that faith could not reside in her heart no more than a fish can reside on desert sand. But little attention is given to faith. Most of her attentions are drawn out toward her appearance and the appearance of others. Other women and girls are the bane of her existence. She hates them for being more beautiful than she. Oddly, she also hates them for being ugly too. Her mind is in constant flux and torture because she is constantly comparing herself, her face, her body, her clothes, and so on, to other women.

She cannot help but percolate green as her sharp penetrating stare undresses and critically analyzes other women around her. Her psyche is steamrolled by the day's onslaught of younger and more beautiful women whom she will never be and she can never look like. She is addicted to shopping like a gambler to the slots because, in her view, she is just one outfit away and one product shy of perfection. Perfection is elusive and youth is a dream to chase but she will run that race even if she has to knock down every female contender in the way. Her life is one big huge unhappy struggle against nature, time, and the Omnipotent.

She sleeps in silence. The slightest noise awakens a multitude of jarring anxieties and it will take her hours to fall back to sleep again. Her mind is always running with thoughts of what she should be doing and what others have done to her. Ever running and ever restless, she can never be left alone because the silence is a harassing wall of demonic noises that chase her through the dark. Voices, so many voices from the past, play in her head telling her that she is never enough. She is angry and the source of her anger is the ever-elusive dragon's tail many steps ahead of her grip. The anger is like a jigsaw puzzle that can never be solved. It erupts like a volcano.

She is angry at men. She hates them but she needs them. She is certain that men will always leave her. She feels frantic and panicked when men leave. "They must never leave me again," she tells herself. Because of this, she must never let her emotional volcano, years and years of stored hurts and slights built up and spewing radioactive darts and erupting tempestuous and sentimental trash and ash, touch the men in her life because, if they were exposed to her real self and her anger, they would surely leave her. Something so painful has happened to this woman but, of what, no one can know. She must keep everything a secret. She had to place her hatred for herself somewhere. She had to place her anger at men on someone. Then God gave her a daughter and I was born into her violent storm.

I began life with many things stacked against me. My father had passed away when my mother was around three months pregnant with me. After I was born, I would suffer with chronic infections that would plague me most of my young life until I was diagnosed with a rare immune disease. I would then require a plasmic ooze of strangers' blood, the vital life force, infused into my veins or my fat to gain the upper hand in my ongoing life-long fight against infection.

Fighting to feel marginally good would not be my only fight. I would fight for love. I had to fight to be loved for love never came easily to me. All I ever wanted was true love. Not the kind of sappy romance novel love but the kind of love that is loyal and kind. The kind of love that never leaves and never betrays. Why was this love so hard to find? As often as my heart was broken, as often as men and women would crush my spirit into tiny pieces, I would rise quickly from the ashes to search for someone else to fill that lonely, chaotic, wearing, and empty space in my heart so lacking in even basic love that I was left with no inkling as to what love really was. I was like the motherless ugly duckling going from person to person asking, "are you my mother?" How do you find love when you have never had love?

As a child, you are supposed to know that your family is a permanent fixture in your life and they have your back. No matter how dysfunctional family can be, they are your family and, thus, you will love them. I would not know this. How could I? When my father died, my mother remarried for a third time. Alec would first appear to be our saving grace, and he was for a time, but then his absence became the source of much pain.

At this point in time, my mother had already had numerous, no countless, fights with Alec. I knew every detail of when and why they fought. My mother told me everything. Alec never became loud but he did not have to. My mother was and is a professional and distinguished arguer. I once had a second-grade teacher with a Southern accent that would say in her southern drawl, "kids, it tayyykes two to tayyyyngo!" I remember thinking, "lady, you haven't met my mother because she can tayyyyngo all by herself." My mother could keep an argument going for days. She could make you question reality by repeating things over and over until you just plain gave up out of mental and emotional exhaustion which I learned later were characteristic of interrogation techniques and brainwashing. She had the ability to get Alec to admit to and apologize for things that never happened. Alec would do anything to avoid angering my mother, even to the point of kicking out his own sixteen-year-old daughter.

I will never forget that traumatic day when my sixteen-year-old stepsister was pushed from my once-safe childhood home for something trite and simple. My mother was so jealous of Amber, my stepsister. The two were like fire and water. My mother, the fire, and my stepsister, the innocent waters of girlhood trying to be loved like children desire. She was sassy and a rebellious teen at times but these were cries for love and attention.

I remember one particular time when Amber was just a little girl about twelve or thirteen and she was sitting on Alec's knee enjoying the blissfully sweet and innocent shared company of father and daughter when my mother walked into the room and the room instantly grew quiet and frigid. Immediately, my mother found the parental displays of affection as revolting and an affront to all that is good and beautiful in the world. She shot Alec the sort of look that makes all men tremble and, with great suspicion, she implied something grotesque and improper was occurring between father and daughter. Alec withered with embarrassment under the false implications and immediately pushed his daughter off his knee. Amber, with her great ability of discernment even as a child saw that she was slowly losing her father to the suspicion and jealousy of my mother and she began to fight for what was God-given to her, the love of her father.

My mother was terrified of being replaced or rejected for another woman or even a little girl like Amber or like me. In weakness, Alec often succumbed to my mother's great irrational fears that incest was just around the corner even when it was not. What happened to my mother? This would be the eternal question of my mind to try and flesh out the reasons why I grew up in a house filled with suspicion, distrust, jealousy, anger, hatred, and ultimately rejection.

I was adopted by my mother's new husband, Alec, when I was eighteen months old. Alec's Samoan family which was from New Zealand created this wonderful vision of what heaven might be like. This picture would beckon me from heaven's open door and I would find that I can't feel at home in this world anymore. My biological father was taken by death at the age of thirty-six but he was replaced by Alec's tightly knit family and, boy, did they understand community. I grew in my formative years with grandparents whose first language was Samoan. Anyone that spends any time around a Samoan community will understand that my family was one big party of food and song. They taught me everything I needed to know about being hospitable. Nana's and Pops' (Alec's parents') house had a drop-by-whenever-you-want, open door policy with food ever ready to be served and shared. Nothing was held back from anyone. It was an environment where whatever is mine is yours too. Family and friends were always loved and always welcome. Neighbors and church members always visited during the week without calling first and were never turned away. It was not unusual for Pops to pick up a ukulele or sit at the piano and have a spontaneous hymn singing session. A great portion of my life was spent trying to recreate this beautiful scene that disintegrated and faded away when Nana and Pops got old and died and when Alec and my mother started to break apart. I would desperately clamber to create a family that existed now only in my memory. Only in heaven will this family circle be restored to its former glory.

One fall afternoon when I was twelve years old, Hugh, my uncle, came over to the family home to "take pictures" of me. This uncle was the kind of uncle that I spent my childhood adoring. I would run up to him and fling myself into his arms. Once he just happened to mention that he liked

Beethoven's Für Elise. I then spent an entire year perfecting my performance of the musical piece to impress him. I brimmed with excitement at the thought of the pleased look on my uncle's face when I played the piano piece perfectly for him. He was very interested in the family's Scottish heritage and one day he brought over kilts for the entire family to dress up in and wear out to dinner. He was fun.

He was also a professional photographer and I overheard family gossip that he often photographed women in the nude for erotic magazines and he was coming to photograph me. Sitting next to the hole in my wall that allowed me to eavesdrop into my parents' bedroom, I could hear my mother wailing away with her typical dramatic flair like she was reenacting a scene from a drippy romance novel. "Alec, how could you let your brother kiss me like that with his hands all over me! He had his tongue in my mouth, kissing me with passion. Why didn't you do anything?" Alec would reply, "Oh stop it! My brother is harmless. He's like that with everyone." My uncle was like that with everyone as I was soon to find out...even me.

My mom had helped me do my hair and makeup for this photo session that my parents had set up. My mother wanted me to go into modeling and my uncle was going to shoot my head shots. So far, I was having fun. I was wearing this beautiful black Chinese-style cocktail dress. Usually my mother was moderately careful that I did not look too seductive but that dress would break all the rules and open the floodgates thereafter to wearing whatever I wanted. I appeared to be ten years older than I really was in that dress. The dress was a black satin Cheongsam with a mandarin collar and it had gold Chinese birds embroidered on the fabric. It had cup sleeves and was the shortest dress I had ever worn. The hem fell far too many inches above my knee. This dress stands out so dramatically in my mind because I remember it was the first time I really felt like Alec would never be my real father. The dress would mark an end of innocence and coming of age much too early.

Hugh arrived and started setting up his camera equipment. My mom and I emerged from my bedroom and proceeded into the living room where my uncle was waiting for me. Alec was also there talking to Hugh. When I walked out, Hugh looked very excited to see me. I was bashful. The whole idea of having everyone's attention on my appearance frightened me.

My mother had always valued my level of outgoing creativity accompanied by childhood excitement but, by the time I hit my pre-adolescent years, my creativity was being squashed by a deep desire for others' approval. My mother did not see how terrifically her daughter was struggling in this area and she sought to push me to be more outgoing than I felt I really could be or was capable of. She saw me as this goddess of a stage actress when I felt more like a little child craving her mother's protection.

My uncle had me sit on a piano bench. I was then

instructed to sit in a very sexy pose. At 12 years old, I was very uncomfortable but did what the adults told me to do. Both Alec and my mom noticed how embarrassed I was and they jeered, "if you want to be a model you better get used to this." "I didn't know models my age had to pose like this," I thought. My parents watched a lot of movies with the kids around which included sex scenes that were never censored. I would be home sick from grade school watching fully naked men running through the forest in one of my mom's favorite movies. My parents' favorite movie had a very graphic sex scene that they would let all of the kids watch with them. I knew all too well what sex looked like. Sitting on that piano bench I thought, "I look like sex right now." I felt dirty and humiliated to be looking like this in front of my favorite, well maybe not so favorite anymore, uncle.

I could see my uncle was really excited by the photo shoot. The perverse energy was palpable and my stomach was growing sicker by the moment. I kept telling myself that it was just a photo shoot and nothing more until I heard someone blurt out, "all the boys are going to want to [expletive] you in that dress," and then I heard, "if they don't want to [expletive] you then I will." At that moment when I heard those comments from the men in my family, who I had been told that God had sent to replace my terrible biological father, betrayed me and shattered my young heart into a million pieces. I felt like someone had punched me in the stomach and I realized that the men in the room, my family, were looking at me like I was not family at all.

I think, at that moment, my uncle, my mom, and Alec were involved in sexing me up so much that there was this mood in the room and they simply blurted out what they thought sounded clever. I heard agreement that I looked like a "sexy girl." I felt disgusting. But then came the words that struck horror in my heart. My uncle said, "now it's time for her to be photographed in her bathing suit." "Why in the world does a little girl need to be photographed in her bathing suit? Why did I need these kinds of photos? I had no idea that I would have to do this!" My mind raced at a confusing pace. "What was going on?"

My mom walked with me back to my room and pulled my bathing suit out of my drawer. I stood there looking at it. It was a one-piece bathing suit in a sexy 1950s style with a tiny light blue and white checkered pattern. It had tiny little spaghetti straps and the bust line was low and straight across. I stared at it some more as my mother tried to hand it to me. I said, "no," and backed away from the swimsuit. My mother could tell I was disturbed and I could tell she was too. I knew in my heart that the comments from a few minutes ago would make her jealous. I felt like even she was looking at me differently now as if I were a woman to be jealous of instead of a scared little girl, her little girl. I wanted so badly for her to be my mother in that moment. I wanted her to say, "No more! No more pictures!" I wanted my mother to see how brokenhearted I was to hear my family state out loud that they did not really see me like a daughter. I wanted her to see that I was so hurt that my favorite uncle would treat me like a piece of meat. I was slowly realizing that life itself turns on this thing called sex. Sex had power. It had power to make men turn against their daughters. Sex had power to turn mothers against their daughters too. I was learning that when men looked at me all they saw was a big S-E- and an X.

"Please mom? I don't want to wear my bathing suit." I was begging my mom not to make me go back out there. I was so ashamed of my body. I did not want my uncle to cast his lusty gaze at me for another moment. I could feel a huge lump in my throat as my eyes started to moisten. I did not want my uncle or Alec to know that I had been crying. I tried to hold back my tears but I could not. I felt like my childhood home had been a huge lie. Why was my uncle so excited by all this? I did not understand what was going on at all. I only knew that it made me feel like I did not belong in this family nor did I want to at this point. I wanted to run away from these people.

Mothers teach their daughters the power to say, "no," and they can also take that power from their daughters by not showing them how to stand against wrong. Just by saying, "no," themselves, mothers can teach their daughters how to say, "no," too. Children cannot stand for themselves. They depend on their parents to stand for them. The world is filled with hurting men and women who struggle to stand for right and for themselves because they simply do not know what it looks like or how it is done.

"I really don't want to do this," I said again to my mother. I looked into her face searching for some sympathy but none was there. I had a difficult time wearing my bathing suit in front of my female friends let alone for pictures and in front of my uncle too. I had all these emotions that I wanted her to explain to me. Her face was numb and hard like she had been here before. I could hear my uncle and Alec moving outside to the front yard to set up the camera equipment out in front of the house. My mom started helping me unzip my dress. I felt like Adam and Eve naked for the first time in the garden of Eden in their shame. My mother examined my body with her eyes in a new way. I could see that she was wondering what about me would make anyone say what was said as if it were my fault. For the first time in my life I felt uncomfortable naked in front of my own mother. I longed to cover myself but I was exposed. My mother's upper lip grew narrow in a sneer. My mother was sneering at me. I could not grasp all of the dynamics that were taking place in that whirlwind of a moment.

From that time on my mother would insist that we share a dressing room together at stores whenever we shopped together. Any opportunity my mother had to see my naked body she would capitalize on and it made me feel as small as the smallest creature because I could never understand my mother's focus on and competition with my body, the body that had grown in her womb. My mother's cunningly cold, assessing gaze of my nakedness would forever bring me back to these moments for the rest of my life. In this moment, I was begging my mother to stand for me but, instead, she thrust the bathing suit into my hand and said with half indifference and half disgust at the sexual excitement of my uncle, "Just do it. Just get it over with."

I stood outside in my bathing suit being forced to pose this way and that against the arches in front of our family home. I felt betrayed and defeated as I was told to put my chin down and lean against the arch. In this moment, I learned a lesson that would guide the rest of my young adult life and would be the cause of countless sexual encounters that I did not want. "Just do it. Just get it over with." I would hear my mother's voice telling me this. I learned that I did not have the power to say, "no." I learned that all men want one thing and they will hurt you to get it. I was starting to understand why my mother hated men so much and I was starting to hate them too.

The pictures resulting from this photo shoot could definitely be viewed as very inappropriate if not child pornography but I stood there with my mother's betraying words echoing inside my head. "Just do it. Just get it over with." My mother stood back with her arms folded in a pout behind my uncle as I was forced to pose uncomfortably in my bathing suit. She looked at me with a hard gaze in her eyes like she was in another world and on another planet. "Where was she?" I screamed in my spirit. "Where is my mother and why won't she help me?" As the camera's shutter snapped and snapped, I felt like the sacrificial lamb being offered on the altar of my mother's inability to admit she had a problem.

Chapter 2

The School Trip

As I left girlhood and entered my teenage years, I constantly had this craving to be noticed by men. This would be my greatest addiction. Beyond cocaine, better than ecstasy, more powerful than any earthly power were the first days and weeks of new love. New love meant that I had won and I had succeeded. I felt empowered to do anything in those early days of love. But it was not really love. It was a feeding frenzy, a binge, of my starving insecurity. If I, with my fat face, rubbish teeth, flat chest, and dull brain, could get this boy to look at me, to like me, even more to act on it then, just for a few moments, for a few days, I felt like I was not so hideous. The relentless insecurities would abate and I would feel high on endorphins from this new thing in my life. As soon as those endorphins, those precious bodily chemicals, drifted away like a low tide into the recesses of my brain, I realized I was starving again for the same experience like a vampire craving new blood.

"I am sick," I told myself. I felt sick. I felt like a slut. I was ashamed that I craved this attention. I could not even sit as a passenger in the car without fixing my thick blonde hair perfectly around my face and willing every man that passed by to look at me and be attracted. It was like a game to me. If they looked and did a double take, I won. If they ignored me or, worse, looked and did not care, it was true that I was the ugliest person in the world. My obsession with appearance was well beyond adolescent insecurity. I thought for sure it was my fault that I constantly felt like I was not only the ugliest person in the room but the worst person in the room in regard to my thoughts. I was surprised when anyone liked me. Looking back, I see everything that built me into craving love like a dope fiend. So many things made me that way.

I am not quite sure if it was guilt or neglect that gave my mother the idea that she could let a thirteen-year-old do whatever they wanted or get whatever they asked for. A toddler will often cry for another delicious cookie until the delicious cookies make them vomit. It is a parent's job to say, "no," and do whatever it takes to protect their child from harmful things and even from themselves.

My mother would often say that I hit thirteen and, suddenly, I was totally out of her control and, therefore, she gave up trying to be a parent. But rebellion in child development does not work like that. There is a progression with rebellion. Sin is like yeast, it steadily grows. There are always red flags and warning signs that a child is hurting and struggling before they dive into the deep end. It is a parent's job to pay attention, to know their child well enough, to see when their child needs help. My mother would say that she did try to help me but dropping your child at the feet of the altar of therapy and walking away is not true help, especially when my parents were very much the source of my hurts and pain. It is almost as if every psychiatrist and counselor my mother took me to see was to make herself feel better instead of I. As soon as the counselor mentioned that my mother might share in some of the responsibility of my troubles, we no longer went to see that counselor.

When a child is drifting away from their parent, the parent must do whatever it takes to win their child's heart back to them. Sometimes that requires parents to ask forgiveness for hypocrisy, broken promises, whatever hurts, or other pain they may have caused their child. Sometimes that means spending extra time doing what that child enjoys. Sometimes parents need to spend time listening to their child and asking questions. To my mother, I was a sharp reminder of her failures. It was easier for her if I were out of her hair. My mother realized that I caused her stress and, therefore, if I were gone, she was no longer stressed. Even though my mother would like to say that I turned thirteen and a switch went off in me like an exploding bomb spraying a parasitic rebellion to infest my host of a body, that is not how it happened. It was a slow progression. For her, though, it is much easier to just blame a thirteen-year-old girl with no life experience than to take responsibility for not being a parent.

By the time I was thirteen, I was already experiencing quite a bit of my illness. I was exhausted. I felt older than I was. I went in and out of homeschool. My brother was getting ready to start his senior year and he started taking trips to check out colleges. One particular trip was to Walla Walla

---

College in Washington state. I had a family friend my age up there and I asked my mom if I could go with my brother to visit Walla Walla. I am not quite sure what my mother was thinking. I was a thirteen-year-old girl attending a long trip by plane and bus with little to no supervision with a bunch of older high school kids from a few different schools. Because I asked for it, I got it. Remember the toddler with the cookie? I can hear my mother's voice saying, "if I didn't give you what you wanted then you would threaten to kill yourself!" It's true. When I was about fifteen, I started telling my mom that if she did not get me cigarettes or alcohol I was going to kill myself.

There are two very important points in that sentence. One, I was a fifteen-year-old foolish kid and, two, I was smoking! If my teenage kid did that to me today, I can promise you that he would be too terrified to try to manipulate me like that. I would put them on a home suicide watch and not let them out of my sight. Children are quickly taught what they can get away with. It is not acceptable for a parent to ever give in and give up and just start being a part of the problem. No matter what age a child is, they are worth fighting for no matter what they threaten to do. As a parent, I live by the phrase, "How would Christ handle my child in this situation?" It is not easy but my children are worth the stress and all the effort.

I did not have to threaten or manipulate my mother to go on this trip to Walla Walla. My mother just arranged it thinking that I would be out of her way and my older brother, with all of his friends, would just watch me. What seventeen-year-old boy wants to watch his younger sister with all of his friends around? I was a young thirteen-year-old girl all by myself with a bunch of older kids from three different private schools and I was traveling with little to no supervision. What could possibly go wrong?

At thirteen I was very emotionally intelligent for my age. Because of my mother's mood swings and propensity toward enduring periods of unexplained anger, I had to learn to survive. A shadow would fall over her face. When I was little I would ask constantly and obsessively, "Mommy, are you mad at me?" I always thought that the anger and mood swings my mother had were all my fault and that I had done something to make her so angry. As I grew older, I learned not to ask questions but only to try and dodge the nasty bullets that were mostly aimed at Alec but, now that I was older and more beautiful, I was slowly and gradually becoming more of a target. In later years, I would be the sole target for my mother's hate.

By that time, I had acquired quite a set of coping skills. I could walk into a room and acutely sense the tension between the people who did not get along or read the body language of attraction between the two people who like each other but cannot seem to say so. I could read envy in women's eyes as they looked at each other. In fact, it was truly awful at times to be in a room filled with people as they betrayed themselves with all their dynamics and emotional garbage that I was picking up. I would frequently come home from school, church, and other functions utterly and totally emotionally exhausted from just watching other people relate to one another. My mother could not understand why I had to run to a retreat of complete and total aloneness for a time after being around people.

Sometimes I wished to be like other people who could not feel everything everyone else was feeling. To walk through a room of people and pick up absolutely nothing from them would be a blessing to me. Instead, I picked up every micro expression, body language, every social lie, every malicious lie, every look, and I could feel everything. This ability served me well at home because I could read my mother's face like a book and it helped protect me from her wrath but, out in the world, I became very emotionally over-stimulated. I think this is very common for people who have experienced abuse. It is out of pure survival that you learn very quickly how to read the face and the body of your parental unit.

I write all about my deep ability to feel because it is a vicious cycle. We wonder why people who are abused continue to find abusive relationships and keep experiencing abuse like they have a target on their back. I have had people ask me, how can one person (me) experience so much rape and abuse? One reason for this is because people that are abused have had their eyes opened to evil, like they have plucked, not of their own choice, the fruit from the tree of the Knowledge of Good and Evil. I have spent hundreds of hours watching interviews with pedophiles and pedophiles will state over and over that they could "just see in the eyes of that girl that she had been abused before." A girl of thirteen is not physically prepared or emotionally ready to experience the deep emotions of sex any more than a boy is ready to have and financially provide for their family as a child. It is just not supposed to work like that.

My first real sexual interaction was on that trip to Walla Walla. His name was Andre and he was eighteen. He knew that I was much younger and he knew that he could take advantage of our five-year age difference. It was evident that no one was watching me and I was on my own.

Our eyes locked immediately at the airport. He saw me and I saw him merely in passing but that was enough. We could tell in each other that we longed for the same thing or so it seemed. He was broken too but in a different way than I was. We were attracted to each other's rebellion. Like seeks like. As a young girl, his tall frame and dark hair were much like the romance novels and movies I had filled my head and heart with. He was at least six feet and I was a small petite five foot two inches. He was Colombian and very handsome for his age. I looked at him bashfully, innocently, even though I very well knew that I was sending him the looks that would alert even the most stupid and dull male that I was interested in something more than playful looks. Oh, how I desired to taste real love but did not even know what that was. I thought I was toying with love and taking the necessary steps to get love but I was only toying with the dangerous fires of lust. I was like the gazelle on the African plains unaware that a lion is stalking in the distance.

Andre joked and laughed with his much older friends as I was standing near the boarding entrance with my mother and brother. This was prior to September 11th when people without a boarding pass could stand in the boarding area. My mother did not notice that suddenly her daughter was casting knowing stares at a young man in the distance and that these looks were received and returned.

My mother was an embarrassment as she stood next to me, totally preoccupied by her own drama. She was upset that a friend of hers, whose husband had had an affair on, was supposedly snubbing my mother and only talking with the wives of other doctors and dentists. My mother was enraged that this dentist's wife who had stood in our kitchen crying her heart out and vowing revenge on her cheating husband would suddenly pay her so little attention. My mother's histrionic personality had misread the situation completely. As a thirteen-year-old girl, knowing what side my bread was buttered on, I had no choice but to indulge my mother's fantasy life. "She thinks she's so great just because she's a dentist's wife and I'm not!" said my mother ever fixated on wealth and status and the fact that she had none of those things. My mother was completely determined to elevate herself by bringing others down.

One example of this was when my mother started getting into a vegan lifestyle in the 1990s through our local church. There was a group of women at this church that were "educated" as my mother called them like she was calling them a dirty word and these "educated" women were the bane of my mother's existence. Every Sabbath, after we came home from church, my mom and Alec would engage in a verbal dinner where they would eat these women and their families alive metaphorically by picking their every action and word apart with biting criticism. My mother hated any woman who had not decided to "stay home with their kids" and instead decided to work and go to school. My mother was not only threatened by and jealous of any woman with a degree but she wanted to take them down a peg or two.

One Sabbath one of these women brought doughnuts to Sabbath school for the youth department. This simply did not jive with my mother's newly found vegan diet. My mother pretended to be filled with righteous indignation as she strode up and down the church sidewalks, rallying the other women to action. She clucked and cawed until she had a small little band of a faithful few to help her fight her mighty and just cause against the evils of doughnuts at church. She took this very grave and serious issue, in her mind at least, to the church board. Every church member heard about how awful this "educated" woman was for bringing doughnuts to church and my mother triumphed in her ability to humiliate this "educated" woman.

I was not going to let another "doughnut war" break out in the airport especially within earshot of my new love obsession. My mother was still chattering away when my older brother, feeling the turbulent winds of my mother's wrath, decided to walk away and leave me to soothe my mother's theatrical and over emotional performance as would be his custom for most of my teenage years. He was humiliated by her too and who could blame him? We were about to board a plane for a trip and my mother was absolutely consumed by the fact that this dentist's wife was not devoting her undying attentions to my mother. I was so frustrated because my mother's perceptions were so warped. I had, upon arrival, seen the dentist's wife wave to my mother and offer a very pleasant hello as she then moved on to talk over some trip details with the other ladies who were not all doctor's and dentist's wives. Any normal person would not have been offended but I was not dealing with a normal person. My mother would stand there and watch the dentist's wife talk with her friends for as long as she could. My mother, forever the voyeur.

"They all think they are so much better," I heard my mother's voice say but I was daydreaming again as I gazed off in the distance to offer Andre another look of longing to keep his interest piqued. I came back to reality and offered my mother a verbal token of peace, "I'm sure she didn't mean it like that, mom." My mother snapped back, "What do you mean she didn't mean it like that? Didn't you see her walk right past me as if I were two feet tall?" "An exaggeration," I thought. I see my mother's upper lip thin out into a sneer. "You didn't see her look over here at me and give me that look?" "Oh no! Now she is aiming her anger at me," I thought again. Her face starts to turn red and a vein on her forehead starts to bulge. "Whose side are you on young lady?"

There it was. Now I'm the enemy. Quick! Disengage! Abort! Abort! Fire up the thrusters and divert this line of conversation before she says you cannot go on the trip and you forever lose the chance to be with Mr. Tall, Dark, and Handsome over there with his friends. So I said, "Yes mom, I totally saw her look at you like that. She's acting like she is so much better than you. Who does she think she is anyway?" My mother's angered face started to relax. Her lip returned to its former shape and her forehead vein retreated. I breathed an inner sigh of relief as I knew that I had just dodged losing the trip and spending the rest of the week being my mother's therapist as my mother endlessly analyzed and discussed this "great snubbing."

My mother continued staring at the group of women. I was dreading the possibility that my mother would start talking about the dentist's wife again when I was suddenly saved by the bell. Our flight was boarding. What a relief. My mother mustered up a false smile but her tone conveyed only annoyance as she tried to focus on me but I could tell that she was still staring at the women out of the corner of her eye. She tried to be motherly by peppering me with an onslaught of questions she already knew the answer to. I gave her a hug and said my goodbyes before boarding the plane. As I turned my back and started walking to embark on my first real trip without my mother, I felt happier with each step away from her. "Was this what it was like to be free of her?" I wondered. I felt so full of possibilities. I put my carryon in the overhead bin and settled into my chair by the window seat. I always had a CD player and headphones with me to use especially when my mother became too much to handle. I turned on some *Nirvana*. The sound of Kurt Cobain screaming balefully into my ears made me want to run up and down the aisles of the plane playing the air guitar. Suddenly, I felt a tap on my forearm. "Who is disturbing my worship at the altar of grunge music?" I thought to myself. I turned to see that a tall, dark, and handsome Colombian had seated himself right next to me.

I was embarrassed that I could not control my emotions. I was panicking, thrilled, excited, and nervous all at the same time. My heart was racing like I had just strapped on a parachute, opened the emergency exit of the plane, and jumped out! I felt my face turning red which made me feel even more humiliated by my lack of control over mind and body. I was not able to eke out the words I wanted to say. It was like being in one of those dreams where you are being chased by an axe murderer but you cannot scream for help. I looked bashfully up into Andre's dark brown eyes for a fraction of a second and then looked away again, terrified of eye contact. All my flirty braggadocio and boldness that I touted in the airport had melted away into anxiety now that Andre and I were face to face and I was expected to hold a conversation. Typical little girl as I was, I could not stand the heat and very much needed to exit the kitchen. I had learned from movies and books how to appear like a grown woman but I was far too young to actually act like one.

Andre let out a breathy snicker at my discomfort. He brushed his hand through his shaggy but luxurious shiny black hair. He had perfectly smooth dark skin and was much more handsome up close. I felt like a hunter that had tracked and killed a lion. I was victorious! "A young man of this caliber is interested in me?" I thought with deep satisfaction. I was too innocent to realize that I had just spent almost an hour giving this young man the kind of sexy and "come and get me looks" that say I am up for more than just conversation which I was carefully mimicking from the movies I had been allowed to watch. Of course he wanted to sit next to me. He thought I would be willing to engage in sexual activity but I actually believed in my heart that he might want a relationship with me. Oh how foolish I was.

A couple of the female senior high school students threw knowing glances at each other throughout the airplane as Andre laughed and flirted with me, a very young seventh grader. He made me feel more at ease as he spoke to me but I could still feel my jaw clenching and my shoulders up around my ears with anxiety. He slouched down in his chair so that he would be eye to eye with me instead of towering over me. The further he slouched in his chair the less leg room for his long muscular legs. "Truly, he was more of a grown man than a boy," I theorized in my thoughts. He appeared relaxed and I was trying so hard to match him but I was so anxious that I would say something stupid and forever regret it. Andre was sarcastic and had a sense of humor like he had seen way too many *Friends* episodes. I laughed at his jokes even though I was hardly listening to a word that was coming out of his mouth. I was trying hard not to look too nervous and his conversation was not too difficult to track.

"He is not that intelligent," I decided, but what he lacked in brains he well made up for with his tragically good looks. Every time I worked up the nerve to make eye contact with Andre, I imagined myself swooning like the girls in the romance novels. We were an hour into the flight and I was starting to be more at ease around him. I was able to ask intelligent questions and feign total and complete interest in him which I cleverly strategized would keep him talking about himself so I would not have to come up with too much conversation on my own. I was downright scared when the conversation started to lull into awkward silence. The silence made me very uncomfortable so I would ask him another question about himself and that started him chatting non-stop again about something else. I was so thankful he liked to talk because there would be no way I could talk as carelessly as he did.

Again, the conversation died out and I felt self-conscious as Andre just sat staring at me. I turned to look at the view outside my window. The puffy white clouds had parted to reveal the beautiful tree-covered forests of Northern California. I was admiring the epic scenery when I felt a hand on my leg. By this point, Andre and I had made physical contact by sheer clumsy chance of our knees knocking together and shoulder brushing against shoulder but this hand that first landed closer to my knee was now purposefully sliding up my thigh. I felt my heart racing again and my face turning red. I did not know what to do. I did not want anyone else in the plane to see what was going on. That would be humiliating. I was shocked at the speedy pace by which Andre was operating. "Did relationships really move this fast? We just met! No hand holding or hugging? Just straight to his hand on my thigh?"

This was my first touch from a young man and I was agitated by this new experience. I did not have any reference point to know if this was good or bad. I froze. I thought that I could pretend that I was not noticing that there was a hand making its way up my leg. Out of desperate panic, I continued to stare blankly out the window like I was oblivious to Andre's touch, like if I pretended he did not exist then maybe he would go away. I was very confused at how I could get out of this tricky situation without losing Andre's interest. I wanted to say, "no," and slap his hand away but I felt this terrible pressure to, "Just do it. Just get it over with." And, I felt this awful and curious feeling of shame at the thought that if I did, in fact, say, "no," and slap his hand away, that I might hurt his feelings. I knew he was a total stranger, a guy I had just met, but I felt like it would be my fault if he were offended if I said, "no." I wondered at my own emotions of shame as I cared more for his hurt feelings than my own. What I did know from experience was that, when men looked at me, they saw S-E-X. "This is all my fault," I internalized. "I bring this out in men."

Suddenly, I felt a warm breath on the side of my neck, whispering gales of warm gusts into my ear, and it gave me chills. He was whispering into my ear. So many sensations at once! His hand was gripping my thigh and he leaned in to kiss my neck. I was so focused on the physical feelings that it did not immediately register as to what he had said. When I overcame the initial shock of Andre's boldness, I understood what he had just said to me. "Wanna join the mile high club?" I did not know what that was. Out of curiosity, I quickly turned my head to meet his up close and personal gaze. His body was leaning against my shoulder. He was so close that I half expected him to kiss me at any moment.

"What's the mile high club?" I asked while scrunching up my nose at the weird phrase I had just heard. Andre replied with a wild suggestive look in his eyes, "it's having sex on an airplane!" "What if someone sees us?" I said quickly trying to hide my shock and disgust. "Well, I would get up like I was going to the bathroom and use the bathroom in the back and then you get up after me and meet me in the bathroom."

Unbelievable. My stomach was in knots. How would we pull this off without getting caught? I could just visualize a teacher or a flight attendant pulling Andre and I out of the bathroom in front of everyone. I was so embarrassed at the horrific thought of being discovered in such a state. I could not think straight. This was happening way too fast.

"C'mon! No one will catch us. I promise. And, if they do, I'll take the blame for both of us. Pleeeease?" He gave me puppy dog eyes and interlaced his fingers through my fingers. He was holding my hand. I could have been happy for a lifetime with just holding his hand. My heart swelled within my chest as I looked down at my small hand completely wrapped in his large hand. I was defenseless. I could not say, "no," to him. I seemed unable to say, "no," to any male.

Andre read the undecidedness on my face. He took my not-a-yes for not-a-no either and responded, "All right. Wait three minutes then go to the bathroom in the back on the left. I'll leave it unlocked." With those words, he jumped up and was gone down the aisle toward the back of the plane. "Oh my goodness! This was happening! How could this be happening so fast? He's gone. He's going to be waiting for me back there."

I felt like I was going to throw up. The seconds ticked

by so slowly that I could mentally focus on the spaces between the seconds. My face felt like it had completely drained of its color. Three minutes came and went. The pressure was agonizing. "What if I did not meet him back there and he came back to his seat and was angry at me?"

I worked up some bravery and stood up, wrapping my arms around my torso as I was feeling like I was going to vomit. I must have looked airsick to the rest of the passengers. I started stepping my way down the aisle toward the back like I was walking the plank. I felt like I was walking toward my execution. "Did I really want to lose my virginity like this?" I pondered. I felt like I was in a dream. Just a few hours ago my worries seemed so trivial. I felt heavy with fear and anxiety. I looked at all the faces of the other passengers in their seats and I felt like every single one of them knew my thoughts. I felt naked.

I knew that once I was near the back of the plane I would have to jump in the bathroom fast so no one would see that it was really occupied. My main concern was being caught. The moment of truth came as my hand gripped the bathroom door handle. I opened the door and slipped inside while locking the door behind me.

I stood in the bathroom like a child bride trembling on her wedding night. Only I was crowded into a smelly airplane bathroom. The blue water sloshed back and forth as a little bit of turbulence shook the plane. Andre and I were smashed together by the limited space.

He grabbed me and started kissing me, no slobbering on me, with his tongue out like he was going to eat me. His hands migrated all over my body like he was a grubby little boy furiously unwrapping his Christmas gift only I was not his and he had no right trying to take what would one day be another man's gift. I was left in great disappointment. "Was this sex?" I wondered. He was all over me with fury trying to remove my clothes but the space was limited. It was gross and sloppy. He tried all sorts of ways to make sex happen but it was just not happening.

He could not accomplish his goal in that tiny little space and I surely did not know what to do either. He had sucked all the makeup off my face in one foul swoop of kisses that seemed more like he was slurping soup. I was really disturbed. I was consumed by the thought that our bathroom escapades were responsible for shaking the entire plane and everyone outside was wondering who was in the bathroom. I just knew that the moment we stepped outside we would be met with great humiliation. Would I be sent home?

He seemed to be tiring himself out and this gave me the courage to whisper, "maybe we should get back before we're noticed." He stopped and looked displeased with the whole situation and I felt responsible for his displeasure like I had ripped a piece of candy from a baby. "Maybe we can try again later on the trip," I said, offering up a peace offering like I had utterly failed him in some way. "Yeah," he sighed.

We made our exit plan. I would step out first. I was

petrified. All it would take to get caught is for just one person to be outside waiting for the bathroom. I just knew that an entire punishing army of high schoolers was awaiting me outside this door to execute my dignity, though I felt my dignity had already been robbed of me by the slobber king. I was now more scared to go outside the semi-safe bubble of the bathroom than I had been scared to come into it but, the longer I lingered, the more the chance of being discovered.

I opened the door just enough to slip out of the bathroom. I slowly raised my eyes to see how bad the situation was. As I peered around the plane, to my shock I observed nothing but the back of people's heads. It was peaceful. No one had noticed the two missing students that were not in their seats. No one had heard us in the bathroom. I could not believe it. I hung my head as I quickly shuffled back to my chair. I slipped into my seat, buckled my seatbelt, and grabbed my makeup bag out of my purse. I had to assess the damage that Andre had caused. I felt a sense of shame slowly creeping up on me. I was embarrassed to see him again. I was dreading him returning to his seat. What would we say to each other now? I had never felt more like a little girl. I just wanted to go home now. I felt sick to my stomach and now the mother that I was annoyed with earlier, I wanted very badly. I felt alone and I felt sad.

The rest of the plane ride was an awkward interchange of bursts of conversation followed by inevitable silence. He was not as charming or funny when he was not trying to get something from me, I keenly observed. I felt like I had done something wrong. It was strange that, although I could hardly say I enjoyed our little tryst in the bathroom, now my embarrassment and shame were leading me to a stronger desire for Andre's approval. Just being physical for a few moments had created a bond between us. I did not like the feeling that he was slowly rejecting me with every passing minute we spent together. I wanted to win him back and make him like me. I wanted the feelings I had before we went to the bathroom and attempted to pluck the forbidden fruit.

The plane landed in Oregon and we boarded buses bound for Washington. Andre disappeared into the crowd. I was crushed but not completely surprised. I reached for my headphones as I melted back into the comforting familiarity of heavy metal notes screaming into my ears. My visions of Andre dutifully attending to me the entirety of the trip had died. I felt used for a moment until I pushed my feelings away. I did not want to feel like that. I was not going to feel like that. "I will not be one of those girls who follows a guy around like a little lost puppy," I thought to myself with pride ignoring the fact that I had just allowed a complete stranger, five years my senior, to feel me up in an airplane bathroom. I was longing for a deep connection with something or someone but I did not know how to get it.

On the bus, I could hear Andre joking with a group of girls. Very cautiously, I tried to appear casual as I craned my neck so I could get a good look at what he was doing back there. I hated not being able to control my emotions. I wanted so badly to just be numb all the time and not feel a thing. Instead, I felt strong waves of envy and jealousy. Exodus 20 defines envy as wanting what someone else has and jealousy is the fear of being replaced and I was consumed by both. I wanted Andre's attention on me instead of on the other older girls. I was afraid that Andre had used me up and was on to the next girl. My chest literally ached like my heart was going to explode. "How is it possible to feel this much for someone you just met?" I felt hollow like he had too much power over me, the power to hurt me. By not saying, "no," I had given Andre the very real power to hurt me.

We had stopped at Multnomah Falls and Andre ran ahead with his friends. I walked up to the falls by myself with my precious headphones while feeling extra lonely. After that we were bussed all the way to Walla Walla. When we arrived in Walla Walla, I parted with the high school group to go stay at a friend of the family's house that I had grown up with and Andre was staying in the dorm with the rest of the high schoolers. My brother and I had not spoken one word to each other since we left the airport. I stood in the dark and empty parking lot next to the bus waiting for my ride watching my brother go with his friends into the darkness toward the dormitory buildings. There were too many black shadows in the night to tell where Andre was. I was depressed and my chest felt heavy as it started to sink into my heart that I may never see Andre again when a figure came racing out of the gloom. It was Andre!

He came running toward me with his hand outstretched, holding a ragged piece of paper. He shoved it into my hand and said, "you can get a hold of me here. Call me and I'll tell you where we can meet."

I was ecstatic! I was thrilled not so much that I would have to endure the slobber king's attentions again but more because he had not rejected me. Now the ball was in my court right where I liked it. I felt on top of the world. My ride arrived and I was extra happy to see my childhood friend and her mother but they would not know why. I had a secret that I knew my friend could not understand. I felt older and more experienced now. As I sat in the car heading toward my friend's house, I dreamed little girl dreams of Andre and I being married and living together happily ever after. If I had carried a notebook with me, I would have written his name and mine together a thousand times in a thousand ways. I could barely talk to my friend and her mother as I daydreamed of the future. Little did I know that I was not storing up love for a future marriage but playing a dangerous game of the heart, the kind of game where little girls like me get very, very hurt and change the course of their life. In my head, my thinking and my experience told me that the only way to get male attention was by playing the sex game. I did not know any other way. I had been taught to play and play I would. If only I had told my friend's mother what had happened to me on the plane, how uncomfortable it made me feel, how embarrassed I was, how empty I felt afterwards. Even after feeling all those negative emotions, I felt I needed Andre's affection in some strange instant kind of Stockholm syndrome. My friend's mother would have likely reported what had happened being that Andre was an eighteen-year-old young man and I was a thirteen-year-old girl like her own daughter was.

I managed to call Andre and find out where he would be. We met up at a very large antique store in Walla Walla. Between the old dishes, furniture, and odds and ends, Andre grabbed me again but this time with more decided force. I wanted the relationship, the talking, the hand holding but without all the sex stuff. My little girl mind was self-conscious of all the makeup being sucked off my face. Thank God we were in a public place so Andre did not try to get further than he had gotten in the airplane bathroom. After the antique store, the last time we saw each other was on the bus ride home. He slipped me his home number that I would call on multiple occasions and get no answer.

I got off the bus technically still a virgin but a far more used-up one. I literally felt like I had used my own fingernails to crack open my chest, tear through the muscle in order to squeeze my beating heart, ripping it out from my chest while spraying blood on everyone around me so that I could, standing there bleeding from my gaping chest wound, hand it to Andre and say, "There. Are you happy with what you've done?" But no such theatrical scene occurred. The parting of

Andre and I was far too uneventful considering how I really felt inside. I wanted the world to stop turning and the sun to stop shining. Instead, I simply got into my mother's car and stared grimly out the window in silence with a look of desolation all the way home.

As we came closer to home, I felt as if I had changed and did not recognize my own thoughts. I could not think happy thoughts or even daydream of the future. I just wanted to crawl into bed and listen to dark and depressing music so I could make myself cry. I wanted out of myself. I wanted to feel different. I did not want to be me anymore. I felt like Andre had taken a hot knife and dissected my insides for kicks and giggles. I felt empty and alone. No one noticed that I was different. I did not want to tell anyone what had happened. I was afraid that, if I told my mother just how deep the ache in my heart felt, she would freak.

"I wish I could talk to my mom about things," I thought. I curled up into bed and let the tears stream down my cheeks. Thirteen-year-old girls are not very good at adult-style flings. One night stands are damaging to anyone and especially to a thirteen-year-old girl.

It was hard to tell my mother anything because of how emotional or angry she became. If I could have depended on the fact that my mother had good judgment, I would have spilled my guts to her on a daily basis, but this was not the case. It was a toss-up, a gamble, on how she would respond at any given moment. Would it be a huge drama? Would it be ignored (which often hurt worse even though it had less collateral damage)? Would she make it all about her? I did not know. One time my mother was terribly offended because a friend of hers had told her that she reminds him of a high school girl that never grew up. I agreed. I could not tell her anything I was thinking so I suffered in silence. In reality, I should have shared my plight with my mother regardless of how she reacted.

No matter how annoyed I was at my mother, I wanted her to succeed at being a mother. I wanted to be proud of her. All children want to be proud of their parents. Children, no matter what their age may be, never criticize their parents to hurt them, even though it may feel like that to the parents, but rather the children desire their parent to be Christ-like. "And the glory of children is their father." Proverbs 17:6. I was a thirteen-year-old girl, like all thirteen-year-old girls, who may act annoyed by their mother but they desperately crave their love, approval, and attention. I was hurting and I desperately wished I could curl up in someone's arms and have them tell me that everything was okay. This little girl had learned well how to behave like a sexy woman and it was tearing her apart.

Chapter 3

Cooler Than I

My life-long illness which forced me to struggle with chronic infections had acutely manifested itself by this age. The field of immunology was not as far along at that time so it would be a common occurrence for my doctors to intimate that I was feigning illness. I will never forget one particular pediatrician who referred me to a therapist and told my mother that I was faking my symptoms of high fever, swollen lymph glands, fatigue, etc. Days later, she called my mother and I back into her office for an emergency meeting to declare that I had the highest viral load of Epstein Bar that she had ever seen. It was not unusual for me to have chronic strep infections. I always felt run down but I was not one to be stuck at home. While other kids faked being sick to get out of school, I faked being healthy to go to school.

Due to these issues that were unknown to me at the time, I was often put into school only to be yanked back out of school for health reasons. I would then be homeschooled for a period of time and try to get back into school again. I was a fabulous student when I was homeschooled and had the advantage of a one-on-one teacher but I struggled in a classroom setting especially when returning to school after long absences. I was always behind in math. The rest of the subjects were easy since I was a ferocious reader. I have found that all children are excited about learning when learning about their interests.

However antisocial I tried to appear, I loved being around people, at least for a while. It was not unusual for my mother to drop me off at a church near my school. Everyone from my school went to this church with their families so, if I wanted to see my school friends, this was the place to be. Strangely, my parents had stopped attending church when I was about thirteen. Alec was struggling to find a job. Well, to be perfectly honest, he thought there were other more effective ways to earn money rather than at a typical nine-to-five job. My mother just wanted Alec to make a living wage instead of the entire family living off of the checks that came from my biological father's death. This was the cause of a great many battles between my mother and Alec.

Often, my mother would load the kids up in the car and drive to the mall to go shopping. The malls my mother liked were usually an hour or so away so, for that hour, I heard every negative detail about my mother and Alec's marriage. I heard it all. My mother told me everything about our family's finances. Children are not capable of sharing these burdens. According to the definition of gossip, if the person you are confiding in is not part of the problem or the solution, you should not be sharing the details with them. I was not part of the solution to my mom's marriage nor was I part of the problem. The totality of the relationship between my mother and I was me listening to her bitterness toward

Alec while shopping.

To my mother, shopping was like a sport. Every shopping adventure was like a hunting expedition. She was and still remains the best shopper I know. When she was shopping she was calm and at peace, goal oriented, and even happy. I could see the endorphins pumping through her veins like she was high on cocaine. She loved shopping more than she loved anything else. She appeared energized as she systematically tore through those shops picking out her new wardrobe items. These items would temporarily relieve her stress and satisfy her aching heart. It was a quick fix, a bandaid, a very expensive cure. My mother hardly ever left the mall with a mere item or two. There were bags and bags and there were times when these shopping excursions would take place daily. My mother, in a single shopping trip, would load the back of the minivan with shopping bags and it was my job to help her sneak those bags through the back door while my mother distracted Alec at the front of the house. Whatever my mother felt on an emotional level, she worked out in the stores. My mother swiped her credit cards like there was no tomorrow to the point of bankruptcy. For my mother, instead of therapy, there was shopping.

The credit card debt from the shopping put even more pressure on the marriage. Alec got odd jobs here and there. One such job was for a local video store. He struck a deal with the owner of the video rental store that he would fix their broken or damaged video tapes for money and free video rentals. Alec would come home with bags of videos to fix and then we could watch the movies.

Hypocrisy is usually the main reason why children learn to hate their parents' religion. I will never forget my family sitting at the kitchen table playing a rousing card game on a Sabbath afternoon together. I have many pleasant memories of family game time. Even my grandparents would sit for hours playing canasta with us. This is how I learned to add and subtract at an early age. However, this one particular Sabbath, a family from our church arrived at our doorstep unexpectedly. I watched quizzically as my parents freaked out and, with one quick swipe of the arm, scooted all the cards off the table cleanly into a box, to hide the "evidence" of our family card game. I was confused and disappointed in my parent's overly frantic behavior to hide the cards. "If cards were so bad that they must be hidden in front of pious church members, should we be playing them?" I naturally questioned. I remember thinking that our family card game, a time when our family had great positive interactions and bonded, could not be that bad to elect that kind of panic.

I was even more dumbfounded when Alec brought home the broken video tapes from the "adult" section of the video store. He was fixing pornographic video tapes and I knew he had to watch at least some of it to know if it were fixed or not. As my brothers and I rifled through the bag of video tapes, we wondered what some of the titles meant. I mostly wondered at my parents' hypocrisy. How are cards bad but pornography is okay? I remember my parents being very worried that church members might see the porn videos we now had in the home.

Alec had applied for numerous job positions and never seemed to land a job and this had worn him down. My mother was angry all the time about money and the mounting credit card debt. Our home was a tinder box waiting for a spark to set it alight with marital discord. Being around my mother was like walking through a minefield. If Alec got the slightest whiff of a looming argument, he was out the door leaving us to deal with my mother's utter despair. Our home, from the age of thirteen on, felt more like a war zone. More than a few times, Alec would leave the house for a separation period due to my mother threatening divorce if Alec did not get a job.

During these times when Alec was gone, my mother would alienate us as far as possible from Alec. She wanted all of the kids to hate Alec as much as she did. She needed all of us on her side and she would tell us the most awful things about the man that was supposed to be our father. When Alec returned, we were supposed to just somehow flip a switch and love Alec like a father after being told that we should hate him. It was a constant roller coaster ride with my mother as the driver. Alec was not the leader of his home anymore. I am not quite sure exactly when he abdicated his position of "man of the house" but, somehow and someway, he had little-by-little given up his role as a leader.

Looking back, I can see that compromising by allowing pornography into our home was a turning point for his role as the spiritual leader. To this day, Alec still blames all of his children for the cessation of our nightly family worship. He argues that the kids did not want to come to worship anymore. We were kids and if we did not want to come to worship then it was his job to have worship regardless. On judgment day, God will not ask the children to give an account for the family. Instead, He will turn to the father to answer for his family. Never compromise with evil and never cease to pray as a family. If the children refuse to come to family worship, keep having worship. Do not let the patients run the asylum so to speak.

Once Alec compromised with evil and allowed such terrible tools for the devil into the home, it was like the angels were chased away and no longer did a Godly spirit exist in the home. There was a price for playing with evil and it was paid in blood, our blood, the blood of the children. It will always be the children that suffer for the sins of the father and suffer we did.

Movies were played non-stop throughout every day and, slowly, my family stopped going to church. By the time I hit my teen years, my parents had completely left their church. They were both bitter at God for their own reasons. As a result, when I did get dropped off at the church by my school, I was unsupervised. A young girl needs supervision. Dropping me off at church to be beholden to my own devices was a very bad idea.

Parents often think that religious environments will make a child religious. If a child is rebellious, they will be rebellious in every environment. Simply dropping a child off at church does not put church in that child's heart. Wherever they go, a rebellious child will look for opportunities to get into mischief. I needed constant supervision and strong guidance from my parents but this would never happen. If a parent stops going to church, it is almost better for that parent to keep that child with them than to send their child to church alone and vulnerable. In the Bible, Deuteronomy 6:7 shows that parents are to teach children what it means to be a spiritual person by keeping that child or youth near to the family circle. This duty does not rest on the pastor, the Sabbath school leader, or the school teacher. The responsibility of teaching a child and a young person what it means to follow Christ at every age and stage of life falls on the parents alone.

One Sabbath my mother dropped me off at church and I quickly found a group of teens that hung out in an outer building on the church property. Most of these teens had their parents present at church to call them into the church services but not I. I perceived a freedom that I did not have to oblige any parental authority by tolerating the church services and I felt proud of myself. I was independent and on my own without anyone to boss me around while my friends had to sit through church services. At my age, I failed to see that I was alone and that made me extremely vulnerable. One older boy, nearly two years older than I, saw my lack of supervision and vulnerability as his opportunity.

I had never been particularly attracted to this older boy but his attention gave me some sense of complimentary fulfillment. The boy had a reputation for getting into trouble. He dressed like Kurt Cobain and he looked a lot like him too. I knew that whatever time I spent with him, it was not likely to turn into anything deep or serious. This boy was all about fun and his life was as chaotic as mine. I wanted deep and serious but his attention toward me was an opportunity to receive the attention I craved and this I could not ignore or pass up.

"You wanna get outta here?" the boy asked in a I-could-care-less-about-life monotone.

"Sure!" I knew I sounded way too eager and very uncool as I jumped at the chance to be alone with this ultra-cool character. He was so much more interesting than I was. His grunge-looking hair and punk-rock clothes were just what I wanted in a guy. It seemed too good to be true. The girls I had seen this boy with were always older than he and so much more beautiful than I. I wondered why there was a sudden interest in me. Where would we walk? What would I talk about?

"Where do you get your clothes?" I asked with a Pollyanna expression.

"At the [expletive] thrift store." He sounded annoyed

and I felt embarrassed as my cheeks grew hot. Such a stupid question. I started mentally flagellating myself, "I read more than anyone else I know! Why does everything I say come out sounding so unintelligent?" As we walked out of the church parking lot and into the streets of small town U.S.A., I started hating myself and mourning my fleeing I.Q.

"Don't be an idiot and sound smart," I told myself so I blurted out too loudly, "do you like Marilyn Manson?"

The boy snorted, "Marilyn Manson is retarded!"

"Oh." I suddenly felt like I had touched the flame in the fire. I shrank back insecurely and I was quiet and ashamed of myself and my fondness for Marilyn Manson. The boy was so much cooler than I. What secret cool club did he belong to? He probably sat around with cool people snapping his fingers to spoken poetry while a stand-up bass played in the corner of the room, talking about cool things, and knew about way cooler music than I could ever dream of knowing. I was on a constant search for new music that would open portals of coolness that were once closed and forbidden to me. If only I knew that I had over-romanticized ideas of this boy and I, in fact, was way more intelligent and imaginative than this boy would ever be.

This boy was merely a mush of hormones, carbon, water, hormones, teenage angst, and did I mention hormones? The boy had a one-track mind and the railway was a non-stop ride to the city of sex. He had no more ability of thinking varied and complex thoughts than a chimpanzee. I had attributed a level of coolness to this boy that simply was not there. I thought he was cool simply because he was able to successfully bully my intellect and slap down my comments and attempts at a real conversation with ease and I let him do it. He was a professional at dismissing my every thought and I let him. For whatever reason, some girls think that being shot down is attractive and they let men do it. Some girls think that men who are emotionally and intellectually elusive are mysterious when these men are truly lacking in intelligence and empathy.

I did not even care where we were walking. He knew the way and I would dutifully follow. The more time I spent with him the more totally uninteresting I felt. The only music I could talk about was what I heard on the radio. The only political issues I could spout was what I heard other people talk about. I felt so unoriginal and unimaginative. I needed to expand my mind and my experience. Around him I felt inspired to be even more rebellious.

All these varied thoughts were hurrying through my mind like traffic on the 101 to Los Angeles. If someone could be allowed a portal into the mind of a teenage female, they will see a hurried amount of thought-filled multitasking. I was single-handedly conducting a self-help seminar in my head, complete with checklists of ideas for self-improvement. I need to be more original, check. I need to learn more cool band names, check. Never mention Marilyn Manson again, check. I need to look more punk rock, check. I need to adopt a social issue to protest, check. All the while, I was valiantly attempting to persuade the boy that I am really a very interesting and complex person, a fact I needed him to see but that I thought was very much a lie. I was much like every other insecure female. If only every teenager could understand how insecure everyone else really is around them. But, to the teenage mind, everyone is looking at me and everyone sees my thoughts because the world is all about me.

While I was internally over-analyzing myself, the boy, the meaning of punk rock, and the possibility of a thrift store shopping spree in the near future, I realized we were far away from the church and walking up the driveway to a home I did not recognize.

"Do you know who lives here," I asked.

"No, but I don't think anyone is home."

I immediately felt alarmed as we walked right up to the stranger's home. Was he planning on robbing the house? He acted so comfortable like it was his house and it was not. He brazenly circled the home looking boldly into the windows. I started scanning around the neighboring homes to see if anyone was watching us stake out this home. Surely someone would see us. I could just imagine the cop cars hastily skidding into the driveway to arrest us. But, if you act like you belong, people will fail to question if you really do. The boy acted like he belonged there, like it was his property.

The home was completely locked up but the boy walked past all the cars in the driveway and into an open covered garage. With comfort and ease he plopped down on the concrete in the middle of the stranger's garage and sat cross legged. I was amazed at his entitled arrogance. I surveyed my surroundings again looking out for neighbors that might have caught sight of the foreign invaders. I just knew that, at any moment, the owners of the home would pull up in their driveway to catch punk kids hanging out in their garage. I felt like Goldilocks waiting for the bears to come home.

The boy had no such worries. At first, he sat cross legged. Then he stretched out his legs and reclined and rested on his elbows. Before I knew it, he was lying flat on the concrete garage floor like he was ready for a nap but I wanted to leave. I did not want to get caught breaking and entering but the boy beckoned me to sit down next to him and when I replied with an emphatic, "no!" the boy rolled his eyes in total annoyance and ordered my compliance.

"C'mon! Chill out a little! What the [expletive] is wrong with you?" he said before softening his tone a great deal. A "come hither" expression came over his face as he patted the floor next to him. "Come and sit over here next to me."

I swallowed hard and looked around again at all the neighboring homes. I released a huge sigh of anxiety as I shuffled slowly over to the boy. I sat next to the boy while keeping one eye on the driveway. I could not shake the feeling of impending doom when I realized that the boy had sat up and was placing his arms around me. I had not planned this and it was too awkward for words to describe. I was at a heightened state of anxiety and therefore I could not be, and I would not be, coaxed into a mood to even remotely enjoy this experience. I did not find the arrogance of this young boy appealing in the slightest. I was unsure of him.

Next, he started to plant long kisses on my face and lips but, to me, he was blocking my view. How could I keep my eyes closed and do my utmost to be a good kisser when I needed to be alert? The boy could tell that his plan was not well thought out nor was it appearing that he would be successful at his goal so he changed tactics.

He returned to his prone position. He lay flat on the floor and undid his top button of his jeans and unzipped the zipper. I was shocked! What was going on? I had not anticipated this. Between the anxiety of the foreign and potentially threatening environment and the boy's privates splayed out before me, I could not think straight.

I should have run away. I thought of the route that would take me back to the church but I simply did not know how to get back through the tangled streets. What should I do in this situation? I sat there thinking and my limited teenage logic provided very few solutions. I had never discussed anything like this with my parents. I had genuinely trusted the boy and I did not know where I was or how I would get back or whose house we were at. The desperation that I felt was mingled with panic when these emotions were shattered by a wrecking ball of humiliation as he ordered me to do something I was completely shocked by.

"What?" I said.

"Do it." He said

"No way!" I replied in meek disgust. "I have never done that. I don't know how to do that."

"I'll show you. Just come here and try."

"No! What if someone sees us?" My stomach was in knots and now I was terrified that people would see the boy exposing himself and that we would definitely go to jail. I was sick with anxiety. I just wanted to leave. I longed to be strong enough to pick the boy up, who was lying down on the floor as large as life, and run. The thought never occurred to me that I could just leave without the boy. Why did I think that I needed him to get back to the church? I do not know.   I had little time to think and I was so confused when, all of a sudden, the boy grabbed the back of my head and forced me to do what he demanded. This was the most unromantic and foul experience. I was paralyzed, and in my state of paralysis, I was annoying the boy even more.

"Just do it so we can leave! I'm not going until it's over." he said. With those familiar words of, "just do it," I felt numb. I was humiliated in every way. I did not like this at all. I was internally distraught. I did not even know if I liked him or not and here I am being made to do this with him. I felt like crying but I was too embarrassed to cry. My wrists ached. I needed to think, to get away and analyze the situation, but it was too late for that. It was I that submitted to his forceful demand as though he had an invisible weapon. He saw a vulnerability in me and took advantage of it. He got inside my head enough to make me feel as though I had no other choice but to do exactly as he said.

Despite my discomfort and protests, the boy gave me specific instructions of exactly what to do. I just wanted to go home. "We can leave when you're done." he said. I felt sick. I just knew that the entire neighborhood could see me doing the worst thing ever. I was terrified every second that elapsed that the home owners would come home and catch us.

Every moment seemed to lag and several times I stopped and said, "I've had enough, let's just go!" This only elicited a cold and firm command with crude and derogatory remarks. I had never felt so stuck in my entire life but I could not go anywhere. I was frozen with fear. I could not even get over the fact that I was doing this with someone who I did not even like nor was I attracted to. I felt like a slut. I thought of myself as a slut.

"What kind of nasty, white trash, slutty girl does this with a guy on a garage floor? You're disgusting!" My inner dialogue was raging against me. I knew I would have to hurt myself later, to punish myself. It was only right to make myself suffer for being such a terribly dirty girl! "I hate me!" I screamed inside as I did this disgusting thing to this disgusting guy in a disgusting garage. Disgusting, disgusted, disgust!

Even if I had possessed the wherewithal to run out of that disgusting garage, I doubt my legs would have carried me. I was stuck in the swamp of pleasing this ungrateful user who would use me to his heart's content. Sadly, if there were a possibility that he might rescue me then I had to give it a try. I had never seen this boy as a possibility before but he was giving me attention and perhaps he was the one I was looking for who would get me out of the purgatory that I was trapped in. I wanted help. I would take help from anywhere. What I mean by help was escape. I wanted to escape and be rescued from my family that did not even know I was emotionally dead inside and I wanted rescuing from my parents who had broken my heart and left me to figure out life on my own. I wanted someone to listen to me, to really listen. Even if what I had to say was totally and completely hate-filled and wrong to say, I wanted someone to hear it and when they heard it they would not leave or reject me.

The boy could tell, like many boys could, that I was desperate. Desperation is an emotional stench that is easily detected by others. Most people can smell desperation a mile away. I was one desperate little girl in search of love. If the devil himself promised me love, I would have sold my soul for it. The devil comes in many forms, even the form of a boy.

What many people struggle to understand is the need for victims to please the person that is abusing them. In those moments when I wanted to run, I stayed still. I wanted to cry but I remained silent. I did not want to do what I was being told to do but I did what I was told to do against even my own wishes and desires. Why? How is it that a person of reasonable intellect and a measure of logic will come to feel completely trapped and helpless by another human being? Though there were no bars, I felt imprisoned. Though the boy had no weapon, I felt as though he were holding a gun to my head. I felt like he was a thousand feet tall and I would have followed any command he gave. Though I barely knew him, I felt some sort of strange loyalty to please him. How is this possible? I was completely dependent on him for his acceptance of me in that moment. Without the protection of my parents, I was vulnerable and completely dependent on others to accept me.

By God's standard I should have seen that the boy was leading me into sin and acting the part of the serpent at the Tree of the Knowledge of Good and Evil. I wish that I had been raised to talked about these things openly with my parents. My mother should have schooled me in what to do in a situation like this. I should never have felt safe to walk off alone with a boy that I hardly knew to a secluded area that I was unfamiliar with. Any one of those neighboring homes had a phone which could have been used to call the police if I had not felt that to call the police would be a humiliating experience in and of itself. Yes, to scream and run and pound on a neighboring door would have been embarrassing in its own right, but it would not have been nearly as embarrassing as the flood of shame that compassed me after the boy declared that the disgusting act was over.

He lifted himself off of the garage floor and said, "let's get out of here." I dutifully and happily obeyed his command and followed him. I was so relieved to be leaving this place. I never wanted to think of it again. I wanted to walk away and leave this memory behind me, never to be thought of again. I had told myself that I just needed to do the disgusting deed so that the boy would return me safely to the church. Without him, I would be lost and did not know how to get back to the church. My mother would be expecting to meet me in the church parking lot and she would be angry if I showed up late and with the appearance that I had not been to church at all. I was frantic to get back to the church quickly.

The boy did not say one word as he trudged down the driveway, leaving the garage behind. He did not care that it was not his home, not his garage, not his driveway, and I was most definitely not his property but, he acted entitled to it all. Owner of the world was he. It is men like this who are easy criminals, victimizers, and abusers. They believe they are entitled to what is not theirs and they rob and destroy with the ease of locusts stripping the fields of their bounty. He came like a thief in the night and stole more of my quickly diminishing innocence.

Before we exited the driveway to leave the home behind, the boy exploded into an angered frenzy and began kicking and breaking the carefully placed outdoor lights that lined the driveway in a wake of destruction. He kicked and shattered every one of the lights. I wondered at his wrath. "I should be angry, not he," I thought.

At last we reached the mailbox and the boy turned to me and said, "I'm headed home. You know the way back, right?" I was shocked. He was planning on leaving me all along. I expected a kind gentleman to escort me back to the church. How was I even a little surprised that this brute had no intention of being kind or a gentleman? Looking back, I wish I could shake and slap my younger self. I was so naive to the wants of boys and men. I thought most boys to be of true and honest intention. I lacked an understanding of the world. All people are battling the battle of self. Many men are battling lust. God is a holy and restraining power on most people's depraved inclinations. Thus, without God, many men are filled with their own natural inclinations which lead down to Sheol. It was naive of me to expect that this boy wanted to spend time with me alone for any good purpose and I was naive to think he would do the right thing and steer me safely to the church. I had a Pollyanna view of the world that would be short lived. My Pollyanna view would last but a few more months when the realization that the "human heart is desperately wicked, who can know it" would become Scripture-come-alive and demonstrated in my life. I would meet and interact with every kind of evil. My feet were swift to evil and my companions were rebels.

The boy turned and walked away from me. I stood

there watching his figure slowly disappear around a corner. I felt an immeasurable amount of shame. I was angry but mostly at myself. I should have been angry at the boy. I should have told someone. It would take years for me to tell my stepsister. My stepsister pried the details out of me like rusty nails coming out of rotten wood. When I gave bits and pieces of information she exclaimed, "You were raped!"

I did not feel raped. Rape required a great bit of screaming, yelling, and kicking in protest. I had done none of those things though I wish I had. My picture of rape was from violent scenes from movies I had seen. It never occurred to me that there are many forms of rape. I rationalized that it was all my fault. I had let it happen. I had failed to resist when my head was grabbed by the boy. I obeyed his intimidating commands. Had I said no? Many times I had said, "no," and communicated my utter and sheer discomfort but, I was met with arm twisting at every turn. I never thought of it as rape. It was all me just being what I was, a little rebel girl. I was asking for it.

I had done something to pull this boy toward me and make him behave in such a disgusting manor. I let him do things to me. I could have stopped it. Could I have stopped it? I knew in my heart that I had absolutely no power to stop those events in that garage because I was frozen in fear. I did not know what to do or where to go or where I was. If my parents had known but a sliver of the emotional pain I was suffering, they might have better protected me, right? No, I was a problem to my parents. My constant need created a constant bother. Was I raped? I would not even begin to think in terms of rape for another fifteen years. Until that time, I deserved what I got. Even to this day I still struggle with this event not being my fault.

I remember pushing away every urge to cry. I had nothing to cry about. It was all my fault. My brain started to work to protect me from the traumatic and unwanted event. I started to grow extremely numb. My wrists ached and pulsated with physical pain. I alternated squeezing both wrists with my hands as I, in a growing panic, walked the streets surrounding the church trying to remember the way we came. I was lost. I did not know how I would get back. I wished I had not been so chatty on the walk away from the church. I wished I had paid close attention to my surroundings and landmarks, a mistake I would never make again. I was a young girl who was completely lost.

My adrenaline pumped harder and harder as I knew that I was losing precious time. If I were late, I was terrified that my mother would have cause to question me and then she would discover that I had left church and done the disgusting deed. I would be in big trouble. I always wondered how some children could get sexually assaulted and their rapist tell them that if they tell anyone, they will be in big trouble, and the children believed that lie. In my very childlike mind, all I could see was how much trouble I would be in. The sad thing is, I am not entirely sure that my mother would have seen the disgusting deed I had done as anything but my fault because she has spent a lifetime denying her own abuse.

I was extremely grateful to come upon a man in his yard watering his grass. I said, "excuse me sir, can you tell me the way back to the Adventist Church?" The man looked at my apparently panicked countenance but asked me no questions and offered some directions by landmarks that would take me back to the church. I was relieved. I started walking and then I found myself running. I could see the cars pouring out of the church parking lot as church was over. The cars and the people were filing out into the sunshine and promise of a beautiful sunny afternoon but, for me, it was night in my soul.

We can never underestimate the power of shame. I honestly believed that if anyone found out about my disgusting deed that I would be publicly humiliated in front of the church. I did not have any confidence that my parents would meet out proper consequences or deal justly with the situation. I knew all too well that my mother's emotional response would be over the top or underwhelming and her focus would be how she might dramatize the circumstances for her own personal gain in an effort to maximize the spotlight and attention on herself. Children need to know for certain that, if the truth is shared, their parents will not react from a place of selfishness by responding with a great show of emotion.

For instance, when my child shares with me the truth of what they have done wrong, if I want the full truth and nothing to be hidden from me, I must respond to my child how I would want someone to respond to me. If I give a sudden outburst of tears and/or anger at my child, they will immediately clam up and there will be no more truth coming from my child's mouth. Children naturally want to unburden themselves and share with their parents but parents teach their children over the years exactly how much truth they are willing to hear from their children.

Children do not just choose to hide truth from their parents in a vacuum. Somewhere along the way their parents have taught them that the really ugly truth, the fact that they have sinned and fallen short of the glory of God whereby we are all guilty, is an inconvenience to the parents that wish to idolize their child and make the child above sin. If every parent could, first, understand that it is not a matter of if their child will make a mistake but when and, second, tell their child that they commit to hearing the truth with a calm, rational, and selfless attitude, then children might feel less of a barrier to unburdening themselves to their parents.

We underestimate the power of irrational thinking. A person's perception, however ridiculous, is their reality. Our actions and attitudes are a product of our thoughts. Our thoughts are a product of our hearts and our hearts will reflect whoever or whatever we have devoted our heart to. For example, parents should make every effort to gain their child's heart. When a parent has their child's heart, then the parent is capable of guiding and directing their child's perception of the world around them to shape their reality. When a parent does not have their child's heart, the child will allow any influence that holds their affections (i.e. friends, sports heroes, movies, music, etc.) to guide their perceptions of the world around them. This will allow a warped and immature reality to take shape. This will also allow children to be easily convinced of lies by others.

In my shame, I had convinced myself that if anyone really knew of what I had done, the disgusting deed, that I would be in big trouble and publicly humiliated. This was a lie but it was my perception and my reality. If my parents had my heart, I would have been able to know the truth from more mature adults. But, many children believe the lie that they will be in trouble for being a victim of rape, molestation, and incest. However ridiculous this may sound to the rational mind, please do not underestimate the power of this thinking in naive little children that grow into adults.

I quickly dashed through the church parking lot. When I became one of the many people in the parking lot, it looked as if nothing had happened and as if I had been there all along. It looked as though I had never left. I stopped running. I began to walk in pace with the other church members. In the reflection of a window I smoothed out my clothing and my hair. I then looked for my mother's car in the parking lot. My mother had just pulled into the parking lot. I was not late but actually early. I had made it. I headed toward my mother's car and, when I reached her car, I opened the car door and slid into the front passenger seat. My mother knew nothing. She saw nothing to raise her suspicion. She was unable to detect anything odd in my behavior as she immediately dove into the drama of her own day. My mother commenced her chattering and was none the wiser that her daughter had just had one of the worst days in her life.

My cover was secure. No one knew of my disgusting deed. "No one will ever know," I thought. "I will tuck this away in my mind where it will never bother me and I will never think of it again," I comforted myself. If only that were true. Emotional pain is like playing whack-a-mole. Tuck the pain away and ignore it and the pain will pop up somewhere else, in another form, on another day. When not properly dealt with, emotional pain will return with a violent vengeance.

Chapter 4

Not Today, Kid

Everyone remembers their first boyfriend. I had lots of boyfriends in seventh and eighth grades. They were fun little play things to me. I wanted my boyfriend relationships to be real and intense but I was dating boys my own age so they were young as was I. Thus, we had young love. It was mostly innocent and naive. We did not know what we did not know. It was the kind of naivety that believes that anything more than hand holding might get you pregnant, the kind of relationships that are together at morning break and broken up by lunch recess. The kind of silly little test-runs that are a kind of experimentation for the real thing. You get your heart broken and rejected just enough to come to the realization that relationships are a very serious thing and very grown up which makes you want to have a real relationship even more, especially if you have raging "daddy issues" like I did.

I was a little girl on the hunt for an adult relationship and this looked as ridiculous as it sounds. I was attracted to the older boys but it was difficult to get them to see me as anything more than a little girl. That is when the makeup and the alluring clothes came out. There is only one reason why a little girl wants to dress like a woman and that is male attention. If a little girl is a little girl she will look like a little girl. But I wanted to be an adult. I wanted to look like an adult, act like an adult, have adult problems, have adult relationships, so I could run off and get married like an adult, to be whisked out of my terrible wretched family so I could finally be happy.

Even as young as I was, I honestly thought that anyone I dated I might marry. The problem was, I may have looked like an adult, or tried to anyway, but I was very much working with the brain of a child. Because of the risks, teens are fragile creatures equal to babies. They are starting to appear like an adult while having a brain that is yet to be fully formed. If we were evolutionary creatures and not creatures created by design, we would have brains that form before our bodies. Instead, we look like adults first then our brains take their sweet time to develop as our frontal lobes fully form into our early twenties. This was a Creator-designed feature. In one respect, we will require parental oversight well into our adult years. Unfortunately, I had very little parental oversight.

I craved a man in my life and I would have done anything to fill this vacuum in my soul. I craved a deep relationship. I felt lonely all the time no matter how many people were around me. I remember one day when my older brother left to go to work at a summer camp and I felt suicidal. I felt a deep emotional pain because someone who I enjoyed talking with would be gone for what seemed like forever. I remember watching the car, that contained my brother and all his earthy goods, pull out of the driveway and I watched from a window and cried for him. I knew that there would be little meaningful connection in my life without him around and I was deeply and profoundly sad.

Love is a big word that we use casually for just about anything. We can love ice cream and love our children. But love toward our children, in the truest sense of the word, encompasses the concept of having someone's heart. God designed us so that we would crave the experience of having our heart go out after Him, "My son, give me thine heart, and let thine eyes observe my ways." Proverbs 23:26. The insurance God put into place to guarantee that when we "search for Him with all our heart, we will find Him," Jeremiah 29:13, is to, first, experience His earthly presence through the love of our father and mother. What more could a loving God do than to make us babes, small and cute, chubby and smooth skinned, totally helpless, smelling sweet and new, with hope abounding for the future with joy and two parents who are bound by a biological and chemical response to that babe's smell, look, touch, and sound. The first heart experience we will have is being loved by our parents and needing them in return.

When we are little babies and toddlers, it is easy for parents to have our hearts because our wants and desires are to be fed, to be clothed, to be hugged and kissed, to be warm and safe, and so on and so on. As we start to get older and we learn to talk, we want to be heard and we want our questions to be answered too. This is where we start learning by the age of six (sometimes much earlier) if our parents are interested in having our heart or not.

To us as humans, there is nothing more revolting, more insidious, than the harming of a baby or child but, sadly, it happens. What happens to God's original roadmap for our lives? It is utterly destroyed and God must use other profound ways to woo us toward happiness. Those who have been betrayed by the people who were designed to love them most will struggle in life due to a fundamental building block of life being missing. Like the game Jenga, in the late childhood and teenage years you will see many children who seem to collapse into chaos because they have been building life with missing pieces. There is only one solution.

There is no story more poignant than the story of David and Absalom. David lost the heart of Absalom by allowing an injustice to take place without enacting consequences or meeting out justice on the guilty party. Tamar, Absalom's sister, was raped and David failed to punish the rapist. This became a source of division between Absalom and his father. The story of Absalom in 2 Samuel 13-19 details how King David lost Absalom's heart. David took no action to avenge his daughter's ruined honor and punish the guilty party. Failure to enact the appropriate consequences and to communicate appropriately on David's part and a subsequent seven years of silence provoked Absalom to wrath.

A father must be seen, first and foremost, as a father. Absalom was treated like a subject instead of a son. Thus,

Absalom plotted to usurp David's throne. So Absalom "stole the hearts of the men of Israel" by doing what he wished his father would do to him: by listening to the people of Israel, talking with the people of Israel, and touching the people of Israel. Like all children, Absalom wanted his father. All children crave their parents' love and acceptance. If parents only understood the strong desire within children to be loved by their mother and father, they would not take hurts so personally, they would carefully guard their language, and endeavor to learn the greatest parental trait of all: selflessness.

Parents frequently become hurt when their children criticize them. They take it as a personal slight. This is very easy to do since we love our children so much that we would give our lives for them. Children critique their parents from a place of wanting their parents to be all that they envision their parents can be. All children want is to be proud of their parents. "Fathers are the pride of their children." Proverbs 17:6. There is no one in the world who will hold a person in higher esteem than a child holds a Godly parent. If you spend time listening to your children, talk and ask your child questions about their interests and hobbies, if you share with your child your thoughts and stories, if you show your child praise and loving affection, then you will be the most loved and adored parent by your child. Fail to do this and someone will step in to do it for you.

If my parents were not going to have my heart then I

needed someone to have my heart. I innately knew that these young boys my age would not be up for what I wanted. I was consciously on the lookout for a relationship. Like a hungry animal seeking sustenance, I was craving love. I was putting it out there that I needed as much male attention as I could get. There are girls who hang out with only boys because they are tomboys and can play rough and tumble with the best of them and then there are the girls who hang out with only boys because they need boys' attention. We all know the one, the needy and desperate little girl who needs all the boys in the room to look at her and prove her worthy. But this is pointless and extremely detrimental to find love through male attention.

During the summer of my freshmen year of high school, I spent a great deal of time hanging out at a youth pastor's house. This house was the kind of hang out that kids dream of. It is technically the youth pastor's house so it sounds really appropriate to parents who care where you are going but, upon arrival, there are kids hanging out in every room with little adult supervision. It was an older home built in the seventies and it was within walking distance of the church. It was a small home, yet it would be large with life and laughter as all the kids slung themselves over the furniture, loudly ran through the halls, and kept the refrigerator door constantly opening and closing. I was desperate to get away from the doom and gloom of my home and I made this place my second home.

This is where I met Erik. Erik was about five foot ten inches and very skinny. He was like a tall pole in the mud. There was nothing very special about his appearance. He was an average guy with a below average weight. People would often ask me about what I saw in him and why I liked him. Then I was told how pretty I was and how I could do so much better but I can look back now and write exactly what it was about Erik that attracted my attention.

Erik had a commanding and larger than life personality and a high intellect. He could have done anything or been anyone. He had a quick wit, a sharp tongue, and I was attracted to his strong opinions and unwavering sense of self. He was not insecure like I was. He did not care how he dressed or what he looked like. His parents loved him. Erik could declare that he was planning on blasting off to the moon if he got the notion and they would sell their every earthly possession to buy him the spaceship he would need. He was secure because he had security. I wanted to be secure too. I knew he had something that I needed. I flirted with him casily using my own sharp intellect. Because I read far more than the average girl my age, I was readily able to casually banter on any number of topics. Oddly, I found Erik's ease at insulting me very attractive.

Still, to this day, I am not quite sure why women find men who insult them attractive, but they do and I did. It is a major red flag of a controlling relationship. It should serve as a definite warning to women that they are suffering from fatal insecurities when they are attracted to men who are comfortable administering sharp little barbs to put them down. It shows that these men are also insecure but, far from recognizing it, they are quite happy to shove a woman's face in the mud to feel better about themselves. Run from men like these!

I, unfortunately, did not run. I chose to fall into what I believed was mad and crazy love. The truth is, I desperately needed Erik. I needed him to drive his little car to my house and get me away from my family. Erik helped me escape and took me places where my family was not. He asked me questions and he listened to my answers. He would most often disagree then tell me what I really thought and I was happy to adopt his opinions as my own. I was very good at becoming what people wanted me to be. I would have become anything or been anyone for Erik. He was my knight in shining armor and I would learn what it meant to be his faire lady. He, in a way, owned me. I would not then know how much he owned me until I tried to break up with him. He spent time with me and he was kind and affectionate. He would win my heart almost instantly. A man had not had my heart since I was a young girl. In fact, I know exactly when my father lost my heart....

Most girls can pinpoint the exact moment their father lost their heart and so can I. I can still see my father walking down the hallway after he shattered me into a million pieces. He may have delivered the fatal blow but my mother handed him the weapon. It was the summer before Junior High. My mother likes to say that it was like someone flipped a switch and I became an awful and rebellious teenager but kids do not suddenly just become something out of nowhere. Nothing happens in a vacuum in a child's life. There are natural laws at play thus for every action there is an equal and opposite reaction. If I suddenly became rebellious, it was because my very own parents hurt me beyond what I could bear.

It was summer time and I was free from the responsibilities of school. I loved the smell of the early morning summer in the desert. It was like bottling the fragrance of possibilities. I felt as if I could do anything at that age. I wanted to conquer the world. My dad had started going for a bike ride every morning. He rode about three miles. I convinced him that I could do it and not slow him down. He was not sure at first but, eventually, he decided to let me go. I was going to prove to him that if he would just let me tag along that I would never slow him down. I wanted, ever so desperately, to be with him. I wanted to be like him. I wanted to hear what he had to say. I idolized him. He was a thousand feet tall to me. Even if my legs were bloodied and about to fall off, there was absolutely no chance that I would let him down or slow him down.

After the bike ride my day got even better. My dad took me out to his favorite breakfast spot and I got to listen to my dad and his buddies talk shop. Listening to my dad and his buddies converse and debate the finer points of Chevy versus

Ford was like flipping through the pages of an auto magazine and I was interested in every word. If my dad would have offered to show me how to put together an engine, I would have enthusiastically volunteered to get my hands dirty. There I was, having the time of my life in a scuzzy diner, in a bad neighborhood, with a bunch of grease monkeys, and I was the happiest girl in the world. Parents do not understand that they do not have to do anything special with their kids nor do they have to be perfect. Just let the kids spend time with you doing what you do. After breakfast, my dad swung by his parents' house. I gnawed on a piece of zwieback bread that my Nana made while we all laughed heartily with canasta cards in hand. Summer bliss! I rolled down the window of my dad's beat up brown van as we blasted country and classic rock and I thought life was as good as it could get.

My ears thrilled when my dad said, "same time tomorrow, kiddo?" as I bounced out of the van to the concrete. "Uh huh!" I shouted back with enthusiastic gusto. It was still morning in the high desert and I had nothing but summer as far as the eye could see. When a girl is at peace with her father, she is at peace with the totality of God and man.

Morning after morning passed with continued bike rides. I noticed in the mirror that my legs were starting to swell with the muscles of a biker. I was biking at least three miles every morning, five days a week. I felt so good. My dad liked country music so I started to turn away from the music I liked and I started liking country music too. He wanted to work on cars so I wanted to work on cars too. I no longer wanted to get attention from other boys. I just wanted my dad's attention and I wanted him to like me. Now that we were spending all this time doing stuff together, I began to really care how he saw me as a person. This summer was the happiest I had felt in a long time. Sadly, it would be my last memory of happy summers for a long while. Unconditional love gives a girl something that nothing else can give. A father's love gives a girl security. Embarrassment is no longer so embarrassing if you have your father's acceptance and worries are no longer that worrying if you know that he is around.

We were riding our bikes every morning for weeks and I was falling in love with my father just the way God intended. Unfortunately, my mother noticed my love for my father and she could not understand it. She knew that fathers and daughters should love each other on an intellectual level but to actually see the father and daughter relationship in reality stirred jealousy within her. With every husband my mother has ever had, she has sought to destroy the father-daughter bond between them. There are four daughters without fathers in this world because of her jealousy. I listened through the hole in the wall to my mother's protests and abject jealousy of my relationship with my father. I hated what she was doing. "No, no, no! Don't say that!" I thought as my mother hammered home the point that my father was spending too much time with me and that she thought it was inappropriate and suspicious.

"I mean what are you talking about with her down there at your parents' house? Are you telling her nasty things about me? You all just can't wait to talk about me when I'm not around! Why does she want to be with you so much and not me? Why can't I come with you two? I would like to go on a bike ride all morning! It's really suspicious that the two of you don't want me to come!" She yelled loudly.

I dreaded every word that came out of my mother's mouth. My stomach started tightening into knots. I did not want my father to stop taking me with him and I knew that if my mother pressed hard enough, all would stop. I whispered to the air, "please don't say it, please..." That is when I heard it.

"I mean if people didn't know any better, they would say that there's somethin' goin' on between you two!" My mind cleared. I immediately became numb like all emotions had just been swept into the garbage can and were no longer present with all their complications. I was so anxious that she might stop this good thing I had with my dad and now I knew she had done just that. I knew that this would be the sick statement that would make my dad feel weird about me. She had suggested that something sick was going on between my dad and I.

"How could a man look at his daughter the same after that?" I questioned. If Alec had only had an ounce of bravery, he would have stood up to my mother and told her that there was nothing wrong, just a dad and his daughter spending time together like they should and to knock off her sick imaginings but, unfortunately, he was a coward. He did not like to fight and so he never fought. Sadly, this meant he never fought for me either.

I will never forget the next morning. I was up extra early. The house was filled with all the unique noises that a child learns to notice when they are growing up. I knew the sound of the water in the pipes in my bathroom that would let me know when my parents were up and getting ready. I was an expert on their morning routine. I put on my shorts, my socks, my shirt, my tennis shoes, and I got ready to go meet my dad to go on a bike ride. I was going to go on a bike ride with my dad no matter what my mom said. I just wanted to will away my parents' awful fight. The force of positive thinking was ever my friend. Time and time again I would choose the happy side of things even when things were dark.

The pallor of my parents' fight hung low upon our home. It was like a musty and stubborn rancor that summer morning. I just knew, if given a chance, I could prove my mom wrong just like I had proven I could keep up on my bike. I did not want my dad to go without me. "That would be the worst," I reasoned. Thinking of him on the bike trail all alone and doing all the fun things I liked to do without me was like a knife stabbing in my heart. I could not think of my dad leaving without me. I knew he could not do that to me...or could he? I pushed that sacrilegious thought away and thought, surely, he can take me and would not ride without me. I sat on my bed ready for a bike ride and waiting to hear the particular click of my parents' room door opening for the day. I knew that my dad would then stride loudly down the hallway filling the house with his larger than life presence and the smell of his hair tonic and shaving cream.

I opened the door of my room just as my dad was walking past. "Good morning Daddy!" I bravely announced with a huge smile on my face that only a little girl with the love for her daddy can offer. "I could love him even if he did not love me," I thought. "I could love him for the two of us," I thought with decided courage. I thought those wonderful positive thoughts until the words of unimaginable painful rejection reached my ears.

"Not today, kid." He said curtly and with a tone of annoyance. He sped past my shocked and hurting face while avoiding eye contact. I slowly turned around and walked toward my window and watched my dad load his bike up in the van. I watched that old brown van take off with such speed like the hounds of hell were after it. And, in a way, I suppose my mother was right. A switch in me somewhere did get hit but not like she thought. She won the fight and my dad surrendered but, what he ended up surrendering was the love and devotion of a daughter. That summer morning, my father lost my heart.

After that summer, my dad and I were never close

again. I would never spend much time with him ever again. Though I would call him, "dad," to his face, I would thereafter refer to him as Alec in conversation. Because I was so hurt and it was never dealt with or repented of, I would slowly start to nurture a deep hatred for him. Even more, I hated my mother for her insinuation that my love for my father was something dirty when it was as pure as the driven snow. That morning would result in me facing a big bad world all alone without a father or mother to run to. That morning I learned to never trust my parents.

Chapter 5

You Promised

Right after Erik and I first met, we began our romance by telephone. We discussed every topic from politics to books and everything you are taught not to discuss with people you first meet. Both of us wanted a deep relationship. He wanted to know what I honestly thought and I wanted to know what he honestly thought. We truly listened to each other and valued, better yet, clung to each other's every word.

Our romance began with all the thrills and butterflies that most romances begin with. I remember my heart racing when the phone rang. Like Pavlov's dog, my brain flooded with endorphins when the shrill ring of the phone echoed throughout the house. When I heard, "It's for you," it was like the heavens opened up to pour out its light and wonder on little ole' me. I had never felt emotions so strong. Someone to listen to me, to hear me, to transport me from my wretched miserable state of being into a superhuman state of mind. I was convinced that I discovered a new way to live in the world. I had transcended my comfortably numb emotional state and entered into a world of bliss. It was a world filled with rushes of brain chemicals like oxytocin, serotonin, and dopamine. I loved every second of the twisting turns and rushes of emotion that I felt. When my face would grow hot because Erik walked into the room, when my hands would sweat because he was looking my way, when my heart would race because he was walking over to me, when my stomach would multiply with masses of butterflies because he was talking to me, all this and more I learned would temporarily cure the pains that ailed me. I was in love with falling in love. That surge of endorphins masquerading as new love would become an addiction for me.

Really, it is not love at all and I disdain the use of the word, "love," to describe simple teenage infatuation. Love is such a complex word with so many levels and meanings. Infatuation fades and will always, after a time, fail the inevitable test of self-sacrifice but true love will last and selflessly give all to the bitter last drop. All relationships come to the point where their strength is tested. The sign of a mature relationship is when both participants can put away pride and self-interest to serve one another. Love is offered without requiring anything in return. To love someone in this way is to take the ultimate risk a person can take. Why? Because risk, in the sense of the heart, is fraught with emotional and physical danger of hurt and rejection but love soars beyond fear and loves anyway and in all things. Teenage relationships are rarely capable of this kind of loving service and vulnerable surrender.

Erik was going into his senior year and I was a lowly freshman. But, as I said, I was not just any freshmen girl. I was unknowingly and subconsciously looking for a serious relationship. I was looking for a father. I needed a man to guide my life and, even though Erik was far from understanding what real manhood entailed, he would suffice.

We went to a smaller private church school that sat on a few acres in an outlying community of Riverside County. I will never forget the back-to-school night for the high school where Erik and I fulfilled every idea we each had in regard to romanticism. We had both had our heads filled to the brim with scenes of romance from books and movies. We wanted to make our idealism tangible.

On a crisp fall evening, the rain started to pour down. Erik and I were running and skipping through the football and soccer fields like a scene from *The Sound of Music*. The school had large rolling hills with beautiful grassy knolls and it was scenic enough, green enough, to play the role of the gleaming meadowland required in any tale of Renaissance-like romance. Erik and I ran and played and spun in the rain like we were on a movie and being filmed. Through our giggles and high-spirited game of tag, I waited to hear the dramatic music and the crescendo of the orchestra. This was no movie although I was all too happy to act like it.

We were the only people braving the downpour of desert rain. More than one hundred adults and parents filled the school gym but we were alone in our fantasy world. I believed, although I was only fifteen, that I must be a very mature fifteen-year-old to be capable of feeling such powerful emotions. My chest felt like my heart would swell and come ripping through my chest. Our game of tag in the rain was building into so much more. Until this point, Erik and I had not had much physical touch but our romantic play was reaching a denouement.

I had kissed before but those past kisses were for the sake of the act of kissing alone and not a kiss with the desired emotional and romantic setting. I felt that kissing to express my feelings toward Erik in this moment would be perfectly normal. It seemed like a natural thing to do as a physical manifestation of what was occurring between the two of us and I knew Erik felt the same way. Like any romance scene out of a movie, Erik and I ran toward each other from opposite corners of the grassy field, the rain having drenched us to the bone, laughing and screeching with full knowledge of our corny play on every cliché. We ran toward each other mimicking the ballet but, when we fell into each other's arms, we sealed it with a kiss.

As usual, I expected the orchestra to commence their performance or for angels to sing and, as usual, I was disappointed. Growing up as a young girl and fed on a steady dict of romance novels and movies, I expected there to be some sort of ecstasy in kissing or for it to be more than it was. I was left to conclude that I must be, or we must be, doing it wrong. There was no explosion of fireworks nor was there a physical rush. It was anticlimactic at best and kind of slimy and gross at worst. But, when you believe that you are in love, you will make yourself think that this kiss is the very best invention since sliced bread and you will do it more and more and think to practice something that is dangerous. It is dangerous because infatuation is a drug and drug addicts will state the very honest fact that, where once a little hit of drugs was needed to get high, now a lot is needed to get high. Soon enough kissing is not enough and the proverbial envelope gets pushed and the boundaries of what a girl will and will not do when it comes to sex gets pushed further and further into what she will do. Many people do not think that having sex as a teenager is a problem. Keep reading and you will see a clear and definite life-long consequence of teenage sex.

Erik and I kissed and kissed until our lips were chapped. We agreed that we were officially going out (meaning dating, going steady, whatever you want to call it). From that moment on, Erik and I were inseparable. I felt my insecurities melt away with the assurance of his strong presence and listening ear. He would listen to my day with deep sympathies and sooth all my concerns and fears. When I got to school in the morning, Erik was there. When I walked to class, Erik walked with me. When I came out of class, Erik was waiting for me. Soon Erik was often dropping me off at home and even taking me to school in the morning on most days. As soon as Erik rushed home from dropping me off, he would call me on the phone and would tie up the home phone line until I went to bed. Heaven help the person who needed to make a phone call (these were the days before cellular phones).

It soon became such that I hated being home with my

parents because Erik's familiar and sympathetic presence was not there. I longed for the morning when Erik would pick me up and I dreaded the long nights in my bed when Erik and I had to be separated. I would fall asleep most nights with the phone attached to my ear so Erik could talk to me until l went to sleep. I needed Erik to feel okay. I no longer needed a parent because Erik filled the role of my parent. I no longer needed God because Erik filled that role too.

My worst fear was a fear of needles second only to my fear of spiders. I had spent such a great part of my childhood getting poked and prodded with needles that I feared needles to the point that I was not above physically assaulting doctors, nurses, and lab techs to get away from needles. My obsessive need for Erik was so extreme that it posed a problem if his parents set limits on what he could and could not do. No young boy is really capable of meeting the expectations of a young girl who has made a god out of him. What I needed was a father. My father was capable of meeting my needs but Erik was not. That was a problem.

My health problems were starting to rear their ugly head. I was intent on ignoring them but my mother was intent on addressing my health issues. I needed to get my blood drawn but there would be no way that I would get my blood drawn without Erik by my side. Erik promised that this would never happen. He promised to be there. Of course, the weather was completely out of Erik's control and the weather set its face against the Romeo and Juliet couple that we were.

As a fifteen-year-old girl, I was not about to acquiesce to a snow storm, dangerous icy conditions, or terrible driving visibility but Erik's mother had every intention to bow in respect to the limits that nature sets on us all. Erik was barred from driving down the dangerous mountain to be by my side as he had promised. This gave everyone an opportunity to see how dangerously Erik and I had become attached. Separating Erik and I was like separating mother and child. It was ugly, violent, tragic, dramatic, and every other word you can think of to describe sudden and unpredictable emotional chaos.

I screamed through tears and sobs into the phone, "but Erik, you promised me that you would be there!" Erik did his best, "I know! I want to be there!" The thought of getting a needle inserted into my forearm and the blood gurgling out into a little tube without having the loving face of my true love right near me just about shattered me. What drama! But that was the reality of the situation. I really believed at certain times that death was better than living without Erik and Erik really believed at certain times that death was better than living without me. Such is the unpredictable nature of allowing a young girl to pour herself into a male figure that is not her father. A father is most prepared to deal with his daughter's heartfelt emotions but a boy is most definitely not.

I felt as though Erik had committed a crime against me. It was as if the realization had suddenly hit me that Erik may not always be in my life for the rest of my life. I honestly believed that I had found the person I would spend the rest of my life with. I felt like Erik and the rest of the world had dealt me a purposeful blow in allowing me to be alone in my perceived greatest hour of need. To me, the needle prick would cause certain death! Do you see how my teenage mind was incapable of rational thinking?

When a little girl's kitten dies, to her the entire world is crying in the tragedy of death. It does not occur to a child that the sun will continue to rise whether or not their problem is resolved. Adults have perspective on problems. Most of us know that trials will pass as quickly as they come. There are good days and there are bad days. To a child with no concept of time, bad days last forever and it feels as if it will never pass. In these instances, fathers and mothers must be fathers and mothers first and foremost. As parents, we must be willing to pay the price. The price is whatever it costs us to be a parent first and foremost.

For instance, if your little girl's kitten dies or a friend has broken her heart and she calls you on your cell phone crying and hurting and you are at work and just about to close an important business deal, you do not tell your daughter that she must wait until your important matter is finished and you will deal with her later that night. You must be willing to pay the price for admission into your daughter's heart. By the time you get home from work, someone else may have ministered to that hurt and the matter is resolved. No, you must tell her that you will drop what you are doing to come soothe her pain. That is what it means to pay the price. There is nothing more important in this life than gaining the hearts of our children. There is nothing more costly and painful than losing the heart of our children. We cannot afford to lose the hearts of our children.

This whole situation would have been a perfect time for my father to step in where Erik had unwillingly failed but that did not happen. True to form, I became so emotionally worked up at the sight of the needle and blood that I passed out cold on the hospital floor. When I arrived back home, I was pouting and miserable that Erik had not been able to come with me. My parents should have observed my immaturity and tried to stop my relationship with Erik then because trying to stop our obsessive and exclusive relationship later on would be totally and completely futile. There were windows of opportunity where my parents could have stopped us early on. The more time we spent together, the more impossible it became to tear us apart. We became so close we were like a married couple and, like married couples, we were becoming one person. How do you separate a person from themselves? Not without great and terrible ripping asunder.

Erik and I had talked about sex. It seemed like a natural step. We were so close that most people thought that we were having sex before we really were. The night that we chose was a school trip. I detail this because I think it is important for adults to know how sneaky and decidedly secretive teens can be. Things can also happen in a very short amount of time.

It was at a school Knott's Berry Farm trip. Erik and I walked hand in hand through the park with our friends but we were mostly focused on each other. We both had dropped our friends and never really socialized without each other present. I cannot remember how it happened but somehow Erik and I had a disagreement of sorts and, representative of our relationship, it turned into a massive and dramatic fight to rival any Hollywood script. Erik started yelling and I started crying and I walked off in a huff.

Erik was not going to allow me to walk through the park with my friends without him so he followed behind me. Every turn I made he also made while staring angrily into the back of my head. Instead of getting an adult to deal with Erik's intimidation tactics, I purposed to ignore Erik and I laughed loudly with my friends so that Erik could hear my sheer happiness with being away from him. Was I happy? Absolutely not. I hated the feeling of being vulnerable without him. I felt naked without his presence to tell me what to do and where to go and what we would do next. I recall just wanting to smooth everything over and just get back to being together but I knew that Erik was angry and I was scared of him.

Erik started to look scarier and scarier as his eyes grew dark. His pupils dilated and he looked like a shark that just caught the scent of blood in the water. Erik could sense my fear. With every person I talked to and every word I spoke, I glanced at him out of the corner of my eye to make sure he approved but I was becoming more and more alarmed because I could see that Erik was only getting angrier. My fear started giving way to bursts of adrenaline and I knew that all this pressure was mounting up to something. My friends were growing more and more disturbed with my shadow boyfriend who looked like an axe murderer. All my friends decided to go on without me because they were feeling like this situation was about to erupt and so was I.

I walked up to Erik and confronted him. He clenched his jaw so tightly that I could see all his face muscles through his skin. Veins I did not know Erik had were visibly pulsating through his skin. I was terrified! Men do not realize that they may actually be only a few inches taller but anger makes them seem like towering giants. I thought Erik was going to hit me. I could picture it.

I am not at all proud of what I did next but I did it because, in some strange world with topsy turvy logic, I thought it would help disrupt the flow of events and perhaps calm Erik down. I did it because, ultimately, I was afraid of what was coming next and I did not know what to do. My action disrupted the events all right. As Erik stood clenching his jaw so tight that I thought he might break his own teeth, he was talking through his clenched teeth in a very exaggerated and angrily calm voice like an extremely frustrated mother speaks to her child in the very public grocery store. I had had enough of being stalked, of being patronized, of being afraid. As Erik was in mid-sentence I suddenly leaned in close and kneed him square in the groin. Erik immediately stopped talking and his eyes grew extremely large. He even stopped breathing as he tried to gasp for air. I felt my head quizzically turn to the side as I wondered why he had not fallen to the ground?

Again, movies played a major part in this unfolding scene. In every movie I had ever seen as a child, I had observed that, when men are kicked in this area, they immediately fall to the ground. I was waiting for Erik to fall to the ground because that is what I had expected which would give me ample opportunity to run away and escape my shadow boyfriend. But alas, Erik stood like a statue letting out tiny gasps of air. I figured since I had never done this before that perhaps I had done it wrong so, again, I raised my knee and gave it the good ole' gold star try by kneeing Erik as hard as I could two more times. I stood back to see if, this time, my efforts had succeeded. Erik fell to his knees on the concrete and a small crowd gathered around him as he lost all ability to breathe for what seemed like an eternity. He was letting out sounds like moaning and he appeared to be crying.

I quickly realized that I was in deep trouble. Assaulting Erik was not a good idea. I felt terrible. I loved Erik. How could I hurt him? How had this spiraled so far out of hand that I was willing to physically assault my boyfriend? I ran off into the crowd. I felt so alone and without a friend in the world. My best friend, my very best friend, was lying flat on the concrete. How could he ever forgive me now?

It was like I had forgotten the simple thing that had made Erik so angry. It was as if I had amnesia and Erik was some kind of hero in my mind. "I had wronged Erik by kicking him," I thought as I tucked away the memories of Erik stalking me to the point that my friends were afraid to be with me because they might get hurt too. Did I forget it all and go running back to Erik? Yes, I did. About an hour later, enough time for me to go into Erik-withdrawals and feel totally and utterly out of control, Erik saw me from a distance. It was like we had been reunited after years of absence. All was forgiven and forgotten and we held each other like the couple on the movie poster for *Casablanca*. Cheek to cheek we leaned on each other in every line for the rides. We made those around us positively ill with our affection and oaths to never hurt one another again. Oh how could we have been so blind as to think we could breathe air without the other?

It was under this thick cloud of drama that Erik and I consummated our relationship in the back of his parents' minivan. No one would suspect a thing because we left directly from the school and Erik was supposed to drop me off at home. I was regularly lying to my mother now. I could write here that I was becoming an expert liar but that would be a lie. I was a terrible liar and, for convenience, my mother chose to tolerate my lying.

I had told Erik many times that I was a virgin but, when we engaged in intercourse, there was no sign of my virginity. Erik was baffled and suspicious that it was so. After all, he had learned everything there is to know about sex from pornography and the locker room and nothing was as he had imagined, he said, which hurt me terribly. The thought of me spoiled by another man disturbed him so greatly that he pressed me about my so-called virginity. This was incredulous. Years later I would become an expert car stereo system thief. I stole thousands of dollars' worth of car stereos and I felt entitled to those car stereos until the night that my own car was broken into and my own car stereo system was stolen. "How could they," I incredulously bemoaned. This was Erik, bemoaning the possibility of another man stealing what he thought was his while stealing what belonged to another man.

I swore to Erik that I had never had actual intercourse with any other man. I was telling the truth but Erik did not believe me. I felt such shame. I wondered why I had not been like a virgin since I was. Erik could tell that even I was disturbed. He was convinced that someone along the way had done something to me that I could not remember. He dropped me off at my home. All of this took place in a matter of thirty minutes or less. In thirty minutes or less a thief can come in and steal what is not theirs for life. I felt incredibly dirty. It was an awful experience and my high hopes were dashed. I could not believe that sex was that mechanical, awkward, and shameful contrary to what I had seen in movies. When I walked in the door, I felt more than ever a little girl who had no business trying to be a woman. I wanted to go back to the lack of knowledge and inexperience I had previously possessed but, once something is learned, it can never be unlearned just as the forbidden fruit can never be put back on the tree.

I felt so ashamed and Erik was, again, angry with me. Erik was so bereft at this situation that when he arrived home he called a psychic hotline. The "psychic" on the line told Erik that I had been raped and my conscious mind had buried the painful experience in my subconscious mind. This satisfied Erik. He called me on the phone. I was sobbing with shame and Erik comforted me and told me about the psychic.

"I'm so sorry! I was so wrong! I know you weren't lying now. I love you so much!" Erik offered all the comfort he could muster to soothe my aching heart.

From this point on, Erik and I entered into an even deeper level with one another. My mother, from time-to-time, would resurrect her efforts to separate the two of us but she was met with such great resistance from me that she would give in when she should have stood firm. This taught me that, if I pushed hard enough and stood strong enough, I could force my mother to give in to my wants and desires. What a huge mistake for a parent. You can never surrender into known sin. Never accept anything less than God's best for your child's life and, when that child seems bent on destruction, fight until the war is won. Never give up. If a parent surrenders to destructive forces even once in their child's life, those destructive forces will only thunder louder and more aggressively. Each and every time my mother tried to resist evil and then gave in, she would find that it was harder and harder to resist that evil. Sin will always struggle for the mastery. When we make up our mind to save our child, we must be in it to win it for the duration no matter what it takes.

Chapter 6

A Loose Screw

By this time, I had tried smoking. My biological father was a chain smoker and I took to smoking like a duck to water but, there was the problem of access. Though I loved cigarettes, I could not easily get them because I was only fifteen but, when Erik turned eighteen, he started smoking and, thus, we started smoking. I loved it. I loved the quick release of tension and the smack of smoke on the back of my throat that hurt. I loved that I had something in my hand to fiddle with. Mostly, I loved that I had something to help me with my anxiety and nervous energy.

The problem with smoking is that it smells like smoke. Where there is the proverbial smoke, there is the proverbial fire. I became incredibly addicted to cigarettes at the age of fifteen. I was too young to consider how smoking was threatening my already vulnerable immune system and challenging my health even further. I was too immature to think about how smoking would affect my appearance in later years. I was just like my biological father. Where other people could smoke one or two cigarettes a day, I wanted a cigarette every moment of the day and I quickly became a chain smoker. I itched to get out of school so I could light up a smoke.

At first, my mother resisted my new habit. Initially, I

tried hiding it from her. I will never forget one bright and sunny school morning when Erik had picked me up from my house to take me to school. My brothers and I went to the same school but I only allowed Erik to take me to school. I arrived at school and my mother was standing there to inspect me. She said with an investigative look in her eyes, "I smell smoke on you!" My reply came without thought, "Erik and I were kissing and he smokes so I smell like smoke." For whatever flagrant reason, the fact that I sucked the smoke right off Erik was an excuse worthy enough to satisfy my mother. At fifteen, I suppose my mother was more content to have me kissing a grown boy rather than smoking. My mother gave a hearty, "oh," in agreement and I walked away from her thinking that I had dodged a major bullet. If that had been my daughter reeking of nicotine, confessing a seemingly smaller known offense to cover a seemingly larger one, I would have ripped her out of school that day and taken her home away from Erik where neither smoking nor kissing was easily accessible. If my mother had done that at this time, I might have turned around. I would have kicked and screamed and caused major trouble and even threatened to kill myself but my mother would have shown me that she was the boss. I mistakenly thought that I was in charge of my life. I was no more in charge of myself than I was able to quit smoking or kissing.

It is easy for parents to put their heads in the sand. I would tell my parents that I was doing some activity with

Erik and, since I was a terrible liar, I would, in fact, do that activity but Erik and I would limit the duration of the activity to the bare minimum and leave an ample enough time for us to stop and "park" somewhere. I would come home with all my makeup rubbed off, hair messed up, and clothes ruffled and disheveled. It was plainly and evidently clear what we were doing.

One evening Erik and I broke down in his car on the side of the freeway. We used this opportunity to get very physical in the back of his car. This is further evidence of how illogical the teenage mind can be. We did not consider that we were on display for every car passing us on the 10 freeway despite the heavy fog that had built up on the car windows. To our shock, we had multiple police cruisers pull up to investigate our situation. I was utterly and totally humiliated as I rushed to put my clothes on. Buttons snapped off and zippers snagged. I got dressed in mere seconds that felt more like an eternity. I could hear the officers discussing among themselves how young I looked and I knew that we were in trouble.

As soon as we were dressed, they ordered Erik out of the vehicle and asked for his license. They ended up letting us go but, looking back, I wish they would have made a bigger deal out of the situation. It would have been better to have a little trouble early on than greater trouble later. This would not be, by any means, my last run-in with the law. This would be but the first sign. A couple of months later, Erik would want to see a movie. A dilemma arose when my mother declared that I could not go to the movie without doing my chores. Erik suggested that we play "doubles" on the highway and roads all the way to my house. This would give me enough time to do my chores and make it back to see the movie. We ended up being pulled over doing over 100 miles per hour in a 55 zone. We were pulled out of the car by the CHP officer and ordered to exit the vehicle with hands on our heads. As I knelt on the hard asphalt, I started to think that maybe Erik was not okay.

Yet again, Erik and I easily escaped trouble. The CHP officer knew Erik's parents and let Erik and I off a great deal easier than he would have let anyone else off. I often wonder if, had Erik been arrested, this might have given Erik and I the warning we so desperately needed that we were existing in a state of dangerous recklessness. Erik, often in fights, would use his vehicle to display his teenage frustration and he and I are blessed to be alive.

I did not even know what "doubles" was until I noticed that the speed of the car picked up at a tremendous rate. It did not alarm me because I thought for sure that Erik would never do anything to hurt me. I must admit that, when I thought that it might be possible to get home faster, I liked the idea but I trusted that, whatever Erik did, he would do with my best interest at heart. It was only later when Erik's mother scolded me, "how could you let him go that fast?" that it ever occurred to me that Erik could do something wrong. This was the beginning of the end: the realization of the fallibility of Erik.

My naivety started to fall from my eyes like scales as I started to note the unpredictability of Erik's moods. The more I questioned Erik and failed to demonstrate my total confidence in him, the angrier Erik became. We fought and fought and fought like a raging sea. I will never forget one particular fight because it seemed as if Erik had a break with reality.

He was driving his mother's forest green minivan and we were down in the bustling city of Redlands. This is where Erik and I went to meet up with other kids our age and visit coffee shops and roam around with each other. I cannot recall exactly what kicked off the fight but the fight was on. We fought over the most insignificant things. We both easily suffered hurt feelings. Both of our egos were as sensitive as baby skin. If ever there were two people who should not be in a relationship, we were those two.

Usually it was jealousy that really got Erik going. We were both very jealous and controlling. Erik's fears were very difficult to assuage and I was very difficult to say, "no," to. We were both equally stubborn though I was the lesser creature in stature and age. I was afraid of Erik. His ability to simmer for hours scared me. Erik was alight with rage and his anger was palpable. I could feel his turbulence the second we got in the minivan to go home. His quills were razor sharp and his tongue was skilled in the art of verbal death blows. I would offer back what I could but I was always cautious not to go too far because I knew that Erik could explode in ways I had not yet seen. To some degree, Erik's anger was an unknown entity to me. I knew it was there but I did not want to learn how bad it could get.

As Erik took the freeway onramp to start the thirty-minute drive home from Redlands into the surrounding mountains, a chill gripped me. The look in Erik's eyes was like looking into the fire. There was a destructive force in those eyes and I was afraid of getting burned. I am not exactly sure of what I said that started the screaming but I am certain it was none too wise nor kind. In any case, Erik started screaming and he said, "in the name of Satan I command you to crash this car." At this point, when Erik started speaking as if there were a third person present, I was beyond terrified. We were traveling at top speed down the 10 freeway and Erik was calling on evil forces to crash the car. I was not too sure, at first, as to how serious this was. "If he wanted the car to crash, wouldn't he just crash it?" I wondered. Then Erik started hyperventilating and talking nonsense. Erik completely let go of the wheel and we started to veer off into another lane of traffic. I had never driven before and I had no idea what I was doing. I screamed, "Erik! Erik! Drive! Take the wheel!"

Erik acted dazed and confused as he pulled over. Was he faking this to manipulate me? Was he really losing it? At fifteen, I had no idea what to make of this episode. Erik managed to pull it together enough to pull the car over to the side of the road but he was still muttering unintelligibly and acting as if he were seeing things that were not real. I was so afraid. I did not know what I should do. I did not know what my options were. I did the only thing that I thought was available to do: I got behind the wheel. This would be my very first experience with driving.

I told Erik to move over to the passenger side and I took my place as the driver. My hands were shaking and sweating. I felt sick. I had never even desired to drive before. I had not thought of getting my license prior to this. I was perfectly happy with Erik driving me around. I wanted him to be the responsible one and now I was called to lead and I absolutely hated every minute of it. I was so angry inside that Erik had the nerve to break down when I needed strength. Erik twitched and muttered in the passenger seat as I slowly paced the minivan up a long curvy mountain road in less than desirable weather. Erik continued to call out to satanic forces as we drove home. I did not know what was real and what was for show. I was so confused and alarmed and scared. My teenage brain failed to see the extreme danger in the situation and the great need for parental guidance. I only focused on my own heart-felt needs. I was broken-hearted, broken-hearted that my perfect Erik was far from perfect and, lately, starting to appear further and further from being mine.

It was awkward as Erik's dad drove me home after I safely drove Erik home. Erik's dad was a very kind man. I wished he were my father. He was not sure what to say to the young, blonde, fifteen-year-old girl who was now starting to dress like the poster girl for *Nirvana*, who reeked of cigarette smoke, and whose eyes were red and swollen from crying. What to say? This night was a turning point for Erik and I. I had grown exhausted of Erik's outbursts and instability yet I was too afraid to let him go. I wanted to be with Erik forever but, at the same time, I knew that Erik was incapable of offering me what I was craving. The infatuation was steadily fizzling out like a balloon losing its air. We were up and down and chaos all over.

Erik and I would attempt to reignite our passion for one another, over and over again, by fighting. It was terrible. His friends did not want to be around him because of the torrid drama and, my friends...well...I did not really have any friends by this point. The up and downs were so dramatic, who could stand it? Any one of my peers who got involved with me as a friend could quickly observe that I was in a very abusive relationship but what could they do? Those who tried to help would get burned themselves. Anyone who put all the effort into trying to help me out of the relationship would only hear my resolve to stay away from Erik and then observe me running back to him and vowing my undying love. I needed my parents to intervene. My parents did not know what to do and they were afraid for my safety. Everyone was. My relationship was the very definition of a flaming roller coaster ride. Even roller coaster rides come to an end.

Our breakups were marked with hang-up phone calls, screaming, a torrent of tears, and, many, many times, Erik would pull up to my house with screeching tires. He was not going to let me go. If I broke up with him, he would resolve to do whatever it takes to get me back. If he struck back at me by breaking up with me, I would panic and resolve to get Erik back. I knew he and I were ripping each other apart but the memory of the safe moments in our relationship, when I felt completely okay in myself, were like a drug beckoning me back to that first high. Why did I need him so badly to feel alright? Why did I have such great anxiety when I was away from him?

I had a couple of girlfriends who tried to help me out and have me over to their home all day, every day, and my parents were so happy that I was not with Erik that this became the measure of what was good for me. "As long as she's not with Erik," became the standard. I could do anything under that banner. I hitchhiked for the first time, tried my first beer, huffed paint, continued to deepen my smoking habit, and hung out with all manner of strange and random boys. But, all this time, I felt great anxiety like I was desperately trying to dig my way out of a deep hole inside me. I ached to have Erik back in my life. He was like a security blanket. I often found myself stranded without rides and I confused the fact that Erik had a car and could get me out of sticky situations as Erik being safe when he was just a method out of the madness. Erik was my version of organized chaos. Still chaotic but a known quantity that I could manipulate to a degree. Though the crew had mutinied long ago, Erik was like a maneuverable ship on a vast turbulent and uncontrollable sea.

I will never forget the times Erik called my house after a violent fight. He had worked himself up into a frenzy. He called my house fifty if not one hundred times. My parents were fed up with the ringing. I felt really bad that Erik was now holding the family phone line hostage with his incessant phone calls. Erik decided to up the ante by coming by my house and parking outside.

Alec was sick to death of this teenage drama and he made it known. He could not say Erik's name without adding an air of expletive-filled sarcasm. In his larger-than-life Samoan way, he stomped down our long driveway to the street. We lived on a cul-de-sac so Erik's exits were very limited. Alec was, in a word, intimidating. Any normal young man should have been terrified to see this large Samoan heading toward him. Alec was utterly annoyed and pounding the pavement with his gigantically wide feet in Erik's direction but Erik was not normal.

Erik had exited his vehicle and was now standing in the middle of the street just outside our home and loudly screaming my name into the night sky. Erik's repeated incantations could be heard all over the neighborhood. I was utterly humiliated.

I must admit that my stomach was in knots as I

watched Alec confront Erik on the street. I will never forget peeking through the blinds of my bedroom window. Who was I rooting for? I was team Alec all the way and, if they had come to blows, I was still team Alec. I would have been team Alec at any point in my life if I had known that I could safely do so without fear of rejection, criticism, or hurt. I was incredibly disappointed in Erik's unpredictable behavior and this was way more drama and attention than any fifteen-year-old girl was prepared to handle.

After an exchange of words, Alec determined that Erik had a screw loose and therefore Alec decided to leave Erik screaming in the street as he pulled our front gate shut. Erik did just that. My mother would forbid me from meeting Erik's demands which were, of course, for me to go outside and speak to him. This would not be the last time that Erik would scream in my street nor would it be the last time he unleashed a telephone campaign against me. Erik was stubborn but so was I. Usually, Erik grew tired and went home wherein he proceeded to call my house or I would feel bad for him and I would go running out to talk to him. We would both scream in the street at each other until one of us conceded defeat at which point we would both cry and declare our love. God bless my neighbors for not calling the cops on me any more than they did.

I think the story warrants sharing how truly disappointed I was in Erik's behavior. I had expected Erik to be a perfect savior for me and he was turning out to be anything but. I could feel the depression sinking back in. Like an old friend, the depression returned, slinking leisurely through the door of my heart. When once with Erik I felt self-assured and strong, I now felt self-conscious and chaotic inside. I felt myself starting to look for someone else. When things were good with Erik, I felt completely happy with him but, now, I felt completely out of control and like I had a deep need to look around for someone else. This would cause more fights.

Erik had been everything to me. I was losing my best friend and a pseudo-husband. He had rescued me out of terrible situations. One Thanksgiving, my mother had invited my uncle over for a holiday meal. I had told Erik of the horrific photography session and Erik listened to my tale of woe in shock and horror that my mother would have allowed such things to happen to me. I yelled and screamed in protest at my mother for allowing my uncle to come to Thanksgiving dinner but that meant nothing to my mother nor to my family. Instead, Erik came to my rescue and facilitated my escape. He took me to another home and to another family where I licked my wounds. Although I was hurting, I was pretty good at bouncing back mostly because I would pretend that, instead of being a guest in someone's home, they were my actual family. I did this all the time. I was an expert pretender.

As the months wore on, it was more and more difficult to pretend that Erik and I had something good. Between the fights and battles and raging of our romance, it was extremely evident that something had to give. Around this time, Erik and I had started hanging out with a punk rock group that, oddly enough, studied the Bible. I started attending Bible studies and gaining strength. When Erik and I had a ridiculously outrageous fight, it was easier, this time, for me to find the strength to resist Erik's pleadings to come back to him.

I told myself that, this time, I would be strong. I would resist, I would do better and change my life. We were broken up for good and it would stay that way, I resolved. I had new friends at the Bible study who were willing to help me stay away from Erik. I needed that. All of my friends, if you could call them that, were Erik's friends. I needed my own group for support and the Bible study group provided just that. These friends were much older than I but I felt like I was enduring the kind of trials that girls my age could not identify with.

Chapter 7

The Shortcut

One problem with being younger was that I could not drive. I was scared of driving now and not at all interested in learning or getting my permit. This made me dependent on my friends for transportation. I certainly did not want my mother driving me places though she often did. Thankfully, everyone at my new Bible study was extremely helpful and they offered to give me rides to and from Bible study.

I had not been together with Erik for nearly a week on one particular Friday afternoon. This was a record time for me to stay away from him. Bible study was tonight and I readied myself for it. I had been offered a ride to Bible study by one of the guys that attended. He knew the terrible dilemma that I was having with Erik and he always offered his assistance to help me get away from Erik. He was ten years older than I and nearing his twenty-fifth birthday. I had known of him in the past but I had never spent any time alone with him. He was quiet and had an angry look in his eye. He attended Bible study and had very strong opinions on everything. He still lived with his parents and he was very overweight. I did not find him attractive in the slightest but, if he was offering friendly company, I was naive enough to accept it.

I still remember his little truck pulling up to my house. It had a camper shell on the back. I will never know why my mother was okay with her little girl going off alone with an older man. I think the words, "Bible study," gave her a false sense of security. This man was supposed to be taking me to Bible study. He was supposed to be safe. Everyone that goes to Bible study can be trusted, right? Not at all.

I will never forget driving down the 10 freeway away from my home and I will never forget Byron pulling off the freeway to "take a shortcut." I was not yet alarmed at this point. Byron drove further and further out into the middle of nowhere. The high desert boasts some of the most picturesque nature scenes and I loved to go on nature walks and explore but I was starting to get nervous as I noticed that there was nothing around us. We were obviously not going to Bible study and I was starting to get scared. In fact, I was so scared that I started to feel myself freeze up once again.

I was too afraid to ask what was happening. I was too afraid to inquire if we were really going to Bible study or not. I was getting a sick feeling in my stomach. Mostly, it started to sink in that something awful was about to happen. "Again?" I thought to myself. "Must this happen to me again? Why does this stuff always happen to me?" With the boy at church, there was an initial interest and I could somewhat hold myself responsible for following him to a strange place. I had thought that boy was the epitome of coolness but Byron was not attractive and I only tolerated him as a friend to get a ride.

As Byron drove further and further away from

civilization and out into the desert, I was completely frozen in fear. I did not know what to say or what to do. I was just a young girl. I remember Byron carefully navigating his truck down the dirt paths and I remember him putting the truck into park. I remember the look in his eye as he avoided eye contact with me. I remember his hands going down my pants and I remember resisting and I remember saying, "no." I had no control over what happened next. I had no ability to fight off a grown, six-foot-tall, twenty-five-year-old man who was at least double my weight.

Byron said, "I am just going to give you a massage so sit back and relax."

"A massage? Yeah right," I thought.

"I don't really want a massage," I said to which I was told that I did, in fact, want a massage.

I again declined the massage but it was too late.

I stared out the car window into the wilderness and saw no escape as things were happening to my body that I did not want or sanction. In that moment, if I had possessed the physical strength to kill a man, I would have killed Byron. I would have sliced him open and watched him writhe in pain. I could have tortured him a thousand ways and enjoyed every second of it because that was what he was doing to me. He was torturing my soul and he was doing it for his own satisfaction.

At a certain point during the rape, my mind went numb and I lose some of my memory. When Byron was finished, he talked to me as if I had enjoyed it and like I had wanted these things to happen. I sat there thinking that I was going crazy. Had I somehow communicated to Byron that I liked him? Was I betraying myself somehow and making these things happen to me? I felt like I was going to vomit. I did not understand how rapists groom their victims. I was shocked and horrified as Byron talked to me like I was now his girlfriend. I was not his girlfriend! He was fat and ugly and annoying and I hated him now.

I stared blankly out the window as Byron talked. I tuned him out. My mind was in a fog and I had to protect myself and keep myself from going stark raving mad by making myself go numb. I wanted to change my body like I changed clothes. Could I simply take my body off like a pair of dirty jeans that needed to be washed? I hated my body. It was dirty and in need of a good washing. The car stopped and we had arrived at Bible study. Oh yes, Bible study. I had forgotten all about Bible study. Would Byron seriously walk into Bible study like nothing had happened? Would he pretend to study the Bible and still offer his annoying opinions on everything? Yes, he would. It was like nothing had happened.

It was as if time ticked on as a cruel joke. The anticlimactic way that life simply went on always mocked the trauma of my experience. The fact that the police did not immediately pull up with sirens blaring and the fact that every event went on like nothing had happened made me think that, if the world would simply carry on, then so would I. I had to. No one cared about me. No one knew what had happened to me.

I was terrified to get back into the car with Byron for the ride home but I had no choice. I had no way of getting back home. I had to endure an entire thirty-minute car ride home with Byron and I think he drove even slower to have more time with me. He spoke to me like I was his property. It messed with my head. He was an expert groomer. He made me question myself and he made me think that I had caused what had happened and deserved it too.

When we finally got to my house, I exited the car before it had even stopped. I slammed the car door in a fury and ran inside my house. I ran through the garage and inside through the kitchen to my room. My family could tell that I was upset and my mother followed me to my room.

I was so angry at what had happened to me. I was furious! I had merely tolerated Byron out of the need for a ride but now he had taken liberties with my body as his own and without my permission. As I heard my mother walking down the hallway to my room, I resolved not to lie to her but to tell her the truth. I wanted recompense for my suffering. I wanted justice. My mother opened my room door and asked me what was going on. I knew my older brother was behind her and could hear me. I told her that, "Byron drove off into the middle of nowhere and did stuff to me."

According to the law, my mother could have called the

police on Byron based on the simple fact that Byron was ten years older than I. She could even have taken me to the hospital and had a rape kit done and they would have found Byron's DNA. She could have done quite a few things and I was expecting her to be furious. I wanted her to be furious. I needed her to know but, instead, the worst thing happened and I felt raped again. My mother got this deer-in-the-headlights look on her face like she had not heard a word I said. It was like the lights were on but nobody was home. She simply said, "okay," in a Stepford wife tone and then turned around and walked straight out of my room and went back to whatever it was that she was doing. Nothing happened and no one said anything. This was the worst part of it all.

The next torturous part happened the following day. I went to church and, as I rounded a corner that led out into the church lobby, I stopped short and started to panic. There was Byron. I was frozen in fear. I could not move my legs. He saw me and he acted like I was too dirty to even talk to. He treated me like I was a dirty little whore. This was his plan. After all, it was all my fault. I had "forced" a grown man, ten years my senior, to do all those things to me down a deserted dirt road. But wait, my heart pounded so loud in my chest that I thought I might pass out. There was my brother walking toward Byron. My brother had heard everything that had happened to me. Surely my brother was going to punch Byron in the face.

They had never been friends and Byron never really

liked my brother. I stood there, frozen with anxiety, waiting to see what would happen next. Byron could see me standing nearby and I knew that he was aware that I was watching. To my total shock and betrayal, Byron singled out my brother and held out his hand for a high five from my brother. I felt sure that my brother would never agree to such an alliance and betrayal of his own sister. Byron looked up at me and made eye contact with me as my brother's hand met his own for that great big high five as if to say, "no one will ever believe you."

As I watched my brother enjoy getting attention from Byron and Byron's group of friends, I felt like someone had kicked me in the stomach. The air was literally knocked out of me as I watched my brother laugh at Byron's dumb jokes. Byron had never cared to spend any time or be friendly with my brother before but now he did. Byron was assessing my brother's behavior to see exactly how much my brother knew or if he knew anything at all. I felt totally and utterly betrayed by my own flesh and blood. Never before had a feeling of total and complete loneliness set in like it did now. I felt like the only person on the face of the earth and like a cloud had settled on me. At times, I had felt as though I had left my family for Erik but now I knew that there was no family to leave for Erik. It felt as though they had never truly been a family to me. My mother was only interested in that which was convenient or that which served her selfish endeavors or made her look good. She had taught my older brother to be the same way.

I was alone. I was at church and surrounded by people but I was alone. I was heartbroken and used up. I wanted to crawl into a small space and shake all over with hurt and pain but I knew that no one would even care if I did. I was an inconvenience to my family and nothing but a little whore to the rest of the world. I did not know what to do so I did what I knew to do. I went and found a telephone in the church office and I called Erik's house. I knew he would be home on a Saturday morning and, when I heard his voice on the other end of the line, I started to cry. I was like a dog crawling back to its vomit. It was what was familiar to me and the only family I had. I needed rescuing and a ride away from the abuse. I wanted to change my body, my family, and my surroundings and I thought Erik could do most of that for me.

Erik eagerly came to my rescue and was there at the church in what seemed like only a few minutes. I hopped in his car and left the scene of the pain. I left it behind like an old story. My family would not even care where I had gone. As Erik drove down the freeway, I rolled down the window and let the breeze carry me off somewhere. I smiled at Erik and held his hand. "Erik was safe," I thought. "As messed up as he is, at least he doesn't rape people," I thought. Erik knew something had happened to me but I could not bring myself to share all the details with him. After my mom and brother, I could not bear another person's betrayal on this issue. I knew that what had happened was bad but the fact that my family had treated me like it was not a big deal baffled me. I put the entire ordeal out of my head and decided not to think about it, ever. But it is never that easy.

In an abusive relationship, things are always good for the first couple of days after getting back together or after a fight but there is an underlying feeling that will not go away. It is like sleeping with a bowling ball under the mattress. You can sleep on the bed and happily pretend it is not there but, eventually, someone is going to get a backache and declare the issue. Erik and I had major issues. I was not the same after the rape. I was more irritable and angry. I got angry at the slightest things. If Erik failed to buy me something I wanted, I would blow up at him. My anger at Byron came out at Erik and, thus, our relationship was that much more volatile.

It was now the summer and we were able to spend even more time together. This was not good. The more time we spent together, the more we fought. There was a huge wall between us. Erik had started drinking with one of his friends and I started drinking with them.

I took to the numbing effect of alcohol like a bear to honey. The rape had left me feeling anxious and jumpy but, between the cigarettes and alcohol, I was effectively numbing myself. Now I really did not want to go anywhere where I could not smoke or drink because I was completely addicted to the cigarettes and I craved the alcohol-induced numbness. I felt chaotic inside and I had no peace. I was restless and not inclined to rest. I was not sleeping well and I had nightmares. I was not feeling well either. My health was declining and I was having more strep throat and sinus infections. Things were going from bad to worse to catastrophic.

Chapter 8

At The Beach

Erik's family was a very active and social family. They were very involved at the private school where Erik and his brothers attended. Even though it was summer, they had organized a 4th of July trip with the other parents from Erik's brother's class. The trip was organized so that a large group of parents would all chip in for a single hotel room in La Jolla, California. The hotel was right on the beach so the kids could all come and go and use the hotel room as their base of operations. The California beaches on the 4th of July are swarming with people and La Jolla is a city that boasts some of the wealthiest people in the nation. It is a beautiful city with many shops that sell beautiful works of art. Erik was going and, thus, I was going. He was excited to go but I was ambivalent. I did not want to be around all the people and the other kids I was envious of. It was becoming very evident that, when it came to family, I had drawn the short straw. I was drinking the poisonous cup of bitterness and I had a very low tolerance for other kids my age who seemed to have perfect lives and perfect families. I was a disturbed young girl who was crying out for help but nobody heard me.

Of course, a day at the beach would not be complete unless Erik and I were fighting. True to form, as soon as we arrived at the hotel room, Erik was being friendly with the other girls my age and I became jealous of his friendly conversations and lighthearted mood. I was not happy and I did not want him to be happy. I wanted him to only want to be with me and I did not want to be around all those happy kids and happy parents. I wanted to be alone with Erik under my dark little cloud. I wanted to wallow in my self-pity and misery and I did not want to do it alone.

Erik was not having it. We were on his turf. His family had organized the day and it was his family's friends. He wanted to enjoy himself and not engage in another fight with me. I should have been happy that we had managed not to fight. Everyone present that day was walking on eggshells waiting for Erik and I to erupt in a plangent, catastrophic, earth-shattering conflict but it did not happen. Everyone breathed a sigh of relief.

Once more, I had walked out of the hotel room and left the premises and I knew that everyone would be happier for it. I was irritated and alarmed by the most frightening thing on the planet to me: Erik was indifferent to me. Indifference to me was greater than hate and greater than contempt. Love me, hate me, react to me but never ignore me. As the door to the hotel room slammed and locked behind me, I caught sight of Erik seated in a lounge chair on the hotel room balcony and he looked happy. I flagellated myself with the thought that he was better off without me.

I decided, at first, to walk around La Jolla looking for candy but then I realized I did not have any money. So, in the hot and crowded beach city, I walked from art studio to art studio looking at expensive works of art. At first it was fun but I felt, again, like I did not belong. I made my way to the beachfront. I did not care if I got lost. I did not even care if I made it back to the hotel. I had only been gone for an hour or so and I knew that no one would be looking for me. I sat in the sand and gazed out at the beautiful Pacific Ocean and I felt as empty as the sea is full of water. A terrible wave of depression overtook me and I sat on the beach and cried. I was surrounded by people and no one saw the young girl crying tears of woe. If anyone had stopped to ask me what was wrong, I might have poured out my story to a stranger. But, the people moved past me just like I was truly invisible.

After a long cry, I finally got up and walked along the boardwalk. I wished I had brought my skateboard that day but, since I had not, I walked along begrudgingly as I stared at the cruising skateboarders. I found a nice spot that had a railing I could lean against. From my vantage point, I could look down on the shore and watch the waves come and go and I could also watch the surfers. To my left were the stairs that took beachgoers down to the shoreline and the tide pools. The sun was getting low in the sky as the beachgoers were scampering to and fro to find the perfect spot to observe the fireworks.

I stood still. I was like a statue in a time-lapse piece. All these people moved around me but I stood still. I had been gone for two hours and I was starting to feel a bit worried that some of the parents might get angry with me for being gone so long. I pushed those thoughts away and continued to gaze out at the beautiful blue ocean in its incredible vastness. I thought about the other lands and nations on the other side of that great watery expanse. "I wish I could travel," I thought. I wish I could leave here and become someone else. I felt the deep sadness that had settled in my chest while I pondered the great questions of life. Where am I going? Where am I from? What purpose do I have? Who loves me? All of these questions elicited great emotional pain because the answer to every one of those questions was nowhere, nothing, and no one. My chest ached even more.

My heart felt like it was breaking but I did not know why nor could I put words to what I was feeling. Was it grave disappointment or utter despair? There was a general overall void where God was supposed to be. All the places in my life where something was supposed to exist were filled with absolutely nothing. My parents had no place in my heart. My family had no place in my heart. My hopes and dreams seemed dashed to pieces. Love had piddled out and drained from my very being. I had no peace. I was adrift and tossed by the wind whatever way it blew. Where was my leader to lead me? Where was an anchor to secure me? I knew in my heart that I was a lost sheep but I was also sure that there was no shepherd to notice I was missing and come find me. I felt so alone.

It was as I was thinking these dreadful and hopeless thoughts of loneliness and self-pity that I heard his voice. Like Eve when she heard the soft and beguiling serpent in the Garden of Eden, I heard a soft, deep, and masculine tone reach my ears like a welcomed melody. I turned to see a beautiful figure of a man. He looked like a Greek god, standing there shirtless with his skin glowing in the hot summer sun. His voice made the hairs on my body stand straight up. His appearance frightened and thrilled me at the same time. He was the most handsome man that had ever as of yet spoken to me.

"Are you all by yourself here?" he asked. At first, I assumed that he was perhaps lost and needed assistance but, as he spoke and asked me numerous questions, he leaned against the railing with me in a relaxed and charming manner. "He is choosing to spend his time with me," I thought with amazement. I felt honored and my mood went from depressed to elated as I carefully watched this man leisurely lean against the rail. He had a charming and winsome smile that sparkled. His eyes were blue and alight with the intelligence of many years. His hair was wavy, dark, and speckled with gray. His skin was deeply tanned and he towered over me. I could not believe that this man was spending time with me.

At first, I felt incredibly shy and I stammered as I spoke to him. As the time passed between us, my self-confidence returned and I was able to weakly offer some girlish flirtation in return to his much more experienced sexual innuendos. I was only able to offer the most basic of questions. I had often mocked the other girls my age and their inadequate ability to hold a conversation. "They are so immature," I often told myself and others. To me, the other girls seemed only capable of scratching the surface when conversing among themselves. I, on the other hand, was much deeper and adept at holding an intelligent conversation that went far beyond the mere pleasantries of life. But, there I stood, leaning against a rail with one of the most handsome men I had ever gazed upon in my young life, and all that seemed to come out of my mouth were words that failed at being anything remarkable. Next to his intelligence, his beauty, and his age, I felt so very plain and even somewhat dumb.

"How old are you?" I nervously and shyly inquired.

"I am too old," he laughed! "No, really," I pushed being that this was the only question I could think of.

"How old are you?" I asked again.

"Well, I am almost forty."

"Oh," was all I could say in return for his brutal honesty. He did not look forty years old to me but more like a young man in his twenties. It really was his appearance that made him look so young. He was dressed like a surfer or a skater with his board shorts and flip flops. If it were not for his salt and pepper hair, he could have lied and told me that he was eighteen and I would have believed him.

"What kind of car do you drive?" I asked. "Oh man. Why do I have to sound stupid? Why can't I think of something to say that sounds brilliant and more sophisticated?" I silently chastised myself.

"I drive a Toyota Land Cruiser," he said in a tone that suggested shame. I had hit a nerve. He explained that it was his mother's but that he would not be driving it for long because he was getting his life "back together."

Again, he pressed me to know what a girl like me was doing all alone on a beach with no friends or family nearby. I did not realize how terribly I stood out. I had porcelain white skin that was rarely tanned by the sun. I was wearing long jeans, Converse shoes, and a thinly knit thrift store t-shirt. I looked more like I spent my leisure time loitering and smoking cigarettes outside a coffee shop or like an alternative rock band roadie than a beachgoer. I was like a giant, red, sore thumb or a huge target. It was as if the beach scene was playing a big game of, "one of these things is not like the other, one of these things just doesn't belong," and I was what did not belong. Like a wounded gazelle on the African plains ripe for the picking, I was easily spotted and cried out as the limping prey fixing to be someone's lunch.

The way he was able to maneuver through the conversation with such smoothness and direct flirtation was a spectacle to behold. Only in my dreams could I be that polished and easy with my words. It always took me a long time to warm up to people so I could converse with ease but this guy was all out and in full force for me to see. He used his language like an artist painting a murder scene because that is exactly what was happening. However, this murder of the soul, this poisonous snake, was slow to strike. He groomed me like a rake grooms the sand. It was nearly professional. I have often wondered how many girls went through what I did by this man because he was too good to not have had practice.

His flirtation grew to downright pushiness and his suggestions transitioned into commands. First, he suggested that we kiss. I immediately felt the blood rush to my head as I stood there thinking of poor Erik back at the hotel room waiting for me. "This cannot happen," I thought. "Not again!" I had not the words to describe what I felt. Was it a trapped feeling? Did I feel trapped? Why weren't my feet running away like I wanted them to? Why was I just standing there? I felt...I felt obligated. This was way worse.

It is a well studied fact that, once a child experiences childhood sexual abuse, that child is 2 to 13.7 times more likely to be re-victimized (more on this in chapter 14). This is because sexual predators can easily seek out the vulnerable and they can observe that this individual has been traumatized before. The bitterness, the knowledge of good and evil, and the lack of childhood naivety is written on the countenance for predators to easily read like a children's book. We are low hanging fruit for another's perverse pleasure.

He read my thoughts and played on my feelings like a musician on their favorite musical instrument. Because he was so handsome, so much older than I, and had spent so much time talking to me and greatly bolstering my ego, I felt that I owed him and that I could not hurt his feelings by rejecting him. He knew this. He said, "you aren't going to hurt me by telling me, 'no,' are you?" I felt trapped. He attempted to kiss me but I was terrified that someone who knew Erik would see me so I pushed him away. He was irritated and then was downright angry but then quickly transitioned back to charming. He skillfully maintained a charming affect while simultaneously intimidating me. He smiled at the throngs of people passing by but grabbed my hand and tightly squeezed it.

He gestured to a dark set of stairs that led down several flights to the beach. "Let's go down there away from the people," he directed. The sun was setting and the beach was now cloaked in the tendrils of darkness. People were scurrying to get to their places before the patriotic fireworks started but I silently complied with my new fearless leader. I followed him down the dark steps until he stopped, turned around, threw me up against a rock, and forced himself on me. I said, "no, please don't, I have a boyfriend." I felt as if I were a mouse in the presence of a lion as I quietly said, "no, no, no," repeatedly into the air. Up above me, I could see the many legs of the masses of people moving about. I could hear the sounds of people laughing and talking but they could not hear me. No one could hear me now and I knew that resistance was futile. I was between wanting someone to hear me and hoping they did not hear me because I was so ashamed. I was completely and utterly frozen and I was so panicked by the thought of Erik. In this moment, I wanted Erik so badly. I wanted to be home so badly.

I was so incredibly embarrassed and embarrassed of what I had become. I blamed myself for everything. I was a slut. I was a dirty whore. I deserved everything I got. I was a rebel girl who needed to, "just do it and get it over with." So, I did. Under the loud, pounding explosions of 4th of July pyrotechnics with the subsequent cheers and screams of a gleeful and patriotic audience, with thousands of people around me, a complete stranger raped me.

When he was done, he adjusted himself and looked at me with little interest. I was all used up now. Oddly enough, in that moment the way he now looked at me hurt the most. Where was his charm and flirtatiousness? He now looked at me with an air of disgust as he craned his neck to look this way and that to see if anyone had witnessed his dirty deed perpetrated on a fifteen-year-old girl. His caution was too little, too late. No one had seen us but he was hardly concerned in the beginning and now he seemed filled with embarrassment.

My body hurt from being slammed into the surrounding rocks. My feet were completely drenched from standing in the wet rocks that border the little tide pools. I wondered how I would hide what had just happened to me from Erik and his friends and family. I wanted to return to the part where the strange man and I had just been flirting. I had felt on top of the world then. And now? Now I felt used and dirty. I wanted to peel my skin off my body like a piece of fruit shedding its bruised peeling and leave it behind at the scene of the crime. I wanted to throw myself off the rocks into the ocean. The ocean was full and I was so very empty.

He turned to look at me but his eyes were full of fear like he was worried that I was going to scream and alert everyone around us to the deed that had been done with a fifteen-year-old girl right under the noses of all humanity. He nervously spoke to me. Gone was his alluring charm. Gone was the flirtation. Gone was the incredible high that came with his attention. Every high has a low and this was very, very low. I appeared to him like a penny that had lost its shine and I felt the great loss of my shininess.

He would not look me in the eye as he said, "so, uh, thanks for the good times." He said this to me like I had been a willing participant in this tryst. This attitude toward me really messed with my head and caused me to question myself. "Was I this kind of girl? What had I done to appear welcoming to this?" He reached around me to give me a hug but I shook my head, "no." He shrugged his shoulders to show me that he could care less if I rejected his affection because he had already taken what he wanted. He felt the frigidly cold mood I was in. His enthusiasm toward the idea of leaving me right where he found me was palpable.

"Well, take care! I gotta go do some stuff! See you

later!" Without fanfare or ceremony, he abruptly ended our brief encounter without even the pretense that he was going to ask for my phone number. At this moment, I thought that, if he asked for my phone number, the dirtiness of what had just happened would not sting so much. He used me for what he wanted. He turned and walked away so quickly that it seemed as if he would break out into a run if that would not make him look more suspicious should I decide to, at last, scream in front of all these people. But, I did not scream. Instead, I watched his tall, dark frame fade into the sea of people never to be seen again. I pondered his words, "see you later," and I knew that I would, in fact, never see him again.

I had little time to sit and ponder these facts before the panic and realization that I had been gone for hours and hours hit me. I was turned around and I knew that, by now, Erik might be looking for me. I did not even know what I was going to say to Erik. My stomach was in knots and I was panicking. My heart was beating so fast and my anxiety was so high as I thought of every worst-case scenario. "What if I were left at the beach? What if Erik finds out about the strange man on the beach?" I was so worried that Erik had seen me with the man on the beach or that, somehow, I would run into the man on the beach again and he would reveal my new secret to Erik. I was in a panic to get back to the hotel but I was lost. The night was dark and growing colder and colder by the second. I had no idea how I would get home if I were left behind by Erik's family. I had no money and, thus, no way to make a phone call home for help. Calling home was my absolute last resort. Calling my parents out of their home this late at night, to make a nearly two-hour drive to the beach, was not an option. I would never hear the end of it if I inconvenienced my parents in such a manner.

I walked back to the railing and determined to retrace my steps. Standing back at the railing made me think of the man who had just left me. The events that had just transpired were such rapid ones. I went from spending the day depressed and alone to meeting a charming man who raised my romantic hopes and my devastated self-esteem so high, only to leave me worse off than I was before. I struggled to process and rationalize the realities of the day.

I needed to carefully concentrate on the direction of my feet and what I was going to say when I got back to Erik. But the man on the beach intruded upon my thoughts like a skilled cat burglar. He was going to break into my mind no matter how hard I tried to keep him out. He was there now, in my mind, and there was nothing I could do to make him leave. He will forever be the cat burglar intruding into my thinking to ruin perfectly wonderful days without any warning. It takes but a smell, a song, or fireworks, especially fireworks, to trigger a break-in of his memory.

"I can't think of this now," I told myself. "I need to get back to Erik and then I can think about this." I made my way through the celebratory events of July Fourth. Every happy scene of the day seemed to mock my trepidation and pain. I had backtracked my steps from the railing, through the crowd, and past landmarks that I could recall from earlier in the day. Soon, all too soon, I was standing outside the hotel door that I had let slam on Erik only hours before. I had worked up a story in my mind that sort of made sense to me but I was not completely sure how I would get through with the lies that I would have to spin and then confidently stand by.

Suddenly, like a dream, I was standing before Erik and his friends. "Where were you?" asked Erik, half annoyed and half concerned. "I was looking all over for you!"

What came out of my mouth was part genius and part verbal diarrhea. It was one of the best lies I have ever been able to concoct in my entire life. I have always been a terrible liar but this lie was amazing because my mind was trying to convince even me that it was true and that this thing called rape had not occurred. I wanted to believe my own lie. I wanted to believe that, if anything, I had met a man and willingly engaged in a romantic affair. "I was not raped," I told myself.

"I walked around all day," I said to a group of kids only a little older than I in an innocent and exasperated tone so no one would question my impromptu tale of woe. "I sat on the beach then I decided to go down into the wading pools. I sat on a rock watching the sunset for so long that I didn't even notice the tide coming in around me. I was stuck on a rock for a long time before I decided to just brave the water." I checked and double checked the faces of the people I was talking to in order to make sure that I was believable. Everyone seemed satisfied with my story, everyone but one.

One particular girl, only a year older than I, apparently had a gut feeling. She looked at me with a discriminating glare and started questioning my story. She was taller than I and, in that moment, she seemed to stand like a giant. She had the power to destroy my story if I let her. My jeans were only wet around my feet from standing in the tide pool with the man from the beach. She questioned me, "you were sitting on a rock that entire time? It doesn't look like you swam through water."

"Well, I did!" I said with feigned outrage which only quenched her curiosity a little. I could tell that this girl knew just what a liar looked like and she saw a liar in me. She knew I was lying and I would have to do some verbal acrobatics to convince her but I was very aware that, if I kept talking, I would betray myself so I gave the inquisitive girl the cold shoulder and iced her out. This secured her silence. The one person that could have discovered the truth was not an adult but a girl like me and, therefore, she had no real power to out me and I knew it.

As soon as the conversation moved on from me and my whereabouts that day, I felt a great sense of relief. The entire day seemed like a video game. I jumped through one hurtle just to come upon another and, once I had found my way back to the hotel, I had to convince Erik. Once I had convinced Erik and his family, I felt triumphant. I was elated that I had not been left behind by Erik and his family and, therefore, my parents would not have to be told a thing of the day's events. The feeling of doom was lifting. I was just about to sit and enjoy the rest of the evening with a happier Erik, who had missed me while I was missing, when reality started sinking in and the cat burglar returned.

Erik and I, with other kids, piled into our respective vehicles to make the long, two-hour journey home. I tortured myself with the day's events and I tried to rewrite its history in my mind with the, "what I should have said," and, "what I should have done," mental torture. Everywhere I looked, I thought I saw his Land Cruiser. Mostly, I quietly cried. I cried the entire way home. Erik noticed my mood and sought to discover the reason for my despair but I iced him out too. I said nothing. I was silent. I had no words to describe what had happened. I knew Erik would only rage if he discovered the truth and even blame me for talking to a strange man in the first place. So, all I could do, the only solution for the moment, was to cry salty tears.

Chapter 9

Apple in the Sun

After that July Fourth, things would never be the same again between Erik and I. There was no particular fight that soured things. It was a slow and steady descent into contempt for one another. I had become a prickly pear. I did not want to be touched but I was a walking contradiction as my appetite for all things sexual waxed and waned. I was beginning to see sex as a form of power. Whoever dominated in the sexual relationship had the power. I wanted my lost power back. I was just beginning to understand the tremendous power that sex had over men and I wanted to learn to use this power against others before it was used against me again. I was turning sixteen and I knew enough to be dangerous to myself and to others.

If anyone had been paying closer attention to me, they would have noticed that I was withdrawn, isolating, and I was intent on getting wasted on whatever I could get my hands on, wherever I could, with whoever I could. I was demonstrating risky behavior such as hitchhiking for no good reason other than that I could. I was moody and depressed. I was constantly acting out to get attention but my parents had no idea what to do with me. My mother often laid me on the altar of therapy but to no avail. The right questions were never asked of me so that I would be forced to break my silence and express the pain and inner turmoil that I was experiencing.

The great drama that typically accompanied Erik and I was ever present but we were like an apple left out in the sun. Our love for one another began to slowly rot and then decay. Any onlooker may have observed our disintegrating romance. We rotted in the sun until we decomposed and, one day, through a process of decay, we were no more. Totally unlike our epic fights and sagas, step by step, we naturally grew apart and broke up.

I wanted to get as far away from Erik as I possibly could and, naturally, my family wanted to get me as far away from him as possible too. Although Erik was graduating from high school and would not be attending my small, private, church school any longer, they and I thought it would be a good idea to steer clear of that school so I enrolled in a public school. For me, starting over was like being raised from the dead. I could be a new girl in a new school. For all they knew, I could be a Russian spy. I enjoyed the thought and practice of wiping my slate clean and starting over. Often, I had felt that my life was over but, to the contrary, it was just beginning. For once I felt excited about the dawn of new possibilities.

New people, new friends, new teachers, everything was all new. Some people find the newness of change a daunting concept, so daunting that they avoid it. Not I, not this time. Recently, I had felt like an outsider and so I enjoyed my alone time. I enjoyed isolation until I did not. I enjoyed the silence until I did not.

In my efforts to start anew and get away from all things Erik, I had started hanging out with an old friend from my brief stint at Beaumont Junior High. Kate was sweet and kind and empathetic toward my family situation and my bad breakup with Erik. She hung out with a bunch of gutter punks from Banning and I was all too eager to break into a new scene and distract myself with the originality of it all. New friends, new music, new clothes, new politics, a new religion (atheism), and even new food (veganism) seemed to accompany the newness of it all. I was reinventing myself into someone who was stronger or so I thought. I was not going to get taken advantage of or messed with ever again. I was learning a very valuable life lesson: to have close girlfriends rather than supposed "guy friends."

I enjoyed my friendship with Kate. She was fun and she was always doing something. She was very kind to me and so unlike the catty girls that I had suffered the displeasure of interacting with. I needed a friend like her. I needed some semblance of loyalty. I needed to be able to trust someone even just a little.

Kate knew a lot of people. Between the two of us, we always ended up hanging out with kids older than us. In addition, because we were two young and blonde females in California, we always knew where the local parties were. One particular party would change my life forever.

We ended up at a house party in Cherry Valley. The

goal of the party was to paint some girl's room. "What a silly idea," I thought. I would take the chance, any chance, to meet people, hang out, and, most of all, flirt. I craved male attention and I was evolving into a shameless flirt. I could not figure out if most of the girls did not like me because I was pretty or because I was guilty of flirting with every guy in the room. It was probably a mixture of both. Most of the time, I would zero in on a particular guy that I observed observing me and then I would focus my energies on him but all stratagem was cast aside when I saw *him*.

When Jacob walked into the party, it was like the waters of people parted to greet him and make way for Jacob and his brothers. His entrance into the party was like a scene out of a movie because the music played and the light shown around him like they were playing to his every move. He was the center of everyone's attention. I am not sure why but he and his brothers were like small town royalty. Maybe it was the sheer size of his family that required notoriety, the fact that his family had owned a frequented shop, or the fact that all the boys were handsome and in a band. Jacob was a tall and muscular six-foot-three and had brightly colored, auburn-reddish hair and light brown eyes. Wherever he went, the girls became giddy in his presence but he remained cool unless he was stoned. In that case, he was giggling with them. He was popular and well-liked by adults and his peers.

Typically, a guy like this that appeared to have it all together was off limits for me. I did not like rejection.

Rejection felt like a cruel burn that would never heal and it took me ages to recover from a bout of it. I avoided rejection at all costs for reasons of self-preservation. I sought out situations that were predictable, situations where the odds were stacked in my favor. "This would be off limits for me," I postulated. "This was way too risky," I reasoned. I stood there at the party analyzing my prospects. He was far too popular with the girls and, if I threw my hat in the ring for this outgoing, charming, and handsome guy, I would have plenty of competition and I could get very, very hurt.

I stood there watching Jacob from afar. He was telling and re-telling his unfortunate run-in with law enforcement that very evening. He was totally high and he had been pulled over by the cops for rolling through a stop sign. The cops had not detected that he was under the influence but they still gave him a ticket. He would be in a lot of trouble with his parents. He seemed in good spirits for having such a rough time of it. He seemed very capable of being positive. I could not stop watching him. I noticed other girls watching him too. I did not appreciate the evident and blatant competition. I decided to leave him alone. "He is not for me," I concluded.

As he was talking to another group of kids, he noticed me out of the corner of his eye and I noticed him noticing me. My friend, Kate, said, "I think he likes you," with an elbow nudge to my arm. My face grew red. "No way," I silently responded with self-assurance. If I thought in terms of having no expectations then maybe I could not be crushed if I were disappointed. I liked him, though. He began to walk toward me and I felt as though my legs would give out. I felt myself disobeying my own self-preserving orders and self-made rules. When I first saw him walk into the party, I knew I was diving right into infatuation but my life jacket of self-preservation kept me from total submersion into puppy love.

He kept walking and I did the typical checking behind me to see who he was walking toward. He introduced himself and he wanted to know who I was because he had never seen me before. He was charming and asked me a lot of questions. He was a huge flirt and he made it evident that he was interested in me. I was shocked. We talked and we debated but mostly we laughed. I came off as strong and intelligent for my age but, mostly, I conveyed how extremely fun and unpredictable I could be. This was only partly true. I was the girl who came up with some sort of prank or weird thing to do that usually involved some amount of danger and breaking the law. I wanted attention and to stand out from the crowd and I was willing to do whatever it took to accomplish that.

I cannot say exactly what attracted Jacob to me but I can say that I found him easy to be around even though he was often the star of the show and that was something that was hard for me to reconcile as "safe." He was a drummer in a punk rock band and he had his own style of dress. He was intent on inventing himself on his terms and being different from the cookie-cutter mold. He liked what he liked and he did not think he had to get anyone's approval to be himself.

He was unapologetically himself. He questioned everything. I found him absolutely irresistible. He wore bowling shoes that he had stolen from a bowling alley. He chose that style of shoe in a small protest to the name brands and labels necessary for popularity at school. Even though I knew he was stoned out of his mind and his eyes were practically closing involuntarily in a marijuana haze, I thought he was one of the most brilliant people I had ever met. He was the most unusual, unique, and winsome person I had ever come across. I thought that, for sure, whatever his level of interest in me, it would be brief. A guy like this would not want a girl like me.

With these thoughts of self-doubt swimming in my head, I willingly removed my life jacket of self-preservation and totally sunk down to the bottom of the pool of infatuation. I was love drunk. I left that party knowing that I must do whatever it takes to see him again. It was risky but something about him drew me in.

Unfortunately, I had been dating other guys up to this point. I had a so-called relationship with a homeless gutter punk named "Hanky." Sadly for him, this was just a filler relationship until the next best thing came along. I knew that this relationship with "Hanky" would not go anywhere because he had nothing to offer me. He had no car or way to get around. He had no way to call me unless he asked a friend to use their phone. He was living on the street in protest to the establishment but homelessness, even in protest, definitely does not lend itself to charming girls. I was impressed with the level of dedication "Hanky" had to making a statement but needing to pay for his meals and worry about where "Hanky" was going to sleep that night put me off. However against the government one may be, the attractiveness of a secure man cannot be underestimated. No matter how closely one holds to feminist ideals, it is not attractive to have to take care of the "man."

"Hanky" was one of Jacob's friends and a nuisance because I knew that I had to get single fast to appeal to Jacob. Poor "Hanky." He was but a casualty of the dating wars. He had to be sacrificed. I figured it would be easy to do. I knew from dating Erik for so long that there was nothing between "Hanky" and I. We barely saw each other. I was merely having fun but I underestimated how "Hanky" felt about me. I tried to break it off in the back seat of a friend's car.

"Hanky, we never get to see each other so I think it's best that we break up because I am starting school soon," I said trying to muster up as much empathy as I could. Empathy or no empathy, there was nothing I could say to soften the blow. Being rejected hurts no matter how little we saw each other or how soft I tried to make the death blow of a break up. It is painful to be broken up with. It is like getting stabbed in the back by a trusted friend. You bare your soul and become vulnerable and show sides of yourself to one person like no other. Then you start holding hands and getting touchy feely and this physical contact works like glue.

When you might naturally just break apart because there is nothing in common and no real attraction to the heart and mind, the glue of being physical with someone holds you together when nothing else will. The power of touch is incredible. It works like nothing else to win hearts and minds. Unfortunately, I had won "Hanky's" heart and now I was crushing it. I had underestimated the power of holding hands and even the shortest of make-out sessions. The power of touch had won and "Hanky" did not have the advantage of being emotionally numb like I was. I started to notice a very advanced ability in myself to marginalize and trivialize human suffering and box it up and put it out of thought like an item thrown in the trash. Get hurt enough and, at times, it feels just and right to be the one to hurt others.

I was hurting "Hanky" but the worst thing "Hanky" could do was to show me how hurt he was and cling to me because that made me want to run away as far and as fast as possible. I did not want the responsibility of another person's emotions. This should have been a strong indicator that I was not capable of having a healthy relationship but I was a mere teenager and incapable of drawing these conclusions. I seemed to never question if I should be in a relationship at all but it was all about finding the right relationship. I failed to see that, even though I had picked some real head cases to date, perhaps I was the problem. I needed help. I did not want to be empathetic toward another's emotional pain because no one had ever been empathetic toward my own emotional pain. I did not have the slightest clue as to what true love really looked like.

So, most tragically, I watched "Hanky" react in hurt and pain by opening the car door and threatening that, if I did not love him or want to be with him, he would kill himself by throwing himself out of the car. His friends tried holding him in but he was sure that he wanted to die if he and I could not be together. I felt very bad that I was hurting "Hanky" but I had someone else on my mind and I did not want to be with someone like "Hanky" who needed me that badly. As "Hanky" hung himself out of the car door, I hardened myself to his suffering because I could not take the feeling of being forced, yet again, to do something that I did not want to do. I wanted to be free and I felt like "Hanky" was a chain around my ankle. He was weighing me down.

The late-night calls from a payphone in supermarket parking lots where "Hanky" was sleeping that night slightly annoyed me. It was novel, at first, to have a homeless boyfriend but the novelty wore off and the reality of "all the things that we could not do" starting sinking in. I wanted someone older and someone to get me out of my house. As "Hanky" hung out of the car with his friends screaming at him, I could see the hard, black pavement whizzing by under the car but I turned off my emotions and readied myself for what could happen next. I prepared myself to see blood. Dating was, in fact, a bloody sport. It always drew blood, it always wounded, it always hurt. Love was a battlefield and someone always got mortally wounded.

I found myself screaming, "fine Hankey! If you want to kill yourself over me then go ahead! I don't care!" I was a little girl playing with the issues of life. I was way too young to be dealing with such critical decisions but I won this round. I had called "Hanky's" bluff and he closed the car door and sunk down in his seat with his arms crossed and tears running down his cheeks. He felt the full force of rejection but I watched as he quickly replaced it with hatred for me. That is what happens in dating, the person you loved and shared everything with, were vulnerable with, becomes someone that you have to hate because loving them is now impossible. There is no such thing as "being friends" in reality. People may make a valiant attempt at "just being friends" but, in truth, someone is left hurting and still hoping and wishing to get back together. "Hanky" skipped the "just friends" portion and went straight to being bitter and hateful toward me. I did not care. I had Jacob on the brain. I wanted to find where he hung out and be there and that is exactly what I did.

It was not hard to do. Between the band practice, the dirt biking, and the half pipe they had in their backyard, everyone hung out at their house. Everyone could hang out without much supervision. The house was on many acres of property and the boys in the family had their own separate kick-it spot on the land. It was the best place to hang out and lots of kids did. Jacob's room was painted black and had lots of black light art on the wall. He had wall-to-wall candles in his room. I could read a lot about Jacob's personality by just reading the walls of his room. Band names, brand names crossed out, interesting words, all these were written in black light paint across the walls of his room while bean bags graced the floor. The room had a pungent aroma of incense, cigarettes, and weed. Jacob's room was where everyone seemed to sit and talk and thrift store chairs and couches welcomed all the after-band-practice crowd.

I noticed that I was not the only girl chasing Jacob. Normally this would discourage me but Jacob kept giving me little shows of affection to encourage me to not give up. In his presence, I felt like I was living life again. For the first time in months, I was not being tempted to call Erik. I felt like I was saved. Jacob was the better man. I felt like the fresher part of my fresh start. This was the best I had felt in months. I liked my interesting friends and the interesting things we did. I liked attending all the punk rock shows and hanging out. My parents liked this fresh start for me too. No, the punk rock stuff was not my parents' first choice but the punk rockers did not do drugs or drink alcohol. It seemed the better of two evils to my parents. Their daughter was intent on hanging out with rebels and, as far as rebels go, this group seemed okay.

I was now running around with Jacob and his friends. He had a twelve-seater van to carry his band equipment in and I was trying to find any excuse to ride with Jacob and his friends. Jacob had met my mom a couple of times and, each time, he charmed her. He was good looking and, with my mom, that helped a lot. I knew that I had to make myself stand out. I went to use the bathroom at Jacob's house and I noticed that his bathroom was filthy with the filth of years of not being cleaned. It was a dirty job but I cleaned that bathroom from top to bottom and got Jacob's family's attention. Manipulative? Definitely.

Anyone that says that the marketing and ecstasy modes of the dating relationship are not manipulative is living in a dream world. We all try to look our best and cover our flaws to appear more attractive to others. The important thing to know is that everyone does this and to wait to make any critical decisions until you have seen the real version, the un-manipulated copy, the un-edited version. No one is perfect and "love covers a multitude of sins." Every guy I ever dated was perfect in the beginning. By the end, I would convince myself and others that I was dating Charles Manson himself.

During this time of extreme-best-behavior mode, I was still very sick and my health situation was being investigated by a physician at Loma Linda University Medical Center. I would get tired quickly. I went to lay down on Jacob's bed and found myself drifting off to sleep when I heard Jacob marching up the stairs to his room. I instantly felt creepy for being alone in his room and asleep on his bed. I did what any girl would do, I pretended to be asleep. "It was believable," I told myself, "I fall asleep all the time during band practice." I felt totally ridiculous trying to pretend to be asleep and, just when I thought I would end the show and pretend to wake up, I felt Jacob kissing my hand thinking that I was fast asleep. This gave me the biggest thrill and then I knew that, as hard as I was making a play for him, he was returning the affection. This was all that I needed. My next moves would be more direct.

I cannot remember when our first kiss was or where it was. All I remember is that things were moving fast. By the time school had started, Jacob and I were formally dating. I was a sophomore and he was a senior. This was no big deal to me but, to everyone else at school, it was like I had swooped in and stolen away their most eligible bachelor. The girls at school were not too fond of me. I had hoped to start at a new school with a clean slate but dating Jacob made that impossible. I became that blonde girl dating Jacob.

I was hardly paying any attention at school. I was completely focused on Jacob and I could not wait to sneak away from school and be alone with him. I would lay down in the back of his van and, being a senior, he would sneak me off the school's property and then bring me back in time for my mom to pick me up from school. Leaving school like this caused us to have lots of free time together. We drove all over and had more fun than I had ever had. It was fun being with Jacob. We laughed at the stupidity of others which made us feel better about ourselves. We played cruel practical jokes on others. He was positive and upbeat and I knew, from dating Erik, to be careful of my jealousy so I tried hard not to show

Jacob that part of me. I only wanted Jacob to see the "fun me." I showed him an adventurous risk taker that loved to have fun. What guy could resist the most fun girl in the room?

One evening, Jacob and I made the drive to Redlands to a coffee shop where Erik and I used to hang out. I knew that, if I took Jacob there, we might run into Erik. I wanted Erik to see Jacob. Jacob was like my crowning achievement. I was so proud of him. He was everything Erik was not and Jacob's gregarious and über-charm made me look so emotionally healthy so I could disprove all the lies Erik had told our mutual friends about me.

As Jacob and I walked hand-in-hand up to the coffee shop, I could hear Erik's laugh and excited chitter-chatter. I thought to turn around and leave but Jacob looked at me like he was concerned and sympathetic which made me feel safe enough to tell him that we were walking into the proverbial lion's den. I quickly explained that I thought we were going to run into my ex-boyfriend and I quickly gave Jacob a rundown of the "purgatory" that I had escaped from. Jacob, true to his nonchalant and settled way of thinking, soothed my concern with his encouraging words and nudged me forward. He said he did not care who we might run into. If he did care, he hid it well.

Jacob and I walked up to the coffee shop holding on to each other. I can look back and I cannot remember exactly what he smelled like or how his hand felt in mine but I do remember that I felt very secure. He held the hope of a father, brother, lover, and a friend all in one person. He was stronger than I and he was kind to me. He gave me a security and a pride when I was with him. Just being with him made me feel like a better person.

When Erik saw me as we approached, he stopped talking and looked like someone had kicked him in the stomach. Jacob was athletic looking (even though he hated organized sports at the time) and he was tall and too big to say anything off-handed to. I knew that Jacob's handsome form would totally consume Erik with anger and jealousy. I momentarily felt bad for Erik. He was seeing me move on with someone who was everything he was not. Erik turned every shade of red. He reflected all the pain that we had caused each other. The hurt came flooding back and I stopped, actually froze, with fear as I stood wondering why I had even wanted to come to this place at all. I guess I was the kind of girl who felt more like keeping her hand in the flame rather than safely withdrawing it. More accurately, too many times others held me to the flame and I learned to suffer the heat. If drama were not following me, I turned to chase the drama.

Jacob saw my level of discomfort and walked right up to Erik. I immediately assumed that Jacob and Erik would fight. Jacob's quick saunter was unique. He walked with his chest out and toes facing outward like he should be wearing a zoot suit. I observed him walking that walk right up to a stunned and speechless Erik. I think Erik was afraid that Jacob would take a swing at him and Erik puffed up like a peacock splaying its feathers and preparing for a scuffle. Erik's fist tightened and he arose from the table as a hush fell over his friends. They all turned to look at me and then their faces grew tense in preparation for the coming conflict.

But Jacob didn't swing at Erik even though he may have wanted to after knowing all the stuff Erik had done. Jacob did the very best thing anyone could do to a person's ex-boyfriend. He did the most mature and charismatic thing he could do. Jacob enthusiastically extended his arm out to Erik, palm up and fingers spread out as far as they could go, offering a friendly handshake.

"Heya, I'm Jacob. Nice to meetcha!" he said with a genuinely toothy smile. Erik looked shocked and I saw Erik's eyes dart around Jacob's face, trying to detect any hint of sarcasm or insincerity. He was frozen in place and then he looked to his friends. Kindness won out at last and Erik shook his hand begrudgingly at first but then in surrender to chivalry. It was two different personality types colliding together but there was no insincerity to detect in Jacob. Jacob's way was and is to always overcome awkwardness with friendliness. Erik was somewhat confused and begrudgingly settled into the new reality. I observed that Erik began to display normal breathing patterns again. Even though Erik's level of fight or flight response was leveling out, he could not hide his contempt for me standing there with my new boyfriend. Everyone there knew that this was the best revenge that anyone could ever have on an ex. How could Erik not be jealous?

I was not only moving on but moving on with an über-handsome guy who was not only attractive but also had an awesome personality. Jacob stood conversing with Erik like he was an old friend. Erik looked at Jacob with suspicion and jealousy. What could he do? How can you fight charming and friendly? You can try but you will only end up looking like the crazy one. Erik's knees slowly bent and he sat down in his chair again while staring up at Jacob and answering Jacob's quasi-interested questions about this and that. Inside, I felt like I was the cat that got the cream seeing Erik get schooled in the art of moving on by my new man. Because of Jacob, after many lost battles with Erik and the loss of all my friends, I had just won the war.

This was way too weird for me. No matter what I felt inside, I stood still like a sculpted statue, afraid to move or I might shatter the peace like a perfect dream. I thought, "how did I get a guy like this in my life?" I had never been so proud of a single person in my life as I was of Jacob in that moment. We were "adulting" and we were doing it well. I felt like someone had demonstrated to me exactly how to approach awkward situations. I was not only dating Jacob but I found myself sweetly and perfectly looking up to him. I respected him. He was completely winning my heart.

Chapter 10

Hand-in-Hand

Jacob was someone that everyone seemed to admire just as I did. He had a job as a waiter at a local diner at seventeen. He was the hardest working person I had ever met. He was careful with his money and he had lots of energy that he put into his job. The locals knew him well and they loved him too. His bosses at work enjoyed having him work for them and they often grumbled that he was not eighteen yet so they could schedule him even more. If he had only played football or was a fire cadet, he would have been the perfectly well-rounded picture of boyhood American life but he fought the Norman Rockwell norm and was punk rock in every way. At work, he rebelled in little ways: his hair, his shoes, his leather bracelets. These were the minor assaults to the normal Abercrombie and Calvin Klein marketing thrust upon our generation.

Try as he might to be the outcast or punk rock rebel, Jacob was good at making the masses adore him. He would have excelled in corporate America because his expertise was in soothing the inevitably ruffled feathers of coworkers and bosses alike. He was a good listener. The best listeners can listen to a point of view that they do not necessarily agree with and still make a person feel heard. He had a way of making you feel heard. He was an expert at networking. He would be anywhere in the world and yet never meet a stranger. Being an eternal optimist is an amazing way to interact with the world.

Everyone could see how well I was doing with Jacob. My family and those that knew and cared about me all breathed a sigh of relief. They hung their hopes on Jacob. They looked to him to fix me too. In my parents' minds, they had come to accept that I refused to be single and the lesser of two evils in regard to boyfriends. They did not know what to do with me and someone had to help me, right? If Jacob brought peace and calm so their lives could go on, then so be it. With Jacob in the picture, I needed fewer rides back and forth because he drove. I was home much less because I was with him. I was happier when I was at home because I was thinking of him. I wrapped my life around Jacob and my heart around him too. Again, my existence was for another. Again, my depression lifted as I willingly swam into utter infatuation. Again, my schooling and my dreams took second place as I laid my life on the alter of young love or, better stated, getting fleetingly fulfilled by someone who is incapable of fulfilling me. The other shoe would eventually have to drop but, for now, it was bliss, bliss to be shared by all.

My mother was scared to upset me. She was scared to tell me, "no." She was scared I would threaten suicide or run away. The alternative to her was to let me be my own parent which was no solution at all. Thus, Jacob was allowed to come over and spend the night and, at sixteen, I would have my mother drop me off at his house late into the night. My mother chose the easy road of "pacify the teenager so we have peace." She was willing to sacrifice her daughter for the sake of a trouble-free life. Jacob's ease with adults and his ability to charm lulled both of our families into a false sense of security, forgetting that we were still children.

No matter how well we appeared to face the oncoming waves of adult life, we were still very much children in need of supervision and parenting. Many parents think to get their children to their teen years and then their work is done but this is just the point when one may make serious mistakes that will impact eternity. Teenagers may act adult-like but they need supervision and rules. Mostly, they need a parent's love and guidance in all of life's matters. When there was a decision to make or a problem with behavior, I would have loved to have had my parents calmly talk with me regarding my purpose and duty to my God. This may have provoked my conscience. Sadly, I had no guidance, I had a strong will, and I longed to fill the void within.

There were many red flags that started warning my family that disaster was ahead but they chose to ignore them. Spending the nights together as a couple at sixteen was dangerous no matter how amazing Jacob was. Jacob had saved his money up and bought a motorcycle. This allowed him to have more freedom because he no longer had to ask for permission to use the family van. He was able to come see me more at my house and my mother let him. Jacob was far more independent because he was turning eighteen now.

One evening, I remember my family leaving to go to some sort of performance in the Los Angeles area. Jacob and I were supposed to go with my family. I was dressed to the nines in a red, sequined, cocktail dress with red heels. I looked like I was in my twenties. I was so proud of myself and I felt truly beautiful. As was often the case, I just wanted to be alone with Jacob. It was a nuisance to have to deal with my family especially when I knew that, if I pushed hard enough, I could get my mom to let Jacob and I stay home alone together. Sure enough, even though I was dressed for a party, at the last minute I was allowed to stay home with Jacob and we were alone without any supervision knowing that my family was far, far away and would not be home for a long time.

On another occasion, Jacob was to come over after his shift at work. It was very late and I was so excited to see him. My mom was going to let him stay the night. I started lighting candles and I got very carried away as I lit wall-to-wall candles in my room and especially as I tossed a beautiful red cloth over the lamp which created a New Orleans red light district ambiance. I had not made a conscious decision at sixteen to set a seduction scene but I had. I needed an adult to come into my room and declare the obvious that this was highly inappropriate. That did not happen. I needed an adult to stop the "adult train" that was rapidly speeding toward a collision and certain disaster. I needed a "cold shower" to my too-hot-to-trot, know-it-all attitude. I needed a parent to be "the bad guy," to be "the drag," and the baneful and ever so hated guardian to slow me down.

There were many, many more occasions when Jacob was allowed to stay overnight or late into the night. Kids will do what kids will do. They will go as far as they are allowed to go. I had no rules and no limits. My mother knew that I was sexually active. She knew because she had recorded many of my phone calls with Erik. She knew when and where I was having sex and, yet, Jacob was somehow thought to be different. I am not sure what she was thinking. I suppose she thought she would cover her bases when she presented me with a grocery bag filled to capacity with every kind of condom imaginable. I was embarrassed and horrified. It felt like my mother was saying that I was a prostitute and I felt extremely hurt. There was no loving conversation about not having sex. It was just assumed that I would know what to do with three hundred or more condoms. I felt like my mother was releasing me on the world, like she had given up on parenting me, like she had accepted my rebellion. Suddenly, I realized that I was not really able to rebel against a rule or a parent that did not exist. I felt unloved. I was too immature to fully understand that the lack of rules and concern for me and my future made me feel unloved.

If she did not know I was having sex up to this point, she knew when my older brother had the terrible misfortune of walking in on Jacob and I. I did not know that he had walked in on us. I heard about it later from my family. My mother presented it to me in jest and with humor. Yet again, I was surprised at her flippant attitude toward my sexual activity. I thought that she would be angry with me or try to stop me but she did not. I assumed that she was maintaining an "if you can't beat em' then join em'" kind of logic. As a sixteen-year-old girl, I felt as though my mother had given up on me. I was hopeless to her.

As a parent, I suppose we all underestimate how strongly teenagers crave rules and limits. Teens want a fence around their so-called "yard" to push against or even climb over. It is a standing marker for where home is or where the line is drawn. It is a reminder that, if one goes too far, there might be danger. Rules create a sense of security. Rules allow for "greater development of character." A home with no rules is unworthy of the intelligence that God has given us. Though we are free to do whatever we wish, rules also provide protection which is why God allowed the first family to enjoy His holy rules even in a perfect place. How much more then do we need to give our children rules for this imperfect place where we live with our bias toward evil.

Jacob, my family (my mother, Alec, and my little brother), and I were at El Pollo Loco eating lunch on a beautiful January day in California. The air was cool and crisp but, typical to Southern California weather, it was warm and sunny. I remember wearing a cute brown miniskirt with pink pinstripes. I remember my skirt because I felt more like staring at my skirt than my food. The look of my food greatly disturbed my stomach. I felt sicker these days. I thought that maybe I was dying. How could one feel this ill and be healthy? I could not eat. I felt too ill. My mother asked if I were okay and I answered that I felt nauseated. My mother gave an all-knowing look to Alec.

The wave of sickness took me, like a vessel on the sea, and I just had to go with the flow. I felt that I had to escape the restaurant. The smells alone were noxious not to mention the mouths smacking at my table. Watching my family eat was near torture. I went running out of the restaurant and thought that I might vomit in front of all the eating restaurant patrons but, thankfully, I did not. I collapsed on the lawn leading to the restaurant's entrance. I was so grateful for the soft grassy pillow underneath me. I needed to lay there and breath the air. Though we were in the city and the smell of traffic was keen, it was a welcome change from the smell of Mexican food. I laid on the ground, gripping it like it was a security blanket about to drop out from under me like a thrilling roller coaster ride. "What is wrong with me?" I thought. Getting the stomach flu is a fear of mine. Because of my immune deficiency problems, when I get the flu, I get a terrible case. I was mentally preparing myself for a rigorous bout of the flu when I started to feel the wave pass over me for a brief season of relief.

I heard the voices of Jacob and my family coming out of

the restaurant. I picked myself up off the ground and looked to my mother for help. I was really sick. My mother looked at me, examining me from top to bottom. I realized she had been watching me. I heard her say, "I think you're pregnant."

"What?" I gasped! "I'm not pregnant." I unsurely stated. I looked at her with a questioning stare. "Could I be?" I thought. "No, no, I'm not." The thought of getting pregnant had never occurred to me. I thought that, because of all my health problems, I for sure could not get pregnant. I was so often sick with infections. "How could I get pregnant? I was not pregnant," I safely concluded. In my immature teenage mind, I never once thought of pregnancy or that getting pregnant could happen to me. Somehow in my mind, I was immune to pregnancy. "Not me. I can't get pregnant."

I am not completely sure how I had come to the conclusion that I could not have children but, to this wrong conclusion, I had come. It is really important to talk to teens and try to understand what they think from their perspective. Sometimes, the knowledge that we assume is understood as a logical way to think is not what our kids know or think. We have to teach every child about life from the very beginning as if they know very little. Even though my mother had provided me with a lifetime supply of prophylactics, I had no idea how to use them. I knew what they were for but I had no idea how to broach the topic with Jacob, how to ask him to use one, or how to use it. They were, to me, as useless as bullets without a gun.

I got into my mother's car to make the journey home. She stopped at the grocery store and, unbeknown to me, picked up a pregnancy test. She knew before I did. I was in denial. When we pulled into the driveway I spilled out of the car like a sailor kissing the land. I just wanted to curl up in my bed and sleep this, whatever *this* was, off but my mother demanded my presence in her room. Jacob and I filed obediently into her room. She whipped out this blue box and shook it like a rattle. Jacob's eyebrows raised. I do not think he ever thought a pregnancy was possible either. His hands immediately slipped nervously into his pockets as he slowly lowered himself down to sit on my mother's California King bed. He seemed to be holding his breath as he waited patiently for the scene to unfold.

"You need to take this," she said curtly. I thought she would be angrier with us but she had an expectant look and feel about her, like she knew something that I did not know. I meekly took the box from her waving hand and I asked her how to do it as I blankly stared at the positive and negative fields of the test. I had no idea what I was doing.

I was not afraid. I was numb. I was going through the motions and doing what I was told to do. I still did not think a pregnancy was possible. Normally, I would be embarrassed by my mother treating me like a little girl in front of my boyfriend but I instinctively knew that I was in need of some mothering. Alone, I walked into my mother's bathroom. I closed the door like I was shutting out the cold, hard reality.

The bathroom felt like a precious little cocoon of my own. No matter what happened, it would not be real until I emerged from the cocoon.

With a trembling hand, I lowered the stick into the cup of urine and pulled it out. I waited and watched and watched and waited. Time stood still as I processed the possibilities. I still had no fear. Maybe I was too young to fear or God held it back but I was not afraid for my future. I had always known that I was headed for trouble. At that time, no one had encouraged me to go to college or have a life. I had no dreams of traveling or career. All I could ever think about was having a boyfriend. My sad existence was programmed to only see a future if a man gave me one. Maybe I had grown up in the time of feminism and strong female leadership but I was a quaint anachronism of the 1950s. Though I had never imagined a future where I was a mother or a wife, I could not see a future where I stood alone.

"What if I am pregnant?" I thought as I waited. "What would I do?" The first image that came to my mind was of a little boy, a toddler, holding my hand. I do not know when or why or where I got this picture from. It was an original to me. Like a dream, it unfolded before me as I stood there waiting. I saw a mother and her son traipsing happily hand-in-hand through a school or grocery store parking lot. They had smiles on their faces. The picture was so clear and vivid that I can still see it in my mind's eye to this very day. They were in love, one of the strongest of human bonds. I was experiencing such a strong feeling of love for a child in that present moment that I had never known before. I suddenly knew that, all along, I had been craving family, to belong to something greater than myself. I sensed a feeling of purpose crop up within me. The vision in my mind's eye faded and I looked expectantly at my pregnancy test. Now, in this moment, I would have been sad if it had been anything less than positive. It was positive.

I was surprised by my own level of strength. I knew that hard times, very hard times were just outside the bathroom door but I hung, no clung, to that picture of mother and son lovingly together. God had just thrown my unborn child a life preserver, something to prevent his destruction. I felt attached to that child I had just seen but moments before. I already felt a sense of motherly protection toward this life I now knew was growing within me.

I knew that, eventually, I would have to exit the bathroom to tell my family and Jacob. Oh yes, there was Jacob to think about. I somehow knew that he was not the type of man that, because he was, in fact, going to have to man-up now, would leave me because I was pregnant. In that moment, I was more thankful than ever for Jacob's Christian upbringing. No matter how much he and I rebelled, it was a Christian background that gave me some trust that Jacob would do the right thing and be a father.

The one thing I feared was what I would do. I felt things so deeply and strongly that I was afraid that I would ruin everything. I was not yet sure what motherhood entailed. I had never changed a diaper, held a newborn, or even babysat. My complete and utter naivety worked in my favor in that moment. My bravery was out of shear dumbness. I had no idea of the magnitude of the responsibility. I saw motherhood, at that time, in a selfish light as in what a child could make *me* feel rather than what I could bring to a child. I knew that the strong bond I already felt would grow and that I would have something in my life worth dying for. Although motivated by pride and selfishness, behind the bathroom door the phrase popped into my head that, "I could do better than my own mother." I had no concept of how hard it would be "to do better." At sixteen, I felt abandoned by my own mother. I felt like she could never understand me and I knew that she would never try to either. "I will never leave my own child," I thought.

I walked into that bathroom and closed the door as a little girl but I emerged from the bathroom being called to womanhood. I had not grown an inch but I now felt a severe level of pressure that forced me into being older. Was I wiser? No, but I was older out of sheer necessity. I was like those children in war-torn countries that have eyes that look far beyond their years. Yet, they are still children that want to play and be their age. Circumstances forced me to grow up and, unlike Christ who grew in wisdom and stature in accordance with the laws of nature and God, I grew out of bounds. It was unnatural like obesity. Yes, the body is mechanically able to get pregnant at sixteen, but should it? I was an unwed teen mother now. I was out of my depth. The wonderful thing about being young is that you do not know what you do not know nor do you have a frame of reference to cause worry or stress thus you carry on with a sort of ignorant confidence. I was fragile. I was so many things at once. How is it possible to describe the moment in which your life changed forever? A child is a huge blessing to anyone's life but this child came out of order.

I opened the door to wondering and inquisitive faces. I heard my mother and Alec, who had walked into the room while I was in the bathroom, discussing their intent to adopt the child. "Adopt my child? Never," I thought. I would run away and drop this baby in a field before I let my mother get her hands on my precious, innocent baby. I felt bad for Jacob because I had taken so long in the bathroom. He looked completely on tender hooks and I had left him to the wolves.

"Well,…" I heard Alec prompt me.

"It's positive," I answered. There was a silence as I hung my head waiting for the verbal stoning that would inevitably commence. I stood there, like the naked and guilty adulteress that I was, wearing my scarlet letter like a good little shamefaced girl, but the stones never came. If they had, it would have been all too easy to rip through my vision of mother and son and destroy him. My family felt sorry for me. I was more surprised than they and that they knew that I was pregnant before I did. They could see that I was genuinely shocked and that reality was setting in. Reality was cold and hard and offered no comfort.

All the talking that then took place felt very procedural and I could not really apply it to myself. I felt like I was having an out-of-body experience. My mother had a way of hitting us with all of the problems and issues at once. She ran down a list of things that would have to be done and she flew years into the future. My mother turned her wagging finger toward Jacob and ran down a summation of things he would have to pay for up until our child went to college. Whatever feelings I had felt earlier of craving her mothering were gone. I just wanted her out of my life again. Teenage rebellion and the call of motherhood were clashing.

I was romanticizing my role of mother as most mothers do. I was pregnant and I felt it a beautiful thing. I was not going to let my mother burst my bubble of motherhood with her cruel realities no matter how real it was. Then and there I felt like Adam and Eve needing to run and hide from the truth. We had sinned, we had done wrong, but now we had to build a life without the Garden walls all on our own. I clung to Jacob for safety and he was just what I needed.

Many would expect this story to go along the lines of many statistics. Jacob would leave me and that I would then be flung upon the mercy of my family but, for now, the story did not go as such. We clung to each other in young love. Trials test love and our love was being tested and we were winning at the moment. I think this made my mother angry. I think she thought I would fail or that Jacob would fail me and that I would then need her. But Jacob did not fail and, instead, stepped up for me. He became my safe place. I loved him more and deeper than ever.

Jacob and I left my parents' house to go and process this new information on our own and talk. My mother carefully watched us in a strange way like a farmer would watch an escaped horse after the gate was closed. What an odd time to be paranoid about your daughter. It was too late. I was going to have to be a woman now. The time to protect my girlish innocence was over but it was as if the crisis of the moment had jolted her into feelings of protective mothering. I had little time to ponder my mother's odd behavior because I was a mother myself. As I walked away from my childhood home to Jacob's van, I was, with every moment that passed, becoming older.

Chapter 11

White Trash

Jacob and I sat in his van together in silence. I was waiting for him to lead the conversation. The stress of the moment pushed us both toward our shared habit of smoking. Jacob turned to me while simultaneously lighting my cigarette and said, "you're going to have to quit this."

"I know, this is my last one." I answered with decided resolve that surprised even me. His concern for his unborn child helped me know his intent. His urging me to quit smoking told me that he was in this with me. I had started smoking at age fourteen. My biological father had paved the way for a healthy smoking habit and I had a pack-a-day habit. My first cigarette was not taken with the typical coughs and heaving that most endure. I took to the habit of smoking like a moth to a flame. I loved it. Jacob and I would often tell each other how we loved the look of the smoke exiting our lungs and how the vapors curled and wound their way through the air. I loved everything about that gorgeous little hit of tobacco and the sting of it hitting the back of my throat. I loved holding the cigarette and the nervous tick of flicking the ashes to the floor. It was my beloved little habit. I often did and I still do feel nervous around crowds of people and in social situations. Lighting a cigarette was a beautiful solution to my anxiety issues. It gave me something to stare at instead of maintaining eye contact, it gave me an anchor for my jitters. It was an entirely different process taking place while dealing with the issues of life. It occupied my hands that otherwise felt lost and swallowed up in the confusion of dealing with people. How was I going to part with this thing that had become so much a part of who I was down to the cellular level?

Jacob and I awkwardly conversed about the day's events. We both struggled for words. It was hard to know what to say. He, not knowing what I wanted and I, not knowing what he wanted, were both trying to flesh out what each other wanted. Somehow there was a mutual understanding that abortion was not an option.

In all honesty, I am not sure if I could have gone through with carrying our child if Jacob had not been so adamantly against an abortion. How he was so sure on this point at such a young age, I do not know. He somehow knew what I knew, that this child was meant to be here. This baby was spoken into existence from the beginning of the foundation of the earth. He was destined to arrive. He was known to a Creator in a time that had no beginning or end. How does one describe a place that is not bound within the confines of mortality? How does one describe an origin that I have never seen? Somewhere amidst the stones of fire, where the sons and daughters of God shout for joy, this child's and every other child's existence was seen and known. He was spoken of and his genesis was designed for such a time as this. He had purpose before he was born and I felt the strength of his presence inside me. He must survive and he will be born. We both innately knew that this was a decision that was not ours to make because, somewhere, a long time ago, his survival was decided. It was a given. I do not really know how, at our age, we just mutually understood that, whatever the outcome of us, our child was greater than our own comfort.

Then and there in that van, in the shadows of the lowering sun, two teenagers, while smoking cigarettes, decided to have a baby. I still feel that this was a very defining moment. I feel my son has always been the best part and the greatest accomplishment of my young life. There is something special about him. He is the lily that survived the swamp. He has always had a way of taking that which is negative and turning it into a positive. Without him, I would be dead. Heretofore would this story end. Here, at this point, the book would close. An omnipotent Creator cast him a lifeline in vision and signs but Infinite Wisdom comes full circle in later years when this child would, time and time again, be my lifeline.

True to my statement, I did quit smoking. Maybe I could not do what was best for me but I could do it for him. There were not too many things that I was truly scared of but Jacob's mom and dad were one of those things. I was terrified of rejection. They had the power to make our lives miserable. I was so scared to tell his parents that I was pregnant. Jacob would soften the blow for me by telling them alone so I did not have to endure the backlash and, if anything ugly were said, he protected me from it. When Jacob wanted to take me to his parents' house for a family gathering, I was petrified to say the least but I knew it had to happen eventually if we were going to make a go of it as a family.

The drive up to Jacob's house was a nerve-racking one. How sick I felt. The stress of what everyone thought and said was weighing heavily on me. Some old friends had called from my old school to ask me if the rumors were true. How sad I was at the sudden absence of the friends that I thought were true blue. Pregnancy is not usually contagious but many parents treated me as if it were. I do not blame them now, but then, I surely thought less of them as they did of me.

My mother took pleasure in telling my friends of my great failure. Then she would come back to tell me how so and so "shook their head in disappointment." Suddenly, people I did not even know or like were disappointed in me. My mother was the most effective agent in supplying the gossip train. I felt more betrayed by her than anyone else. I expected more from her and I got much, much less.

She would revel in the sympathy that her wicked daughter had done this evil thing as if it had been done in a bubble and she had no part in my mistake. Her favorite saying to this day is, "you turned thirteen and just went nuts and there was nothing I could do." She conveniently forgets that she stopped my father from having any influence in my life and that I became pregnant under her roof while she was home. She forgets that she not only stopped my father from giving me any attention with her envy and jealousy but she went back to work and school and gave up on supervising me. I write these things not to inflict pain upon her but to warn parents to keep being the stick in the mud and to keep annoying your children. It is worth it to be hated for a few years rather than to create an entire lineage of suffering.

Often, my mother would pick me up from school and be frustrated that her steady flow of questions were met with grumpy and curt replies. I was tired and very sick, sicker than anyone knew at the time, and my mother's "how was your day" line of questioning was to me, at the time, an annoyance and I was mean to her. I was a selfish girl and a rebel and I needed to be won back from my rebellion. It is in heaven when the father and mother's efforts will be praised by angels and all heaven will bow in recognition of the faithful parents. It was not until my mother was no longer home that I missed her annoyingness. In fact, I believe from experience that the teen years are the age in which the parent has the greatest identification with the suffering of Christ.

Loving a teenager can often be correlated to the gospel experience. At times, loving a teenager is like loving the unlovable. It is so easy to love a cute little baby who depends on you and needs you for food and nourishment. Little children are loyal to a fault. With a teenager, it is not so. They are sensitive to hypocrisy and this can enable them to be critical. It is a parent's experience to bear the Cross of Christ and often be misunderstood yet be patient and kind, firm and decided. A teenager needs to be wooed to Christianity by loving parents. They are intelligent beings who crave intelligent and thoughtful conversation. They crave guidance and need their parents to instill a purpose in them. All the while the parent is trusting them more and more and giving them more freedom.

Here is the ultimate test of love: a constant loosening of the rope while still holding it tight. What a testimony to the love of God toward us. Everything a teenager needs is everything Christ has shown us in His life here on earth. Christ's relation to people, his self-sacrifice for the comfort of others, is what we must be to our children. Above all, we must never give up. It is never too late to be a parent. It is never too late to start loving unconditionally and attempting to win the hearts of our children and giving them a God-filled purpose in life. Though we have failed today, there is still tomorrow. There is never a time a parent stops being a parent unless they give up. Even if our children "go nuts," God's love is even "nuttier" and "never leaves us or forsakes us."

My mother's newest husband has given her a faulty phrase to live by which has failed her: "never chase after love." They have decided that they should never have to chase after their children but this is not God's way or the gospel message. God's love is ever chasing after us. If it were not so, none of us would ever go to heaven. God is in the very inspiration and idea that brings us back to Him. 1 Corinthians 13 is the very essence of the loving parent. "Love never fails" is the Holy Spirit chasing after us. If God did not continually chase after us, He would be giving Satan an extreme advantage on the battlefield. We serve a God who, as David says in Psalm 139, chases us to the ends of the earth. I feel terribly sorry for anyone whose picture of God is so limited to think of God as proud and aloof and far away. God is close by us, He is humble and strong, He believes in us, and desires us so much that there is nothing He will not do to get us back. As parents, we must understand that our role is to win our children's hearts for God. We are extensions of the heavenly Kingdom and we are, to our children, God on earth. God has given every parent an advantage in that our children crave our attention and approval all their lives.

I remember pulling up to Jacob's family home. What a beautiful and scenic place it was but I could not enjoy the lush greenery and the cool of the evening that graced this little piece of heaven tucked away in the San Gorgonio Pass hills. His mother and father were seated in lawn chairs outside their home. They were lounging in the rays of the pink glow of the California winter's setting sun. At another time, I would bask in the ethereal dream-like lighting but I could not enjoy what felt like walking the plank to my certain death. My stomach twisted into knots as Jacob and I seated ourselves so that our chairs formed a circle in the lawn.

I sat across from his mom and dad with my hands

folded and my head hanging as I was shrinking into my chair. I attempted to be as small as I possibly could be. I was quiet and speechless and I let Jacob lead us into conversation. Yes, they already knew that I was pregnant but this would be the conversation where we were all deciding how supportive his family would be to us. They could, with one word, make our lives very difficult. They could cease to let Jacob use the family van that Jacob used to pick me up and drop me off and then we would be doomed to never see one another. They could decide to be critical and set all of Jacob's siblings against us. This was an emotional time for both Jacob and I. What his parents would say and do was critical to our child's survival.

In preparation for the total onslaught of in-law fury, I had prepared a speech to prove that we, Jacob and I, really could care for a child but the words would not come. There were so many things that his parents could say to us that might have pushed us over the edge. Although we wanted to have the child, we were still only a new couple, unmarried, and unprepared for the stresses of life. Who knows what decisions may have come from just the pressures of life. So it was amazing and miraculous that, even though Jacob's parents could have given us the "I told you so" speech, they did not.

"You guys are about to have your socks blessed off!" Jacob's dad exclaimed in sincere and prophetic declaration. I choked back my salty tears. There were plenty of nasty and unkind words spoken to me but Jacob's dad's words were like an oasis in the desert of lettered expression. By this time, I felt as though I was usually only barely surviving life, hanging on by a nail, ready to crack and trying not to but these encouraging words and various others would be yet another life preserver to hang my desperate and often lifeless soul on. Kindness is a refreshing drink of water to a kindness-starved person as I was then.

I can remember everything that people said to me about my pregnancy, words of encouragement or words to wound. I remember them in a hall of memories because I know the power that words have for others who are struggling through dire circumstances. Though I was guilty of sin and fornication, it did no good to shame me for it because, at night when I slept, I knew what I was. It does no good to rub one's nose in their crimes. I needed encouragement. Words have that power to lift one up or to tear one down. "Death and life are in the power of the tongue." Proverbs 18:21.

I remember my Nana, Alec's mother, saying to me in her thick German accent, "Darling, it's always the good girls that get pregnant because they don't know all the tricks. You will be such a good little mother." When I felt as useless and dirty as a two-bit whore, I felt the grace of the gospel message through people like her who, even though I had let her down, still looked at me as "a good little girl." Some of my friend's mothers like Kathy Espalin, Linda Wagoner, Linda Middleton, and even a shopkeeper at a punk rock head shop in the Inland Center Mall would be surrogate parents to me and a source of much encouragement. I gleaned advice from them about motherhood because they were positive and loving toward me. We have to remember that "it is the kindness of God that leads us to repentance." Romans 2:4.

The words of Jacob's dad were in stark contrast to some other words I heard. Unfortunately, one person that hurt me very badly was my own older brother. One evening, I sat in his room watching television with him. I had felt the sharp disappointment of my mother and my brothers. They, more than anyone, hated me for embarrassing them. My mother made it her duty to verbally chastise me. My heavy weight gain, terrible pregnancy acne, and too-young-to-be-pregnant baby face were her cruel playground where she could be a bully. My older brother followed suit. What can one expect from an older brother who is utterly disappointed? I sat in the corner of his room on an office chair, leaning back slightly, and scarfing down a bowl of mashed potatoes. They were the most delicious mashed potatoes I had ever eaten. Pregnancy makes everything taste better unless, of course, you are hunched over a toilet bowl. I had emerged from the early months of pregnancy and, with that, the nausea had gone and left me ferociously hungry and I was huge.

I leaned back precariously in the office chair that sat beside my brother's computer desk. We faced the television and watched some silly comedy together. I tightly held my bowl of mashed potatoes and enjoyed it immensely. My belly had grown steadily into a gigantic basketball in front of me. It was now obvious evidence of my wrongdoing and my brother was ever ready to cast glances of contempt toward me. When, in my enthusiasm for my mashed potatoes and without thinking, I ate and ate and discovered that I could continue eating while setting my bowl on my burgeoning belly, I embraced the one convenience of being pregnant and made the mistake of using my belly as a surface from which to eat.

"You are white trash!" My brother yelled in my direction.

I startled like a shy dog looking up from its doggy dish. I looked up from mashed potatoes and saw my older brother looking angrily at me from the couch where he sat.

"What?" I shrugged off his comment and said, "it's easier to eat like this."

My brother shook his head and said, "you are such a [expletive] slut. You look like white trash eating like that."

I smarted under the weight of his words and I quietly accepted the abuse like I deserved every word and I believed every word he spoke as if it were gospel truth. My mother never stopped my older brother from speaking these curses to me. My brother and I acted as if cursing were a right of passage and that calling me "whore" and "slut" were merely a consequence of my actions. His sarcastic and sadistic humor at my expense hurt me terribly. It went far beyond the typical childish brotherly jabs. Later on, whenever I had a boyfriend and I stopped hanging out with him as much, he took it as a personal rejection. This was such a tragic shame because I looked up to him like a father.

My brother swims through life as angry as a violent storm. He is charming and funny and well-liked but his eyes reflect an angry darkness. I remember running into my brother at a grocery store and watching him peruse the tomatoes. He looked as if he would viciously murder the tomatoes and chop them into pieces. "What did those tomatoes do to him?" I wondered. As a teenager, I always felt as if my brother were on the verge of an explosion and I felt a sense of anxiety in his presence. His jokes were always mean-spirited and at my expense. He had no one to tell him that the way he joked about women was wrong and hurtful.

My mother's anger at me grew the more pregnant I became. The more successful Jacob and I were, the less we needed her. The more we "made it" and defied the odds of teen pregnancy statistics, the more my mother resented us because she was in no way emotionally prepared for her sixteen-year-old daughter to live on her own and have her own family. This was not wrong but a God-given feeling. Those feelings should have been a good indication that it was a bad idea for Jacob and I to live together.

Shortly thereafter, my mother allowed Jacob to move into our home. This was not the right solution. I am not a fan of allowing boyfriends to move into homes without a marriage certificate. This is just further confirmation that my mother and Alec were checked out as parents. The idea behind this was that the damage was already done so why care now but it is never too late to start parenting. I wish I had been encouraged to marry Jacob. It would have helped me later.

Jacob moved into my parent's home and my childhood room was changed into a mini studio apartment that could serve as our teenage love shack and nursery. Half the time we were going out at night and trying to be teenagers and the other half of the time we were playing the part of adults. Jacob got a job at a local casino and he was able to cover all of my prenatal care. What an accomplishment for such a young kid.

At eighteen, Jacob would start providing for me so gallantly. I am not quite sure why my mother's hatred for me grew but I felt it. Perhaps it was because I responded to it by ignoring her or perhaps because I did not want her involved in any decisions. I did not want her involved in my child's life and I especially did not want her involved in the birthing process. She was persona non grata to me.

I did not wake up one day and just decide this. I could feel her hatred and the state of our relationship slowly and steadily descending into grim and unfavorable waters. I had not heard her speak the words, "I love you," for almost a year. She was bitter at me and she allowed my brother to call me every name that she wished she could say herself. My mother was nicer when Jacob was home but she often gave Jacob the creeps as she would stand outside our shared room and listen to our conversations.

Later, in court documents, Jacob would testify that my mother was weird and that she would walk in while Jacob was changing and, instead of quickly closing the door, she would stand there and watch him. She allowed Jacob to move in and welcomed him in the beginning but, as the novelty of our situation wore off, so did my mother's patience for him. Jacob's teenage arrogance did nothing to help the situation as he, for example, left his laundry all over the floor and expected my mother to wash it.

Looking back, I wish that my parents had insisted that Jacob and I not shack up together under their roof. This set a precedent in the home for future decisions that would cause more heartache. We were having a baby and, yes, the die was cast but the very best thing would have been to secure a commitment from us for the future. The very best thing would have been to present us with two roads to follow: raise the child as a married couple or raise the child together while both pursuing our educational and career goals but while also maintaining a separation in our living situation.

The reason is simply that shacking up together to play house almost always ends in a break-up. There was a baby to think of and the very best thing would be to ensure that the baby had a solid family and marriage creates that kind of solemnity. It is too easy to walk away from a "shack up" type of situation. It is shaky ground. In the case of not being married, it is best if the couple works out a shared custody situation while both pursue their goals. This gives everyone a future. I have observed too many young couples walk away from each other and I know that "shacking up" is not a good idea and will not provide lasting stability for a child. Statistics show that those that live together rather than getting married have a fifty percent chance of breaking up within five years.

I am quite certain that my mother resented the fact that I was a pregnant teenager. What mother would not? I am sure hopes and dreams were shattered but I could never tell whether her anger was because I got pregnant or because I publicly humiliated her or both. A part of me also knew that she was angry that I was shutting her out in regard to my baby plans. This was because I had a warranted fear that she would try to take my baby. I knew that she and Alec had previously discussed adopting my child on numerous occasions.

The day I discovered that I was pregnant, I thought that she would be angry at me. Instead, a few months down the line, I started to take note of her curt replies and short answers. This is how my mother often played the long game. It was a series of passive aggressive plays. Nothing was direct but very covert and indirect. She would quietly ignore me. For me, being ignored was the worst. By the time we did have a confrontation or discussion about why my mother was angry at me, three months to a year or more could go by and I never knew exactly why my mother was so angry at me.

One particular time, when my pregnant belly was just beginning to show, I had grown tired of the silence and the frigidly cold shoulder that my mother offered me. This game of silence was not exclusive to my pregnancy situation. There were many times when my mother would grow silent and appear to be simmering with anger. Weeks would go by and I would consequently avoid her. Avoiding her always made things worse but confronting her meant that I would take a verbal beating and I would always, always have to apologize even though I may not even know why I was apologizing. Apologizing was a problem too because, any time I tried to "make peace" with my mother, I would have to carefully approach her and would try so hard to smooth things over.

By this time, I craved a truce with my mother. There is not a daughter on this planet that does not crave and wish for a healthy relationship with their mother. I am one of those daughters. Sadly, her quick and almost autonomic response was to lift her nose slightly in the air and narrow her eyes with suspicion. She would usually say, "do you know why you are apologizing?" If I failed to guess the right answer (because I often struggled to know why my mother was actually angry with me) then my mother would make a face that made it clear she was disgusted with me and the silence might continue, if I were lucky, but usually this would launch my mother into releasing the pent-up emotional aggression that she was holding against me. It never felt good and sometimes the supposed slight or thing that I had done wrong had not even happened. Sometimes, I could not recall what my mother said I did. This made me question her sanity but, mostly, this made me question myself. My mother had a talent for helping me believe that I did something wrong or I was responsible for causing her anger even when I questioned if my mother were indeed telling the truth. To her, it may have felt like the truth but I knew that I had not even been in the same places or said the words that my mother insisted on.

Not this time, though. This time I was not going to apologize for something that my mother had imagined. I was trying to learn how to stand up for myself and not cower with fear in front my mother. She had the power to destroy me with words and she made me feel extremely anxious when she ignored me for days, weeks, and sometimes months. My mother worked very hard to keep me isolated from my entire family during those times. I did not want my precious child to experience all the pain and hurt that I often felt in my own family. Though my efforts were admittedly feeble, I was trying to learn what to do to stop the cycle. I had no idea that doing this, alone, would cause my mother great anger and contempt for me.

Chapter 12

Don't Hit Me

Yet again, my mother was angry at me and I did not know why. I could feel her simmering with anger whenever I walked into the room she was in. Was she angry at me because I did not do the dishes last night, put the cup in the dishwasher, or because Jacob left an item of clothing on the floor in the laundry room again? I did not know. I wished I knew. I just wanted things to be okay and peaceful. The anxiety and anger were so thick and palpable that they could be sliced with a knife. It drove me crazy. When my mother became like this, everyone in the house avoided her and this made her even more angry. Sometimes, it seemed as though I were the only one that cared enough to approach her and discover what was wrong. Sadly, no good deed goes unpunished. As the scapegoat, I would often take the blame and the punishment for my mother's emotions even when it had nothing to do with me at all.

It was on one of these occasions where I was seeking to just make peace yet stand up for myself and break the cycle all at once. My mother was sitting at her bright yellow kitchen counter. She sat on a stool looking through some papers and catalogs that had arrived in the mail. She always looked so sullen and unhappy. As a young child, I had started blaming myself for my mother's unhappiness and coldness as most children do. I had been feeling my mother's ire rising against me and I desired to head it off at the pass and try to stop a huge fight from happening.

I approached her and questioned her about why she was so upset. I got nothing but a cold response. She continued to rifle through her papers and paid me no attention. She would not even look up at me as I tried various ways to draw an answer out of her. At last, I pressed the matter further by asking her, "don't you love me?" I asked her this considering all the love I already felt for my own unborn child. She finally looked up from what she was doing. She folded her arms over her chest in self-protective symbolism, put her nose in the air, and declared in a monotonous, matter of fact, chilly voice, "I have never loved you. I only love your brothers."

I felt my mouth drop open. It felt like I had just been socked in the stomach. I had always felt that my mother treated me differently from my brothers but to have her state this was too much for me to handle. It hurt so badly. No matter how many times my mother had said she loved me, it only took this one declaration of truth to undo years of love and care. My wrists and my chest ached with emotional heartbreak. It hurt so badly to hear from my only living, biological parent that she had never loved me.

My mother waited to see what effect her words would have on me and she observed the pain in my face and my body language. Her verbal torpedoes had the desired effect. I felt the need to retreat. I slowly backed away from my mother and she sat there watching me and the pain she had caused. She watched as I continued to shrink away to my room. In a way, the lack of response to such a great statement was the worst thing possible. I think my mother said this to incite an argument. She wanted an argument with me and when she saw the resolve in my face to get away from her, she innately knew that she had just caused the beginning of the end of our relationship. I am certain that she had been storing up her anger and resentment toward my pregnant condition for months and now she was releasing her anger on me in her usual way.

I closed my room door behind me and locked it. I sat on the edge of my bed and wept with great salty tears of rejection. Just then, with no knock or warning, the door burst open. My mother brandished a butter knife in her hand which she had used to unlock the door. She stood there, the great mammoth-like figure she was to me, as I remained seated and made a galant effort not to cower and tremble. I was very afraid of her as I stood staring up at this woman who had such great power to hurt me. I watched the butter knife wag back and forth as my mother wagged it in my face while screaming, "you do not lock the door in my house! This is *my* house, young lady, and you are not allowed to lock any door in *my* house." This was a new rule that I had never heard before.

I had grown so weary of this drama and my heart hurt

so badly. I had a sharp chest pain. As usual, my emotional pain was visceral and felt on a physical level. I felt like I was just not capable of taking any more pain. I might wither and die if I were hurt any more by her. I stood up in a calm and purposeful manner and briskly walked to the bathroom which was just outside my room and closed the door behind me. I relished the immediate calm and peace that the small bathroom brought to the situation. I wanted to get as far away as possible from my mother and the pain. I instinctively and without a conscious effort gripped the little lock on the bathroom door handle. The knob was black and brassy. My mother had grown extremely quiet because she was listening for the slight click that the lock made when pressed. My fingers pushed the lock on the door knob and the clicking sound reverberated like a bomb being set off in a quiet forest. I had inadvertently made the terrible mistake of locking that door too and my mother lost it.

She burst into the bathroom and screamed again, "you do not lock the door in *my* house!" She was red in the face and, this time, she was gripping the butter knife so tightly that her hands appeared to lack their vital blood supply. Locking the door was not an intentional act of disobedience on my part but an act of instinctive protection from an outside threat. I knew that my mother was using the lock on the door as an arbitrary rule with which to harass me. This was the first time I had ever heard of the "no locking the door" rule and, in the face of my pregnant belly, it seemed so very silly to just now create this rule. My mother did not care about the rule. She cared about having an excuse to lose her temper. She knew that she had said something that would change the way I would feel about her and she would change the story to blame me as always. At that moment, I could never have guessed how far my mother would take her need to change the story.

She closed the bathroom door behind her so that we stood face to face with each other. My mother was always taller than I but now she was like a giant to me and I held my belly in a protective and motherly fashion. I looked at her like a mouse in the clutches of the snake waiting for her next move. I was terrified. I now understood how a deer in the headlights felt. I was a young girl in front of her mother and I had no idea what her plan of action was. My fear was warranted. I watched my mother do the strangest thing.

"Susanne, stop it! Just stop it! Knock it off! Don't hit me, Susanne!" I stood there absolutely bewildered. The measure of pain I felt was replaced by sheer confusion. I was still and silent watching my mother pretend that I was hitting her. It was the most disturbing and odd drama to ever play out before my eyes. I had no idea what was happening. I never thought my mother capable of such cruel deceit. On the other side of the door and just down the hall, my little brother was in his room and could hear my mother's screams for help though he did not respond to them.

I felt totally dazed and confused as the bathroom door

swung open and my mother burst out of the bathroom and ran down the hall crying all the way to her room. What a masterful performance. I was stunned. I could never have imagined in my wildest dreams that this scene would have occurred. I still had no idea what all of this meant or why she had behaved that way. My mind did not think in terms of manipulative gameplay like my mother's did and I wondered at what had just happened. "Did my mother think I was actually hitting her?" I wondered. I was so confused. I stood there briefly in the hallway in a state of shock and questioned reality as I shuffled to my room. I was careful not to lock the door to my room this time. I was scared of all the unpredictability in my mother's behavior.

I had seen her lose her mind before in a thyroid and hormone induced rage. One day, she had all of us in the car as she drove down from up in the mountains of Southern California. She was terrified that she might drive off the road and then started screaming in the car. She pulled over to the side of the road and continued her screaming at us for our loud and boisterous play in the car. She was out of her mind with hormones, rage, and terror. Granted, we were a major handful but raging and screaming at kids for being kids is never acceptable. Sadly, my mother had herself convinced that these outbursts of anger were an acceptable way to communicate with children and that we would forget that it ever happened. It is not acceptable. It has taken me many, many years to identify my own anger problem and give it to

Jesus Christ, my Lord and Savior, to completely change. I will not live with any amount of anger in my heart.

As Christians, we must not believe the satanic lie that we are allowed to be angry and excuse it by calling ourselves passionate, intense, or any other word to excuse our behavior. As Christians, we are called to manifest the fruits of the Spirit and one of them is meekness, the exact opposite of anger. "Cease from anger, and forsake wrath: fret not thyself in any wise to do evil." Psalm 37:8. Every time I share my testimony, I usually have a number of parents approach me and ask me what my mother could have done to turn me around from my wicked ways. For many years I did not know what to say until I realized the damage that my mother's constant spirit of anger had caused in the home. If my mother had identified, dealt with, and repented of her anger in an open and Biblical way, this would have turned my behavior around.

I sat in my room for many minutes. My brain was playing the scene over and over in my head. I could not understand my mother or what she had just done. If I thought what had just happened was bewildering and evil, I did not need to look any further because the next happening was downright scary and pushed me from my childhood home.

I sat on my bed, bracing myself for the next bit of drama. I felt like I was in a state of shock. I was not sure what to do with myself so I just sat there, waiting for Alec to arrive home like a child waiting for their father to get home from work to get their spanking. Indeed, I was awaiting my executioner.

I heard Alec's imminent arrival and my stomach whirled with nerves. I had no idea what my mother would say or do. I heard the front door slam and I heard his wide and broad gait marching down the hallway past my room to my mother's room. I could hear my mother's shrill voice picking up and taking off like a spaceship lifting off. She yelled on and on, recounting her tale with enthusiasm. I could not hear her exact words but I could make out my own name and I could hear my mother's excited chatter as she used her words in a herculean effort to turn Alec against me. I knew that Alec would be coming to see me next and that this situation would not be a simple thing. This kind of fight could last for months with my mother and, as our fights often did, sometimes even years.

I contemplated my own nervous tension and wondered if all of this upheaval was good for my unborn child when I saw and heard the door moving with the soft knocking sound of Alec at my bedroom door. I stiffened because I knew that my life was about to change. I knew that my mother had been looking for a reason to get rid of me and now she had it.

Alec came into the room and, in his typical defeated and torn down manner, said, "I'm sorry, kid, but you have to go." He then described to me the terrible bruises my mother had all over her arms from my violent and terrible outburst. He said that my mother had shown him and my little brother what I had done to her.

"I did not touch her! I swear! I didn't touch her!" I said as I bristled under the false allegations. I could not believe this. I was stunned, hurt, and rejected by the one person on earth that I thought would love me most. But she did not love me. She hated me and she was willing to lie to get everyone else to hate me too. I knew that Alec believed me. I knew that he was the only person on earth who understood just how sick my mother was and that it was, indeed possible, that my mother put those bruises on herself. He looked at me with sympathy in his face and sadness in his eyes as he said, "I know you didn't do it but you have to go."

"Where will I go?" I asked in a defeated and mournful tone. My mother's hate had pushed my stepsister from the home and now it was my turn.

"Can't you stay at Jacob's place for a little while?" I agreed that it was probably the best for a little while. I left home that day and my mother stood on the porch crying and bawling as if she wanted me to stay. I was so confused. I did not understand these games and neither did my brothers. They thought that I had beaten my mother up and now I was leaving of my own choice. I left for a while to go stay with friends but in a couple of weeks I came back home.

Things were extremely tense with my mother. She looked at me with hatred and contempt. I never knew if she was happy I was home or wanted me to leave again. I knew in my heart that I needed to get away from her, permanently, to protect my baby. My mother scared me and I felt as if I were living in a war zone. From day to day, I never knew if she was going to scream at me or hug me. I would often hear Alec and my mother discussing my mother's feelings about me. It would hurt me so deeply to hear what my mother had to say about me. She talked as if she thought that either I could not hear her or she did not care if I heard her.

Jacob and I ended up coming back home a few weeks after my mother's outburst but that was short lived. The damage had been done. I could never fully trust my mother and my mother resented me and especially hated that I kept her at arm's length.

I was afraid to have my mother present at the birth of my son. After witnessing, first hand, the lengths to which she was willing to go to lie to my family and isolate me, I was terrified by the possibility that my mother could influence the doctors and nurses at the hospital while I birthed my child. I wanted my child to be mine and not to have my mother fighting me for control of my child.

The night I went into labor was surreal. Even though Jacob and I had been to Lamaze classes and I somewhat knew what to expect in a theoretical sense, no one can quite prepare you for the actual experience. I had no way of knowing that these terrible gas pains were the beginning of labor pains. I felt exhausted so I decided to lie down to nap after traipsing through Jacob's parent's beautiful orchard. Maybe it was the running around and excitement that jump-started labor although, more than anything, it was the right time. I did not think that this day would ever come. When you are pregnant and miserable, you long to get this over with but you also dread the unknown of childbirth. Other women's stories had frightened me to death and I was very scared. True to my teenage level of maturity, I put the actual day of childbirth far from my mind and as something "that wouldn't happen to me."

But, it was happening to me. I woke up late in the evening after a long nap, feeling like gas pains would tear me in two. In my childhood room, I was about to pass from girl to mother. In the room where I had played dress-up and dolls with my brothers and friends, I was experiencing the realness of life. Childbirth is a portal through which a selfish girl passes to hopefully become a more loving and selfless woman.

I denied what I was experiencing. Even when I felt the "gas" pains growing more and more painful by the minute, I refused to think of myself as in labor. I was embarrassed to call Jacob to come home from work at the casino if I were not actually in labor. He would get home at around two o'clock in the morning. I told myself that I just needed to hang on until then. I sat on the edge of our black, rod iron bed and stared at the clock above the door. I held the baby secure within my belly and rubbed my extended and large stomach as the pain ripped through my lower back. My stomach twisted with nausea. I instinctively wanted to bring my knees to my chest to push through the pain. Was it gas? As I watched the minutes slip by into hours, I felt the pain become stronger and more intense in steady intervals. The denial was wearing off as I started to acknowledge that I was going into labor.

My chief concern was that my mother not know. It was easy to hide the fact that I was in labor from my mother because she was ignoring me. Family dinners happened without me. She no longer cared to check on me or talk to me at all so I was able to writhe and groan all alone in the awful full swing of labor. I would grit my teethe and grow silent if I heard anyone pass by the door to my room. I stressed about how I might get myself out of the house and into the car without my mother noticing. I knew that if I waited for my mother to go to bed and, if I waited long enough to call Jacob, then he could come home from work and we could slip out the front door and head to the hospital without anyone noticing.

Most girls want their mothers with them during such a time of unexpected pain and miserable blood, sweat, and tears but not I. The thought of having her there made this time seem more stressful. I did not want to have to worry about how she was feeling or how this was affecting her. I needed to focus. It was ingrained in me to put my mother's feelings first but I knew that this baby needed me to put him first. I needed to protect him, love him, and give him better than I had experienced. I knew that I never wanted him to feel like an outsider in his own family.

I felt stuck. The stress of the simultaneous back-breaking pain, not knowing what to do, and whether I should call Jacob or not while trying not to be loud with my miserable pain was too much to bear. The contractions were coming on stronger and more often and it started to sink in that this was it. I was scared but I also felt strong that if I just focused on the seconds and minutes at that moment, I might survive. I decided that, if I did not want to have this baby in my room and subsequently give my mom an opportunity to control me and my baby to her advantage, I had better call Jacob.

I dialed the number to his work and I nervously asked for Jacob. Personal calls were frowned upon unless in an emergency. Everyone at Jacob's work knew that I was pregnant so my call was met with a lot of excited voices. Jacob's voice was a welcome sound to me. It had been a long and lonely few hours trying to brave the pain and the stress all alone. I suddenly realized how much I needed Jacob and his support. I did not want to do this alone.

"Yello," Jacob said in his chipper and upbeat tone.

"I think I am having the baby!" I announced. I could not hide the fact that I was in pain and Jacob heard the tears and emotion in my voice.

"Okay!" His tone changed from chipper to sympathetic and concerned. I was worried that he would drive home too fast. "I'll be right there." Jacob added as he hung up the phone to rush out the door. I have no idea exactly how he got home so fast but he managed to arrive home very quickly and

I was so relieved to have him by my side. I breathed a sigh of relief as he walked through my bedroom door.

Jacob found me sitting on the edge of my bed, staring at the clock, and waiting patiently through every minute for him to get home. By now, my mother and Alec had gone to bed. It was about thirty minutes before midnight so I was worried that my mother would awaken out of her usually light sleep and notice that Jacob had come home early. The fear that she would put two and two together and insist on coming to the hospital with us was very real. Jacob could sense my fear and he shared the fear with me.

In a great silence, we operated like a secret agent conveyer belt, picking up the things we might need and the things for the baby, without uttering a single word. It was quiet and methodical as Jacob grabbed our new diaper bag and a hospital bag for me. He opened my bedroom door and checked to see if the coast was clear and nodded to me as a signal to walk through. We were like covert agents moving under the cover of darkness as we traversed the dangerous journey from my bedroom to the home's entryway in order to escape out the front door to safety from my threatening mother but also to exit my childhood and enter into womanhood. We walked out the door and into the night. Jacob left the car lights off as we silently pulled out of the driveway to make our journey one town over to the hospital.

Most of us do not go around remembering every moment of life. There are snapshots of events that serve as symbols of certain things. Having a baby, for a young girl who managed to avoid thinking of the pain her entire pregnancy, was shocking as the realness of becoming a mother started to sink in. I remember having contractions all the way to the hospital and pushing so hard, with my feet up on the dash, that I cracked the windshield. It was like a dream. The pain put me in a state of mind that felt like I was out of my body. I hardly remember being wheeled from the hospital lobby up to the labor and delivery ward of the hospital. I do remember crawling into the bed and crying for relief. I tend to internalize pain so I was screaming loudly on the inside. I did not think that anyone in this much pain could live. I began to think that I was dying with every contraction. I clung to my bed until the pain ferociously ripped through my back and belly and I turned over to be on all fours and felt myself starting to stand up in the bed. I kept trying to move to different positions as if, if I could change positions again, I could somehow manage to escape from the pain. At last I cried out, "I want an epidural!"

A nurse had me lie down in the bed again to check my progress and I was almost too far along to have an epidural but I begged and cried for relief. The time seemed to drag on. "I am dying!" I told Jacob. "How does anyone live though this? How can a person be in this much pain and it not be deadly?" I thought. I was certain that I was dying. Jacob's face looked concerned and I could feel that he felt helpless. He wanted to help me but childbirth is a road that every woman must walk through. There is no way to escape it. It must be faced.

At last, the anesthesiologist arrived and I hunched my back as was needed to do the epidural. The best and worst part is the contractions happening while you are getting an epidural. You cannot move to change positions while they are inserting the needle into your back for the epidural but you know that, if you suffer just a little bit longer, you will soon have relief and you will do just about anything to get an ounce of relief from the misery.

After the epidural, I started to feel some relief and at last was able to look up at Jacob, who was standing next to me and holding my hand, and smile. I saw a look of relief come over Jacob's face as he observed the old me return. It was only minutes later that I was told to push. Without any fanfare, I went through the work of pushing and laboring. We had arrived at the hospital at around midnight and, only three hours later, I was pushing to bring my new baby into the world.

I pushed and pushed and soon I felt the great pressure of the baby in the birth canal and that caused me to push harder. I felt the pressure in my pelvis and I wondered at why I felt anything at all, not understanding that an epidural cannot take away all feeling. At last, I heard the nurses exclaim that they could see a head. I could see my baby's head in my own body reflected in the eyeglasses of the doctor in front of me. I was kind of disturbed by all of the blood. I was embarrassed by my own bodily functions and I felt self-conscious.

There was no time to dwell on my self. I was having a baby. Finally, after a few more great pushes, at 3:18 AM, my little man-child arrived. I thought that maybe something was wrong with me because I had watched so many birthing stories on television and had seen nearly every woman cry when her baby was born. I did not cry. I could not cry because my eyes were trained and focused on my baby's little head and body. I was paranoid that someone would see my incredible blessing, undeserving and immature as I was, and forbid me from keeping my baby.

I was so young to be given a life, the most precious and fragile thing in this entire world. A life was being entrusted to my care. I was sure that social services would burst into the room and take my baby at any moment. I failed to realize that my fear and strong desire to protect my baby were God-given motherly instincts. I wanted to hold him and never let him go. I wanted to protect him from anyone and anything that might hurt him.

Despite some of the awful things that had already happened to me by that time, I saw my mother as the most dangerous thing that could happen to my baby. I thought that she might want to take my baby away from me if she could and I knew that she would be very angry with me once she found out that I had gone and had a baby without her. It was like a snowball effect. I knew that the fact that I had not told her that I was in labor at home and had not called her when I arrived at the hospital would enrage her. Every moment that went by without a call to her made it worse but, still, I was afraid of her anger.

Eventually, I worked up the nerve to call home in the wee hours of the morning and I was extremely grateful when Alec answered the phone. He greeted me with a hearty "congratulations!" I knew I was blessed that he had answered the phone and not my mother because I am sure that Alec took the outrage that my mother dished out when she found out that I had already had my baby and had not uttered a word to her. She had planned on being in the delivery room with me and figured that I would be so miserable and in so much pain that I would call out for her and that she would have to help me. Maybe she put off reconciling with me and gave me the cold shoulder during those long months of silence because she thought that the birthing experience would bring us together when months and months of time did not.

Whatever my mother's reaction, it could not dull the joy of my new little baby. He was perfect. From the moment the nurse laid him in my arms, all I could do was stare at him. He was the most entertaining thing I had ever seen. I could spend hours and hours just looking at him as if his growth could be seen by the human eye. He was fascinating to watch.

He cried and cried with great gusto in the delivery room after being born. They put him in the infant warmer and he screamed even louder until his daddy walked over to him and started speaking to him in low and comforting tones. It dawned on me that my baby could feel things. I know people already know this fact but, as a young and new mother, it never occurred to me that my baby could feel emotions before this moment. "How will I ever put my little baby down in his crib when he can sense that he is alone?" I immediately thought. At my age and in a time when the "attachment parenting" ideology had not yet become mainstream, I started the practice of attachment parenting without even knowing what I was doing. It was natural to me.

So began my own journey in learning to be a mother apart from my own mother. Most girls learn how to mother from their mother. I knew that many things about my being a mother had to be different from my own mother if I were going to have a healthy relationship with my son and not hurt him the way I was hurt by my own mother. My mother had always told me, "I hope your children grow up to be as terrible as you are," or, "I hope that your kids are just like you," always with the meaning that I was the worst kid ever. I really wanted to raise a child that did better than I could do as a parent. The truly God-fearing parents want their children to grow up to be a better person than they are. I was experiencing the truth of parenthood: it is a road of total self-sacrifice for another. Being a parent is the "laying down of one's life for a brother." I wanted to do for my children what was not done for me. This became my sole purpose.

Though I felt my entire life's purpose newly revealed to me, I struggled with my teenage urges to run wild. There were many months when my son and I stayed home and did nothing but cuddle and play. Those times of being still and peaceful with my child are the most precious. But, in that time I often felt alone and depressed. I missed my family and my mother was not speaking to me.

To keep peace, Jacob and I had to move out of my mother's house again so we moved into Jacob's parent's house at first. Jacob was working hard and I was happily caring for our sweet little son. I enjoyed being with Jacob's family but I longed for my own mother. She was angry with me and again and, as always, I did not know why she would not speak to me and this went on for over a year. My mother has often missed huge chunks of our lives. These lost times would never be redeemed. For whatever reason, the standoff between my mother and I went on and the fact that I was a minor but had been legally emancipated did not help.

I was frightened and it felt illogical that I could take my son to the doctor and sign for my child but I could not take myself to the doctor and sign for myself because I was still a minor. I really wanted to be able to take care of myself in every area. It was always a very frightening reality that my mother could call the police on me and say that I was a runaway and that she could even fight for custody of my child as long I was a minor. I wanted the security of knowing that I was declared a legal adult to protect myself and my child. I was completely on my own with no help from my family and I wanted the law to recognize that fact.

A family friend who was a malpractice attorney drew up the papers to declare my emancipation. Many families had witnessed the fact that I was on my own and that my mother wanted nothing to do with me. This family was just one among many who had seen my stepsister kicked out of our home at sixteen and I was out roaming the streets and getting into a lot of trouble at fourteen. It was not a stretch for this family to observe my predicament. The legal papers were drawn up and taken to my parents to sign. It really made sense since I was now a mother with a young child. I was, in a way, divorcing my parents.

Many teenagers may wish to or, in a tongue and cheek way, say that they are going to be emancipated but it is an entirely different thing to actually go through with it. To emancipate yourself as a minor, you must show that you willingly live apart from your parents and that you can financially support yourself with an income that is neither illegal or from your family. The emancipation process is a process that shows the court that a minor is better off without their parents and sadly, ever so sadly, this was my case.

I remember when my family friend (the lawyer) filed the paperwork and a signature from my parents was required. I thought for sure that there would be resistance in signing the necessary paperwork and that this would be a huge fight but it was not so. My friend went to my childhood home, Alec invited him in, and they simply signed the paperwork. That was it. A part of me wished that my parents would have said something along the lines of, "we love you, come home," but this was not said and I got the message loud and clear that perhaps it was just better that I go away. Thus began a long period of silence between my mother and I. It would be nearly a year before I heard from her again. She would miss so many special things and I missed her but I could not bear her hatred for me and the venom she cast my way. It was sad without her in my life for the special moments in my son's life but it was a huge relief to finally, after all these years, be free of her. There is not a child alive, no matter how abusive their parents are, who does not crave their parents. It is a natural impulse within us to need our parents and to want them. No matter how close our children may become to friends and other adults, no matter how happy they seem, nothing can ever replace a parent.

I stood before the judge and heard her say that I was now an emancipated minor. There are very few minors emancipated per year in Riverside County (or anywhere else). The numbers range from zero to ten in most years. It is not a common practice of the courts unless there are extreme circumstances. I thought that being an emancipated minor would cause me to suddenly feel very adult-like but it did not. It was a cold comfort. Comforting, in the way that I knew that my mother could no longer withhold consent on trivial paperwork, but cold in the way that all that I ever wanted was a solid, loving, and involved set of parents. On this point, my mother would sharply and excitedly protest. She would say that she did offer me unconditional love but love never fails and my mother, by coming in and out of my life and then lying to my brothers and telling them that it was I who desired separation, failed me. I have never wished to cut my mother out of my life but longed for my mother to show me a kind of love that did not require me to be her marriage therapist or her scapegoat. My mother always put me on a pedestal to be her mother and, when I failed to meet her requirements, she cast me down to the ground and tried to destroy me.

So many times I would come to talk to my mother and it would not be a good time for her due to homework, shopping, or other goals she had in mind. Then days or even months later, when my mother came to speak with me and I had already found someone else to meet that need, she would be outraged that I did not confide in her about my life. Children need to see parents, first and foremost, as parents. When we have children, we may still be a doctor, a lawyer, a writer, or some other profession but, first and foremost, we must be a parent. It should be number one. I must be willing to stop whatever I am doing and be a parent, first, regardless of my own goals in life. Goals are excellent and children need to see hardworking and driven parents but they must know, beyond a shadow of a doubt, that their mom and dad would do anything for them. They would swim across shark-infested waters to bring them a lemonade if they had to. Our children must see us completely dedicated to the task of raising them. Even in writing this book, I have to manage my time to make sure I meet the needs of all five of my children, from adult to infant, first and foremost.

There are appropriate times to talk to children and each child has a unique personality and I, as a mother, need to learn the inner workings of each unique personality gifted to my care. When I would get in the car after school, my mother would be very frustrated with me if I did not want to talk. I am, by nature, an introvert. I have to exert an extreme amount of energy in not appearing to be an introvert so I am always exhausted after I am around lots of people. Back then, it was not yet known how sick I was.

After school, I felt as though I would collapse. It was a mix of pure emotional exhaustion and physical exhaustion on an extremely deep level because my immune system would struggle as I was exposed to a vast number of germs at school. I would get to the car and feel as though I were crashing and my mother would be questioning me and I gave one word answers in reply. This she would take very personally and then scold me all the way home about my bad attitude. All children are not alike and they share things in a unique way. Some of my children cannot wait to tell me everything and some of my children need a little time to process the day first and then they will come out later while I am cooking dinner and open up to me.

Children depend on our maturity as adults that we can take rejection and not take their sharing, or lack thereof, personally. Each child will share things differently and at different rates. I know my mother envisioned her daughter being this extremely chatty person and share everything with her so that she might live vicariously through me and that I would help her process her emotions. I was neither emotionally or physically able to fulfill her vision so her vision died and, as a result, she began to deeply resent me. I am careful not to envision what my children will or will not do. The future belongs to God. In each moment, the most important thing is that I make myself available at all times for all of my children, that I do not put unrealistic expectations on them in any area, and that I respond to them in a Christ-like manner.

Chapter 13

My Friend Crystal

Months sailed by as Jacob and I enjoyed the blissful early months of our baby's life. This was a relatively peaceful time in my life as I took on the role of stay-at-home mom with gusto. I surprised myself with how much I enjoyed the nursing and care of a baby.

At this point, I think it is pertinent to mention that, when my father died, he died because of gross negligence on the part of his treating physician. On New Year's Eve, my father passed away when medical intervention could have spared his life. The treating physician was under the influence of alcohol and, thus, my father died in a hospital choking on his own fluids. My mother sued the hospital and won a sizable settlement paid out to her and to be paid out in future installments to my brother and I when we reached a certain age. This money, rightly handled, should have been a blessing but it turned out to be more of a curse.

I used these funds (the first pay out was $20,000) to move Jacob and I out of our small town to the much larger neighboring town of Redlands, California. We leased a cute and sizable two-bedroom apartment. With my little nest egg, I was able to buy a little SUV for cash, get some furniture, and set up my own home. It was my own little sanctuary or piece of heaven and I was very happy during this time with my beautiful baby boy and his father. Unfortunately, we would not live together there for very long. I wish that I could say that Jacob and I stayed together for the long haul and that we defied the statistics until the end and made it through the hard times. We were teenagers playing a dangerous game. When a relationship falls apart, it is a wound of the worst kind. A break-up causes the most severe heartache. Some have said that a break-up is worse than death because death is not a rejection. A break-up or a divorce is a wound of the heart that never fully heals but rather fades away with the passage of time. The worst part about our break-up was knowing that we had failed our son. We were both guilty of breaking apart his little home.

Breaking up, although people say they do not want their children to observe the conflict or a loveless environment, improves nothing. Breaking up made nothing better. What was stressful was even more stressful as a single mom and what was lonely was even more lonely. I would forever be cursed to deal with a string of girlfriends that came into the life of my son's father and disappeared as quickly, never to be seen or heard from again. I, too, had my string of boyfriends and thus my son was cursed even more to live a life of carefully measuring his every emotion as to not love so much that he could not lose a person.

It was and has been awful to raise my son in separate homes. My biggest regret is not trying harder to keep my son's home intact. I gave away my influence to the other women that play the role of mommy all while my son longed for his real mommy and I could not be there all the time. Women think that, if they can just get away, things will improve. It never improves. You just end up settling for alternative versions of the stress and it is even more stressful trying to co-parent because it is rarely ever done in a truly successful manner. As long as we live, we can never truly repair the damage we have done in breaking up our little boy's home.

"I'm not happy," I said, as we both sat out on our apartment porch smoking cigarettes together. Jacob replied, "I'm not happy either." He curtly stood up and walked inside, shutting the door behind him. I had expected him to fight a little more for our relationship and I underestimated the effect the words, "I'm not happy," would have on Jacob. He took my words to mean, "I want to break up." The past month had been quite revealing to me about Jacob's character and controlling side.

I had bought Jacob a motorcycle and a few other things and I saw that my money was quickly being depleted so I went out and got a part-time job as a sales associate at Sears in their men's suit department. Jacob worked nights and I worked days. I also enrolled in college courses. Jacob was not happy with these decisions.

One day we were driving down the freeway in our new little SUV and he turned to me and said, "you better not come home and try to teach me whatever it is you think you're learning at school." He did not like it that I was working and he did not like it that I was trying to gain an education. Instead of seeing my desire to advance as a testament to the security he gave me, he took it as a threat to our happiness.

He started hanging out at his friend's house when I was at work. These friends were into raving at the time and I assumed that Jacob was consistently around drugs and girls and this scared me deeply for us and our little family. I still thought that we could work all these things out so I was utterly shocked when I arrived home to our little apartment, my little slice of heaven with our baby on my hip, and it was being emptied out by Jacob and his parents. They took everything they could. It did not matter if I had paid for it with my money. Everything I owned somehow belonged to Jacob.

I stood there at our formerly shared living room apartment window looking out at the parking lot where Jacob and his parents were loading up the vehicles to move their son back home with our baby in my arms. I watched them drive away with nearly all of my things, my SUV that I had bought in cash (which Jacob would total only months later), and the motorcycle I had bought Jacob. They carried everything they could out of that apartment and I was left with nothing, nothing but my baby. I was terrified that Jacob would try to take him too so I did not let Jacob have a moment alone with our son for months which is something that Jacob held against me for years.

I stood there tightly holding our baby in a ransacked apartment with no car, no food, my bank account had equally been ransacked, checks had already been written that I could not cover (this would ruin my credit for years), and I knew I was up against a rock and a very hard place. I had no way to make rent and no way to feed our baby and I knew that Jacob and his family would be coming for my baby next. I had no time to sit and think of my heartache or of how quickly my savior and prince charming had turned against me. I never thought that Jacob would ever turn against me but he soon would become one of my greatest adversaries. While my baby played on the living room floor, I quickly went into survival mode. There was only one thing left to do and that was to call my mother.

I was technically an adult now and she did not need to take me home but I had no money and I was now a single and unwed mother. I had nowhere to go and I did not want to live on my own anymore. I was humiliated that everything had fallen apart just as everyone said it would. The year and a half that Jacob and I stayed together, with every passing month that we managed to hold things together, seemed like a rebuke to the naysayers and I felt a deep sense of pride that Jacob and I would be different. I thought we would not be "just another teenage romance." We would go the distance so everyone who judged me would see that I was right and they were wrong. Most people could see the forest from the trees and the writing on the wall. I could not. I was shattered when things fell apart but I chose to sweep my pain under the rug, always waiting for another day which was something that would come and bite me later. Worse than that, I was humiliated and humbled to tell people that Jacob and I had broken up. I did not want to be that girl or a failure and, in my own estimation, I was exactly that.

Looking at my son was like proof positive of all the wrong I had done. I had done wrong by getting pregnant and now I was doing wrong by breaking up the home and hating his father. I wish I had gone to Jacob and tried to work things out but I did not and he did not come to me. It was a standoff that entered the court system. I encourage anyone who has a child and is not married to the other parent to, please, try to work it out on your own without the courts. Talk to each other and, as much as you may hurt because of each other, try to put your child first and work out a shared schedule together. Once in the hands of the court, you lose control and lawyers can make things more warlike and it is awful.

I spent a lot of money and fourteen years trying to do what a little humility, kindness, communication, and sharing did in a few seconds. I thought that, eventually, I would get full custody but I never did. Jacob never got full custody either and that is because a child is meant to be shared, not split in two. I believe the story of King Solomon and the two women fighting each other over the baby is a good example of what the courts do to a child. The parent that truly loves the child will stop the cutting and do what it takes to save the child from being ripped in two.

I wish I could say that I had effectively done that. I was young and foolish and, in all those years, no adult told me to try to peacefully work things out with Jacob. I was always encouraged to fight it out in the courts. After a while, I realized the very best thing for my son is to love his father. To this day, I love his father even though he has wronged me, he does not deserve it, and we are not bosom buddies but I love his father because of Christ. It took years of maturation to come to this place which is why teenagers should not have babies but they often do anyway.

If you are a teenager with a baby, I encourage you to do all you can to find forgiveness for your ex-partner and do everything you can to keep peace and stay out of the courts. It is worth it when the child is a teenager. It is completely worth it to be selfless instead of selfish and work together for your child. I wish I would have had the strength at the time to be a strong woman instead of a foolish girl contending for my rights. Of course, in instances of abuse, this advice is null and void and you must protect your child as their life depends on it.

My level of foolishness was only outweighed by the emotional pain I was experiencing. My mother, much to her credit, was always there to pick me up and take me home when I hit rock bottom but she would often be the reason why I was at rock bottom to begin with. She encouraged me to leave Jacob and I could see that she had a sense of satisfaction that I was coming home as a failure. I had failed miserably and I crawled home to lick my wounds. I registered in school and I saw how the other girls my age were living and I was envious. I longed to join the girls that were free without a care in the world.

Admittedly, at this point I would have been happy if my parents would have taken my baby from me because I felt defeated and I knew that I had miserably failed my son. I had never seen stability in my life so how could I create it? My mother was a constant push and pull of emotion. She was never happy in her marriages. She was always angry and my parents were often fighting. Down deep inside, I knew that things with Jacob could have been saved and that we had just sabotaged something good and I regretted it deeply. I did not realize that we were also experiencing the consequences of living together outside of marriage.

Not more than a few weeks after Jacob and I had ended almost two years together, I was back home, enrolled in college, and I met an exchange student from Germany. He drove a Jeep and he was deeply homesick. He spoke broken English and lived in a small apartment in Loma Linda. I enjoyed spending time with him and I especially enjoyed the fact that he could whisk me away from my life for a time in his Jeep but, the moment he broke down and cried about how much he missed his homeland and family, I bailed on him. I could not handle his deep emotions because I was making a conscious effort to run from my own. My worst pain was now coming from the fact that I loved my son tremendously but I did not want the responsibility of taking care of him all on my own. I deeply and profoundly grieved losing his father from my life. I had no one to share the amazing things my son did and said with. When two people break apart like we did, they often work as hard as they can to find the worst in the person they used to see the best in. I worked hard to turn my love for Jacob into hate. It hurt too much to love him so it was easier to hate him.

It was too easy to break apart. One day we were living life together and then we were not. It hurts even more when you know that you are partially to blame for the state of things. As time went on, I took pleasure in the game of meeting people and breaking it off just when things started to get a little serious. I did not want to feel a thing. I committed to not feeling anything and doing whatever it took to accomplish this. The problem was that my son made me feel love and loss and I struggled to run a delicate balance between being a loving, young, single mother and a party animal who could care less.

It was like living two lives. I would come home from a long night of club-hopping in Hollywood and check my nose for bits of cocaine before entering the door to pick up my son and play mommy to him. Of course, I loved him dearly but I was in my own personal version of purgatory and I felt like I had to run from myself. My mother once told me that I would pace back and forth at home just itching to leave and get out.

I felt like I had to go where the party was and lose myself because I hated myself.

I partied hard. I drank and drank and raved and took ecstasy and anything that anyone would put in front of me. I knew that drugs were a destructive thing but I did not care. I never thought that I would live past my twenties. If someone asked me, "where do you see yourself in the next five years?" My answer would have been, "dead." I became obsessed with death and the question of when I will die and I longed to die but I did not know how to successfully kill myself either. Most of my suicide attempts were a cry for attention from my parents. I also did something as harmful if not more harmful than drugs: I slept around. I used my body like a weapon to hurt others and hurt myself. I let men use me and abuse me in the worst ways. I knew I needed help but I did not know how to really ask for help or who to ask.

It was during this turbulent time, when I needed my family the most, that my family broke apart. My mother and Alec were getting a divorce. My mother often complained to me that, "you were never there for me during my divorce like your brother was." I would walk past my mother's bedroom and see her crying on my brother's shoulder and I remember thinking how wrong it was to lean on a teenage kid that way but I also thought that I was glad it was not me that she was using to lean on. I had been through so many fights and false alarms of divorce where Alec would move out and go back to his parents' house. I can hardly ever remember a time of peace in the home though there must have been some. There was a constant Cold War threat of divorce growing up so I compartmentalized the divorce as been there and done that already. I already felt divorced from Alec so why not truly be divorced?

However, I severely underestimated his impact on my life. His very presence seemed to be a check on evil in the house. Fathers keep the home secure and, even if he was emotionally checked out as a father, he still kept a measure of discipline in the home. As soon as Alec moved out of the house, it was an all-out free-for-all for all of us. I turned my childhood home into a party house and my mother let me. She would complain about how afraid she was of me but I was trying desperately to tell her that I was desperate for help. I needed her. I was eighteen, a mother, and lost as can be. I did not know what was wrong with me and I trusted her to help me.

My success would ebb and flow. I would try to get myself together during the winter but, by summer time, I would lapse back into party mode. I wanted to do well but I did not know that I had a giant God-sized hole in my heart that needed filling. I was trying to hold down a job and go to school. I would just barely make it through a semester and then fall back into old behavior. I was my own worst enemy and I sabotaged my own success. In many ways, I wanted my life to be as big of a mess as my heart was so that it would be abundantly clear that I was hurting.

Then I met Crystal. She filled my life up and brought me comfort in ways that I never dreamed before. She became my best friend. There was only one problem, Crystal was not a person. She was methamphetamine and she became my precious comfort in so many ways. Whatever I was missing, my mother, my father, my God, she became. When I felt shy, she made me strong and, when I felt tired, she pushed me forward. I could get everything done in a day. No more depression. No more illness. No more pain. The very first time I met her, I knew that I never had to feel a moment of pain ever again. I was hooked and I loved it.

I had done drugs before. I had taken ecstasy pills and I had also done cocaine. Cocaine made me want to party and therefore I did not feel like it was something I could do around my child. Ecstasy put me totally out of commission for the night. But Crystal, she was different. In the beginning, it felt like I could very much use it to get things done and to feel better. My health was ever on a decline but doctors would struggle to learn exactly what ailed me until 2008. So, for the time being, Crystal felt like an answer to all my life questions.

Suddenly I had loads of energy to do everything on my list and, not only that, I did not need to sleep or eat as much. I also felt pain free from all the aches and pains that usually bothered me. Wow! I was impressed and I went from trying it once on a weekend to wanting to get more and more and more until I was an everyday user.

In the midst of my drug use and club-hopping, I met

Damien. I met him one night at a club in Riverside. He was tall and built. I came upon him when I noticed this huge crowd of people surrounding this gorgeous break dancer. He whirled and twirled on the floor in an acrobatic fury. Not only was he an awesome break dancer but he was smart and good looking. He had the typical German face: a strong jaw line and a perfect nose. He was blonde and blue eyed and he could have been a male model. I stood in the crowd as the music blared watching Damien move around with ease and support the entire weight of his body on one hand. He could do a one-handed push up. The crowd surrounding him clapped and cheered as he did these impressive moves. I cheered too.

The song was ending and the crowd started to dissipate. Damien felt the presence of the crowd leaving and looked up to see me. I felt intimidated by this huge man that looked straight at me with a penetrating, blue-eyed gaze. He stood up tall and I felt weak-kneed looking up at this six foot three strong and handsome guy.

"What's your name?" he said through a smile. He was wearing a ridiculous, all white Adidas sweat suit get-up because we were at an all-white club party. He wore it well. He had a way of making me feel like I was the only girl in the room. "He could have talked to any girl in the club that night so why is he talking to me?" I thought. I pondered the fact that I, clearly, still had massive self-esteem issues as I looked up at this vision of perceived perfection in front of me. "I must not say anything stupid," I told myself. "Be smart!"

Since I had given birth to my son, I had acquired even more significant body image issues than I had before. At sixteen, I had become pregnant and, at seventeen, I gave my body up to the birthing process and it had taken its toll. At eighteen, I bore the marks of a woman who has had a baby. It is only natural. Men are supposed to love the woman that gives life. This is what is natural but I failed in seeing my body as a beautiful testament to self-sacrifice for the life of another and I hated my body.

I worked hard to cover my stretch marks with makeup. I often used body makeup and foundation to cover my body completely. One time I got up in the morning and had left makeup marks all over the sheets of a paramour. I went running from his house in utter humiliation but I kept wearing the makeup because I was intent on erasing what God and nature had blessed me with.

Damien was smart although he dumbed himself down with weed and alcohol. He was pushy and persistent. I attracted jerks like moths to a flame. What I thought was boldness was really pride and arrogance and usually severe anger in addition. Damien grabbed my hand in the club and trotted me out to the smoking section where he asked me for a cigarette. He smoked my entire pack of cigarettes that night. Later, I would buy him beer too. What a guy.

I shyly gazed at him and allowed him to talk my ear off. It was easier to meet these really bold and presumptuous guys that made their wishes immediately known because it was easier to navigate. I knew where I stood immediately and I was willing to surrender to a controlling man who would bluntly dive right into, "I like you," and, "I want you to be my girlfriend," rather than attempting to navigate the waters of carefully getting to know a person with the terrible threat of rejection. I hope that my daughters learn that rejection by any man is not the end of the world. I pray that my daughters are close enough to Jesus to hang their identity on Him instead of any man that comes along.

I was not there yet. My father was out of the home now and my mother was struggling to "find herself" again after the divorce. She was dating various men and, any time I spent time with my mother, I was hit with a barrage of hateful rantings about Alec. "Do you want to go shopping with me?" meant what it always had and, even more these days, it really amounted to, "do you want to listen to everything I think and feel like a therapist would?" My mother's bitterness toward men was palpable and, for this reason, I avoided her. She was incredibly toxic and it hurt me deeply to be around her.

I was vulnerable to the creeps. No father at home to cause the creeps to second guess their intentions and no mother to hold me accountable anymore. She would text me from time to time to ask where I was but there were no consequences for anything. I thought that, even if I was up to no good, what would she do about it? Anytime I needed money for Crystal, my mother gave it to me. Most of the time, my drug habit was supplied by my mother. It was easier to give me the cash that I was demanding instead of holding me accountable and helping me get treatment.

Chapter 14

Armed to Kill

Damien came into my life like a bandit in the night. He was a narcissistic, spoiled brat who managed to manipulate me into being just what he wanted. I was afraid of him. I met him at the club and one week later he was my boyfriend and attending family functions with me. He slid right into my life like a snake and, like a snake, I was terrified of him and he was poison to my life. Are you noticing a theme in the men I chose to date?

He kept me in the dark about who he really was. I was not allowed to ask him any penetrating questions about who he was, where he came from, or what he was doing now. He used his size to intimidate me. Occasionally we would rough house and pretend wrestle. He would pretend to "kill me" and wrap his hands around my neck and then let go and laugh. I knew that there was some sort of element that was deadly serious in our play. I slowly started to grasp the fact that he was so vague and unwilling to share about himself as a negative thing instead of a shy and reserved thing. I started to understand that he dealt drugs for a living and I also started to see that he was dangerous and kept weapons with him.

Ladies, play acting and jokes are indicative of real behavior. If a man jokes about something, take it as a window into his soul and inner workings. Damien joked that he would kill me because, when he got angry at me, he really did want to kill me.

I could feel a sense of looming danger when I was around Damien. Then there was the problem of my son. I did not want to bring my son around Damien so I kept him away and this eventually became a problem. He wanted to meet my son and I refused. In a very short amount of time, Damien became controlling and wanted to know every detail about when I saw Jacob and how we talked when I picked up my son or dropped him off.

In the beginning, I was brainless enough to think of Damien's jealousy as endearing and I took this level of jealousy and control as some kind of deeper level of commitment. "He just wants all of me which means that he is invested in this relationship," I concluded. It would not be until years later that I would learn that the most jealous guys are the ones that cheat the most. Those who are guilty are the most suspicious.

I would hang out at Damien's apartment. He would invite me over every day. He wanted to be with me all the time. He kept me so close to him that it was nearly impossible for me to be alone and have time to think and identify the red flags. He also started getting angry with me when I spent time with anyone else.

One night Damien had been drinking and became very angry with me and I did not know why. He thought that I would break up with him and so extracted promises from me that I would never leave him. He threw me down on the bed. I could smell the beer on his breath. Sometimes, he was so drunk that he wet the bed. He would keep jars of urine next to his bed because he often got too drunk to get up to go to the bathroom. Charming guy, right? He drank to the point of blind rage and, tonight, he was raging and I did not know him well enough to know what to expect next. Was he going to hit me? What was the limit of his madness?

He threw me down on the bed and demanded that I get undressed. I said, "I don't want to." I tried to refuse his demands but I was scared and he was much bigger than I. I could not fight him off. I kept pushing him away but he wielded his strength like a force over me and I was helpless. When he forced himself on me, there was nothing I could do but lie there. That was when I noticed that Damien had marks all over him and I was not sure what it was.

Damien made remarks that I was his in a sort of fumbling, drunken language. I may not have understood exactly what he was saying but I understood what he was doing. He was marking me. He was making me come down to his level. Damien had a sexually transmitted disease (STD) and he was giving it to me. Like a reverse vampire he was giving me microscopic death blows to my self-respect. He was delivering the venom, the poison, and he knew exactly what he was doing. I tried to fight but it was useless. I could not stop what was happening so I gave up and let my spirit get broken again and again. He knew he was bringing me down to his level so that he could keep me from ever leaving him. Now, I know that this is assault with a deadly weapon to knowingly and purposely share an STD. This kind of assault was brand new to my thinking. I never dreamed that I could feel this invaded down to the fiber of my being. Violation is not a strong enough word to describe what I felt that night.

Contracting an STD is just as much a psychological experience as it is a physical experience. The medical community often talks about the health ramifications of an STD but forgets to talk about the effects of an STD on the mind and the heart. STDs are often a consequence of violating the marriage bed. For me, as a young girl, I felt that I was now dirty and forever tainted. The entire experience of going to the doctor and having to state that I was sleeping around was too humbling for me to bear. Thankfully, the STD was not a life-long STD and was cleared up with medication but it left me feeling no better than a two-bit whore.

After that, one would think that I would have run from Damien but I clung to him even closer now. I had a sort of Stockholm syndrome again. I thought that no one would ever love or value me ever again. I was now more damaged than ever and I would never be able to recover. I was humiliated when I went to the doctor and she gave me a round of medication for the STD. The doctor pressed me about where the STD had come from. I protected Damien. Why did I protect him? I felt a strong sense of loyalty to him now. I felt like I deserved him and that I would never get anyone better. He had successfully manipulated me into being his lap dog.

I spent a lot of time over at his apartment and I started noticing that his "roommate" gave me the worst glares and treated me with contempt. "What was her problem?" I wondered. Instead of listening to this nagging feeling I had, I ignored it and decided not to be "that kind of girlfriend" who second-guessed their man all the time. I surrendered my God-given wisdom to a man in every way. God never intended for women to surrender their individuality to any man and, oh, did I ever surrender myself.

I would ask Damien, "what's wrong with your roommate?" He would brush off my concern in a cool and calm manner that was trying too hard to be convincing but I did not notice this until later. One rainy and cold day I went over to Damien's apartment, knocked on the door, and his roommate answered the door. She stood in a silky robe and I remember thinking and hoping that she did not dress like that when Damien was home. Again, I dismissed my inner voice screaming at me. It was this nagging feeling that I had taught myself to ignore. The earlier in life one learns to heed the "still small voice," the wiser and happier we will be.

"Damien isn't here," She said in a cold and curt manner. I stood outside the apartment shivering in the rain.

"Oh." I sweetly replied to her stinging hatefulness. My sweetness and naive innocence softened her. She begrudgingly invited me inside. I accepted her offer hoping to win her over to liking me. I could not understand why she hated me so much. She sat on the couch and I sat next to her. She was really pretty and I considered our similarities in appearance. I thought to myself, "we really do look like sisters." Still, my naivety kept me so very blind.

At last, the sisterhood of women came breaking through the clouds of jealousy and hatred. She softened and asked me, "what in the [expletive] are you doing with Damien, anyway?"

"What do you mean?" I had no idea what she was talking about. Damien was good looking so I was taken aback by her question and a little shocked. She continued in a very blunt honesty much like a big sister would talk to a little sister. She pitied me and, after spending just a little bit of time with me, she could see that I had a very Pollyanna view of the world and had no idea what I was up against.

"You seem like a nice girl." She took out a glass pipe and loaded it with glass shards. This would be the first time I would smoke Crystal. Between her inhalations, she said, "why would someone like you be interested in Damien?"

"I don't know what you mean. You don't like Damien or something?"

"I love Damien!" she exclaimed, "but he is a tool and I should know because I am his girlfriend."

Suddenly many things clicked for me. I began to realize that this "roommate" was not really a "roommate" at all. They were together and Damien simply marched me straight into his apartment whether she liked it or not. I was the other woman. I was shocked and surprised as the scales fell off my eyes. How could I be so blind? How could I have been so trusting? She asked me, "do you wanna try this?" At that moment I was low, very low. How could I be so stupid? "Yes, I do." I grabbed the pipe and took my first draw on a glass pipe of a substance that would make me fly and feel clean and sharp in my head. I had all these ideas and I knew I had to break it off with Damien immediately.

I learned a lot from the "roommate" that day including how to effectively smoke Crystal. I also learned that Damien never paid the rent on the apartment that he shared with his "roommate." I learned that they had been together for many years and that she simply suffered through his infidelities but that she was fed up with Damien's antics so she was moving out which meant that Damien would be homeless in a week or two. She told me how Damien lived off of women and how he thought that women should pay for his way through life. He was basically a gigolo, wanting women to keep him in the lifestyle of which he was accustomed.

As I sat there taking in the words the "roommate" was sharing with me, my estimation of this strong and good-looking man fell lower and lower. I no longer thought of Damien as the giant that he originally was to me. He now seemed dirty to me and a waste of my time. I thought back to the night that he threw me on the bed and I felt sick that I let this man take so much from me and then, in turn, give so little in return. He was just that, a taker. I started to feel a hatred for him crop up as Crystal took control of my thought process. She made me feel so very brave and like I had the courage to stand up for myself. I felt like I was pumped and could take on any man. Just let him try throwing me on the bed now with Crystal by my side. I would never be caught off guard again.

Crystal made me feel tough and street smart. I was angry at the mess that my life had become. It just kept getting worse and worse. I was so angry at those that had failed me and the pathetic slant that was now the struggle of my life. I never wanted to be a statistic and, now, I was. I was also feeling like the punching bag for sociopathic men. I felt like I had a sign above me that read, "victim right here!"

What I did not know is that, by hating my mother and Alec so much, I was becoming more and more bitter by the day. That bitterness could be seen in my eyes, my face, and the way I dressed. I did not know that the way I was presenting myself to the world was attracting the wrong kind of men and the wrong friends.

Bitterness and rebellion are contagious and, when you are a rebel, you look for other rebels to associate with. The old saying, "birds of a feather flock together," is most certainly a fact. If you want to know about how a person sees himself or herself, look to see who they surround themselves with.

The Department of Justice Office on Violence Against

Women released a study in 2012 that states, "numerous studies suggest that sexual victimization in childhood or adolescence increases the likelihood of sexual victimization in adulthood between 2 and 13.7 times." It seems like a cruel trick that life throws at you. Why is a woman who has been raped once so unlucky to be raped again? It has nothing to do with luck at all but the cold hard nature of sexual abuse and assault. Women who have been sexually assaulted in the past subconsciously live their life in a trifecta of the perfect storm.

One, we are easier to groom, manipulate, and accept the blame for the assault or abuse because it is familiar and we know how to live carrying the load of blame and silence. This burden is often visible and predators can see us coming from a mile away.

Two, we who have been assaulted and who become bitter at those that have offended against us start to hate ourselves and our bodies as much as we hate those that have offended against us. We feel that our bodies have betrayed us by being the vessel that received the criminal act and, if we could trade our bodies in for another, we would.

We fail to respect ourselves and see ourselves the way Jesus sees us. This makes us not only a target for predators but makes predators a target for us in what researchers and psychologists call re-traumatization compulsion. We associate sex with violence as one and the same. We believe that we do not deserve any better. We believe we are worthless and we accept people into our lives that we should not because we believe we cannot get any better than the worst nor would anyone any better see us as valuable.

Third and last, we become bitter because it takes divine help from Christ to forgive our offenders and bitterness translates to predators as vulnerability. Predators look for the rebel, the loner, kids not getting along with their parents, girls who seem angry with life, and those who seemingly have emotional problems.

I would like to take a moment and recognize the ugliness that had become my life. Hang on to your seats because it gets much, much worse. Drugs and alcohol allowed me to have even more casual sex. The friends I hung around with acted like it was no big deal to have one night stands. Some say that it is a right for a woman to do with her body as she pleases and men have casual sex so why can't women?

Just because I am free to do what I want with my body does not mean that I ought to. What kind of freedom is it to have the right to cause damage to my own mind, body, and soul? Just because I can choose something does not mean that I should. I have the choice to choose death but there is no joy in that choice. True freedom is living within the design of God's natural laws and divine law. I had been violated by other men but I also put myself in the fire and violated myself by daily going against God's original design for my body. God never intended that we give ourselves away repeatedly and so cheaply. It took a toll on me.

I missed Alec and his attentions. I did not know how to

get his attention or how to manage the conversation that I had become caught up in their divorce and picked my mother's side when I did not mean to. I was too emotionally immature to form those words. I needed an adult, Christ-like male, to say those words for me and ask my forgiveness for the pain that men had caused me. I needed a Godly person to tell me to repent and turn from my ways. There were times when I may have received these kinds of words and repented. I was not sure what was wrong with me but I knew I was chaotic inside my heart and mind and the only time I felt better was in the chaos of the clubs and nightlife.

Without a boyfriend, I was back to hunting for another man to fill the void. I kept meeting men and maybe they would last the night or maybe they would last a week and, once in a while, they would last a month but then I would toss them out before they realized how disgusting I believed I was.

More than cocaine, more than alcohol, more than Crystal, I was again growing in my addiction to men. I loved the immediate fix. The dance, the game, whatever you want to call it. I craved the attention of a man wanting me. I enjoyed walking into a club. The pulse-racing music combined with the lustful stares of men. I could see them all looking and I welcomed it. If they did not look, I immediately ran to the bathroom to check to make sure I looked okay. I started shopping for clothes that were excessively revealing and seductive. I looked like a hooker most nights but I wanted that attention. I had to get it. When I caught the eye of a man, I loved the initial butterflies of our first conversation. I could lie. I could say anything about myself. I could be a pilot, a teacher, in law school, in med school, I could be anyone.

They did not know me or the truth and I knew that I would never keep them around long enough so I could invent any kind of reality I wanted to. I was someone else every night. I learned to morph into what I thought the man I was talking to wanted from me. If they said their mother had died, I became ultra-sympathetic to their woes. If they said their last girlfriend was too jealous, I became the most passive and laid-back girl. Whatever they said, I adjusted myself to become whatever they would fall in love with. I was learning to be the ultimate con artist.

Then, in the morning when they asked me for my number, I was gone. When they wondered why I stopped answering their calls after a week and they cried in their voicemails, I would feel inwardly satisfied. I enjoyed and detested their tortured pleas to call them back or to stay. "It was pathetic," I would tell myself on the way out the door. Man-eaters do not just appear. They are created. Do not feel too sorry for these guys. Most of these guys were not the cream of the crop of society in any manner of speaking.

If I simply turned the circumstances on their head, they were using me as much as I tricked myself into thinking I was using them. Sex was usually involved and I was becoming an expert on what most carnally-minded men wanted. But, there is a price to pay for giving your body away to anyone who wants it. You lose pieces of your heart until there is nothing left. You lose a little of yourself each time until you find that there is not much left. Though I thought I was free and living wild and how I wanted to live, I was lost and losing. I was losing myself and, more than that, I was living as a slave to my body and the lusts thereof.

When I slowed down even a little, maybe I did not go out for a night, I found that I could not stand to be alone with myself for even a second. I had demons and they were raging/ I felt like I would burst apart if I tried to stay at home. The drive and the urge to party was no longer a desire, it was a need and a thirst that cried out to be quenched. I was now nineteen years old and had acquired too many sexual partners to tell. I had joined up with many different scenes and moved on looking for something else. I would casually drift from raves to Hollywood clubs. I would be at college parties one night with nice all-American boys and be at gay clubs the next night.

I felt like I was looking for something that was elusive so I looked in every place that presented itself. I went from Hollywood to biker bars and gangs, to transvestites, to hip-hop break dancers, to coffee houses, to goths, even to Wall Street types. I was walking through scenes like they were rooms as if I were searching for my lost keys or something. When I did not find what I was looking for, I would move on and leave behind paramours and friends with no feeling of earthly loyalty at all. I had no problem saying goodbye to those who did not meet my temporary cravings.

When one lives doing whatever is right in their own eyes, the descent into madness is quick. Even if I still thought I was okay in the head, whenever I drank it became evident that I was in need of help. Like Saul and Solomon, the price to pay for giving your heart to whoever and following after them and being "a strange woman" is losing your soul.

My mother was now completely terrified of me. Most days I was wearing all black including a long black cape. I often looked like Lara Croft the Tomb Raider or like a dominatrix. Most days I wore long black gloves with a fitted, long, black cape and tall, black combat boots. I kept my long, blonde hair bleached white but occasionally I died parts of it black before it became popular to do so. I wore all black because I felt all black on the inside. My heart felt loveless. My life was void of love and I felt cold and compassionless.

I started to surround myself with people who were involved in the occult. My interest into the supernatural had started when I was young. It is only logical that a person who has loose morals will then descend into a theology that fits their morality. The occult offered me a false power, one I could master and control myself. Herein is the ultimate selfishness to believe in designing and forming your own destiny for yourself and to believe that everything is in one's self.

I knew that I was dark and tainted but I no longer trusted a God who allowed bad things to happen to me. I was unwilling to suffer, unwilling to submit, and unwilling to be broken. I was anti-God. I knew He existed but I railed against him and "kicked against the pricks." I vowed my allegiance to Satan and prayed to him. I ripped up Bibles and blasphemed against my Creator. The rejection of one's Creator is the ultimate hatred for one's self. I never felt so alone as when I rejected my God and joined the army of the enemy.

Chapter 15

The Fence

The long road into the occult happened over many years. Around the same time, I started hanging out with some heavy metal bands. I had again received money from my father's death and this was catastrophic for me. Instead of being low on the food chain in the drug world, I was flooded with thousands and thousands of dollars in cash and I skyrocketed up the food chain. I had a lot of money to buy meth and I began to carry a suitcase on me with every kind of drug but I mostly dealt my old friend, Crystal. She was always faithful to me and I could count on her, at least for a while.

I was becoming ruthless and violent. I was regularly getting into fights and hurting people. I walked into homes at night without a care. I would get an itch to hurt someone and hurt them I did. I was regularly spending the night in graveyards. I was the literal demoniac of the Gadarenes.

During this time, when I had successfully managed to turn my childhood home into a party house, I met Kane and Dillon. I met Kane at a friend's house I was visiting during band practice. He was a guitar player in a heavy metal band. He seemed friendly and nice and he was attracted to me although he played it cool. He had a nice truck and a job working for the cable company. He was six-foot-seven and very handsome. His mother was Irish and his father was

Japanese but, somehow, he ended up looking more British than anything else. He had sandy blonde hair and darker skin. He had Japanese tattoos all up and down his upper arms but did not get fully sleeved at this time because of his work. He was an athlete and a musician. He played every kind of sport. Again, as was my custom, I assumed I was not worthy to have a guy like this. I had the accurate reputation of being the crazy drug dealer around town and I had not had a steady boyfriend since Jacob.

One afternoon, Kane drove up to my childhood home. I happened to be sort of calm because I was using less Crystal that day. I had my son home with me and I tried to shield him from the chaos of my life as best I could. I know my son perceived the trouble I was in but I tried hard to switch into "mom mode" when he was around despite my heavy reliance on Crystal. My "mom mode" was attractive to Kane. As he parked his little white truck in my driveway, he saw me standing in my yard playing with my son. Kane's mom was a drug addict and she had abandoned Kane and his little brother so many times. They lived in San Bernardino in a little apartment in a rough area but Kane had a good job and he seemed to be doing well for himself. He and his brother and dad all lived together as comfortably as one can live in a rough part of a big city.

He missed having a mother and craved a sense of family so seeing me dutifully care for my child was like catnip to a cat for Kane. I was wild and crazy. He saw that, of course, but he also saw my mothering side and he really started to care about me because of this. Watching the two of us fall for each other was like watching a storm within a storm brewing. My entire life was now a storm so adding yet another serious relationship to it was pure insanity. We were two broken people trying to bring our brokenness into something that had a semblance of wholeness. I could not even care for myself at the time so having someone care about me again started to awaken emotions that I had no desire to feel. We fought as was my typical type of behavior in a relationship but Kane was not like the other guys that would fight and fight and fight with me. When he was sober, he was a gentle giant and would quickly say things to soothe my spunk and angry sass. He was sweet and, one day, he did something that I will never forget.

We were playing house at the time, better known as essentially living together. Kane would frequently stay the night at my house and then drive out to his work early in the morning. We were sleeping together as in actually sleeping when together and not having sexual intercourse. Maybe this is why we lasted a little longer than usual. Because Kane was not anxious to use me and lose me, I actually started to feel safe and secure around him. Before he went to work, Kane would kneel down by my bed for a few minutes and watch me sleep or just talk to me. He really desired closeness and a family and I was starting to feel things for him in a way that I had never intended. I was getting close to him and this was scary. His kneeling by my bed gave me some reminder of my childhood and the family worships we used to have and this was endearing to me. I was starting to, yet again, give my heart away to Kane and this caused me to feel a great deal of anxiety and reluctant vulnerability. True to form, we both started to sabotage things and this was, not coincidently, around the time we consummated our physical relationship.

As soon as we slept together, it was a like a bomb went off in both of us. Kane started to hang out with his buddies more and with me less as the newness of our relationship began to wear off. In the beginning, he would come to see me almost daily. Now I found myself begging him to come over. I hated the smell of desperation on me so I was thrilled when his truck started to break down and he needed me to drive him to work in the mornings.

It was a long drive through curvy mountain highways to drop him off at his cable company job in Riverside but I loved his dependence on me. Dutifully and cheerfully I drove him to work and I played the role of partner quite well which seemed to pull Kane back more from his friends and more toward a serious relationship with me. I found myself discovering that I was tired of shallow and meaningless relationships and, if Kane were interested, I would like to stay together as long as possible. It was anyone's guess if he really wanted the same thing. He kept saying words like, "let's take things slow," and I really wanted to speed things up. I was willing to become whatever he wanted me to be.

Girls can be shaped or molded but a woman is who she is. I had not learned that individuality is far more attractive than total surrendering of one's individuality. I was so accustomed to morphing into whatever I needed to be according to the man I was with. I liked whatever they liked (whether I truly liked it or not) and I did whatever they did. It would take me years to actually learn what I really liked and did not like.

I would go to Kane's shows and watch him play guitar with the fury that every metal guitarist pours into their performance. I bounced and nodded to the music like any dutiful girlfriend does but I could not stand the music. I spent a lot of time going to his shows and band practices. I look back at all the time I spent going to boyfriend's performances as a waste of time. It was something I thought that I should do so I did it, even if I did not want to go or did not feel well. Even with the rides to work, it was not long until, once again, our one-on-one time with each other waned and we were spending more and more time with other people. We settled into a casual rhythm of a relationship that Kane was content with but I wanted more. I wanted more of a commitment from him.

The only demonstration of affection I could seem to extract from Kane was when I could make him jealous. Believing it was love, I sought to engender and secure a reaction by making him jealous. To accomplish this, I decided to throw a huge party and have lots of people over. Whether my mother liked it or not, I was in control of the house. What I needed was a mother to call the cops, possibly get me arrested, chase everyone away, and put me in some sort of drug treatment. But she did not do any of these things because she was afraid of me and it was easier for her to just let me do my own thing rather than upset me. I wish she would have taken the risk and upset me. We cannot enable our children. We must do what is right. These parties that I was subjecting my mother to were wrong and I needed her to stop me.

These outrageous parties were becoming a regular thing at my house. We had an entire full-size refrigerator dedicated to the storage of alcohol and I had my regular suitcase of drugs. At this time, I was making frequent trips to Orange County to get mushrooms and any other designer drug I could get my hands on. These parties became amazingly outrageous. We were loud, had fights, and had all kinds of madness transpiring. I am certain that the fact that we were on private property was the reason the cops were not there every night but not for the lack of trying on the part of my neighbors. Years later, when I grew up, I went door to door to apologize to my neighbors for what I put them through in all these years of extreme partying.

During this time, I did not have a care about the noise or the out-and-out debauchery I was creating because my conscience was being regularly seared with a hot iron. When you work so hard to justify your actions (being in and out of whoever's bed whenever) you begin to justify anything. The human mind can rationalize *any* sin.

I kept throwing party after party and, at most of these parties, there was a disproportionate ratio of guys to girls. I was not as fond of girls as I was of guys. My mother had taught me this. She struggled to hang on to female friendships for as long as I can remember and, when she found a female friend, she squeezed them so tightly that they either went running from her craziness or the relationship would sour. My mother often said the most terrible things about her friends and their appearance behind their backs. We used to call it "finding mom's ugly person of the day." Whenever my mom went anywhere, she had to find and point out an "ugly person." This was characteristically shallow. Competition toward other women had been modeled to me my entire life and it destroys friendships. Later, I discovered that it is, sadly, not unusual for women to compete with each other.

I never felt as comfortable around girls as I did with a group of guys. These parties and the guys I surrounded myself with were causing problems between Kane and I. He did not like it that I was constantly surrounded by a bunch of guys and I did not like it that he was constantly taking off to wherever with whoever. We were meeting at an impasse and neither of us would budge. He wanted the freedom to do whatever he wanted. I wanted him to be with me and my son to create our own little family. He was unwilling to do this and I was unwilling to budge. Of course, I did not really tell him that I wanted to settle down with someone like him and that, for the first time in my life since Jacob, I felt like I could see a future for us. It came out more like, "you don't care about me," and, "where the [expletive] were you?"

Why was I incapable of saying what I really felt and meant? I was used to game play and hiding my vulnerability under a guise of street toughness. Some people play games because they are downright manipulative but most people play games because they are afraid of rejection and tired of getting hurt. I was terrified of rejection. I could not tell him how I really felt and I doubt it would have mattered anyway.

Around this time, the outrageous parties had morphed into nonstop parties which turned my childhood home into a "flop house" of sorts. My mom was gone to work all the time and I felt the sharp absence of Alec too. I kept a lot of people around me in an attempt to drown out the loneliness that was taking up residence in my life. I had met one of the kids hanging around the house at a rave and his name was Max. His parents were divorced and his home life was awful, at least according to him. His mom had sent him to live with his dad in Pasadena but he called me and begged me to come and get him so I did.

My mother still, to this day, vents her resentment toward Max for "taking advantage" of her by staying at her house and eating her food but no one takes advantage of us unless we let them. This kid was a runaway. One call to the cops (which my mother should have done) and Max would have been shipped back to where he belonged, his parents' house. Since I was nineteen, I could have technically been charged with kidnapping for picking up a sixteen-year-old kid and hiding him from his parents but none of the adults called the cops and none of this mattered to me because I was a rebel.

Max had a lot of raver friends that would come over and hang out. Our parties were especially loud and drug-fueled. My childhood home became the epicenter for parties in the area. It was the place to be. I have never done anything "half way" in my life. These parties were no exception. I would have multiple DJ's in multiple rooms and all kinds of wild things going on with large numbers of people. I was, at last in my own mind, the cool kid and everyone wanted to hang out at my house.

One kid that came to hang out was a friend of Max's named Dillon. Like most of the kids that hung out, Dillon did not have a father that was active in his life. In fact, most, if not all of the kids that hung out at my house had absent fathers. That should serve as a warning to anyone reading this. Consequently, one particular Father's Day, I threw a party and invited anyone who did not have a father or who hated their father to come and get drunk with me. Dillon was one of those kids who came to this party to angrily rage against the paternal absence we all shared. His mom worked hard all day to provide the things they had and Dillon was going through a rebellious phase.

Dillon had an interest in raves and especially "rolling," better known as ecstasy. Whenever anyone does ecstasy it has to be approached cautiously because the come-down is brutal. For hours and hours, you are thrown or encapsulated into the most beautiful and amazing feeling that words cannot describe. The pleasure centers of the brain fire off with full force and a feeling of "all is well on the earth" takes over. For a few hours, you feel no pain and have no worries and suddenly become the friendliest person around. I bought ecstasy, or pure MDMA, from a drug dealer on an Indian reservation. I had the best ecstasy that anyone ever tried or would ever try. After reaching the peak of the drug, the coming down (or trough) was brutal and it was not unusual to feel severely depressed or suicidal.

I really enjoyed taking ecstasy but I did not enjoy the come down. In my life, drugs served a purpose. I always felt terrible or was sick and I wanted to take things that made me feel better, not things that totally knocked me out or made me feel worse. Sometimes it was about getting high and, sometimes, it was about feeling better. Dillon was different. He wanted to take whatever would get him as high as possible without overdosing. He would do ecstasy so often that he often battled severe depression for weeks and months at a time.

Dillon was a sweet kid that had sort of lost his way. At almost seventeen, he was five foot eleven inches tall. He had really dark skin and looked almost like he was Italian or Hispanic but his hair was too light and his eyes were too blue to be considered anything but Caucasian. He was a good-looking kid and very much tall, dark, and handsome. He was also incredibly charming and mild-mannered. I often compared him to a lost puppy dog. I was older by two and a half years which is not a big deal now but, when you are nineteen and someone else is still a minor, it is a big deal. Notwithstanding our age difference, I found his sheer devotion to me sort of endearing.

Our friendship grew while, simultaneously, I could not get Kane to spend any time with me. Dillon was willing to follow me anywhere and everywhere. If I had to go to the grocery store, Dillon would come and help me load the groceries in the car. If I had to go to the mall, Dillon would dutifully follow behind me without a single complaint. For someone who was eternally lonely even in a crowd, it was such a comfort to have someone who was so willing to find any task interesting as long as we were together. There is a lot to be said for patient endurance.

Even though Dillon was young, he seemed much older than Kane at times because I knew that Dillon was starting to have feelings for me that were way beyond friendship. Dillon never complained when I went off with Kane even though I knew it hurt him deeply. Dillon would quietly acquiesce to my decision and be kind about it. He would wait for me to get home or meet up with me the next day and never chide me or scold me for doing what I did. Comparatively, Kane would get angry and demand that I stop hanging out with other guys, namely Dillon. Kane used to look so strong and capable to me but now, compared to Dillon, he looked foolish and juvenile to protest so vehemently at my friendship with Dillon. It seemed so hypocritical of Kane to demand that I be so exclusive and available to him while he wanted to evade any kind of commitment to me. Our fights sounded like this, "why should I cut off all my connections to my friends while you hang out with all your friends?" Any relationship that has a tit-for-tat tagline is not a good one.

I tried to convince Kane and myself into thinking that boys and girls can be this close without sex getting in the way. Sex always gets in the way. In my experience, it is very unusual and nearly impossible to carry on a platonic relationship with a person of the opposite sex. Kane was not fooled so he demanded that I stop hanging out with Dillon while Dillon demanded nothing. My attractions were shifting toward the one who put no demands on me but I was completely turned off by the age difference between Dillon and I. I did not want another kid in my life.

I was not, by any means, Dillon's first love. There had been a girl before me that he had dated for a long time and I certainly looked a lot like her. If Dillon had a type then I was definitely it. Down deep inside, I knew that my friendship with Dillon was only thus because I said so. If I wanted more with Dillon, he made it clear that I could have more but I was determined to put Dillon's feelings off and try to work things out with Kane. The biggest problem was that I wanted them both. I wanted the incredibly tall, stoic, manly, and older Kane but I also wanted the devoted, sweet, loyal, and always available for me Dillon. I wanted the best of both worlds. What was a girl to do? I have never been a person to carry on two relationships at once and I was incredibly bad at it. I could never lie very well or hide the fact that I was torn and both Dillon and Kane sensed my disloyalty.

I always felt Kane pulling away from me whenever we started to get close. Ultimately, I knew that, if Kane left me, I would be crushed and would want someone as backup to take the sting away. Kane often left for periods of time so I was fully aware that it was only a matter of time. If ever there were a girl who needed a man to manage along in life, it was I. The thought of being "manless" terrified me.

This particular evening, Kane had dropped by my house to pick up some of his stuff which was another sign that he was leaving me. Why did he need to get his stuff? Was he breaking up with me for good? His brother was waiting for him in my driveway. My heart literally throbbed inside my chest as I watched him packing up some of his shirts and other things in my bedroom. I choked back the tears as I tried to understand what had happened and why he was so numb and nonchalant about our being together and, yet, other times he was furious at me with jealousy. "I truly do not understand him," I thought as he drove away with his brother. What I had not factored into our relationship (and it is awfully silly of me looking back) was how our drug use was affecting our relationship. Kane was not an everyday user like I was but he used meth and cocaine from time to time, just enough to mess with his brain chemistry and behavior. We were two broken people from broken families with broken lives. How could we ever expect to form something whole out of all the brokenness?

As indicated by Kane's picking up his things, our relationship was not going that well but, at the same time, it was not going that badly either. The honeymoon phase was gone and over and sealed with a sloppy, drunken kiss never to be heard from again. Kane had taken off to go be, and by, "be," what I really mean is party like it is 1999, with his friends, leaving me behind and unable to get in touch with him. I felt like such a fool as I called his house over and over to beg him to come back to me. He was at home all the way down in San Bernardino and I was at home all the way up in Cherry Valley and the distance between us felt like a thousand miles and I desired to shorten the distance. I wanted Kane back and here with me. The one shred of hope was that, even though Kane packed up some of his things, he still had a number of items at my house including his truck. He had to see me one way or another and I would do whatever I could to have an excuse to communicate with him.

Much to my chagrin, every time I called, his brother answered the phone. He could sense my desperation and I

270

hated the fact that I sounded like the crazy girlfriend who would not take, "no," for an answer. The first time I called, I could hear Kane in the background laughing his particular and noticeable laugh that clearly told me that he was drunk. There was a one-of-a-kind way Kane slurred his words and laughed when he was drunk. Most of the time he was so serious, soft-spoken, and a man of few and poignant words but, when he was drunk, he was loud, outspoken, and had a giant grin on his face that death itself could not wipe away. I hated it when he was drunk and ridiculous like this. His sheer size made this loud and obnoxious drunkenness extremely intimidating. Because of these mannerisms, I could tell just how drunk Kane was in the background.

"Eh! Tell her I'm not home!" He laughed loudly in the background. This hurt me so badly that he did not want to talk to me and, even worse, he did not care if I heard him telling his brother to lie to me in the background. I heard the crackle as his brother quickly covered the phone receiver with his hand.

"Shhhh! She heard you, dawg!" Kane's brother tried to do his best to soften Kane's imbecilic drunkenness but nothing was going to work as the alcohol had done its job to rob Kane of a heart. I heard Kane's friends say things like, "tell that [expletive]," and laugh and joke as to what Kane's brother should say. My heart felt like it was slowly melting away inside me. It hurt to be alive. It hurt to feel my heart pumping. It hurt to have a heart. I trusted Kane and he promised he would never hurt me. I promised myself that I would never get hurt again and here I was freely and willingly opening myself up to the pain of heartbreak. I felt a huge and giant piece of my heart being ripped away, packaged, and shipped to an apartment in San Bernardino to a man so drunk he did not even know or care.

Kane's brother got back on the phone and attempted to respectfully end the conversation but this was impossible with the friends they kept who were laughing and egging Kane on. Even if Kane had taken my call, he was surrounded by goons who had no respect for women at all. He had to save face and anything he had to say to me could not be said in front of these guys. I tried to console myself with the thought that, because of his friends, this was not the real Kane but I was heartbroken and resolved to stop the pain. I hung up the phone and was not quite sure what to do with myself now. I sat in my room and felt like I needed to run away from myself. I was so angry at Kane that I wanted to get back at him for hurting me so badly. How could I let him get away with partying it up without me and just sit here and be miserable? If I had my way, Kane and I would sit together and just watch a movie but that was not going to happen.

I heard a knock on my bedroom door. It was Max and Dillon looking concerned because they were standing outside my room and listening to me crying and trying to get in contact with Kane. One of our friends had gotten a hold of a bunch of ecstasy pills. "Do you want 'em?" Max asked me

272

knowing the answer. Of course I wanted them. I never ran into the arms of a drug so quickly. As fast as I ran into the arms of a drug, I also ran into the arms of another. Dillon was there that night and partying with us. I thought for sure that Kane and I were over so I found comfort and solace for my heartache in the arms of another whom I found comforting and loyal.

As we smoked a cigarette, Dillon worried, "is Kane going to beat me up?" I found his worry and self-preservation very unattractive but I knew that, compared to Kane, Dillon was much smaller. "No, I will make sure he does not find out." I knew that, even if Kane and I had broken up, there was the real possibility of getting back together again since we often repeated this cycle. Kane hated Dillon with a passion because I spent so much time with him. It was okay for Kane to spend time with other girls but not for me to spend time with other guys. I found this kind of male hypocrisy to be maddening. Yes, Dillon was a little younger than I but he was kind and loyal. Was I willing to make a trade on tall and handsome for taboo devotion? I was not so sure.

I found my conscience quickening as the drugs were wearing off as is usually the case. "You have to go!" I declared as I jumped quickly to my feet. I started gathering up Dillon's stuff and shoving his clothes into his hands. "You can't be seen in my bedroom. I don't want anyone to know that we were together like this." I could tell that my shame was hurtful to Dillon and I felt bad for hurting someone so devoted to me. It had nothing to do with Dillon, personally, but had everything to do with the age difference. On a deep level of my conscience, no matter how far I ran from God, I knew that what I was doing was wrong and I felt like running for cover from the examining eye of God.

Dillon quickly got his stuff together and scurried out the door to go lay down on the couch so everyone would wake up from a long night of partying and see him on the couch and suspect nothing. There were so many people hanging out that any one of them could tell Kane the truth and I would be toast. As soon as Dillon left the room, I closed the door and locked it and quickly searched my room for that comforting glass meth pipe. I hit it as I watched the white smoke curl its smoky fingers, combing the air, and dispersing the odor of death. Ahhh, my old friend Crystal. Here to save the day, numb my pain, and chase away the nagging feeling of my wretched conscience. I very nearly hugged the pipe. I loved how it made me feel nothing at all. Well, almost nothing.

I remembered the terrible telephone saga from the night before and I pulled the telephone near me. I picked up the receiver and I called Kane's house again. Even after a night with Dillon, I was fixated on what was elusive and awful. I wanted the thing that I could not own or control. I could not take the rejection and I wanted to solve the puzzle. I wanted to figure out a way.

Kane ignored my phone calls for two days and Dillon,

hurt by my callous disregard, tucked tail and went home. I could not talk to Kane nor did I even know where he was. He simply fell off the radar. I felt like my world was, as always, crashing down and I started to mourn the death of my visions of Kane and I together with my son, trying to raise a family. It simply would never be and, as painful as it was, I began to strive to close the book of "us" and put it away on the shelf. Some relationships felt like a chapter and some felt like a paragraph while yet others felt like incomplete sentences. This relationship had evolved into a book in my mind. I had started to envision Kane and I together for the long term but I had no idea that he could be so careless and insensitive. He seemingly dropped off the face of the earth and apparently did not care where I was or who I was with. I also knew that, if Kane found out about Dillon, he would be outraged and there would be no hope of ever getting back together.

As the day wore on, I was sick of waiting around and being sad as I reached day three of Kane's disappearance. My friends were going to go visit another friend's house and they wanted me to go with them. Of course it was a guy's house and his name was Troy. I did not want to go anywhere. I wanted to stay home and get as high as I possibly could but I was afraid to be alone and in this much pain so I went. We were not going to do anything special, we were just going to sit around and drink some beer and smoke some weed and look at Troy's collection of ninja stars and other weapons. I was happy to sit there nursing my wounds but it felt good to get away from my house and my own bedroom that reminded me so much of Kane. Now I had the added weight of knowing, even if Kane and I did get back together, what I had done with Dillon. I did not know what the future held because I could not even get Kane on the phone to ask him if we were really done or not. I needed to know where we stood. Emotionally, I felt like a powder keg ready to blow apart with the tension that uncertainty brings. Then, as a group of us were sitting in Troy's house, I heard a commotion outside.

At first, I could not make out the words but then I realized that my name was being shouted outside Troy's house. He pretty much kept his house boarded up like a dungeon so I could not see who was outside through a window. "What in the world," was my first thought as I headed to Troy's front door and unlocked it to go outside. Instantly, I felt the wonderful feeling of a princess being rescued by her white knight. There was Kane in a car with a bunch of his friends and he was standing outside Troy's house shouting my name. "Maybe everything will turn out okay," I thought. Wrong. It is always way worse to feel those immediate feelings of elation and rescue then to realize the opposite is actually true. It's like a cold, hard slap in the face to remind you that you are, indeed, on planet earth and all is not well. I sighed deeply with hopeful relief and ran to meet Kane with a hug and a kiss like in the movies and he put up his hands to stop me as if to guard himself from any kind of estrogen spell I could cast upon him. I felt my hope shrivel up and die. I knew my face was reflecting the pain that this sudden dose of reality cast upon me.

"What's up?" I curiously questioned while eyeing the car of guys behind Kane. Kane met my question with a question.

"What are you doing here?"

I returned the favor while gushing pure astonishment at the entitled nerve and sense of ownership over me that Kane held.

"What am *I* doing here? What are *you* doing here?"

Kane quickly snapped, "Who is this Troy? Is this your new boyfriend?"

I let out a sarcastic chuckle. "Are you kidding me! Is Troy my boyfriend? How can you even ask me that? You came and got your stuff like we were breaking up and wouldn't answer my calls and have been M.I.A. for the last three days! Where have *you* been?"

Everything I said fell on deaf ears. Kane answered me as if disappearing for three days were totally normal and acceptable, "you have no idea what you've done!"

I threw my hands up in the air. "What *I've* done! Oh wow!" I was now yelling and the entire neighborhood could hear us.

"Yeah, I made all my friends drive out here because, while I was with them, I realized how much I've missed you and I want to try to work things out with you. Then I drive to your house and find out that you're with some guy named

Troy! So it takes a couple days and you're with some new guy already! I see how it is!"

"I'm not with some new guy, Kane! It's Max's friend and I am not even here alone with Troy! I have no idea where you are for three days and you expect me to just sit at home and be at your beckon call? You're such a jerk! I am so done with this and I am done with you!"

The words just came flying out of my mouth before I could stop them. I was so angry. I really did not want to end things but I could not believe that Kane was being this controlling and unreasonable. I had no idea at the time and would only find out later that he had been smoking meth for three days and could not tell his foot from his elbow at the moment. I was trying to reason with a totally irrational person who would not understand a logical statement if it were a large zoo animal wiggling on his nose. Ironically, I had cheated on him the night before but not with Troy and, conveniently, I compartmentalized my guilt and failed to mention that to Kane.

Kane turned on his heel and yelled back at me, "whatever!" With that totally noncommittal phrase, he got in the car with his friends and drove off. He may have intended to come and show me his undying love in some grand gesture but, in his mind's eye, he saw all of this happening at my house where I would be waiting for him and not already moving on with someone else. Whether it was true or not or his friends had made too many joking comments, he could not get past the fact that I was at another guy's house. The hypocrisy was rife as Kane had just spent three days getting high with his "friends" and partying with a bunch of girls. I had, very evidently, observed that what was good for the goose most certainly was not acceptable for the gander except that, apparently, I was the gander.

I did not see Kane again for another two days. Just like that, he was gone and I missed him. I tried to have fun and party but it was impossible without him around. I felt a deep longing for that possibility of a real life with someone and now I felt like the almost-adopted child being flung back out into the cold night. When Kane finally showed up at my house one night to get the rest of his stuff, I really wanted to try to save things, explain myself, or at least go out with a bang. I still was not sure from Kane's "whatever" if things were really over.

I was not going to let Kane grab his things out of my room in peace. I was not going to let him walk away whenever he wanted and on his terms. If he had not taken off for days at a time like he did then we would be totally fine, or would we? I was longing so much for Kane that I was starting to forget what the problems had been in our relationship. I was missing my fantasy of our relationship so badly that I was totally ignoring the truth of what our relationship actually was. How many girls and women do this too? We sacrifice the reality of the situation for the dream even if the dream is actually a nightmare.

I needed to know for sure that things were over so that I did not hang on in a vicious limbo of guessing what he was thinking or doing. If anyone thought that I would press him regarding his true level of commitment in a healthy fashion, let me disabuse them of that notion. I was going to fight hard to extract an answer regarding his intentions for this relationship and do whatever it took to get him to make a final declaration. It was either fish or cut bait at this point. This would not go well, not at all.

As Kane packed up his things with his typical rhythmic "I am not in a hurry but don't slow me down" pace, I could tell that Kane was stalling and packing his stuff more slowly than was necessary. I could tell that he was really sad. He looked like he may want to fix things. He was being really soft-spoken again per his usual way when not drunk or high. He was sober now and regretting his ludicrous actions. This was really confusing. I cared about the Kane who was soft-spoken and so strong but I hated the lack of consistency and the roller coaster ride that we were currently riding.

I kept talking or, better yet, drilling down on him to strike some sort of emotional reaction. I was pushing him toward the edge. An emotional reaction, any kind of reaction, anything at all from his stoic and tempered way of being in this world (unless he were high or drunk), would be like gold to me. He was always so measured and cautious not to give me too much of what I wanted. Why? "Just give me the love that I want!" This was my soul cry to someone who could not possibly fill this desire.

I wanted him to be totally open and honest with me. I wanted him to feel something for me and stop trying to hold back so much. It was like he was behind some sort of mask or murky partition wall that I wanted to break open and see clearly. I wanted black or white but Kane was grey all over. He sat up high on top of the fence and I was going to make him pick a side even if it split him completely in twain.

"If you leave now then we are over. I am not joking! If you walk out that door then we are done for good and I never want to see you again. I am not going to call you or bother you. It will be over!" I used my most serious voice to hit home the point that this was it. I was trying to impact him and tell him that I was not going to accept him walking out on me and then take him back again and play these games. My heart was racing and aching all at once. It hurt to hear my own words coming out of my mouth. I was not as strong on the inside as my words made me sound. I was not the girl on the inside that others saw.

I could hear Max and his friends out in my garage kicking back a few beers. It was that time of day to start cracking open the beer fridge and get the party started but I was not in the party kind of mood. I knew that it was likely that everyone in the garage could hear our fight but I did not care. I needed to say what needed to be said. There comes a point when you have lost the ability to pretend away the reality of the relationship. In the honeymoon phase, all the red flags get overlooked. Now, the red flags were like sharp stakes sticking in my heart and relationship-death was imminent. I was feeling all the pain and emotions that yet another failed relationship brings. I was ashamed of myself for failing again.

"You are [expletive] crazy," he muttered under his breath. Wrong thing to say to any woman at any time. "Oh! I am the crazy one?" I snapped back as I stood there, feigning shock and dismay. "I'm the crazy one? You go and party for days at a time and expect me to be waiting for you then accuse me of cheating! Who's the crazy one? Why don't you get your stupid little truck off my property and get your stupid stuff out of my room!" I folded my arms across my chest in a brazen show of strength.

"I don't have to deal with this! You're a [expletive] psycho and a [expletive]!" We were both shouting now at the top of our lungs and we continued to hurl names and accusations at each other. Kane may have originally come to get his stuff and hoped that there might be hope but I cured him of that false idea by being unwilling to accept anything less than a complete and total attitude of apologetic and humble surrender. I wanted him to tell me that he was wrong and that he would change and that he did not want to break up but that was never going to happen. Both participants, minds cloudy with the long-term effect of drugs and alcohol, unwilling to bend in the slightest, took love (if you can even use that word) and perverted it until it looked nothing like itself, if it ever had.

With that, Kane rapidly gathered his things and marched out the door in a loud show of force. He mumbled, leaving the words behind him like a trail of crumbs, "I'll be back to get my truck as soon as I can get my dad to help me pay for the tow." With that, he slammed my room door and let the house door slam behind him too. It was an audible exclamation mark to emphasize the finality of the ending of "us." I was emotionally exhausted and I wanted to be put out of my misery. Max came to check on me and found me in quite a state as I laid crumpled up into a despondent ball on the floor of my room. I was weeping and the mascara was dripping down my face like the rain was watering the ground with black ink.

After a desperate theatrical performance to rival any theater troupe, I picked myself up off the floor, wiped the tears from my face, and announced to Max that I needed to be alone now. I was done crying and I was done with Kane. The suicidal ideations had left as quickly as they had come. I realized that the sun would continue to shine and today would indeed lead into tomorrow and time would carry on even though I was heartbroken. The world did not stop like I thought it should to match my life. Life simply did not stop. I wished it would. Since I could not die then I must, like Scarlett O'Hara, live to be victorious another day. But not today. Today, I would shrivel up into the fetal position and cry myself to sleep in my bed.

"I'm going to bed," I said in a monotone, robotic-like voice to Max. "I'm going to bed and I don't want anyone to bother me."

"Okay!" Max replied in a very annoyed voice to my sudden switch from I-am-going-to-die-without-Kane to exhausted ambivalence. Sometimes you just cannot give anymore to anyone and emotions require a greater amount of energy than anything else. I could not feel anymore and, with that, I closed my bedroom door and crawled into bed. The pillow that Kane slept on still smelled liked him. I inhaled deeply to smell that familiar smell. I rolled over on it to use it as a body pillow as if Kane were still there. I fell into a deep sleep, a sleep like no other, the kind of deep, healing sleep that a body like mine needed and would need for the trauma of the next few days.

Chapter 16

Death Warrant

It was that kind of deep sleep that allowed me to completely sleep through the pounding on my room door. At first, I heard pounding in my dreams. Something was breaking into my dreams. I was still curled around the pillow as I opened my eyes. It took me a little while to remember who I was and where I was and why the pillow was now covered in black mascara marks. For a moment, when I woke up, I was pain free until I remembered Kane and then I wished I had not opened my eyes. At last, the pounding registered. "Someone is pounding on my bedroom door." I heard my name being yelled. I thought that something must have been on fire which would not be out of the realm of possibility considering the hooligans that were always drinking at my childhood home. "Is the house on fire?" I did not care. I could not care about anything. I was numb. But the pounding and shouting of my name persisted so I arose from the comfort of my bed and the pillow that smelled of Kane to go unlock my bedroom door and inquire as to the commotion.

I opened the door to find Max standing in front of me with eyes as large as tennis balls. "I tried to stop them." He put his hands up in a guarded and self-defensive motion like I was going to hit him.

Still in sleep mode and annoyed I said, "what are you talking about?"

"All I have to say is I tried to stop them."

"Stop what?" By the look on Max's face, I knew that something very big and very bad was happening. My stomach tightened. "Max? Stop what?"

"You have to come and see." He turned his back on me and walked out of the house into the early morning darkness. He hurried through the garage which made my curiosity grow even more. He walked out of the garage and to the side of the house and stopped in front of where Kane's truck was parked.

There are certain moments in life where everything you have ever done catches up to you. This was one of those moments. I knew right away when I saw the sheer destruction of Kane's truck that my reputation was going to make it impossible for the truth to be believed. I viewed the demolition job in shocked and awesome silence. My hands went straight over my mouth as I gasped and circled the truck to take in the total devastation. I had become well known for stealing car stereos out of vehicles to pawn the stolen items to provide the alcohol money that our parties required. Everyone in the town knew that I was a seasoned thief. Quiet and stealthy, I learned how to remove the stereos from vehicles in record time. If I did not like someone, I would smash their windshield. Crystal bestowed upon me all of these pleasant little behavioral gifts. I was her slave and, when she said, "jump," I asked, "how high?" I had a reputation for messing with people's cars and now it would be utterly impossible to convince Kane that I had nothing to do with this. It was my typical modus operandi yet I had nothing to do with it and he would never believe the truth. He was going to kill me, literally kill me.

"What happened?" I gasped while trying to push the words out of my mouth. I conveyed my consummate horror perfectly because Max immediately started shedding the verbiage that explained much and so little all the at the same time. I did not understand how this had happened.

Kane's truck was a white, souped-up Chevy S-10 that had a minor engine issue that could have easily been fixed at any mechanic in a matter of an hour or less. He had failed to actually take it in to get it fixed because he could not afford the towing cost. He had almost saved up enough to get it towed and fixed and then he would be back on the road as usual. He hated having to bum rides. He loved being independent and he could not wait to get his truck fixed. It was top on his list of things to get done. Until he could afford to get it fixed, he was parking it on the property. But now it was barely recognizable. He had worked throughout his teen years to save up money to afford this truck. This was the biggest investment he had ever made. He had built it up to have an amazing sound system. Everything on the truck was special order and custom designed. It was his pride and joy. A pride and joy that he was still making payments on.

I continued to circle the truck, unable to believe my

eyes. First, I saw an expletive carved into the shiny white paint on the hood of the truck. The windshield had been smashed to bits as the side windows had been as well. The high-end stereo system had been yanked out of the truck's center console and the subwoofers had been taken along with the amplifier. I saw the gas tank was open with cap dangling and, upon further examination, I noted the smell of urine emanating from the gas tank. My hands went to my forehead as I stood there in total grief for Kane. Every part of the truck had been destroyed. Every step I took made a crunch, crunch, crunch sound due to all the bits of truck and glass on the ground. It finally settled in that the truck was totaled beyond repair and that I would be blamed for this because the truck looked like the kind of damage that any angry ex-girlfriend might inflict. This was over the top and it was totally believable that my hand had caused the ruined devastation.

Kane would no longer be able to get to work. He could lose his job and then he would still be on the hook for the truck payments. This looked like something I would do and definitely had done in the past. How was I going to get him to believe that I did not do this? Who could have done this and why?

"Who did this, Max?" The tears in my voice told Max that the situation was even more dire than he knew. Max was very worried that my consternation would be aimed at him and he sought to assuage my growing vexation but he was nervous and talking too fast with exaggerated hand motions.

"Vigo, man!" Max seemed unable to finish his sentences as he raised his hand to wipe his forehead in exasperation.

"He thought he heard Kane hitting you when Kane and you were fighting in your room last night. He heard Kane being a jerk to you last night. Then he drank a ton of whiskey and beer and he got totally wasted and said, 'no one is going to treat a woman like that in my presence and get away with it.' Then he just grabbed a baseball bat and went psycho. I tried to stop him but I couldn't! He just started going crazy on the truck. Then he called Joe to come and get the stereo system out. I tried to wake you up but I couldn't!'"

Hearing how it happened made it seem more real. This was not a dream. It was a reality. I stared and stared at the truck as if staring would somehow stop the nightmare or repair the ruins.

"Max, go get me my phone. I need to call Joe and at least get that sound system back here." I called Joe and he refused to bring the sound system back. He already had estimated the sound system's worth and was looking forward to pawning the system and getting more beer money. The sad thing was that Joe was actually a friend of Kane's but, when Vigo called Joe to come and help dismantle the sound system, with a greedy eye he didn't bat an eyelash because of the possibility of money. A true alcoholic, Joe went wherever the beer was. He needed cash for beer so he was willing to do anything to anyone to achieve that goal. I threatened Joe and screamed threats at him over the phone while at the same time offering him beer. This was chaos. I really did not know what I was going to do. How was I going to tell Kane about this and what would be his reaction?

Maybe it was the shock of seeing the truck like that or thinking of Kane's reaction but, whatever it was, it made me sick. I ran to the bathroom and found myself huddled around the toilet bowl praying for relief. I sat on the bathroom floor in a ball and cried. I knew that Kane would contemplate killing me and I was dreading him finding out. He would never believe that I had nothing to do with this.

I could not bring myself to tell Kane what had happened. I did not have to. Good ole' friendly and loyal Joe knew that this was a life-threatening situation so he called Kane himself to taint the truth to cover his own hide. He left out the part where he came to help rip out the sound system and I had to threaten and entice him with beer to bring it back. He wanted to make sure that, when the posse came for us all, he was in the clear. He had no idea how the truck got that way so he surmised to concoct his own story on how the truck got destroyed, a story that, of course, left me as the guilty party and him totally innocent.

Kane called me. I swallowed hard and my stomach tightened again in the grip of total anxiety. I felt like I was going to be sick again as I saw his number on the caller I.D. In a shaky and weak voice, I attempted to muster up the greatest of feminine wiles to soften the coming blow.

"Hello?"

"What happened to my truck?"

I tried my best to explain. As I listened to myself explain, even I had a hard time believing my story. I had messed with so many cars at this point that it was a sort of poetic justice. This one time I was innocent, just this one time, and, to Kane, I was as guilty as sin. "I am going to [expletive] kill you! I am going to kill you!" He screamed on the phone. I held the phone a foot away from my ear and could still feel the receiver vibrating with the screams and angry tirade of a man driven to insanity. He was going to kill me. I could feel it.

Kane was in San Bernardino and he had no idea how bad his truck was damaged. He hoped that it was not that bad but calls from his friends confirmed that the truck was totaled. Being raised on the streets meant that he held a street mentality. Respect and "what you do to others gets done to you" is the honor code of the streets. He did not believe that his ex-girlfriend was innocent. She was guilty and she had just robbed him of thousands of dollars invested in his truck. His friends could not help but overhear his phone call and they heard him screaming death threats into the receiver. He was well aware that some of his friends were dangerous. Some were just fun-loving metal-heads but others were straight from the streets of San Bernardino and some were even gang members, especially Carlos.

Carlos was dangerous. He was the gun-toting

psychopath who was void of a conscious. Kane would not have chosen Carlos as a friend but life kind of chose Carlos for him. They had grown up together. Carlos' parents had died in an accident and, consequently, Carlos was left some money. There is nothing worse than a psychopath with a budget. Carlos bought all sorts of surveillance, weapons, and lots and lots of drugs. He was a huge dealer in the San Bernardino area. He had special toilets that were designed to cause anything sucked into the vortex to disintegrate in case of a police raid. He treated women much like they were dogs and he enjoyed any reason to bring out his weapons. He was waiting for the day to use his instruments of torture and ruination. His most prized toys were the implements to assemble a bomb that would inflict maximum destruction. When Carlos heard Kane screaming into the phone receiver, he immediately started packing his gear as though he were a hitman with a new job assignment. Kane's friends gathered around him as Kane gagged on his own words detailing the state of his prized possession.

All of the men stood horrified at the story which was falling on their ears. They all thought of their own vehicles sustaining the same fate by the hands of an ex-girlfriend and every one of them volunteered to go with Kane up to Cherry Valley to exact justice and revenge for the crime committed. They were an angry mob ready to attack like fighting dogs. As far as they were concerned, I deserved the worst kind of treatment but I was ignorant of the imminent threat to my life and the lives of my family.

They drove the necessary freeways to carry them to my childhood home under the cover of darkness. I was told later that they were fully equipped with enough explosive power to destroy my whole house. Kane rode in the passenger seat. They drove up my street with the intent to set a bomb near the outside wall of my home. They passed my house and continued up my street so they could turn around and park on the street just outside where they could sit and have a view of my room window.

When they brought the car to a slow stop, five sets of eyes and five hearts were united in the purpose of seeking out and causing my death. Even in the dark of night, they could see the damage done to Kane's truck and this made them even more intent on my demise. They had everything planned and worked out to avoid detection so they sat and observed the scene to see who was home and who would get caught up in collateral damage. It had to be placed near me and detonated. They figured that near my room window would be the best place to take me out but I had to be in my room so they all waited and watched for me to appear in my room window. They could see right into my room from their street view. Carlos was excited but also respectful of the explosive device that he had the pieces to. It was not a toy or something to play with. Once the moving parts were set in motion then, boom. Short of having the device put together and triggered for detonation, he was ready for "go" time. He was anxious to observe what his weaponry could do.

At last, I walked into my room and flipped on another light. They all sat there watching me and waiting. Carlos was ready and declared, "let's do this!" The guys were all about to get out of the car and get things started but Kane said, "wait a minute." That was not what Carlos wanted to hear but he obeyed. If they were not "all in" then things would not move forward. They had to all be in on this and prepared not to waver should they get arrested.

Kane watched me as I fiddled around my room. Carlos was growing impatient and urged him forward. "C'mon man! Lets do this!"

"Wait." Kane said firmly and kept his eyes fixed on my room as if waiting for something.

Carlos let out an annoyed sigh of frustration but Kane did not care. He was angry and he wanted to kill me but he did not want to regret it later so he sat waiting to be completely sure that he wanted me dead. Would he regret this later? No, he would not. He was ready to destroy the person who had so expertly disrespected him by destroying his property. Just as Kane was giving the "go" sign to Carlos and opening the passenger side door to go commence violence and death, Kane saw my sweet and precious son happily run into my room. He saw my son gripping a toy and showing it to me. He saw me holding my son and playing with him. Kane was frozen in time as he beheld the happy scene of mother and son. With all my problems and crazy and chaotic flaws, he knew that I loved my son. Kane was always melted by the dynamic between my son and I. I really desired to be a good mother but good intentions always seemed to break down in the application phase. The sprit was willing but the flesh was very weak but it was that motherly spirit that Kane always loved about me.

He sat with the car door ajar and one foot on the street outside and one foot in the car, symbolic of the choice he would now have to make. Per the criminal order of things, it is one thing to exact revenge and meet out street justice but it is quite another thing to hurt a child. Kane could not set a bomb knowing that my son might get killed or maimed. He was frozen for a minute weighing the outcomes and the possible risks. He hated me. He wanted me dead. That much was sure. But he still had warm affection for my son. He thought of all the possible consequences. His foot recoiled from outside and he pulled himself back into the car and shut the door to my death warrant. This would not be the last time that my son would save my life.

Carlos was disappointed and tried to urge Kane to continue the plan of attack but, once Kane decided, he was sure.

"Let's go! Not tonight. Not with her kid there. Let's go." He said the words with strength and firmness so that none of the guys would push him on this decision. He would not do it with my son there. He could never hurt a kid. He locked his eyes on me in my room to forever remember the moment because he did not plan to ever see me again. Seeing me with my son made it hard to hate me so much but then he looked to his truck and the anger would bubble up again. He wondered how he could love someone that was so incredibly evil and wondered how I could do the things I did. With those thoughts, the car was placed in drive and they pulled away from their perch at the top of the street and made their way back down into the city of San Bernardino.

I was totally unaware of what took place that night until I was told about it a few years later. This was a good thing that I did not know how close I came to being blown to kingdom come because I was experiencing my own crisis. My life was exploding all on its own without Kane trying to blow me up.

I had been feeling sick for a while but I took it to be my reaction to all the stress. I still had no idea what I was supposed to do with this demolished truck sitting in the front yard. My childhood home, like my life, was messy. And it was about to get a whole lot messier.

Chapter 17

The Squeeze

A week or so later, I was sitting in my room, as usual, and I realized that I had been feeling very sick for quite a while. I was used to a certain level of feeling sick but that was usually due to chronic sore throats, ear infections, sinus infections, bronchitis, and similar maladies, not a constant feeling of nausea. I pondered what could be causing this when I had a terrible feeling of dread come over me, "could I be pregnant? No way!" This could not be a more terrible time in my life to be pregnant. I would be all alone. I tried to think of a scenario where Kane would even pick up the phone to hear that I was pregnant and I could not imagine him ever speaking to me again.

"There is no way this could happen right now." I tried to push the unspeakable thought from my mind but the symptoms begged for an answer. But the incredible inconvenience caused me to dismiss the idea altogether. It was way too untimely to be true.

I managed to crawl through life for a week or two in a mindset of procrastination but I kept getting more and more sick. The circumstances forced me to inquire as to the cause. I went and bought a pregnancy test. I could not even believe that I was buying one. I never wanted to be caught up in this situation ever again but, here I was. Even though I had decided long ago that I would never get pregnant again, my lifestyle was to live in the moment. I did not want to get pregnant but I was too irresponsible to manage the basic steps of birth control and too immoral to practice abstinence.

Ironically, I was totally naive in the area of birth control and, because I was known to be promiscuous, the assumption was always made that because I had a lot of sex with a lot of people that I was educated about sex. Having sex, being educated about sex, and knowing what sex is and its purpose are all very different things. The assumption that I knew how to prevent pregnancy and all my options was a false one. Young girls that are having lots of risky sex with lots of different partners are often the most naive in regard to sex education. They are especially ignorant of the true purpose of why sex was created.

Sex was created to create a loving bond between individuals and they do become one in many ways. It is meant to be enjoyed and a loving experience with the bonds of marriage. Everything that a young girl experiences when having promiscuous sex is far from this design and sex becomes a perverted thing. With every new partner, the promiscuous girl gets farther and farther away from learning how to really enjoy sex within the confines of love and commitment in marriage.

Such was my experience and, as a consequence, I found myself sitting on the toilet in my bathroom, horrified that I was the very definition of stupidity. I was doing the same things over and over again expecting different results. The symbols on the stick indicated a positive. I was pregnant.

The shame engulfed me and overwhelmed me. It so overwhelmed me that I could not even think about it that much. The moments I did think about it, I immediately drowned out my thoughts with a beer or smoked some more of my good ole' friend Crystal. My habit was up to one hundred dollars a day of meth. My brain was fried and I knew that I could not really think straight. I was on drugs, so many drugs. In fact, that month alone, I had done ecstasy, hallucinogenics, drank a truckload of alcohol, and done my typical amount of Crystal.

How was this baby ever going to be normal? What damage had I done to my baby? I knew that I had to tell someone. I could not trust my own brain but the thought of telling my mom, the only person I really trusted at this point, made me feel even more shame and overwhelmed but I knew it was the only right move in the situation. Regardless of her reaction, she was still my mother and I wanted her now. I needed her support. It would have been better for the survival of my baby if I had never told my mother but I did not know that at the time.

I vividly remember walking down the long hallway that led to my mother's bedroom that evening. I swallowed hard as I humbly and uncharacteristically displayed a level of politeness and softness. Because I had not learned my lesson the first time, I had been laid low and humbled in the worst way. It is one thing to be a teen pregnancy and make it through that but, to do it again, means it was not a one-time mistake. I might as well tattoo the red letter "A" on my forehead because I was indeed a whore and a slut and all the things they said I was. All the hard work I had done to prove people wrong about Jacob and I had been destroyed long ago. Never before had I looked back on my life and taken stock like I was now doing. I had to make a change but I did not know how. I thought that this baby would force me to get my life back on track.

On another level of additional selfishness, I considered how much weight I had gained during my first pregnancy and I shuddered at the thought of gaining all that weight again. The one thing about Crystal that I enjoyed was being ultra skinny. I have always been an emotional eater and then would feel guilty about what I had eaten. Once I had tried to make myself vomit after eating an entire appetizer of buffalo wings at T.G.I.F.'s and, although I did make myself purge those delightful morsels, I hated the experience of vomiting. I would rather avoid eating altogether than the binge and purge of it all. Crystal helped me to never, ever, be hungry. I was down to one hundred pounds and a size one or a two instead of the size twelve or fourteen that I was while pregnant.

I always enjoyed the weight loss that drugs induced and I hated the weight gain that pregnancy caused. If I failed to mention this, I would be failing to be honest about the things that teenage girls think about when they become pregnant. The thought of losing our bodies is one of the first things we think about when we find out we are pregnant. It is selfish and awful that this was my primary concern but, that is the point. I was not mature enough to even know that this should not be my first thought. I was too young to be having babies. The rest of the world considered me an adult at nineteen but I was far from being able to manage my own life without the help of a parent. On the inside, I knew this so I made my way into my mother's inner sanctum to tell her my awful and shameful truth yet again.

I sat on her bed which still had the same bedspread and bed frame that she had shared with Alec and I felt sad that we, as women, were alone now. In that moment, I felt sorry for my mom. She would hear this awful news and we would be alone in this. As awful as my mother was, she was still my only family and the only one I could turn to right now.

I told her that I was pregnant with a quivering voice while trying so hard to hold back the tears. I felt like I did not deserve to cry or feel sorry for myself. At this point, I could not tell her that I was a heavy drug user and an addict too. I knew that I was going to get myself off the drugs so I could have my baby but I had to stagger the amount of information I gave to my mother. I did not want to throw everything at her all at once. I knew I needed some kind of help. In my mind, I was picturing being the mother of two babies now.

As I told my mother, I saw her grow increasingly quiet as the information sank in. She had very little to say as she managed her shock. I was saddened by her lack of comfort in the moment but I felt I deserved any verbal or physical blows that she might deliver. I was a social criminal. I was breaking all the rules that society had to offer, not to mention the laws written on my heart by a loving God watching me suffer under the cruel tyrant of sin.

I would fail to get the words of support I so badly wanted. My mother was thinking of all the ways that her own life would be changed which was understandable since I was living under her roof. She and I were fighting on a regular basis over the amount of time she already spent watching my son. I still wanted to hear, "I will help you get your life together," even if that meant that I would have to go to some sort of treatment facility (which should have been on the table but it was not). I knew I had messed up again and I wanted help. She asked, "who is the father?" I had not even thought of the possibility that anyone could be the father other than Kane as I mentally rifled through the files of my various sexual partners over the previous months. "There was only Kane," I falsely and conveniently concluded.

That is when horror squeezed me like a hand squeezes a water balloon. My mother observed me with her watchful and motherly eyes as my hand went to my forehead in emotional agony. She pressed me about what thought I had just had the way mothers do when they can read your face better than anyone else on earth. I confessed the cold hard truth about the ecstasy fueled night with Dillon but I left out the part about the ecstasy.

"Impossible," I declared in unbelief. "That was just one night with Dillon."

"One night is all it takes!" My mom snapped back. That was when the feeling of brokenness washed over me. I felt like flinging myself into my mother's arms to be a little baby again to find comfort and for her to make everything okay. The floodgates of emotion burst open as the tears ran freely and my mouth declared the awful truth.

"Mom!" I cried to her as if at the bottom of a well crying for her help, "I don't know which one is the father."

Every talk show that I had ever laughed at when they did the DNA test and wondered in detest at those white trash, disgusting girls came to my mind. "How could those girls not know? I mean, how do you not know who the father is?" All the names that my older brother called me came back to me now. I was a slut. I was willing, at that point, to do whatever my mother said I needed to do. My mom, overwhelmed with my further descent into failure said, "we will talk about this later," and got up and walked away, leaving me sitting there in a state of fully deserved self loathing.

Later turned into later and still later. Weeks went by as I ignored the evident and the obvious. I felt that, if I procrastinated enough, then maybe nature would take its course and I would lose the pregnancy. This did not happen and my belly started to swell with life. I was desperate to know who the father was. I went to the doctor to find out how far along I was in order to determine who the father might be but this would only leave me with more uncertainty.

Some days I was certain it was Dillon while other days I was certain it was Kane. I went back and forth between the two. I needed someone to walk through this with me. To me, this was my Hurricane Katrina. This was my Tsunami, my earthquake, my "pregnancy-gate" and, like anyone in crisis, I was terrified of going down this torturous path all alone. "I need to call Kane and tell him I am pregnant with his baby," and that day I was kind of certain that it was his.

I picked up my home phone and dialed Kane's home number. I listened to the phone ringing and I could not even begin to anticipate what his reaction was going to be. The butterflies in my stomach felt more like wasps as the typical nerve and pregnancy-related acid reflux snapped and crackled and popped in my esophagus. He absolutely hated me and now I was going to tell him that we were going to have a child together. I dialed the familiar numbers on the keypad and held my breath as it rang.

"Hello?" his brother's familiar voice greeted me and I was happy he was answering.

"Hi. Is Kane there?" My voice was expectant of the coming backlash.

His brother was always so nice to me and part of him always felt sorry for me. He was a thug but he was a sweet kind of thug. He always liked me and he wondered why I would do such a terrible thing to Kane's truck.

"Why are you calling here?" He asked with true curiosity in a voice that said he was tired of dealing with the drama.

"Johnny, I really need to talk to Kane. I really do. I know he hates me but this is really important." I was as humble and sweet as I could be because I really needed to talk to him.

I heard the phone muffle over and I knew that Kane was in the same room at the time. I could not make out the words but I could hear Kane's tone of voice and he was not happy.

Johnny came back on the line. "He really doesn't want to talk to you." I knew Kane was too angry at me to even see straight. Honestly, I was happy to tell Johnny about the current state of things rather than Kane.

"Tell Kane that I'm pregnant." That was all I had to say and Kane was on the phone so fast that it made my head spin.

"You're a liar! You're really going to sink that low and lie to me like this!" He wasn't yelling at me but the coldness in his voice was chilling.

"I'm not lying, Kane. I really am pregnant. I don't know what I am going to do." I could not hold back my fear and frustration. All my fears seemed to be hitting me at once.

In a tit-for-tat tone he said, "Oh! So if you're not a liar then tell me who messed up my truck then? Tell me that!"

"I told you who did that! I am not lying, Kane. I am

pregnant. I can show you the test."

It was useless. Kane announced his last words, "This is some kind of [expletive] entrapment! You're trying to trap me! You're not pregnant! You're a [expletive] liar!" And with that he hung up on me.

I got the five pregnancy sticks that I had used to confirm my worst-case scenario. I threw them all in a plastic bag and got in my car and started to drive to Kane's house. I was going to pee on a stick in front of him if need be to show him that I was not lying. As I started to get on the 10 freeway, I decided to call Kane one more time to tell him that I was coming to his house. I knew that this was a dangerous move. Being on his territory would put me in a danger that I could not underestimate. I was still enemy number one and the prime suspect for the wrecking of Kane's truck but I did not care. I detested that I was believed to be a liar and not really pregnant. It was infuriating to be lumped in with those girls who lied about being pregnant to get their man back. I did not want to be pregnant with his child or at all for that matter.

I was driving and dialing Kane in my fuming anger. Driving while being angry at your ex is just as dangerous as being on the phone in my case.

"Hello!" It was Johnny again. "Are you really pregnant?" he asked matter of fact. I could hear Kane shouting in the background "Don't even talk to her! It's a waste of time! She's such a liar!"

Johnny walked outside away from the infuriated jeers of Kane. His voice became lower and soft toward me and he seemed to want to get down to brass tacks, "Okay, tell me the honest truth. Are you really pregnant?"

With tears in my voice I said, "Johnny, I swear! I am driving down there right now to show you guys the pregnancy tests. I am pregnant!" At this point, I was pleading with Johnny to believe me, "I am not lying!" I cried.

"Okay, okay. I believe you but you can't come down here. You messed up Kane's truck. He'll never forgive you for that. Whatever you do, do not come down here. I'll try to talk to Kane but this is not a good time to spring this on him."

I felt the air being sucked out of me like I was kicked in the gut. A part of me was still hoping that Kane and I could work things out. He had always talked about having his own family. I guess now it would be with anyone but me. I felt more alone by the minute. I pulled my car off the nearest freeway exit so I could turn around and go home. Even if I had shown Kane the pregnancy tests, he hated me too much to ever consider the future with me. There is no loneliness quite as lonely as being misunderstood and falsely accused of these crimes, although I was guilty of many others. It was a sharp, gut-wrenching loneliness that I felt and this made me extremely vulnerable, vulnerable enough to do things that I had never planned on doing.

With Kane out of the picture, I was besieged under the burden of the thought of being a single mom twice over with two different fathers. Dillon had sort of stayed away for some time but as soon as he heard from Max that I was pregnant and that Kane had left me, he just knew that it was his. He knew that I had been with Kane many times but he thought only of our time together and he just knew it was his or assumed as much. One day he showed back up at my house and offered me something I so desperately needed, support. But his kind of support was not really the kind I was picturing. He was younger than I was, without a job, a car, or a place to stay but he did not care.

"I told my mom about us and she says she can help us!" I felt horrified. Dillon practically fell to his knees to beg me to come stay with him and his mom. "I want this baby." he declared. The decisions I had made while totally messed up on drugs were now coming back to bite me. I was ashamed for having been with Dillon and I was not excited about anyone finding out, especially his mother. Dillon affectionately grabbed my hand and sought to cuddle and console me but I was numb and in shock and did not want his comfort.

I did not want to have a baby with someone younger than I, someone under eighteen. Even though it was two years and four months difference between us, I felt as if I were a criminal that was robbing the cradle. I did not want anyone to know that I was pregnant and I took ridiculous steps to try to hide the obvious. I would not let Dillon touch me in front of people or my friends or family. What a mess I had gotten myself into. What a mess.

My mother took note of the extreme amount of stress I was under and the mess her daughter had created. She thought of how this made her look and she did not want another baby out of wedlock. She knew that I could never give up my baby for adoption. Whatever her reasons, she called an abortion clinic and made me an appointment. When she told me this, I was shocked because she had always been staunchly pro-life and an ultra-conservative Christian. Dre, the new boyfriend, was pro-choice and he was urging her to have me go and get an abortion. So the decision was made that I would have an abortion. I weakly objected to the idea. I already had a baby saved from abortion and we made it through okay. Did I really need an abortion? Isn't there adoption?

Honestly, my mother calling the abortion clinic and making the appointment for me took a huge weight off of me. It gave me permission to do what I thought was wrong. I already had the evidence of what kind of precious life comes from an unwanted pregnancy and I knew that this pregnancy might be as huge a blessing as the first. Was it possible that we could just go to a clinic and I could wash my hands of this entire mess? Was it that easy to shake off the pain and hurt of both Kane and Dillon? I was not so sure. I did not feel like I had the freedom to choose. I was not sure about having an abortion and the weight of the decision made my belly ache as if the baby was crying out on its own behalf. I had already begun to think of my belly in terms of there being a baby inside and now to think that I was going to get it taken out of me made me hurt all over.

When I voiced my concern, my mother responded, "if you are going to keep this pregnancy, you had better find another place to live!" With those words, my mother made the choice for me. She forced me to choose between keeping this baby and keeping the child I already had. The thought of being thrown out and having no place to go always frightened me. I had been there before and I had no idea where I would go or what I would do. If I had been forced to make my own appointment and get myself to the abortion clinic, I would never have chosen to have an abortion but I was able to completely tune out reality and "numb up" as my mother walked me through every step as if I were a zombie.

"She is making me get an abortion," I told Dillon. The fact was that I was over eighteen now so she was not really making me do anything but it was easier to allow my mother to bear the brunt of the blame rather than take any responsibility for myself. If I had been strong, and few who are looking to get an abortion are ever completely sure or completely strong, I should have told my mother that I wanted to keep this pregnancy. There is always a cauldron of circumstances that create the seemingly insurmountable pressure in decisions like these.

I felt terrible, just terrible about the fact that I was going to get rid of the child in my belly. I had been pregnant long enough to get used to the baby being there. I thought that, maybe if I waited long enough, the abortion clinic would not take me but I was wrong. I was nearing the end of my first trimester and the time that ticked by was an endless reminder of what I had growing inside me. I felt a sense of anxiety because, if I were going to do it, I wanted to do it now and not wait any longer and "know" my child any better than I already did. The more I knew my child, the more the love was growing for it and, the more I loved it, the more painful this felt. I remember trying not to love anything at all at the time so I even tried to see my son less and less. That was the only way I could survive. I started to count the number of drugs I had done in the last three months and I told myself that, even if I had the baby, it could not possibly be born normal. I created roadblocks to life where there were none. I had a living and breathing being in my body that was going to die before it ever was born.

I knew the abortion appointment was coming up the very week that my first trimester would end and my second trimester would start. I had to drown out the voice of my conscience and whatever faint sound of the Holy Spirit that I could still hear. I did what any person does when they are running from the right decision and the conviction of the Lord, I had a huge raucous party at my house and I got completely and totally wasted. I cracked open my drug suitcase and partook in ways that allowed me to feel nothing at all for my unborn baby and allowed me to further rationalize getting rid of it. I had managed, by this time, to fully convince myself that my baby was likely so disfigured and had too many birth defects to be born. If an ultrasound had been ordered around this time and a medical professional had told me that my baby was healthy and not disfigured, I would not have gone through with the abortion. I was totally deceived that it would be better for my baby never to be born than to be born to a disgusting, drug-addicted whore like me.

Every woman that has a child knows that we sacrifice our bodies from the moment that we know that there is life within. We are no longer living for ourselves but for a purpose greater than ourselves. How awesome it is to have and to hold in these earthen vessels our own spirit but even more amazing it is to carry the spirit of two. As a mother, I have come to know well the feeling of a living and breathing spirit inside me and, on one occasion, I was aware of the spirit of my unborn child only a few weeks after conception. That is to say, I knew I could feel that I was not alone in my own body before I even took the pregnancy test. Motherhood is the ultimate fulfillment of, "greater love hath no woman than this, that a woman lay down her life for her friends." The opposite of this is destruction of the innocent. It is the ultimate form of selfishness. For the sake of convenience, I would destroy my baby who, through no fault of its own, had done me no wrong other than to exist.

The party was raging that night. We had kegs of beer and an entire fridge filled with liquor. People were using acid and shrooms. I was drinking and drinking and drinking some more. I had troubles to drown out so I opened the flood gates and drank more than I had in a long time. The party was loud and there were tons of people there that I did not even know. I was high and drunk and was still trying to converse and play hostess. I could not get rid of the aching in my heart. I was laughing and hanging out when I thought I felt my baby move. It has been said that if you have ever been pregnant before then you can feel the baby move much earlier the next pregnancy. I felt the strong presence of the baby inside me.

I put my beer down on a table and walked past all the people partying and dancing on my porch and in the garage. Their faces were a blur to me as I made my way past them all. The beat of the house music pounded in my ears and all I wanted was to get away from it. The room was spinning and, for the first time, I felt a new emotion emerge through the numbness of the past few days. I felt sorry for my baby inside me. I felt pity for it. It would not be alive much longer and it did not know, or maybe it did, that the one person in this world who was supposed to love and protect it was planning and commiserating to secure its destruction. I felt sad for the baby who had no one to love it. Even with all the people "having fun" at my childhood home, with all the noise, with all the festivities, with all the people I knew and did not know dancing and laughing, I went to my room and closed the door in a quiet place to hold my belly and cry, to say goodbye to my baby that I would kill in just a few days' time.

Chapter 18

Rachel Weeping

The morning of the abortion is a very clear and searing memory to me. I can remember my mother talking as if nothing were out of the ordinary on the way down to the abortion clinic in San Bernardino. She even talked about Alec and her divorce and all the things she hated about him. When she parked the car, she turned to me and said, "are you okay?" The answer was, "No! I am about to make the biggest and most damaging mistake of my young life." But I sat quietly and returned the answer that I knew she wanted to hear, "I'm fine." I felt roped into this and like I could not turn back. I was tired and hungover and I wanted it to be over with now. This had been a long drawn out process and my conscience was continually being tortured.

Dillon and I had fought all night long. He wanted so badly for me to keep the baby. He begged me, practically on his knees, not to have the abortion. His mother was brokenhearted and told him she could not bear to lose a grandchild like that. I felt the pain of sadness, I really did, but my mother's words that I would "have to find another place to live," were the loudest in my mind. It was all well and good for other people to try and dissuade me from having an abortion but were they going to be the one to help me get off the drugs and help me find a place to live and help me provide for my two kids from different dads now? No, no one was going to help me. I was learning that there is rarely any sense of altruism in anyone, especially in my family. My mother had spent a lifetime being against abortion but she was willing to usher her own daughter into an abortion clinic to preserve her own level of comfort and save us both from the embarrassment of not knowing who the father was.

Over and over, I told myself how terribly deformed my child must be from my drug use. It was my mantra as I unbuckled my seat belt. We had been warned that there might be protesters on our way in. I pictured, in my mind's eye, a sea of angry men and women throwing rotten tomatoes at me and hurling insults in my direction. Maybe there is such a scene like that somewhere in the United States but there was not here, not that day, not for my baby. No one was fighting for my baby that day, not even me.

The fact that I might meet protesters or the images of what abortion does to babies terrified me. I braced myself and kept my eyes peeled for these protesters that we were told to be leery of. My idea of abortion clinic protesters was that they were a militant bunch and I expected every kind of name and accusation. When we only encountered a few people that said very little to me, I was surprised. I opened the door and walked inside the building, wearing my loose and comfortable-fitting clothing, for "my procedure" and I immediately questioned the lady at the reception desk, "where are all the protestors?" She said, "oh, there aren't very many out there today."

I took a seat in the small and uncomfortable waiting room. I sat there more calm than I thought I would be. I had been told that I would be given a drug to help me forget and not be conscious of what was going on. "Good," I thought, "can they help me stay that way for the rest of my pathetic life?" I sat there and noticed that my legs were shaking.

It was a normal enough place. It appeared to be like any other medical office I had encountered through most of my life. No one seemed to be too emotional and the very procedural and matter of factness of it all allowed me to think very little of the life-long emotional impact that this would all have on me.

I wish I could write that, in the waiting room, I had second thoughts and ran out of the building but my agony had already come and gone in the garden of decision. Although there are many stories of other girls running out mid-procedure to save their babies, this was not my experience. For me, the decision had already been made. To run now would only inconvenience everyone involved in getting me there. When it was all said and done, I did not want to get kicked out of my house and have nowhere to go. I was a selfish nineteen year old girl who was consumed with my own thoughts of losing the shred of reputation I had left.

They walked me back to the procedure room and prepped me for the next step. They said that the drugs would make me unaware of what was happening. Unfortunately, the drugs did not completely knock me out and I was in and out for the entire procedure. I placed one foot in one stirrup and my other foot in the the other stirrup. My body was wide open and willing to give away God's greatest gift.

Two nurses and a physician attended me. The room was white and cold as I lay there and looked up at the ceiling. I concentrated on the patterns in the ceiling and tried hard to tune out the pulling and stinging of what was going on. I looked to the nurses for help and comfort because I was afraid and loopy so one nurse thoughtfully said, "we are close to being done now." I can still see the doctor hunched down between my legs going to work to remove my child. For so many months when I was pregnant with my first child, I was terrified that someone would take him away from me and now I was not only giving my child away but executing it.

I did not think of my sweet, little, innocent baby who was four months old within my womb and what was happening to him or her. I was not willing to go there in my thoughts. From experience, I know that babies are emotional creatures and I often wonder what kind of emotions went through this little being as it was taken out of me in a most violent and cruel fashion.

The anesthetic I was given did not work like it was supposed to (which has been my experience with most medical procedures) and the procedure hurt very badly. I was in and out of lucidity. Although hazy, I remember parts of the procedure very well. I knew that I was now bleeding. There are scenes that I remember very clearly and then there are moments where I draw a blank but, as long as I live, I will never forget this next scene.

I had been wheeled into this cavernous surgical recovery area toward the back entrance of the building. It was not so much the visuals that shocked me, although it was a stunning sight to see. There were twenty or more young girls recovering from their abortions lined up in chair after chair. I started to come alive and aware from my state of anesthetic-induced intoxication when I became aware of this terrible sound of deep, heart-wrenching sadness. I am not quite sure how to describe it but imagine the sound of ten or more girls, grief stricken and emotional because they have just had their babies taken from their womb. It was "Rachel weeping for her children because they are no more." I imagine this is what war sounds like, the sound of deep agony and wrenching of spirits for something has been done that can never be undone. It was the sound of death and heartbreak.

There was a young hispanic girl one chair over from me. She looked younger than I. Perhaps she was around fifteen years old. She held her head in her hands, shaking her head back and forth, while bitterly weeping. She could barely breathe because she was overcome with grief. My first instinct out of my haze was to jump up and comfort her. I stood up and shuffled just a few steps to her and put my hand on her shoulder and I asked her, "are you okay?" She bristled under the touch of human sympathy and I understood the sentiment. I did not want anyone to comfort me either. I felt that I did not deserve it nor could I begin to tell others what I was feeling. She cried harder and deeper and I could truly empathize with her.

Just then, a nurse briskly marched into our vicinity. She seemed annoyed that I was talking to the other patients so she came over to me and led me back to my chair. She just left the girl there to weep all alone and unattended.

"Please stay seated in your chair until your ride gets here," The nurse said in a cold and do-not-make-trouble-for-me tone so I shook my head in docile agreement. I looked around the room and I could observe two groups of females. Some were terribly suffering with what had just been irrevocably done and the other girls were indifferent or in denial. It should be evident what group I belonged to. I wondered at my own ability to feel so deeply for others but not for myself. I sat and listened to the girl next to me sob and occasionally cry out, "my baby!" and I felt annoyed at the terrible regret these cries brought up in me. I realized this girl and I were feeling the same emotions but she could show it and I could not. I could not cry because I knew that, if I started crying, I might never stop and, if I really allowed myself to feel the gravity of what I had just done, I might go insane and never recover.

Just then I saw the face of my mother. "That was it?" I thought. "It's all over. That was easier than I thought it would be." How could it be this easy to completely sweep my life clean and tidy of a long succession of mistakes? It was all too easy. I came into the clinic with my belly teeming with life and now I felt all alone inside again. The little spring of life that makes one feel that their body is not their own was plucked before it even had a chance to bloom. It was like life would just go on and not even know that it was missing something precious. Life is compared to a seed and I snuffed out its chance to grow. Could I just go on the same as usual as if this had never happened? I wondered if that were even possible.

The nursing staff brought my mother back to fetch me and take me home. She offered me her arm to escort me back to her car but I refused her assistance and assured her that I was able to walk just fine all on my own. Her new boyfriend was there and I remember thinking how strange it was that they had only known each other a few months. I had only met him twice before today and now he is a part of the most intimate decision a girl can make? I was sad that my mother was not taking the time to be with me and talk to me. She was especially focused on her boyfriend. I could never make my mother be there for me anyway and I was exhausted of protesting my mother's decisions and lack of interest in me. I felt as though I was always getting in the way of her love interests and I was just so tired of it all.

I shuffled across the tile floor of the clinic on the way to the car. I was still more focused on the other girls in the clinic than my mother or her boyfriend or my own pain and discomfort. A nurse opened the back door of the abortion clinic to see us out. She handed my mother my post-op instructions and said, "Absolutely no activity when she gets home. She needs to rest." The California sun flooded into the recovery area and it was strange to see the sunshine stream into such a fluorescent inferno. I would have preferred to see the day turn to rain and gloomy fog as the sunshine was a cruel mockery. What a contradictory scene, the sunshine shinning and the girls crying for their children that will never experience a single sunny day on this earth. Seeing the natural sunlight pour in and break through the artificial lighting pulled me outside and away from my own emotions that I struggled to feel. I was all too happy to leave this place.

I tucked myself away into a ball in the front seat of my mother's car. I managed to fit the seatbelt around me as I put my feet up on the dashboard. I sat in the car and waited for my mother. I watched her in the side and rearview mirrors as she kissed and flirted with her boyfriend in the parking lot. I wanted to go home. I could feel that I was bleeding. I wanted the comfort of nothing else than being alone and not having to see anyone. There was no idea more comforting to me than the idea of being completely alone to get high and escape this, whatever *this* was.

My level of irritation with my mother was palpable on the ride home. I felt numb and empty and dark all rolled into this one heart of mine and yet she was in the throws of new love and giddy for it. It was more than annoying to hear the little cute things that Dre did because I could not even begin to imagine being that happy again. I had lost Kane and I had been pregnant and now I was not. I still had my son but it felt like I only had half a son because Jacob and I were continually fighting for him and also fighting for who would take him when one of us had plans. I thought of my life and how I had very little to show for it.

I was still a heavy meth user. I had a desire to get clean but I really had no idea where to start. I knew that I was sitting on a precipice. I could either fall deeper into the pit of despair or start trying to pick myself up by my bootstraps. I knew my mother was aware that I was struggling in life, if only by the way I dressed and partied. I also knew that she had no idea how much I was in danger of dying. I was living the life of a dealer and I was operating like an unpaid prostitute and, at nineteen, I was already reaping the heavy consequences of both.

As we pulled into the driveway, I could see that Max and Dillon were waiting for me in the garage. They both got up to meet me with expectant looks on their faces. Maybe they were waiting for me to collapse into a fit of emotion or maybe they were expecting me to be catatonic and need their assistance to be lifted. It was clear they were there to help but they looked like two little puppy dogs waiting for their master. I appreciated their concern and eagerness to help me but I did not even know what I needed in those moments.

I made my way inside my childhood home with my

entourage in tow. My mother, Dillon, and Max were all staring at me like they were waiting for me to have a meltdown. Everyone was on edge as I settled into a big arm chair that was placed in front of the big screen television in the den area. I could feel everyone walking on eggshells around me and I felt quite humiliated with all the attention. This was far from a private and secret thing now. I really wanted fewer people to know. I was worried that many more people would find out.

"Please don't tell anyone." I looked at their expectant faces and thought to extract oaths in blood if I could but the shaking of their heads in agreement would have to suffice for the time being.

I sat in the big arm chair and I looked at Dillon's face. I found his sad and tragic face to be crushing. It was hard to face him. He sat on the couch across from me and his face looked pregnant with questions he wanted to ask me but he was holding back for many reasons. For one, he was afraid that I would send him home and he just wanted to be with me. I could tell he was also very angry with me. He firmly believed that I had aborted his baby and he was so very upset with me for that. With Dillon on the couch sitting across from me, it made it impossible to sit and rest per my post-op instructions. I could not sit still with myself. I had too many thoughts and too many feelings to sit still. I was the saddest a girl could be and I longed for happier days.

I stood up and my mother asked from the kitchen,

"what are you doing?"

"I am getting up to clean."

"What? You are supposed to rest because there is a risk of bleeding."

"I can't just sit here. I need to clean." The words coming from my mouth were emotionless.

"You had better rest." My mother said with a concerned voice.

"No, I have to clean."

Dillon chimed in, "You have to rest!"

"I can't. Max, go get me the vacuum and, Dillon, help me pick up some of this stuff."

Clearly this was very odd behavior and I was refusing to comply with the post-op instructions. I was seriously disturbed by the day's events and sitting still with myself was not an option. I was not okay and I did not know how to cry for help any louder than to display my eccentricity for all to see. Obediently and dutifully, my friends helped me clean. With that, my mother washed her hands of the day's events as if it never happened. For the next couple of hours, I cleaned away the day like I could wash myself of the memory. I did everything but rest.

I was forced to take stock of my life in the few moments on the drive home from my abortion but, alas, I hardened my heart toward the Holy Spirit and pushed away the voice beckoning me to heaven's open door. The company I kept allowed me to quickly turn from thoughtful thoughts and get busy partying again. I needed an older and wiser woman to sit down and put the questions of life to me. The heartache I was now feeling was leading me to repentance although I did not know it. I would push onward in sin as I was eternally running and finding new depths to my "rock bottom."

I wish my mother would have considered the emotional toll I was paying by continuously engaging in a relationship with this person and that but, we are only as wise as our experiences allow. My mother was eager to free herself of my drama for her own set of drama. I needed a good dose of mothering but she was ill-equipped to help me. I needed someone to take me by the hand and help me get some sort of treatment.

It spoke to my spirit when my mother allowed me to get up straight after a serious medical procedure and clean the house, seeing that I was clearly having some sort of emotional break, and she did nothing to see to my emotional well-being or offer and provide counseling or preventive options. She simply went back to her life as normal and never wanted to speak of it again. I felt abandoned and replaced by her new boyfriend and I was seriously struggling to keep my head above water because the suicidal thoughts started to flood into my thought life and I could not shake the idea that everyone would be better off without me.

Chapter 19

First Blood

The weeks wore on after my abortion. One night, I organized a party as a sort of sendoff because I planned to die that night. I wrote my son a letter on my computer and I took a bunch of pills and drank as much as possible on top of it. My three-year-old son found me curled around my mother's bathroom toilet. It was no accident that I took the pills in her bathroom. I took as many sleeping pills, benzodiazepines, and anti-depressants as I could get my hands on. Many famous people have died from taking similar and a lesser number of pills. I remember fading out and thinking of my mother finding me there in her bathroom and I was happy that, finally, she would know just how bad things were for me. I could never seem to convince her that I was really that bad and that I needed some help. My son went and got my mother and said, "mommy is sick." My heart aches that my son had to see such a sight but, by finding me and getting help, my son was led by a greater power and saved my life that night. At last, my mother found me unconscious, lying on the ground, around her bathroom toilet.

Soon, everyone at my party was in my mother's bathroom and they were trying to wake me up. When I was easily roused, I was tragically disappointed that I was so easily awakened from my hopefully fatal slumber. "I had not taken enough pills," I immediately thought. I was so disappointed with myself. I felt like even more of a huge failure. Then I heard the news that someone had called 9-1-1. I was horrified. Even though I had purposely made a cry for help in my mother's bathroom, I was immediately terrified by the prospect of being in a county hospital on a 5150 hold. I had no capability to think logical thoughts nor should I have been allowed to be in the driver's chair and directing the show. At this moment (and many moments before this one), I showed myself incapable of making my own decisions. However, the crazy show must go on. Before the paramedics arrived, with slurred speech between episodes of vomiting, I begged everyone to tell the paramedics that I was just drunk and not suicidal. For whatever reason, everyone agreed to tell the paramedics that I was only drunk.

I was a poor, pathetic, little thing trying to tell the world or whoever would listen that I was terribly suffering in my heart. After this night, I realized that even suicide would not cause my mother to take action on my behalf. It took me several days to recover from all the pills I took that night. Max nursed me back to health by practically pouring water down my throat. This would not be the last time I would try this method of suicide. It was just the shadowing of the many evils to come.

I subconsciously decided to stop trying to shock my mother and cry out for her attention. However, I knew that I had one last-ditch effort in acquiring my mother's sympathies and concern and, if I were ever going to admit that I was an addict to anyone, it needed to be her. I needed to tell her that I had been using meth. My mother knew, by this time, that I was using something but she was too naive to the drug world to really figure things out. This is the woman that, when my friends blew marijuana in her face, thought it was "funny smelling cigarettes."

All I can say is that, when a child appears to be on something, a parent must do all they can to learn about drugs and the signs and symptoms before it is too late. I know my mother prayed for me and I know she worried a great deal about me. We cannot sit back and pray when God is calling us to act. We cannot be like the priest and the publican when God is calling us to be a Good Samaritan. My mother was enabling my drug habit. She often gave me money to supply my drug habit and she gratefully closed her eyes to what she was doing. Even though she thought she was only buying cigarettes and alcohol, it did not take a rocket scientist to see that I was on a lightning-fast crazy train into the abyss.

One result of my abortion experience was that I was shaken up to say the least. I knew that I had sacrificed my baby because I was on drugs. I told myself that there was no way the baby could be normal with my crazy one hundred dollar a day meth habit not to mention using other drugs on top of that like cocaine, ecstasy, and hallucinogenics. I had run out of money from my father's estate. Every last bit of it had gone to drugs and now I was stealing to support my habit and my mother was my prime target. She was an easy target. She tried to lock her room but I always found a way into her room and I stole everything I could from her that I thought, in my own estimation, was not all that precious. "She was getting divorced so why would she want her rings?" I rationalized. My sense of entitlement was strong and I believed that my mother owed me for the pain she was causing.

She was most definitely causing pain. She was seriously dating her new boyfriend and had little time for me or my little brother. She had promised my little brother that she would not remarry until he was eighteen and could leave the house but I knew that promise would not hold water.

It was absurd in a way. The more my mother gave into my begging and pleading for money, the more I hated her. Secretly, I wanted her to take a stand against me and, at last, be a parent. Every time she gave me money, I knew it was hush money to get me to leave her alone. I was a great big pain in the neck and I used it to my benefit.

After the abortion, I let my meth supply dwindle and I never re-upped on my supply. When I was out, I was out and, when you are withdrawing, it is incredibly difficult to operate when you are that sick. The withdrawal was intense and strong and unlike anything I had ever experienced. My body ached and convulsed and my abdomen cramped with bodily functions that had not occurred naturally for almost a year. I told Max to stand guard over my bedroom and not let me out of the house no matter how hard I begged. I locked my bedroom door and went to bed for almost a week. I slept. I had terrible sweats and nightmares as I went in and out of sleep.

Mid-way through I decided I could not do it and I tore my room apart looking for any tiny little rock that I could find but to no avail. Nothing would replace the one hundred dollar a day habit. I started making phone calls and the desperation I conveyed to my fellow druggie friends was a tragic reminder to them of their own future date with the come-down and they wanted nothing to do with me. I called people who owed me money and, because I was weak and sick and could not make it out of the bathroom, I was no longer feared and no one would pay me back. I called best friends and acquaintances for help but no one would bring me drugs. The friendships I had cultivated in the drug world were the shallowest of attachments I have ever known. There is no honor among thieves and no loyalty among addicts. It is kill-or-be-killed and a horrific come-down for every high.

I can vividly recall my trembling hands as I hung up the phone and realized that I was going to have to get through this alone and there would be no way out, only through. The first three days dragged on and on as I slept and slept and finally, for the first time in months, I felt this terrible grinding and twisting in my stomach called hunger. What a strange feeling to feel hunger for the very first time in ages. It was a painful feeling and not one I welcomed. The pain was so strong that I can keenly remember it. I was sweating buckets and I felt wide awake but in a weird state of twilight all at the same time.

I had been in a heightened state of awareness for so long and now I felt continually dull and asleep. I slowly and steadily shifted down into a depressed state. Even as the days passed into more than a week and I came out of the endless sleep phase, I felt that I would never fully recover my mental faculties. I felt completely and totally stuck in my dumbness. With Crystal, I felt sharp and alert and clever but now I was passive and insipid. I felt as though I would never again produce an intelligent thought. Despair started to grip me until I jumped in my car and went for a drive, a test drive of sorts. Now that I was awake enough and no longer suffering from a withdrawal paralysis, I could get around. This was dangerous though. If I wanted my old friend back, I knew just where to find her. She was calling my name. It would be so easy to get back to my old self and feel alert and awake again.

Although I did not recognize it at the time, I can look back and see how an unseen force and an unseen arm sustained me through a recovery that I walked through apart from human assistance and companionship. I managed to quit meth cold turkey. I cannot emphasize enough how powerful our God is to reach the unreachable. There is always hope. After I had been off meth for two weeks, I decided to tell my mother what I had been going through.

I walked the familiar walk down my mother's hallway

into her bedroom, a walk I had done a thousand times in my life. Sometimes I made the walk because of a nightmare as a little girl and, sometimes, I made the walk because I just wanted to be with my mother. I loved her. I will always love her. Now, as a young adult, I was walking down the long hallway to her room to tell her that, for the last year, I had been using meth. This was a strategic decision to tell her after I was already clean. As a further demonstration of how much I lacked any sort of decision making faculties, what I needed most I feared most and avoided most. I was intent on avoiding any type of recovery program. I could do it myself.

I sat my mother down on her bed and said, "I need to tell you something." Her face drained of all blood and turned even paler than before, "Please tell me that you aren't pregnant?"

"No! No!" I quickly exclaimed.

"Phew!" My mother relaxed knowing that, as long as I was not pregnant, she could handle anything I said.

"Mom, I have been using meth." I hung my head.

She leaned in as if she did not hear me. "You've been doing what?"

"I have been using meth." I said a little louder.

"Oh." She looked bewildered. "What does that mean?"

Are you serious? After all the suffering and everything I have been through the last couple of weeks and my mother does not even know what meth is. Unbelievable! I wanted, at the very least, a pat on the back for getting clean all by myself but there would be none of that.

"Mom! Meth is a drug! I have been on drugs! I am a drug addict."

She sat there staring at me like a deer in the headlights. I went into mother mode toward my mother. She really had no idea what was going on with me or how to help me or anything to do with me. I was on my own so completely that even I had underestimated just how on my own I was until now.

"Don't worry, mom. I'm off it now. I got clean. I'm not using it anymore but I just thought you should know."

"Is that why you are always stealing from me and asking me for money?"

"Yeah. But I am better now."

"Well, okay. As long as you're off it now." She was done talking about it. The continual push and pull between us. She, always wanting to talk about things that I could not care less about, and me, wanting to talk about things she hated to discuss. A round peg in a square hole.

That was so anticlimactic and easy compared to how I thought it would go. I felt a little defeated and disappointed and relieved all at once. I had worked up such an image in my mind of the reaction that would come but, as usual, my mother was numb and not able to deliver the support that I was looking for. It took her a while to absorb what I was saying. Maybe she would say she was panicking on the inside and delivering a cool and calm state of grace or maybe she would say that she never knew how bad it really was. Either way, every part of who I was at nineteen now turning twenty was crying out for her help. I was not living life but life was passing me by. I was not only being passed by and passed over but I was losing time.

While other kids were going to college and preparing for the rest of their life, I was gaining a knowledge of the streets and becoming a violent criminal and an addict. Again and again, I put my "freak-flag" out to fly for my mother to observe and do something with. I flew those colors like the white flown in the midst of heated battle. I surrender, but to who and to what, I did not know. "Where do I go for healing? Where do I go to get back on track? What do I do, mom?" But she was lost too. The blind-leading-the-blind march soldiered on and I was alone and broken in a world that kicks the ones who are down. There is no mercy for the weak in this world. If Darwin was right about one thing it was this, in this world, the ones to thrive are those fit to survive. I was emotionally handicapped and thus, I was ever the wounded gazelle on the African plain, totally vulnerable to the roaring lions.

One of my favorite parables is the parable Christ told in Luke 11. It is such practical advice for those of us that get involved in things that we should not. Jesus in no way makes excuses for sin but He understands our weakness and He gives us mercy, escape, and a better way. He tells the story of an unclean spirit coming out of a man and when that habit, behavior, or thing is finally gone then come seven more spirits that are worse than the first and "the final state of that man is worse than the first." This was always my condition. I would clean up my behavior and chase out one evil behavior to make room for that which was even more evil. Yes, I quit Crystal but I was left depressed and very low and the next best thing to fill the void was alcohol and the final state of the alcohol use was far worse than Crystal ever was.

The alcohol numbed me completely and I drank until I often blacked out and could not remember how I got home. I am ashamed to write that I often drank and drove myself home from parties. I would tell myself that I was being "careful" as I would close one eye to stop my eyes from seeing two roads instead of one. Instead of a state of hyperactivity and paranoia, I swung to the other side of the paradigm and I was sloppy and careless. You can always tell a drunk by their car. My car's side mirror had popped off when I sustained a case of the "bumper cars" in a parking lot. In one single day where I started off with Jack Daniels, I got myself into two minor car accidents. I was slipping and sliding on the shale of rocky bottoms. I was going to dig down into rock bottom to find the earth beneath it. I was intent on making my grave in the pit of the inferno. I found myself wanting to die.

I will never forget the night I said the most regrettable and voidable words, words that were expensive to Christ and cheap to me, words that I could never take back, but words that only He could undo for me. I had spent the night at a party. I was buzzed but not fully drunk yet. It was pitch black outside and I was unusually early as I turned up the long road to head up the hill to my childhood home. This road was a straight road that you could easily race down and many people did. That night the road was empty and I could let go of the wheel of my car and hit the gas. I rolled down my window as I accelerated and let the cool night air pour into the car. I was so angry at God. I hated Him for allowing my family to fall apart and the tears rolled down my cheeks as I remembered what it was like to be an innocent child and have a sense of family. My family was gone, I was no longer a child, and I was so far away from innocence. I longed to be innocent again and, yet, I was so evil.

My sense of dirtiness pressed in on me. Instead of recognizing this for what it was, the work of God's immutable law held up to me like a mirror, I felt my guiltiness and I ran away from God like Eve of old. I shouted curses against God into the night. Not only that, as I rounded the corner on to Mountain View, I screamed a pledge of my soul to Satan. That night I audibly renounced my God and asked Satan to take control of my life, take my soul, and kill me.

Every time I thought I had sunk to all new lows, I was shocked by my ability to sink even lower. That night I went home and cut myself for the first time. It was this amazing release and watching the blood flow down my arms was like a drop of blood in the water to a shark. It became a test of courage to me. Was I brave enough to sink the knife in deeper? Could I take the pain? Was I strong enough to die? I would yell, cursing at myself, as I lifted the knife and dug it into my own flesh. "You deserve this," I would say.

Cutting one's self is along the same lines as an eating disorder. One feels this buildup of anxiety that only cutting will relieve. What I started that night with one cut would follow me everywhere and, as weird as it is, cutting became an addiction. There were nights when, under the moonlight, I would utter occult incantations and raise my arms up with a knife and slice my arms above me.

How disturbing and grotesque to think about now but, then, it was my penance and my self-flagellation like Martin Luther with his whip. If someone hurt my feelings then I hurt me too. If I were rejected then I added physical pain to my emotional pain. If I wanted to get attention then I played Russian roulette to get it. Whenever I was drinking alcohol, I would descend into a fit of rage or emotional outbursts and all of this would culminate with the evening's ritual of steadily slashing away at myself. Most of these were small slits of my wrist but I was working my way up to the big slash that would end it all. Satan had taken control. Wherever he takes control, there is pain and suffering, wounding of the body and spirit, and an obsession with death. "But he who sins against me wrong his own soul; All those who hate me love death." Proverbs 8:36.

Chapter 20

Tug-of-War

One night, I became visibly possessed for others to see. Some of my friends were over at my childhood home and we were all hanging out in the garage. One such individual was known to speak to the dead and be a devout satanist. He had carved a swastika into his forehead to be just like Charles Manson and a pentagram was boldly tattooed on his chest. I was sitting on the old garage couch and several of us sat lazily looking out the garage door at the view from my childhood home. The sun was setting and I sat, watching the cool colors fade, while holding an old acoustic guitar that usually sat on a guitar stand gathering dust. I longed to play guitar but I was never any good at it. I messed around a few times and learned a few chords but I never dedicated myself to it to learn any more than a few basics.

That evening, in the presence of my friends, I asked Satan to use me to play the guitar. That was the last thing I remember. I went into a trance-like state and I lost track of time. When I came to, I looked down at my throbbing fingers to see that my fingertips had been cut by the sheer force of the guitar strings. Bright red blood covered the fret board. I was immediately alarmed by the lapse of time and I was scared by all the blood from my fingers that now throbbed. My friend, the satanist, was slowly clapping his hands with a look of astonishment on his face.

"What happened?" I exclaimed with fright.

"Dude! You just played the guitar for almost an hour like you were Elvis or some sort of professional blues guitarist. I never knew you could play like that."

"Really?" I nearly shouted in an excited voice. "Did I really play the guitar?"

"Yeah, dude. You were rocking out."

I was positively thrilled that I had harnessed such an amazing power. I could not wait to share this new talent with my other friends. I was filled with a strange kind of energy and I wanted to quickly control whatever power this was so I could play the guitar like this again. But, I did not play the guitar like that again and I did not control the power either. Instead, the power controlled me.

I often felt a strong force driving me to the local graveyards and, on occasion, I would sleep in the graveyard. How scary it must have been for the graveyard attendants to arrive at work in the morning and see a scary figure, all in black, sleeping in the graveyard. I simply played it out in my mind that I felt more at home with the dead than with the living. I believe that, wherever there is a demonic stronghold, there is a fascination with death. In Christ, we have life and, by sin, we die. To live focusing and fascinated by death is to live without hope. It is the father of lies that tells us we are hopeless. "Satan is ready to steal away the blessed assurances of God. He desires to take every glimmer of hope; but you must not permit him to do this. Do not give ear to the tempter, but say, 'Jesus has died that I might live.'" *Steps to Christ* 53.

The night of the following Halloween I started to understand the evil that I was playing with. I dressed that night as myself, a satanic dominatrix. I wore all black and a long, black, form-fitting, hooded robe, tall, black, combat boots with long, black gloves, a whip holstered at my side, spiked bracelets, and a belt that had metal chains and spikes. It may have been Halloween but I wore this kind of outfit almost every day now. At least, today, it was somewhat socially acceptable to wear what I was wearing. I was now a full-time soldier in the army of darkness. It was not unusual for me to fly into a demonic rage. During one such rage, I tore apart a Bible and used my own blood to stick the pages of the shredded and desecrated book to the walls of my room. I was Legion. I was the dwelling place for all manner of devils.

That Halloween night, my car had broken down and I had no problem hitchhiking my way from Yucaipa to Beaumont. It was dangerous on Halloween to be hitchhiking as a young twenty-year-old girl but, at this point, even if a serial killer had picked me up, it is a toss-up to say who would have actually been more evil or in the most danger. I hitchhiked my way to a party that my friend, the satanist, was having. This party was a huge gathering place every Halloween. All manner of activities went on there from drinking to séances. This particular Halloween, Max had invited a lot of his friends who were younger and more into the rave scene rather than the gothic scene. Sadly, there was a cornucopia of about one hundred colorful young people gathering to celebrate the day of evil.

At a particular point in the evening, I met Layla. Layla was the satanist's girlfriend. She really did not like me much at the time because of the amount of time her boyfriend spent partying at my house. She was jealous of me and she cast me witchy stares across the party. I hated the tension between us. I had no plans to ever date her boyfriend because he was not someone that I was attracted to in the slightest. I was so lonely for love that I desired a good girlfriend, a relationship that seemed to be the unicorn in the forest to me, rather than yet another boyfriend.

Every day for years now, I felt the chaos roaring within and I longed to soften the hurt, if only a little, with human companionship. I found myself wanting her friendship. Like seeks like. I crossed the party and I walked up to her and introduced myself. I knew that she was a Wiccan witch. The satanist had told me that he was terrified of his girlfriend and the powers that he thought she had. As terrifying as he was, he was childishly afraid of his big bad girlfriend. He told me how he would fasten armor to his chest at night or else he could not sleep knowing that his girlfriend might stab him with a knife at any point during his sleep. I knew how evil I was so to think of anyone being more evil than I, frankly, terrified me. My lack of trust in myself was all too easy to project on to others.

I knew that I was capable of any and all evil so I approached one labeled more evil than I with great caution. I slowly ventured toward Layla who was dressed in a Victorian vampire costume. She looked especially wicked this evening. Her hair was dyed jet black which contrasted against her white skin and made her appear gaunt and dead-like. She had bright blue eyes that only added to the look of extremes that she capitalized upon to look rather terrifying. She was suspicious of me but she quickly melted under my disarming smile and attitude of cautious respect. I was like a submissive cat exposing the underside of my belly to show her that she could be dominant if she so desired. I was working so desperately to communicate to her that I was not a threat.

The alcohol flowed so freely that night that I cannot remember exactly what we talked about or how the conversation ramped up to human sacrifices and blood drinking but it did. The suggestion was made, and I am sure that it was my suggestion, that we should cut my arm and drink my blood. If I could enlist another's assistance to cut into my flesh, I could forego the typical self-hatred I endured when I failed to cut my own arm deeply. I felt like such a weakling when I could only scratch the surface. Before this, I had never had a friend to cut with. It felt like Layla was my soul friend. She understood the level that I was on and she recognized herself in me. We were like two forces combining and we watched the entire party separate themselves from us and move away from the two girls that found comfort in death and evil.

I hardly noticed everyone scooting away from the two of us until Layla pulled out a sharp knife that she had on her person and held it up to stab my arm. There was a sudden gasp from those attending the party as she drew the knife down to make a deep incision into my flesh. The giant gash in my arm was huge and gaping and I could almost look down into it and see the muscle. I realized that I was cut badly but, to me, this was success. I had finally managed to draw the amount of blood that I was looking for. The partygoers stood back in horror as Layla bent low while holding up my arm, letting the blood run down past my elbow and straight into her mouth. "Mmmmmm, that's good," she said as the faces of the onlooking partygoers contorted with pure disgust at our antics. Perhaps Layla was doing it to shock the all-American teenagers that were attending the party but the reason I was doing it was for purely self-destructive reasons and, of course, to worship Satan.

After Layla and I put on our show for the onlookers, the party started to die out. Not that many people want to stick around and party with those that are truly disturbed. Layla had to work in the morning so she quickly jotted down her number for me to call her so we could hang out again. I was excited to hang out with someone else so much like myself but, for me, my evening was just beginning.

I would usually drink until I passed out. My alcohol use

was spiraling out of control. Others could see this but I thought I could operate just fine while intoxicated. I did not stop drinking until I passed out. The new cuts on my arm were very serious. Max looked at my arm and shook his head, "you had better go to the hospital. If it gets infected you could lose your arm." The satanist and his friends huddled around me all looking at the damage I had sustained. "I could go get a needle and thread and stitch it up for you." The thought of Civil War era medicine sent shivers down my spine. The satanist's house was very dirty and filled with all manner of creatures so I knew that letting him stitch up my arm was risking infection also. We all sat and discussed the possibility of my going to the hospital and we all decided that, if I went, I would surely get held on a 5150 and I did not want that. The satanist went to his bathroom and pulled out some expired Neosporin and some old ace bandages to conduct a sort of drunk makeshift first-aid. I was grateful for the attention.

The cuts on my arm were very serious injuries and the major cuts that I sustained that evening were deep enough, painful enough, and potentially permanently damaging enough that I felt ultra-satisfied with the damage that I had done to myself. It was a relief to have such serious injuries. My arm pulsated with the pain and, for the first time in several months, I felt a deep satisfaction and the urge to cut subsided and quieted for the first night in so long. I was able to slip into a long, drunken sleep without feeling the urge to slice and knick away at my own flesh. This was the pacification that I had been desiring for so long and I always knew that, if I cut deep enough, it would make me feel better. The urge to hurt myself could only be soothed when, at last, I was truly hurt.

Maybe it is hard for some to understand but those who self-harm are on a mission to quiet the beast within. It is a beast that is fed only on flesh and blood. Once the bodily harm is achieved, it is like a sense of euphoria washes over the body. I now had a physical manifestation of what my bruised and bloody heart felt like. Now I could show my mother just how damaged I was, how sick I felt, and how heartbroken I was. Now my arms looked like they had been put through a paper shredder so, for whatever reason, I liked to drive with my arm dangling out the window so people could see the bright red cuts up and down my arm. I was desperate for someone to notice my pain and to help me, even if it were a stranger.

As was typical, it was hard for me to go without a relationship to sustain me. I would accept any kind of love, even if it was a counterfeit for the real thing. I sat at the satanist's house and he usually had a bunch of friends over. One such friend was Draven, a six-foot-tall, blonde, blue-eyed, German young man who was a gothic punk. He was not particularly handsome but he was hilarious. He rose to the level of a seasoned comedian as he kept everyone around him in stitches. I adored his comic relief and I chose him to be my next boyfriend like a person chooses the mashed potatoes at a buffet. I had never dated anyone like him and I decided that he would be my next conquest. His larger-than-life personality drew me in, not to mention that he, too, had a fascination with death.

The one time that I had been in his room, I found it covered with pentagrams and death metal and punk rock posters. As usual, though, he seemed way too intelligent, too funny, and too disinterested in a girl like me. "I must proceed with caution so that I do not get rejected," I told myself. I could not handle anything remotely near rejection these days. I was spending all of my time away from home and at the satanist's house and I did not want to ruin a good thing by messing things up with the satanist's friend.

Draven lived across the street from the satanist. It was easy for him to run home and come back again whenever he needed to. On a cold and rainy November night, I went out to meet him on the street. I stood there waiting, in the cold and the mist, for Draven to appear on his way back from his house. I saw him hop the fence and come toward me on his way back to the satanist's house from his house. My stomach tightened because I knew that I was going to declare my feelings and could potentially seriously embarrass myself.

"What are you doing out here?" He said in a cool nonchalant voice. The chains that dangled from his spiked belt jingled as he walked. He had an oversized, soft, all black hoodie on and he looked cuddly to me. I surprised him by throwing my arms around him to hug him and I said, in a very girlish and all too simple line, "I really like you!" This surprised Draven and the ultra-cool facade that he carried melted into the real guy that he was. He said in a very kind voice, "well, I like you too," and he hugged me back under the soft yellow glow of the street lamp outside the satanist's house.

The raindrops were illuminated under the light and the soft rain was a little softer and the light a little brighter that night. My stomach was a flurry with new love and, like an addict taking a hit of their preferred drug of choice, I was sucking in all the love endorphins I could get. I took a step back out of our embrace to look Draven in the face and he surprised me with the unexpected boldness of a kiss. The darkness in me attracted the darkness in him and one cannot underestimate the attraction toward physical affection because I was so lonely and in so much pain.

It is really a toss-up as to whether Draven really did like me or simply decided, then and there on that rainy night, that he would accept my offer of a relationship. I personally think that he never even looked my way until that evening. Maybe he thought I was out of his league. Many people wondered why I went for Draven and not someone else but I liked Draven and, that night, Draven decided that he liked me too. He came across like a lost puppy dog. The only problem was, like me, Draven had a drinking problem and, when he drank, this puppy dog became a pit bull. Draven could get incredibly moody when he drank and he would say the kind of things to me that I found it very difficult to recover from. There was something else in Draven that I found endearing, like an underdog, and very, very safe. Draven had a medical disability that prevented him from ever having sex.

Draven's mother was a meth addict when she was pregnant with him and she struggled on and off with drug addiction after she had him. He was born with deformities and had some health conditions that he was very hush-hush about. He told me that there were times, as a little boy, when he remembered sleeping on his mother's friends' couches while she did drugs. They sometimes had nowhere to stay. He grew up with an addict and now he was dating me. It would be an understatement to say that Draven had demons that he wrestled with. There would be times that he would just sit for hours with a sneer on his face. Like most comedians, there is the funny side and then there is the dark side.

When Draven indulged in his darker side, he, too, would cut himself. We never did this together but we knew what the other one did. The thing about Draven was that he was always like water, slipping though my fingers. When we were together and he gave me all of his attention, we were a happy couple. When he was away from me and with his friends, he could not care less if I existed. He would not answer my calls. He would disappear for days. He would take calls from his ex-girlfriends. He was elusive and I could not figure him out. I wanted to pin him down and be with him. I felt safe with him but so did other girls and his friends loved him. I was in a constant competition for his affections and I found it positively revolting that I fell too quickly for someone like this, again.

The appeal of witchcraft is that the power is said to be all one's own harnessed power. There is no dependence on God or need to yield to the Holy Spirit. I could charge ahead and make things happen for myself. Christianity puts this on its head by stating that all of our strength and power comes from God in the person of Jesus Christ. Witchcraft and spiritualism are all about controlling life through the power within one's self. The two philosophies are, of course, totally different. Christianity is a total surrender of control and power in Christ.

I wanted Draven to be all mine and I would use witchcraft to accomplish this. There are various things that witchcraft offers in the way of casting love spells and, in my mind, they were working. I was addicted to Draven and I did not want him to reject me. I knew that, if I was going to get Draven to feel for me what I felt for him, I would have to play it more cool. He was like most men. He detested needy, demanding, helpless, always available, and desperate girls. He liked me best when I could not care less if he liked me. So began this push and pull, this game, between Draven and I of who could hurt the other the most.

I truly enjoyed being treated badly. I enjoyed it when others came to me and said how concerned they were about how Draven was treating me. Draven would get drunk and publicly lay into me and call me names. He was the quintessential male chauvinist pig. He said things that shocked all of the other guys there who halfway expected me to haul off and slap him but I never did. I knew that Draven held a rage against women so I excused and enabled his behavior because I knew that Draven also excused and enabled my behavior.

When things were good, they were good. Draven and I would smoke pot together and then cuddle under a blanket and watch a movie and eat food. We would laugh and giggle at nothing. Sometimes, it would be like being with your very best friend for days. We had inside jokes. We liked the same movies and television shows and I enjoyed cooking for Draven which is always a plus to a guy. Sooner or later, someone would knock on his door and that someone would usually be a friend of Draven's and then he would be pulled away to go drink and, when he came back or if he came back, he was angry and withdrawn. He would kick me out of his room to go sleep on the couch.

One night I dared to knock on his room door when he was in such a mood. I knew that when he blared *Nirvana* while in a drunken state, nothing good came of it. I carefully cracked the door and saw Draven sitting in an arm chair that was placed by his bed. He was staring off into space, just letting the loud and obnoxious noise surround him like a warm blanket, and he had no expression on his face. He hardly noticed that I had cracked the door so I just watched him from my vantage point. He had been drinking for days. Above his head, I saw a hole in the wall and wondered why he had been that angry.

I saw that Draven had various weapons out on his table and I felt too scared to come any further so I closed the door. I was too afraid to ever ask him if he were "okay." It was too unpredictable. He was too unpredictable. We were both volatile when in that state. A part of me understood exactly what he was going through because I often experienced the same level of depression. It was a kind of brokenness that only broken people can understand. The isolation, the need to be alone, the anger, the hurt, the heartache, the longing for more. I sat on the couch at Draven's house. In fact, I often slept on his couch in his living room like a devoted pet dog not wanting to leave his master but mine was not devotion, mine was self-preservation. I felt safer at Draven's house amidst the darkness than at my childhood home. I would do anything to avoid going back there. On occasion, I would slink back home to wash my clothes or to pick up more clothing to stash in my car.

In my zeal to completely avoid being home, I had taken up Layla on her Halloween night offer to give her a call and "hang out." I cannot remember the first time we hung out because, whenever the first time was, it became the next day and the next day and we never stopped hanging out from that moment on. When I was not with Draven, I was with Layla and, when I was not with Layla, I was with Draven. "Birds of a feather" truly do "flock together." We were so alike and she saw in me a softhearted and struggling person and I saw a dark side of Layla that attracted me to her. She was nice to me but not to be mistaken for a kind person. She worked at a local Denny's diner as a waitress by day and, by night, she was Medusa or an evil witch.

She enjoyed all things evil and the best way to describe her appearance is the spitting image of Marilyn Manson some days and Lily Munster other days. She and I were the epitome of the kind of people you do not want your kids to hang out with yet, we found each other. A rebel seeks out the company of other rebels. I had found my other half. Around her, I never had to be embarrassed about my slashed-up arms or the fact that I was indiscriminately sleeping around with guys. She simply accepted me and wanted to hang out with me. I was happy to have a friend that was not a guy. For once, it was nice to have a female friend. Almost every day, when she got off work, I could count on the fact that she would be calling me to go get a bottle of liquor and get drunk and high that night and every night. She was my home girl who was down to fight if need be to defend me and, fight, we did. We got drunk and we were a menacing, dark force to be reckoned with.

At Draven's house, I had struck up a kinship with his mother. She was a recovering meth addict too but, sadly, I would often observe her relapse right back into meth use. She would get high and want to talk or she would stay in her room and not come out for a few days. She dated an American Indian man and he often gave her money which she used to get drugs and go to the casino. Despite her drug and alcohol use, she was a kind woman and she could see that I was a young girl who was hurting so she, in a way, took me under her wing. She was the first woman who really showed me a firm and guiding hand in my twenties.

At this point, I was grateful for anyone to take an interest in me. My mother, before she met Dre, was off dating this guy and that guy but, when she met Dre, she became engrossed with Dre and no longer had time for her children. She was swept up into a whirlwind romance that included lots of nights out on the town and motorcycle trips. My mother had no time for me or my little brother who was still living at home. If I wanted to see my mother, I had to see Dre and watch my mother play the girlfriend game. My mother was so intent on securing Dre as hers that, to have me around grimacing and rolling my eyes at her fake facade and her dating marketing mode, was a total nuisance so I clung to Draven's mom like a pseudo-mother.

Most of my suicide attempts were a cry for attention but there were a few suicide attempts that were serious. When I was alone and able to think, the hopelessness gripped me like a vice. I saw no way to make my life better. I was spending every day high or drunk and, any kind of vision of what life could be, had faded. I was a dead flower waiting to turn back to dust. I felt that I had missed any chances that I might have had. The friends that I knew with families seemed to have so much more potential than I did. "Potential and success were not for girls like me," I bemoaned. "Whatever success I had would be because I was with someone who had it, not because I could earn it myself." There were times when I just could not see through the haze or the grayness of life. My sins, so heavy when not nailed to the cross, were nailed to me and it overcame me.

I had amassed a small supply of psychiatric medication from my teen years and up. I had been misdiagnosed with bipolar disorder at eighteen after Jacob and I had broken up. The psychiatrist who had diagnosed me had since lost his medical license which did not surprise me at all. He dosed me up on both lithium and Depakote without ever drawing my blood to check my levels in order to monitor my kidney and liver function. I was thrown on a cocktail of medications until I could barely remember my name and I remember thinking that, whatever my psychiatric problem was, it was way worse when on the medication. I had full prescription bottles untouched and stored in my mother's kitchen.

This night, though years old, I downed an entire bottle of lithium and Depakote mixed with Jack Daniels and vodka. It still makes me nauseated to think of the mix. I sat in my bedroom listening to the darkest music known to man and I took the pills until my stomach could not contain any more and I resisted the urge to vomit so that my body would be forced to process the medication. I was alone and nobody was around which was dangerous because this was a very serious attempt to end it all. I had written my family notes on my computer and I was waiting to slip away when Draven called me. I told him what I had done and he begged me to drive to his house. "Drive?!?" I exclaimed in a whispery voice. "I can't drive right now. I can barely keep my eyes open."

That's when Draven made the very real threat, "If you don't come now then I will be calling 9-1-1." I grabbed my keys and staggered to my car with my cell phone in hand with Draven still on the phone walking me through every step. It was about two o'clock in the morning so the road was completely empty and I only had ten miles to go but every mile was a struggle and I had to pull over numerous times to close my eyes and recover. I would wake up five to ten minutes later and hear Draven yelling on the phone for me to wake up and drive a few more miles. At last, I pulled into Draven's apartment complex driveway and I saw Draven standing outside at the entrance waiting for me with the house phone in his hand. Finally. I put the car in park and I opened the car door and fell out of my car. Draven picked me up and brought me inside to his bed. He made me vomit. He woke me up every ten minutes to drink water but, mostly, he let me sleep. I slept for three entire days.

I remember waking up a few times during those days and seeing his face above me. He was watching me with concern and was worrying as to whether he had done the right thing by not taking me to the hospital. He woke me up to eat some food on the third day. I ate a little and went back to bed. My body was taking every blessed moment of rest to recover from the months and months of alcohol abuse and the overdose of pills. I was blessed to be alive. When at last I could form coherent sentences, I realized that I had dodged a huge bullet. I was alive.

I had failed in my attempt to leave this earth but I was happy to not be dead. I thought of my son and how little I had seen him in the last few months and I missed him so badly that my arms ached to hold him. He was the only real thing in this life to me. I was seriously failing at being a mother and I knew it. I hated myself for it but I was stuck in a vicious downward spiral of drug use and hurting myself. I vacillated between whether my son would be better off without me around or if I should try harder for him. It was a constant tug-of-war.

Chapter 21

"Blow!"

As the cold weather melted away into a cool California spring, I started to feel a smidgen more encouraged about life. I knew that I had a large check coming again from my father's estate and the future prospect of having money again without Crystal eating it all up in a month was something to look forward to. The large amount of money I received never lasted very long so I was considering ways, in my immature and crippled way of thinking, that would make this check last a little longer than the last one. Every time I received my check, my mother would take a cut. She said it was money that I owed her for lists that she kept against me. Things like gas and clothes and whatever else she kept track of would need to be paid back when my check arrived. If there were any hope of going to school, it was dashed when I would see a quarter of my check go to pay my debts for the last year. "I never have enough money for school," I lamented and, with that, I would give up. But this year I was going to change all that. I was going to go back into the drug dealing business and quadruple my check. What could possibly go wrong?

This year, I had a plan. I did not share my plan with anyone for fear that reality would somehow get a hold of me. I wish I had. This was before any amount of marijuana was legal. You had to know a drug dealer who had a good supplier to get large amounts of chronic. I took thousands of dollars from my father's estate and I "invested it" in marijuana. I bought an exorbitant amount of chronic, bought the necessary baggies to sell various quantities of marijuana in, and bought a scale.

Just like that I was back in the drug dealing business again. I had been out of the business for a year now and I missed the wheeling and dealing of the street life. Mostly, I missed the kind of power that comes with dealing. I enjoyed being a cutthroat, female dealer and the shrewdness that comes when one dances with the devil. It was a beautiful arrangement because I was not a big marijuana smoker so I knew I would not use my own supply like the last time I dealt. I was really looking forward to seeing the return on my investment and I let all my friends know that I was in business. Where I lived, as in most other places, there was a flourishing demand for marijuana.

Part of dealing is the mission of having something to do. It is like having a very social job. People are always calling you and you are always invited to the party because you are the weed dealer. Layla and I traveled all over together helping me "slang" my weed. We were rolling together like original gangsters and, that particular evening, we were feeling our gangster oats and picked up a bottle of gin and juice. I had received a call from a friend on the other side of town who needed to buy some weed but he did not have a car. Although I was pretty buzzed, I obliged and Layla and I got in my car to go carry out our business.

When we walked into my friend's house, a dirty, little, two-bedroom house in downtown Beaumont, he was in the kitchen cracking open a bottle of Southern Comfort, a sweet-flavored whiskey. Because of its sweetness, it is a whiskey that often gets consumed rapidly and in large quantities. I always had to be really careful with Southern Comfort because it was one of those alcohols that I could drink an entire bottle of without giving it a thought. Layla was not very fond of this particular friend of mine but business was business and I had a ton of weed to sell that week. We took a seat on his couch in his front living room and I whipped out the little bag containing the strongest smelling marijuana that the rich climate of California and Mexico can provide. I kept the bag of weed inside a dark bag which I hid on the floor behind the driver's seat of my car. I was always afraid of getting robbed so I only carried smaller amounts on my person.

My friend seated himself, looked over at the weed, opened the bag, and smelled the telling aroma of chronic. "Oh! That's strong."

"Yup! And I added a little extra for you too." That was a lie. I was trying to make money not run a charity. Although, for Layla who smoked marijuana nearly every day of her teenage life, she never paid. I fooled myself into thinking that I was not dipping into my own supply but Layla certainly could smoke for the two of us. Some people say that marijuana is not addictive and, normally, I would agree but then I met Layla. When she did not smoke marijuana, she was moody and full of rage. I would make her smoke just so I could calm her down. A couple of times we nearly got into a fight because she was so irritable when she did not smoke. Maybe she was always that way or maybe she was that much more irritable without the marijuana.

I could sense Layla's level of irritation rising as she rolled her eyes and sighed in my direction. I giggled a little as Layla made mocking gestures at my friend, our customer, behind his back. I always enjoyed that, wherever Layla and I went, we had our inside jokes that no one else knew about. I knew what she was thinking and I knew her sense of humor, the hallmark of a close friendship. Over and over she kept making faces at my friend, the customer, and I knew that her patience was just about exhausted. She was just like a little toddler throwing a tantrum. The only thing that would help her mind would be to remove her from the situation. If she did not like someone then she simply did not like them and there would be no changing her mind which is what made our friendship so strange.

My friend, the customer, had just been released from jail and he was craving some female company. He failed to read Layla's feelings but assumed she felt warm and friendly toward him and, thus, he kept flirting with her which only made things worse. It was a powder keg situation just begging for a spark. I did not really enjoy my friend much either but I felt bad for him with his stint in the the slammer, though I did not want Layla to get too upset and pull out her knife on him. I was not up for that tonight. I just wanted to make that fast money that comes with selling marijuana.

We stayed long enough to take a few shots of Southern Comfort, sell our weed, get the money, and be on our merry little way. We got back in my car and headed toward the satanist's house. Layla was sitting in the passenger seat as we be-bopped to some hip hop rap music. The thought of nights like these always caused me great anxiety. You wake up in the morning and you never know if this will be a day that is as ordinary and forgettable as any other day that fades into the past or if this will be the day that changes your life forever. This day, that had now turned into night, was one of those days that will never be forgotten.

One choice or one action is always the catalyst to a lifetime of regret. It is a sobering thought. A favorite Christian speaker of mine says that life's major struggle for men is the battle of lust and we, as women, will battle the temptation to fear. It is a fearful thing to consider that our lives and the lives of our loved ones can be extinguished in a single second. To sit and think on the fragility of life is to be humbled. I would usually wash away all my fears with alcohol. I had liquid courage or confidence in a can though this never lasted.

The only thing that can truly stand against the fear of circumstances is the security that comes in Jesus Christ. "I can face uncertain days because He lives," is the only calm in the midst of life's crises. This night, all the fearful burdens that I carried on my own back would come to fruition and the worst part, what is always the worst part, is when I brought the terrible consequences upon myself. I deserved more than what I received. I deserved so much more.

I slid into my car and put away my $60 in twenties into my pill box purse and I threw my weed in the back, not caring if it was hidden properly with the rest of my weed stash behind my seat. Layla turned up my stereo system to a deafening volume. I still had my subwoofer hooked into my trunk so my car vibrated with the bass beat.

I was that person that had the annoying, low-riding car that drove through your neighborhood in the dead of night with my bass speakers booming and breaking the peaceful silence into small sleepless little pieces. The dogs barked and the babies cried when I drove through neighborhoods but I did not care who I disturbed because life was all about me, my fun, and my entertainment.

Here I would like to note the importance of the music I was listening to. Music is a trigger. Music is, for most people, a religion. It was created to be a form of worship and prayer. Each song has a memory attached to it, the anthems of my life and experiences. I will never forget when Layla turned on a particular song by Lady of Rage. It was the kind of music that makes you feel like a boss. It is the kind of music that makes you want to pull out your nine and cap anyone who messes with you. I was invincible. I could fly. I was the dealer again and back on top.

We pulled away from my friend's house and hit top speeds to make our way back to the satanist's house. Back at his house, we were supposed to watch a bunch of heavy metal bands do their band practice. Band practice is just not complete without two goth girls to bounce to the beat and the screaming. Back at the satanist's house, Layla had been encouraging me to date another guy named Nick so I could get rid of Draven. I was leery. It was one of Draven's best friends and, not only that, it was a close friend's baby daddy. I had never done that to another girl. I would not want any of my friends to date Jacob. That would be weird but Layla was sure that Nick and I would make a better couple than Draven and I. Plus, Draven was always ditching me and he would constantly call me to hang out and then would never show up. I would call Layla to cry on her shoulder. She would tell me to "man up" and get over it. She had known Draven for most of his life and she would tell me, "he is the biggest flake I have known! Break up with him!" I would try to break up with him and then, just like Erik, I would get depressed without a guy in my life and I would go running back to him.

Nick was a heavy metal guitarist in a band with the satanist. The bass player was my marijuana supplier. He was the real deal with an Escalade all paid for by marijuana. He had connections to Mexican drug cartels and the drug world on the local Indian reservation. He was ultra-paranoid too.

The bigger his marijuana business got, the more of a target he was for the local police department so he kept a police scanner in his house and had an evacuation plan in case they came for him. He was my weed supplier and he was very skeptical about trusting me. He did not think that I played it safe with my drinking and driving and he was afraid that, if I got caught, I would deliver him up on a silver platter for a lesser sentence for myself.

I was eager to arrive back at the satanist's house but the prospect of dating both Draven and Nick at the same time scared me. I was never very good at being a smooth operator. I was too sensitive to not get hurt by being so double-minded in splitting my affections between two people. It was either all or nothing for me. In between just would not do. I tried dating Nick just long enough to hurt myself and others and then thought better of it. I had sort of learned my lesson from the consequences born, or rather not born, from the Kane and Dillon situation. Breaking things off with Nick was no show of love for Draven but self-serving self-interest. I could not stand myself when I was disloyal but I could not stop myself from playing the field.

I knew that my occasional infidelity hurt Draven badly but I was hoping that it would get his attention and that, maybe, just maybe, he would try harder in our relationship. It was a dangerous game of the heart that I was playing and I thought to force my hand with Draven to make him change into the loyal and loving boyfriend I desired. I lived under the false delusion and sense of puffed up pride that many girls live under and commit to: I thought I could change my boyfriend and make him love me the way I wanted love but this is not love but self-serving gratification that masquerades as romance.

I wanted to fix my brokenness with another's brokenness and it never works that way without Christ. First, the kind of love that I needed was the kind of love that no man or woman can give. Second, to get love you have to give love and I had learned to give sex, not love. I was taught that love is gained by sacrificing self-respect and that it is a feeling based on the level of physical attraction. The more deluded I grew, the more base in my affections I became. I lost all sense of reason and possessed no womanly wisdom. Sin never stands still. It always gets worse and worse. I was getting worse by the day. I was continually evil and a rebel. God was about to wake me up and blow up my life. For some, it takes crisis upon crisis to come back to Jesus where we belong. I was in the dark and God was about to put me under pressures that would crack me open so He could shine His marvelous light into the darkness.

God uses the consequences of sin as the means whereby He pulls us back to Him. Some people look at the bad things in this world and say, "How can a loving God allow that?" First, I know from experience that nothing evil in this world is from God but from the enemy. Second, consequences from sin are the most loving thing that God can allow because our eyes are then opened to the pain of sin so He can take away our sin and we will desire it no more. Third, when we look around at the world and see what Satan has done, we will declare, "heaven is our home." We will have no earthly ties to separate us from the heights and depths of the love of Christ.

I proudly drove on the street, thinking that I was the ruler of my world, and chanting the words to the music. I needed to turn left into the satanist's long driveway. The road into his driveway was a major city thoroughfare and the speed limit was fifty-five. I was speeding along at far faster speeds than that. With an arrogance about life and the bass driving into my body like a force of a thousand drums, I noted an oncoming truck but thought I could make the left turn. I turned to Layla and said, "watch this!" Before she could exclaim, "No! You can't make the turn before that huge truck hits us!" I forcefully turned the wheel of my car to turn left right in front of oncoming traffic. I honestly believe that, at this point, I was totally under the control of evil spirits and that the plan was to kill me that night. I pictured that we would cut in front of the oncoming truck and race into the satanist's driveway as some sort of Nascar heroes I suppose. That is not what happened.

Maybe if I had been going a little faster, I would have made the turn but I was not. The impact was a sound that I will never forget. In fact, most people that heard it that night will not forget it either. People came out of their homes to check to see what was happening. Even months later, people would ask me about the accident because of the amazingly loud sound that this collision made. The airbags deployed and, to this day, if I hear the song by Lady of Rage, I can smell the smell of airbag powder being shot up my nose. My car was snapped in half.

Later, it had to be held together with ropes to even tow it away. Weeks after, I would pick up pieces of it half a mile down the road. The front windshield tented and glass shot into my scalp and into my face. The two of us were knocked unconscious by the force of the accident. The heavy metal band that was practicing at the satanist's house all ran out to see what that awful sound was. Yes, you could hear the accident over the sound of heavy metal.

My dealer came running out of band practice and heard the sirens of cop cars nearing. He saw my possibly dead body slung over the wheel of my car and he pushed my body aside to pull all my drugs out from behind the front seat of my car. He only cared about self-preservation. Although I was grateful, at the time, that he saved me from a drug charge of distribution with intent to sell, it did not matter to him if I were dead or alive, it was all about the drugs and saving his own hide.

When I regained consciousness, I picked up my sore head off the steering wheel and looked around. I was stunned and in shock but I knew what had just happened. Everything had happened in slow motion. I saw the glass break and slowly fly across my face taking bits of skin off my face. Small drops of blood flew by my face in beautiful hews of crimson and ruby red. The airbag had smacked me in the face and it was hot and had burned my arms with its white, chemical-laden powder. That life saving device is like a spanking to the irresponsible. It is hard and forceful but I am thankful for it.

I knew I was in trouble upon impact and I regretted my own sense of hubris in thinking that I could make that left turn. Worse than any feeling of physical pain was the regret that instantly filled me when I came to. It was now extremely evident that I was making very bad choices and I knew that everyone would now see just how messed up I was. I could no longer deny it and everyone around me could no longer deny it either.

At that moment, I felt like a plague on the earth and I wanted to be swallowed up by it. When I could, at last, think beyond the thoughts of my own body that was still somehow miraculously intact, my stream of consciousness turned to my friend. I looked over at her body lying limp and lifeless in the seat next to me. She was covered in windshield glass and smoke filled the air. The scene was positively horrific and movie-like. She had blood on her too. I touched the blood to see where it was coming from and that is when I realized that the blood was coming from me.

I slowly leaned over to shake Layla. "Layla!" I cried out with sudden tears. The thought that I had killed my friend filled me with a terror I cannot even now describe. It was a guilt that is not easy to recount. Then Layla coughed and sputtered and came to. I breathed a sigh of relief that she was alive. She was thankfully coming to and the tears were flowing, running down my face in no short supply. "I am so sorry, Layla!" I was crying and said, over and over, "I am so sorry!" The pride of life had been shattered and I was laid low. I knew I was in deep, deep trouble when I heard the cop cars coming but, in that moment, what I cared about was apologizing to my friend. I could hurt myself but it was more than terrible to hurt someone else.

The cop cars started arriving one by one. It was as if all of Beaumont had nowhere else to be. Then came the ambulance. I had been in accidents before so I knew that, if I went to the hospital or Layla did, the likelihood of me going to jail and catching more charges was high. My concern for my friend came to a sunset and my true character shone forth. I asked Layla not to go to the hospital for treatment of injuries so I would not be charged with bodily injury even though she was hurt. When the CHP arrived, I resisted the urge to run. I had seen many chases involving law enforcement and I knew that, if I ran, things would be worse for me.

I was overwhelmed by the stiff consequences of my actions. The lights, sound, colors, and shock I was experiencing caused a sensory overload so, when I was pushed to the ground and the cuffs clicked around my wrists, I did not even know or care. All I could do was stare at the mangled pieces of machinery that were formerly my car and wonder how I was still alive. I sat there in the driveway of the satanist's house on the ground and handcuffed. Cars were going by and staring at me in my shame and lack of freedom. I was then taken to an ambulance and examined. I lied and said I was fine. My face and wrists were pulsating. "I am fine," I whispered to the EMTs while still staring off into the direction of my car. The truth was that I was still incredibly drunk. I could not feel too much yet but it would hit me later like running full speed into a wall.

"Whoa! We need a breathalyzer over here," yelled one of the EMTs to the CHP officer. Busted. I hung my head in shame because everyone knows that it is very stupid to drink and drive. The line between right and wrong was so blurred now. My decision-making faculties were greatly impaired and, every time I got behind the wheel of a car, I was endangering innocent people but I never thought anything would happen to me. I never thought anymore, period. I needed the full force of the law to stop me like it did that night. This is why authority is so important. God uses consequences to save us when nothing else can. He uses the authorities, be it parents, cops, judges, pastors, bosses, and others to give us consequences to save us from ourselves and the downward spiral that we are on because He loves us too much to lose us without a fight to save us.

"Blow!" they said. I blew and I was more drunk than a skunk and only twenty years old. It was not even legal for me to drink which makes the penalties even stiffer. I had broken the law and the next words to register were, "you have the right to remain silent," and then my mind trailed off and I could not believe that invincible me was getting arrested.

I was going to jail. I was put into the back of a cop car. I was still looking at my car as we pulled away to drive back down the street from whence I had come. Things were so different now as the pride had been blasted off by a truck going over sixty miles per hour. What a difference a night makes in a person's attitude. I was now low, very low.

There is so much that was missing from that night. I found out later about the outraged man that was in the oncoming truck. He was injured and his truck was totaled. I would have to make restitution to him. How I managed to walk away from this accident can only be explained as a miracle. This thought was quickly sinking in as the CHP officer got in the squad car. As soon as he sat down in his seat, I began to sob and sob. I could tell that the CHP officer was a little annoyed but, mostly, he felt bad for me. Anyone looking at me could tell that I was a young girl who was totally lost.

"Why are you crying?" he inquired, knowing the answer but caring enough to ask anyway.

"I have just ruined my life!" I answered.

"Yes, you have."

"I have a son. He's only three years old. Do you know if this will make me lose custody?"

"I can't answer that for you." He replied.

"I was supposed to pick him up tomorrow morning."

"Well, that's probably not going to happen. You will be in jail tonight."

With those words, I started to sob uncontrollably. The mascara had run down my face and mixed with the blood from hundreds of tiny cuts. My face was now swelling with contusions to my cheek bone where my face had been violently thrust into the airbag and steering wheel. My wrist was starting to throb even more and my knees were painful from the impact. I was a sight to behold besides the fact that I was dressed in all black with tall black combat boots. I had glass all in my bloody and matted blonde hair and I smelled like a rotten tavern.

"Please don't take me to jail! Please don't take me to jail! Please?" I begged without reserve or any pride left. If I could have crawled on my knees or kissed the officer's boots, I would have but I was helplessly cuffed in the back of a squad car. I was beyond crying, beyond sobbing, at this point. I was wailing and begging him to have mercy on me. "If I go to jail I will never get my son back! Please?" I knew the freeway entrance was imminent. If the CHP officer turned right to go west on the 10 freeway, I knew that he would be taking me to the Riverside County Jail. If he turned left, I knew that I was headed to the CHP Office in Banning, California.

The turn came and the CHP officer, without a single

word, turned left and took me to the CHP Office in Banning. To say I was relieved is beyond comprehension. I cannot describe the relief that came, knowing that I was receiving the tiniest bit of mercy, even though I did not deserve it. I did not deserve any kindness at all but, somewhere in this CHP Officer's heart, I had struck a chord of sympathy. I am so glad that I did not go to jail that night. Although my wild days were far from over, I know that going to jail would have broken my spirit in a way that I could not handle at the time. God will never give us anything that will break our spirit.

Not going to jail hardly meant that my night was easy. I was ushered into the CHP Office and I was fingerprinted, photographed, and my blood was drawn. It was humiliating to be handcuffed to a metal pole in front of all these nice officers who were upstanding men. "Where had I gone wrong?" I thought. How does a little Seventh-day Adventist girl end up handcuffed in the police station and charged with driving under the influence and destruction of city property? Why was my life spinning totally out of control?

I will never forget sitting in the CHP Office, tethered to the bench, hanging my head, and trying to hide my face in shame while waiting for the lab tech to arrive to draw my blood. The officers made various comments about my all black dress and one officer came over and gave me a stern talking to about drinking and driving. I took it all in. I listened to every word. "I am going to change," I thought. "I am not going to get in trouble again."

"Hey! Call someone to come get you!" Come get me? I never thought that I would get to leave this place. I was stunned and surprised that I would get to go. I thought I would be held for at least a night but apparently not. "Who am I going to call?" I thought of calling my mother. "No, absolutely not." My mother was just newly married to Dre and it was made very clear to me that I was in the way of her matrimonial bliss. She had a new family and I was her disgrace. I was all together certain that, if I did call her, Dre would tell her to let me sit and rot because that was the kind of "tough love" that he taught her to wield against me. I did not need tough love at this point. I had just endured everything that the world can throw at a rebel girl like me and I was terrified and willing to change but totally ignorant of how to change. Who to call? Nick? No. Draven? Yes. I will go back to Draven.

When I called Draven, he did not hesitate for a second to come get me. He had heard the loud crashing sound of my accident and had seen me being taken away in the CHP squad car and his heart went out to me. He was there, in his black Mustang, only fifteen minutes later. I was un-cuffed and given a paper with my looming court date on it. I slid into the passenger side of Draven's car, happy that he was sober and driving. I felt like I never deserved to drive again after all that I had done. Draven started the car and I started to cry again. He reached over and grabbed my hand and we were quiet all the way back to his house. He got me some pain medication and some of his clothes to change into and then, once again, Draven put me to bed to sleep off my injuries and the pain from the long night of drinking and humiliation.

I crawled into Draven's bed and slipped into a deep, deep depression. I was again detoxing from the alcohol though I failed to recognize, at that time, that I had a drinking problem. I was totally oblivious to life and I had no knowledge of the where and the why of my emotions. I was totally numb. I had no self-awareness. Maybe you have met people like this who cannot seem to connect the chaos of their life to their own choices and rebellion. It is always someone else's fault and not their own fault. Living in this particular state of mind caused me to never go deep emotionally and look at why things were happening the way they were. A lack of personal responsibility will always cause mental illness and depression.

Chapter 22

Serial Killer

I was emotionally fragile. I felt that, if I were to talk to my mother and tell her that I had lost my son, lost my car, lost my freedom, and I was in trouble with the law, her condemnation could crush me. There I was in someone else's bed and there I stayed for a month. I shook, rattled, and rolled through the dangerous process of alcohol withdrawal which was far more painful than meth withdrawal. I slept and slept and slept some more. My mother would call and I would not answer. I simply fell off the face of the earth. Somehow my mother obtained Draven's home phone number and discovered that I was at Draven's home, not even ten miles from her. Once she discovered I was not dead but merely staying at Draven's house, my mother did exactly what I knew she would do upon finding out that I had totaled my car.

Layla pulled me out of Draven's bed to take me to get some clothes from my childhood home. Driving up that driveway to my childhood home caused a flurry of unwelcome emotions to wash over me. I longed for my son and I had a giant hole in my heart where every man I had ever been with had taken their cut of me. I walked up to the door and it was locked. Dre had my mother change the locks to the house and I was no longer welcome. I had come home to get some of my things that I had paid for with my own money but I was locked out. I do not blame them for locking me out although I would not lock my own child out when they are finally at the point of surrender. My only wish is that they would have locked me out much, much sooner before God had to use a life-threatening accident to save me.

I instantly knew that my behavior had led my family to turn their back on me. Using my cat burglar skills, I broke into my childhood home. I knew that I would only be able to take with me what I could carry. I was losing everything. At this point, if my mother had done an intervention, offered rehab, or something to help me get my life back on track, I would have taken it with gusto. There was no love behind that toughness. It was only the cold-shoulder to the extreme and I felt a keen sense of rejection from her. I knew that, more than anything, she had ejected me from her life so that I would no longer be an annoyance to her while she created a new family without me. I had never felt so lonely and ready for change in all my life.

I crawled through the window that I was able to get through and walked back to my bedroom. There, on my bed, I saw that Dre had raked up every cigarette on the lawn I had thrown there and had put it on my bed so that, if I came home, I would find no comfort in that life-size ash tray of consequences. Again, I cannot over-emphasize the importance of toughness followed by love. Toughness without love is just anger and that is what causes these types of addictions to begin with. They only pushed me further from my family.

They were the last people I would ever go to for help now and I needed help.

I understood that, most likely, my mother did not know what to do and, consequently, readily followed Dre's suggestions. Dre was not my father and his mean-spirited tit-for-tat demonstrations of vengeance did nothing to help me. If you have an addict in your life, you must be strong enough to love them home. Sometimes that will mean locking them out and sometimes that will mean picking them up out of the gutter. It never means giving them money or doing mean things to hurt them because, rest assured, they are already hurting. This is easier said than done but we must look to Christ as our model in how to treat the seemingly unlovable. Never give in and never surrender because God never gives up on us. I was ready for change but I had no one but my friends to help me and they were as bad off as I was.

I gathered whatever I could in a suitcase as the bitterness of being kicked out of my family started to sink in. I knew that I had wronged them terribly in many ways so I also knew that I deserved much worse than they gave me. It is much, much worse when you can see how you have caused this to yourself. More than anyone or anything, I hated myself. Even though I wanted to hate them, I could not. I loved my mother even more for having some gumption to do something about my addiction and bad behavior. I longed to stay at my home and be accepted and for some change in my life. How does a girl ever have any hope of becoming a woman without a woman to guide her?

Taking hold of my suitcase and every kind of garment that I could grip and get out the door before anyone came home, I walked away from my childhood home as a vagabond and a drifter. I was now homeless and knew that this meant that I could not see my son anymore without a place to live and this terrified me. I knew I was a terrible mother. The burden of raising my child was all on Jacob. It had been two months since I had seen my son and the pain of grief was like a sharp knife to the chest. "This is all too much to handle," I thought as I slumped down into Layla's car. I had managed to stay away from alcohol for a month. I was clear-headed and I was able to think of just what I had done to everyone around me and I was so overwhelmed. "Lets go get something to drink?" I said with my hands up on my head in desperate pain and feeling every ounce of rejection. I was rejected by my mother and now I was rejecting my son. The generations of sin were being passed down as a tightly held tradition.

"Yeah?" Layla said with her eyebrows raised in excitement at the possibility of having her drinking buddy back.

"Yes. I need a drink." I exclaimed with sorrow and defeat. "It's my twenty-first birthday soon anyway," I consoled myself with the fact that I would be the legal age of drinking as all people do when rationalizing sin.

My twenty-first birthday was a day to be literally forgotten. The day was spent binge drinking and I blacked out. Today, it is positively terrifying to me that I could black out and keep operating as if on auto pilot. The lights were on that night but nobody was home. My alcohol tolerance had been lowered since I had quit drinking for a spell. I was not physically prepared to drink the normal amount of alcohol that I typically consumed but I did not consider this. I was on a mission and that mission was to forget and numb the pain. Moreover, I had my court date the next morning and I was scared to death of facing the judge and going to jail.

Layla picked me up in the afternoon after she got off work and we drove through several cities, hitting up a number of bars on the way. We were at one particular bar when this stocky Italian man in his late thirties or early forties with dark hair, dark eyes, and a winning personality approached Layla and I as we slung back our beers at the bar.

"Well hello ladies! Can I buy you a drink?" Layla and I chuckled and scoffed at the typical pick-up line used to win our approval. We cast each other glances out of the side of our eyes. "Will we let him sit with us or not?" We could tell what each other was thinking just by our looks. If a guy appeared to be too wholesome or goody-goody, we would usually rudely dismiss him as "not our type." We both agreed that any guy who is not somewhat evil is not for us. "They just don't get what we're about," Layla said one night when we were discussing men.

This time Layla and I gave each other a knowing nod and let the Italian man take a seat beside us at the bar. We both knew that we would let him buy us drinks and food and then we would split and leave him with the bill. We would tolerate his chit-chat and overly flirtatious innuendos even though it made our skin crawl for free booze. Anything for free booze.

The man slid onto the bar stool next to me and I could smell his reasonably-priced cologne. His dark hair was slicked back. He was apparently a body builder. His muscles declared to the world that he spent an inordinate amount of time working out and maybe even taking steroids. He was, for all intents and purposes, a very handsome man but his football-looking exterior was not my style. I was totally into the antisocial punk rock and gothic lifestyle. If the activity or person was underground or at night and positively evil then count me in. Otherwise, I would pass but I could tolerate mid-level America for an hour or so and let the Italian man buy us one drink after another. First, we were drinking beers and then we graduated to cocktails and, before I knew it, I was taking shots of, you guessed it, Southern Comfort. The taste reminded me of a night not too long ago when I lost everything and the thought of it made me tremble with humiliation. Thinking of my court date the next morning, I felt like I had a secret shame and this made me more vulnerable.

It was time for Layla and I to move on to the next bar. The Italian man had worn out his welcome, despite the awkward amount of money he had just spent on us. I felt really bad that we were going to go to the bathroom and then never come back to the bar. "Let's go!" Layla pulled on my arm to pull me out of the door but I shook her off. "We can't just leave!" I snapped back with slurred speech. I went back to the bar where the Italian guy was seated waiting for us to return to the revelry. "We are going to go now. Thank you for the drinks."

"Oh? Just like that you guys are gone?" The Italian man seemed genuinely disappointed.

I was flooded with a sense of guilt, "Yeah. I'm sorry. It's my birthday and we're bar hopping tonight. But thank you!"

"Well hey! Let me get your phone number so I can at least call you and we can do this again?"

My gut said to say thank you and walk away but the social graces of the moment held me in place. Why do women always feel that they owe men beyond what the Still Small Voice instructs? I was always torn when it came to Draven. Yes, he had picked me up from the CHP office and took care of me the last month and that meant the world to me. He was my family. But lately, the burden of carrying me was weighing on him. I knew that he and his mother were kind of sick of me staying there. The tension was starting to rise and I was worried that I would have nowhere to go. I was at their mercy and I thought that, perhaps, I might need to start preparing backups to take me on. Against all my inward alarms, I gave the Italian man my phone number and then I walked away.

That night, Layla and I hit up two more bars. I had to be told the events of the evening because I had no recollection of my own. I started to black out around the second to the last bar we were at. I am actually very grateful for this because the last place we ended up at was a strip club. I ended up on stage but started a fight with one of the men at the bar and had to be carried out by security, kicking and screaming all the way. By the time Layla brought me back to Draven's, I was vomiting and in and out of consciousness. Again, Draven had to sit up with me all night in the bathroom to make sure that I did not aspirate and choke to death in my drunken stupor. In the wee hours of the morning, Draven finally brought me to bed so I could sleep it off.

I woke up late that morning to realize that I had missed my court date. With charges against me, I knew that I now had a warrant out for my arrest. The anxiety gripped me. I knew that I was only making things worse by not going to my court date but was I supposed to go smelling like the town drunk? No, I had made my decision to not attend my court date the night before when I started drinking and I knew it. I was going to do what I did best, avoid it all. With my terrible hangover and likely alcohol poisoning, I thought to recover by smoking a grip of marijuana that day. I was starting my twenty-first year with a bang. I was drunk, high, and wanted by the law.

But the day was just beginning. I could tell that Draven was planning something. "A birthday surprise? Likely," I thought with little to no excitement. I could care less. I was tired and discouraged by my present state of circumstances and was in the slump that one easily slips into after a night of total drunkenness. It was now a regular assurance that, when I awoke in the morning, my first thoughts would be of my son and this was like being awakened by the terrible agony of torture.

I knew that I was doing nothing to see him and, at the time, he was living with his dad in the same apartment complex. I was not sure how much his dad knew about me so I did what I did best, I avoided facing them both. But I ached for my son. Some nights I would cry myself to sleep and some mornings I would awaken to cut myself because I was, what society loathes more than anything else, a deadbeat mother.

I hated myself for abandoning my son the way my mother had abandoned me. My mother had also had a son, my beloved older brother from her earliest marriage, and she rarely saw him. He lived with his father on the other side of the country. She abandoned him when he was six or so and only saw him some summers. How history repeats itself. For so long I had ridiculously and proudly held my parenting in higher esteem than my own mother's and, now, I was on a cycle to be worse than my mother.

I was sitting on the edge of Draven's bed when he came into his room and was way too cheerful for my liking. "I have a surprise for you!"

"Oh?"

"Yeah! But you have to go with Layla for about thirty minutes to get it!" Draven had a big childlike grin on his face and he was practically jumping up and down with glee.

"Sure." Honestly, until I had figured out a way to see my son again, I could hardly justify being happy.

I walked out Draven's front door to see Layla waiting for me. "Hey! How are you feeling, drunky?" she shouted way too loudly. I winced at the sound of her voice. My head was pulsating with the pain of the hangover. I felt old, really old. I often wondered how much more my liver could take. I sat in Layla's car and heard all about the previous night. I was shocked and horrified at all the antics I was up to the night before. How can I not remember anything? I felt that I had violated myself or that I had somehow betrayed myself in letting "something else" run my body and dictate my actions. I did not want to hear about the night before. Then Layla told me that I had admitted to her that I was secretly a lesbian.

"What?!?" I yelled at her, suddenly paying close attention to the conversation.

"Yeah dude! You told me how much you hate men and how you are a lesbian."

I really did not know what to say. I could not remember anything. All I could respond was, "weird," and that was that. I felt emotionally exhausted and run down when Draven eagerly approached Layla's car. "Okay! I'm ready for you now!" He announced with excitement and a smile. I took in a deep breath and rallied to go see Draven's

surprise but I was not in the mood to care or be happy about
it.

Draven ushered me through the apartment door and
back toward his room. When he opened the door, I could see
that he had hung beautiful, Christmas-like lighting all over
his room. Perhaps if I had been in the mood to appreciate it I
would have said it looked magical and fantasy-like. I knew
that a lot of work had gone into this creation so I worked up
some enthusiastic "oohs and ahs" but my thoughts were on
my son. That is when I noted that Draven had dropped down
to one knee. What was this?

Draven had a very sweet and contemplative look on his
face as he recited all the reasons why he loved me, reasons
that even I did not believe. I was happy to know that at least
one of us loved me because I surely did not. "So," he pulled
out a little black jewelry box, opened it, and presented it
before me, "will you marry me?" I was totally and utterly
shocked. I was a little stunned by this turn of events. I
thought that maybe Draven was perhaps sick of rescuing me
but it seemed as though he was not. What would I do with
my son? Draven and his mom made it clear that they did not
really want my son living there with us. I cannot marry
someone and not have my child with me. This was my first
thought but my second thought was that, if I said "no," I
would have nowhere to go.

I really cared about Draven and I wanted to marry him
but I knew in my heart that it would never happen. In spite of

all that, I replied, "Yes! I will marry you!" With that, Draven slid the ring on my finger and we told our friends that we were engaged. I was willing to push my concerns aside to play house for a while. It was a nice fantasy to indulge in for both of us but we took no steps toward actually getting married.

I am not sure if it was the panic of being engaged and knowing that I did not want to get married that caused me to answer the phone a few days later but, I did answer when I knew, full well, that I should not have. It was the Italian man calling me to arrange a date. At first, I said, "no," because that was just the right thing to do. I had no idea who he was or anything and, staring at the ring on my finger, I felt satisfied with my decision.

Then Draven and I got into a fight the following day. Sadly, Draven started drinking and accused me of being controlling and not wanting him to hang out with his friends. We exchanged insults with each other and called each other names that would make a sailor blush. He decided to take off for the night, the entire night. I had no idea where he was or who he was with. I called and called his cell phone until I realized that his cell phone was in a drawer in his bedroom with me. I felt so sad that our little fantasy was shattering so soon. Every time we had a fight like this it was so over the top and dramatic that we both thought we would break up. Each time, we would get back together again after a brief or not so brief respite from each other. Was even our engagement going to be so? I knew that marriage, at least for me, was off the table.

Because of our fight, my resolve was weak. When the Italian guy called again, I answered the phone and accepted his invitation to go out with him. It was tricky because he wanted to go out the next evening. Draven had come home late that night after being gone all day and most of the night. I no longer had a car so the Italian guy had to pick me up from Draven's house. How would he pick me up without Draven seeing me take off with a super buff Italian guy? I gave the Italian guy strict instructions that, when he pulled into the apartment complex, he would pick me up on the opposite side of the complex where I knew that no one would see me get into his truck. I slipped my engagement ring off of my finger and dropped it into a secure zipper section of my purse. I felt guilty for only a few seconds until I jumped up into the Italian guy's truck. We took off from my everyday life to something altogether new.

"Altogether new" was also quite dangerous. No one knew the Italian guy and no one knew I was going anywhere with him. The thought occurred to me that, if I wanted to, I could simply disappear from my life and no one would ever be able to find me. I could simply slip away from everything.

The Italian guy was not my first choice in companionship. He liked sports (namely football) and he drove a giant, lifted, navy blue truck. I enjoyed the total shift from the typically very high or drunk guys that I hung out with. He wanted to take me to a restaurant and then to a bar for some drinks. He actually wanted to talk. He was very charming and asked me all kinds of questions. He wanted to know all about my family and my home situation. I spilled my guts and I was happy to talk about it. Draven and I avoided talking about painful things. The Italian man was so interested in me and he was so alive and intelligent. I remember his eyes alight with the light of thought and it was so different from the dull eyes of the drunken men I saw every day. Here I was, the unwise girl that always fell in love on the first date. Instead of being measured and evaluating character while keeping my eyes open for red flags, I ignored every kind of warning and drank up the attention (and alcohol) being showered upon me.

At the bar, we took shots of tequila. I was getting hammered while the Italian man was conversing with the bartender and other bar patrons with ease. Yet again, the Italian guy was buying me drinks, one after the other. I considered how gentlemanly it was for him to be paying for everything without considering the fact that I was being plied with alcohol for nefarious purposes. In my mind, all I could see was that he was not like the other guys I hung out with. With those guys, it was more like Layla and I bought the bottle and they would drink half of it. I was so pleased with myself to be in the company of a true gentleman and I felt a proud sense of accomplishment in the new caliber of men I attracted. The dishonest thought occurred to me that, "I must not be all that bad if this guy likes me." The Italian man was all smiles as he suggested we go for a drive. "He is so charming!" I thought. I started out the evening not even sure if I could tolerate the Italian man but now, after so many shots of tequila, I felt myself in love and totally trusting a complete stranger.

I was so drunk that I do not even recall the drive to where he parked his truck but, I will never forget where we parked. He had loaded drunk little me into the back seat of his truck at the bar and buckled me in. He had driven me down Interstate 10 a couple of exits from the bar where we were now parked off of the Ford Street exit in Redlands where the LA Fitness gym exists today. He crawled into the back, extra-large cab space to join me. I remember thinking how spacious the back seat was and marking the door handle in my mind in case I needed to throw up because I was so very drunk and out of it.

Of course, it was to be expected that the Italian man made his advances to have intercourse with me but it was not happening as it should because I was so completely drunk that I was like dead weight although I think that was the point. I lost consciousness for a small time and, when I woke up, the Italian man had turned into a hairy werewolf due to the fact that he was angry and mean. Gone was the winning personality and the flashy smile. Gone was the charm and the allure of a gentlemen. He was no gentleman. I was drunk, so very drunk, but not too drunk to feel the Italian man sink his teeth into my neck and my shoulder. I was not that girl. I did not enjoy pain like this. This hurt and I felt deceived by the Italian man. He was too aggressive and he was hurting me.

"Wait. Stop." I managed to get the words out even though my head was spinning. Fear gripped me. The fact that I had no idea who this man was suddenly dawned on me. He knew everything about me. He knew that I had no family to care where I was. He knew that no one knew where I was at the time and that no one would miss me. He had bought me shot after shot but I could not recall him drinking anywhere near the amount I had consumed. He was breathing hard with totally wild aggression and he was whipped up into a fury.

I felt totally humiliated that I had fallen for this kind of thing yet again. Why did I get myself into these kinds of situations? At that moment, considering the how and why was not important. Survival was important. I was somewhat calm until I thought I saw the glint of something metallic and reflecting the dull glare of the streetlight. Was that a pair of handcuffs? Did I just see what I thought I saw? He was now on top of me and biting me. I could taste blood like I had been hit in the face.

What kind of man plans ahead and carries handcuffs in his car? Rapists and murderers do! I had little time to be terrified. My body was sent into fight or flight mode and I completely surprised the Italian man with my ability to rally from my drunken stupor. I have always been able to handle my alcohol just a little bit better than men assume and this would work to my advantage now and again at a later date in the future. If I did not fight, I could just picture my cold, strangled, bitten-up, and lifeless body being thrown out the truck door on the side of the road.

I kicked and screamed and fought but he would not get off of me until one of my kicks with a combat boot managed to connect with something that hurt. I did not stick around to see exactly what I had kicked. I grabbed my bag that was in the back with me and managed to unlock my door. I opened the door with such great force that I fell out of his lifted truck. I hardly felt a thing as I hit the ground and made a run for it to the gas station. I felt like I was running for my life and that he might chase me so I was beyond relieved when I heard his lifted truck start and skid off in the opposite direction and pull onto the freeway onramp and take off down the freeway.

There at the 76 Station, wondering if I should stay under a light where the Italian man might see me, or if I should stay under the light so others could see me in case he came back, I reached into my bag and pulled out my cell phone. Thankfully it was charged and I had service. I called Draven. Without saying a word of what had happened, I cried on the phone, "come and get me!" Draven knew by the sound of my voice that something was terribly wrong. Without a question, he came and picked me up.

When I got into his Mustang, the bite marks were all over my neck, shoulders, and chest. I tried to hide the ones I could feel the most but I could not hide them all. I looked roughed up with my mascara flowing down my face and my hair tangled and messed up. Draven looked me over with a concerned and quizzical look. "What happened to you?" he asked. "Nothing." I snapped back. I was self-consciously pulling at my clothes as if I was only wearing a single autumn leaf to cover my shame. I suddenly felt as though I could not cover up enough. Every thought I had entertained at the restaurant and the bar earlier was now a cruel mockery of my own making. "How could I be so stupid? This was my own fault." I quietly thought the thoughts of self-condemnation. "If I had not been so willing to cheat on Draven this would never have happened to me," I concluded.

I would never tell a single soul about that night. Too afraid that Draven would find out what I had done, I would never share the details of this night to even my closest friends. To think that Draven did not notice my bare ring finger and bite marks that covered me was wishful thinking. The next day, I was wearing a turtle neck in the summertime and trying to cover the terrible purple wounds with makeup. I know Draven saw it. He saw it all. It made him furious but he would never ask me where they had come from or what happened that night. I think a part of him knew that I had experienced something horrific but, if I was putting up a wall, he gave me the boards and paint I needed to make that wall as strong and opaque as I needed it to be.

Chapter 23

Crossroads

The Italian man was a pivotal turning point for Draven and I. It showed both of us that there was no power in the ring. In other words, there was no engagement that would keep us together. It was a nice idea but neither of us were willing to do what it takes to have a relationship. We were both unwilling to self-sacrifice. Once it was clear that our relationship was doomed due to our unwillingness to serve one another within the confines of marriage, we grew contemptuous toward each other which is only a mere consequence of disloyalty and our relationship disintegrated like a castle built on a sandy beach gets washed away by the tide.

Our breakup was a particularly trying circumstance due to the fact that Draven was drinking and angry. He flew into a violent rage and grabbed my suitcases and the little I had in the way of possessions and threw them out of his house. He grabbed me by my arm and flung me out on my ear like the trash I thought I was. I had to turn around and knock on the door to get my cell phone and charger. Draven's mom was inside and saw the entire thing but even she was afraid to let me in against her son's wishes. I had to go around to Draven's bedroom window and knock on the glass window persistently so that Draven grew tired of my rapping.

"What!?!" He screamed through the crack of his window.

"I need my cell phone and charger!" I hollered back. I thought that, if I could get Draven to just talk to me, I could change his mind. I was terrified because I had nowhere to go and nowhere to stay. If I could not get Draven to change his mind then I would be out on the street.

Finally, Draven emerged from his apartment with a medium-sized box with all of my belongings from his room and bathroom. Even though I had felt that this was a long time coming, I felt defeated and heartbroken. I hated being dependent on Draven for a place to stay. There was such an imbalance of power because of my total and utter dependence on Draven for everything. I had no money, no car, no job, and now nowhere to lay my head. Draven handed me the box of my belongings and turned around and walked back inside. I tried to match his speed to hold him back but he anticipated my desperation and ran from it like a noxious fume. I ran back to his window to try and, once more, yell through the crack to talk him out of his decision to toss me out but Draven turned up his music so loud that I could barely hear my own screams for mercy.

What had become of me? I had no self-respect left. God is not primarily concerned about how we feel about ourselves because how we feel about ourselves is directly connected to and impacted by how we feel about Him. He will allow financial pressures to come to us to get us to evaluate our lives and turn back to Him. Some financial pressures are a consequence of sin. I was on the road back to the Lord but I did not know it yet. I sat on my suitcase and thought of my next move, pushing the Holy Spirit's urging away from my conscience. My adrenaline was pumping so hard, I could hardly think straight. Survival mode does not lend itself to wise decisions. It was not even an option to call my mother because I knew that further embarrassment and rejection lay at the door but, more than ever, I cried for her. I wanted to go home but I was ashamed. I got a call from Layla to hang out and I told her that I had nowhere to go because Draven had kicked me out.

"Come stay at my house!" she responded to my angst and despair with hospitable enthusiasm. I searched the sound of her voice to see if I could hear any hesitation but I heard none. I was so reluctant to walk away from my perch on my suitcase without the door of Draven's dwelling. It would be admitting defeat. I wanted to stay and fight to get back within the good graces of Draven for the mere purpose that I hated the idea of change and the unknown and I also wanted to be the one to break up with him and not the other way around. I had grown quite comfortable with Draven's saving graces and I was anxious in a world without them. Layla arrived and pulled me off my perch of self-loathing and self-pity. She threw my suitcase into the back of her car and drove me to her house to show me where I was to lay my head.

It was hardly a bed and hardly a couch. With the

posters of heavy metal and occult bands gracing the walls, I tried to fit my body on the leopard print chaise lounge that was now my bed in Layla's room. I had gone from the comfortable queen-sized bed at Draven's to a lounge chair. My combat boot clad feet hung off the lounger so Layla gave me a marble stand to try to balance my feet on while I slept. It was the most uncomfortable sleeping situation in all my years. Once more, Layla's parents were hard working people so my habits of sleeping all day and drinking all night were quickly highlighted in the light of their diligence. My habits of getting stoned and eating everything in sight were shown to me and I started to see myself as very ungrateful and slovenly. Every day, I was confronted with the fact that I had a DUI, a warrant, and a suspended license.

I was grateful to Layla's parents for opening their home to me and I tried not to be too much of a nuisance to them. I stayed in Layla's room when they were home and I used the bathroom only when they were not home so as not to see them in the hallways. I was terrified to get kicked out of Layla's house because I would have nowhere else to go but maybe a shelter or somewhere else of that nature. I had no car to sleep in so I was on the street should I get ejected from Layla's house.

When I walked in the door that first night staying at her house, I saw her mother and I was immediately convicted that I had done a very wrong thing by drinking and driving with her daughter as a passenger. I was terrified to ask her forgiveness for my total and completely selfish act in driving while intoxicated and nearly killing her only daughter but I needed to. With a trembling and shaky voice, I meekly repented, "I want to apologize for drinking while driving with your daughter in the car. I promise you that I will never drive while drunk again." Her mother looked at me with soft eyes and a look of sympathy for this lost puppy dog that had landed on her doorstep. "Well, alright. Thank you for saying that. We all make mistakes." I am eternally grateful for her forgiveness.

I was never so motivated to get a job as I was when I was totally at the mercy of the kindness of others. Where does a girl go to get a job when she has no license and has outstanding warrants for her arrest? The traditional jobs were out of the question. I had gone with some girlfriends to apply for a job at a club but I could not work there. At last, I figured that I would go apply for a job where all the criminals I knew were, the local biker bar.

The moment I stepped into the biker bar, I knew I was home. The combat boots, the miniskirts, the leather, the rock and roll rebel vibe, these were my people and my kind of place to work. It was a red building on the side of Interstate 10 in the Inland Empire. It served as a concert hall and a biker hangout.

Famous classic rock bands often played there as did many lesser known cover bands. Its rustic vibe combined with the grunge made it a perfect house of debauchery. Whatever the rock history may be, the fact stands that the place was known in the area as the local Hells Angels and Diablo biker gang hangout. It had changed hands several times but it always remained a biker bar.

I sat at the bar and sipped a cocktail while filling out my application, unheard of at most workplaces. Sitting happily and thinking on how perfect this scenario would be for me, I set my heart on working at this place. There was not even a second look into my legal status. Nearly everyone here had a record.

The owner here, Geneva, was a former showgirl herself. Her late husband was a Hells Angel and she was a tough madam to work for. She wanted her bartenders and cocktail servers to be attractive, skinny, and follow directions, namely her directions and that of her manager. She was short in stature and had short, dark brown hair. Her face reflected the look of being a little broken by the pain of life. Her dark eyes looked alight with the knowledge of good and evil.

She looked me up and down with a critical eye as she did all the women in her company. Deny it though she tried, I was a perfect fit for her notoriously rough establishment. I was intimidated by Geneva which is how she preferred it. I worked very hard to avoid running into her around the venue so I would take alternate routes to accomplish my tasks but the days where she sat at the bar and watched us working were intimidating and it was difficult to escape her glances. She had seen many a worker come and go. Some would steal from the register, some would sleep with all the bikers, some would sell drugs out of the place, and some would turn informant for law enforcement. She trusted none of us though we all tried to gain her trust.

When I got the call that I was hired to work at Crossroads, I had no idea what I was in for. It was quite an experience. I had to adjust to a new culture and it took a learning curve to master. My first night I was thrown into the deep end of biker culture or what I call total immersion education. I was given a tray so I could take alcoholic beverages from the bar to their respective tables. On my tray was a little box to keep money in for change and hopefully lots and lots of tips. In the back and behind the bar, I was shown a little cubby where I could stash my stuff and check the mirror to make sure that I was looking good. "I will never miss a party again because I work at the party." I thought. It was essentially being a drug dealer all over again because I could make money while I served mind-altering substances.

This night I would learn much about the biker culture. First, I was taken to the back of the building and given a rundown on biker gang colors by the head of security named Mark. He numbered the three rules with his giant, Goliath-like fingers on his massive paw. Although this man would become a sort of big brother to me, that first night he towered over me and I shook in my boots.

He held up his index finger as he continued, "Whatever you do, do not wear white." Black and white were the Mongol colors, a rival gang. He held up two fingers, "And do not wear green." Green was the Vagos' gang color. With three fingers raised, "I'm tellin' you that it's best that you stick with wearing black and red for now." Black and red were the colors of the Diablos.

I shook my head in agreement and I took off any green punk-rock pins that I had on at the time or any pins that had black and white together on them. I tucked these things away in my cubby and I took up my tray again and went to the bar to try to seem helpful.

"Hello, new girl!" A sunny voice from behind me greeted the back of my blonde head. I turned to see a figure all in black who appeared in the image of a mix between Johnny Cash and Clint Eastwood. He was weathered by the road, by life, by drugs, by anything and everything that a self-destructive person can destroy themselves with. But, then again, we all kind of looked the same here in this cradle of rebels, this mad band of vagabonds and outlaws. Immediately, with my brand-new crash course in biker gangs, I was able to ascertain by the colors that he wore that he was a Diablo, tried and true. "Hello." I meekly replied with a sweet smile.

"I'm Jack and I'll be your bodyguard tonight."

"My bodyguard? Why do I need a bodyguard?" The fact that I needed a bodyguard should have alarmed me but it did not although I thoroughly enjoyed feigning female helplessness so that I could gain this man's protection in any way. What woman would not enjoy walking around with a bodyguard at her side?

"Well little lady, you'll see!" he said with his eyebrows raised and a devilish smile while pretending to warm his hands in the fire of hell.

I hardly had time to let any of Jack's comments sink in before I was called over to the bar. There was a particular smell in the bar, the smell of raw wood and of ale that rotted on the floor combined with the smell of appetizers in the deep fryer and the cigarette smoke wafting in from the front door. The bartender grabbed me to give me a tour of the facility. It was much larger than I had heretofore thought. The bartender named Stella was half Filipino and half caucasian. I could tell, right off the bat, that she was an alcoholic by the fact that it was only the start of her shift and her speech was slurring.

In the future, I would lose count of the amount of times I would find her passed out in the bar bathroom or the times she would get drunk behind the bar and hardly be able to count the money coming out of the register. However, in that moment, she was my senior as a seasoned biker bartender and she took the opportunity to snootily detail the geography of the bar. I learned quickly that there were plenty of nooks and crannies in this place where I could potentially disappear from Geneva, the owner.

The bar had two actual bars that were made of sturdy blonde wood with metal barstools with padded seats. One bar was in the "red house" and one large bar was expansive in the concert hall. The concert hall that had no ceiling (you can do this in Southern California) was huge and, when there were too many people in the "red house," the concert hall would get opened. The decor on the walls highlighted life on the road with several flat screen TV's. When sports games were not playing, there was a live band. I was excited to be in a place where there was always something going on. It was church for the irreverent. I was slowly becoming a believer. It had the feeling of a highly dysfunctional family but a family nonetheless.

I was instantly attracted to this rag-tag bunch of bandits. They called each other "brother" when conversing with each other. I felt my inner heart swooning for the romantic storybook-like loyalty toward each other. I saw them as a sort of outcast group of disparaged knights. In fact, loyalty and respect seemed to be the anthem that rang between them and the result was my total and complete enchantment. To say I was taken with the sense of belonging that existed within this "family" would be an understatement. Why does anyone join a gang? To the orphaned outcast, whether it be orphanhood of one's own making or not, a gang is the perfect counterfeit to family and faith.

This new job was exciting. I felt a new sense of hopefulness. Was it really possible to party while working? Why had I not thought of this sooner? I could strut my stuff and receive the male attention that was so vital to my existence while having access to a literal pipeline of alcoholic beverages. This was fantastic. From this point on, I literally came alive at work. The environment, the risk of danger, the meat market, my senses fed on alcohol, and loud music. All of this fed my appetite for sin like no other.

Jack sauntered over to the area where I was leaning against the bar waiting for my drink order to be filled. He eyed me up and down in my black miniskirt, black combat boots, and black buttoned-up blouse. "I love what you're wearing but I would like it better if you were wearing black and red." It was like a right of passage to be teased about not wearing the club colors.

"Thank you!" I coyly batted my eyelashes and wished I had a red bandana to sport at that moment. He was a different kind of man than I was used to. He was, in fact, a man and not a boy. He was in his early forties and I was not used to this kind of man who knew how to talk to a lady, if you could call me that. He wore black biker boots in fitted Levis and a tight black T-shirt that read, "SECURITY," across the back. He was a tall and muscled man but, moreover, he was a biker through and through. More than just a biker, he was a died in the wool Diablo.

I cannot say too much about what a Diablo is and does because they are still doing it and I am not willing to put myself in needless danger. To put it plainly, they are a very dangerous gang of outlaws. I saw firsthand what they are and what they do so I will leave it at that. Jack leaned against the bar across from me. His handsome frame made me feel bashful and fidgety especially because he was so forward and leaning into my personal space. I could smell his aftershave and whatever else he was wearing. He definitely had a presence about him that made the ladies sort of shiver in his presence.

I continued to lean against the bar and feel the awkward silence as Jack leaned and stared into my eyes knowing full well and enjoying that he was making me uncomfortable. Our little tête-à-tête was interrupted by the loud sound of a bar stool flying through the air and crashing into pieces behind me. As the sound of the wood breaking into pieces loudly cracked in the air, I turned around to see what was happening. There, on the other side of the room directly across from me, were two men fighting like wild animals. I turned back to Jack for a little guidance to gauge the danger of the situation to see that he had disappeared into the fray. He was security after all.

The men who had started the melee were from rival biker gangs. One man had disrespected the other man and a fight had ensued. Suddenly, two additional men jumped to the defense of the man getting punched in the face which caused even more men to jump to that man's defense. Before I knew it, I was standing in the middle of a huge bar brawl with my mouth hanging open in shock. I just stood there listening and watching the mesmeric chaos of a free-for-all by what I had previously thought were grown men. Fists, faces, arms, and legs seemed smashed together in a glorious scene of anarchy. The blood drawn from various men's faces and knuckles mixed with brightly colored club patches created a feast for the eyes of vivid color and cinematic action.

Two more wooden barstools went flying through the air and crashed against the bar right where I was standing and, yet, I stood still, transfixed like the onlookers passing a car accident. I had to watch. At that moment, Jack, out of nowhere, once more appeared and grabbed me by my waist and lifted me up so that I was sitting on the bar. I was as light as a feather to Jack and I was so glad for his effort to save me. He arrived like a white knight out of a dark forest to rescue me.

After sitting me up on the bar, my white knight surprised me by roughly pushing me off the bar. I slipped right off the polished bar and landed on the floor behind the safety of the bar. I had no time to object to being shoved to the ground before Jack hollered down at me, now on the floor but behind cover, "Don't just stand there girl! Take cover! I've seen people get stabbed in these fights!" "Oh. Well then." I thought. I did not even consider that there was a level of danger. How silly of me. I sat corrected or, rather, huddled behind the bar waiting for the fight to end.

It is so interesting to me how God uses even the wicked for His purposes. As I started to acclimate to biker culture, criminal, clandestine, and occult by nature, my response to their loyalty to one another was to consider my own loyalties. Layla and I rented an apartment together and finally, at last, I had a place to lay my head that was neither a man's bed nor a chaise lounge nor the pavement of the street. It was a breath of fresh air to have some sort of scheduling normalcy so that I could have my son again. I rejoiced to be able to have him spend the days and nights with me. Having a job, making semi-honest money, and knowing that I had a home was a huge security.

Though I had my own bed these days it was not unusual, on the nights that I did not have my son, for me to meet men at the bar and bring them home with me. I took pleasure in the ability to eject these men from my bed early in the morning and kick them out of my house. I would mistreat these men the way I thought I had been cruelly treated and rejected. Layla and I laughed at our ability to use and lose the men the way men often treat women.

Eventually this casual view of sex and bitterness against men plunged me into bisexual relationships with women. It was only a natural consequence and result of gross promiscuity to then continue to move away from what God designed me to be until I was the exact opposite of God's design for me.

The apartment that Layla and I shared was a two bedroom, one bathroom, little hole-in-the-wall but, it was our hole-in-the-wall. We kept our beloved pentagrams hanging on the walls in both of our rooms. I made our living room an altar to dead rock stars. Layla hung the idols of pagan gods throughout our home. We were proud of our little place in the world and we made it fully ours which meant that it was evil.

Most of the time when we walked into Layla's room, we could feel an extreme temperature drop which meant that demons were with us. It was normal to use the pentagram to pray to spirits to get answers for our questions. We would ask the familiar spirit a question and, if the pentagram that was hanging by a chain from our hands swung in a circle to the left, the answer was, "no," but if it swung in a circle to the right, the answer was, "yes." On a handful of occasions, I witnessed supernatural communication using this method. I observed an invisible force move a perfectly still object.

Oddly enough, Layla's deepening interest in a music group that called for the rape and murder of everyone started to concern me. I had a son to raise. Layla's friends visiting our home were more of the same, druggies and evil of every kind. On the nights I did not have my son, it was not a concern of mine. However, everything in the light of my son's wellbeing changed how I viewed rebellion. I started to be convicted that, perhaps, these things I was involved with were not good for my son. I struggled against this quiet voice speaking to my spirit and I worked hard to drown it out with more and more alcohol. I was now fully submerged in gang and street life, a kind of life where talking to law enforcement is forbidden, justice is carried out on the street, and respect is everything.

It was within this period of my life that the voice of the Lord grew louder in an attempt to woo me back to Him. I had felt Him all along trying to warn me and guide me but I rebelliously ignored the pleadings of the Holy Spirit. My journey back to the Lord would often be as bumpy as the road away from Him. I was hesitant to find love and peace in Jesus. I concluded in my ill-fated logic that life cannot be as simple as Christianity painted and I felt that, to see Christ as the answer to everything, was, in fact, corny and idealistic. But still, the Lord was coming after me with a vengeance. I can only imagine the armies of angels fighting for my freedom and just when they gained some ground with me, I would choose the evil instead of the pure and good.

During moments of sobriety, I would consider my life and the Lord would use those opportunities to press in close to me. I could literally feel the Lord urging me to return to Him. In my sober moments, I would be led in thought to my brief knowledge of the Bible. Songs from Sabbath School would burst in on my mind like a flood proving the verse, "train up a child in the way he should go and when he is old he will not depart from it." On one occasion, I even started singing, "Oh be careful little hands what you do! There's a Father up above who is looking down in love!" Layla said, "what is that?" I quickly avoided the question. Our God is the searcher for the lost coin taking every opportunity to search for the lost, find them, and press in close to the wicked in order to save them. "If I make my bed in hell, You are there." Psalm 139:8. I had done just that. I had made my bed in hell and the Lord was there and He would not let me go.

I was now dangerously driving without a license. My little truck would often break down and I would be stuck on the side of the road. Before, Layla would be my first call but now I called Jack. Days when my truck would not start, Jack would come pick me up. It helped me a great deal for the other apartment residents, of which there was a large criminal element, to see this tall and dark figure, dressed all in black, with his Diablo vest come to my humble abode.

My neighbor to the side of me was a meth dealer, one of the neighbors across from me was a known gang member, another across from me was a crack addict, and yet another was a hit-woman. Jack held back the criminals from bothering me. Anywhere Jack went, people made a path for him to pass. He made the criminals that surrounded me quake with fear when he came near. He was not a man to be messed with. His prison tattoos showed from underneath his shirt and he was often carrying a weapon. But he was my friend and I felt so safe with him. This trust awakened trust between us. God used him as my guardian angel many times when I continued to get into trouble.

The first time Jack arrived at my apartment he exclaimed and scolded me when I opened my door to let him in, "this is where you live?" I lowered my eyebrows at him while scratching my head at his astonishment and disappointment, "Yes. This is where I live. Why?" Jack pushed through the open door so he could stand inside and talk with me privately and he pulled me in close and dropped his voice to a whisper sparking my curiosity.

He became serious and stern, "I want you to have nothing to do with your neighbor over there," he said with his finger pointing to my neighbor across the courtyard. "Why?" I questioned. This only exasperated him further. He had some rank in the Diablos so my questioning his orders did not go over very well but he quickly realized that he was dealing with a child and a naive one at that.

"Listen girly!" He stuck his finger in my face like a concerned father, "I don't want you going near that lady over there. You don't hang out with her, you don't talk to her, you don't look at her! She is a hit-woman and she kills little girls like you and rolls them up in carpet rolls and dumps them out on the Indian reservation! Do you understand?" My eyes widened to the size of golf balls and, for once, I stood quietly listening to the instructions of one wiser and older than I. I simply nodded my head in a newly acquired obedience toward Jack.

In that moment, I could have hugged Jack because I saw that he really cared about me and he cared that I stayed out of trouble. He proceeded to soften his voice even quieter in case anyone was in my apartment listening, "you don't tell anyone what I just said. That's between me and you." He continued to talk like he was about to say something that he had been thinking about for a while now but never had a chance to say to me, "And another thing, this life isn't for you! You are going to be offered anything you want but, you say no. Okay?"

I shook my head in agreement. I knew that I would obey anything Jack said. I was only slightly injured by the suggestion that I was not cut out for gang life. And with that, I believe that Jack protected me from the perils of getting in too deep with the Diablos. I had the full protection of a motorcycle gang without ever having to prove my loyalty or get initiated into the group of women that are the property of the gang like most girls do by sleeping with certain (or all) members.

My obedience to Jack would later be tested but, of course, it helped that, on occasion, I had witnessed Jack, as the security of Crossroads, ejecting men from the bar with great force and violence. On one such occasion I mistakenly walked out to the parking lot to see where Jack had disappeared to and to see if he was okay. There, I saw him standing over a beaten and bloodied man that he had previously grabbed by the scruff of the neck and thrown out of the bar. Apparently, the man had done wrong because Jack had a fist full of the man's hair and Jack had punched him numerous times in the face.

I had walked out to see Jack raising his fist once again to strike a blow but, when Jack saw me standing there, wide-eyed, shocked, and scared at this whole other side of him that I never thought existed, he dropped his fist and the man. "Go back inside!" he yelled. I knew he could see the fear and disappointment on my face. I had always seen Jack as an

412

honorable warrior of sorts. Jack followed behind me inside and with urgency attempted to explain his actions. The last thing you want is for the sweet thing that adores you to suddenly fear you. He was trailing close behind me toward my cubby at the back of the bar.

I knew that, if Jack had been around earlier in my life, some of the evil things that had happened to me thus far would either never have happened or there would be have been an eye-for-an-eye type of justice meted out for my suffering. This thought was very endearing to me. Though I did not like to think of it, I knew that Jack hurt people from time to time but I decided, then and there, that they must have deserved it.

In a matter of fact tone, I blurted out, "Jack, if he deserved it then he deserved it." I said this more to myself than to Jack. Although very corny and childlike, I knew no other way to break the sudden tension between us. Jack had become someone I loved and not in a romantic way either which told me that he was someone special. I quickly acted like a wide receiver footballer who had just caught the ball and I ran into Jack like I was running through him while wrapping my arms around Jack's chest in a very childlike hug. He laughed and love melted him. His hands that were, moments before, clenched into fists now were patting me on the back. I refused to see him as anything less than noble. He was my protector. I was loyal to him. If he had asked me to do anything for him, I would have.

Chapter 24

Crash

One night, I was working at the bar and Jack was the security guard that night. The girls that worked at the bar were not usually allowed to walk out in the parking lot alone after our shift because it was dangerous. Jack and I started discussing matters of religion and our beliefs on life. Oh wonder of wonders that Jesus would use a convicted felon and gang member to reach his precious daughter. Jesus will use the most astonishing means to reach His sons and daughters and retrieve them from sin.

Jack escorted me out to my car and opened my door. "Why don't you lock your car door?" He shook his head as he helped me get in my little truck. I smiled and shrugged with a bashful smile as I turned the key to start my truck. Yet again, my little truck would not start. Jack popped the hood and it was not a repair that could be fixed right away at two in the morning. "Well," Jack let the hood slam and brushed his hands together to get the grit off, "I can let you stay at my house and we can come back first thing in the morning to get your truck or I can take you home tonight but it might take me a while to come and get you tomorrow." When Jack said this, I was a little disappointed that he might be making a pass at me and making it easier to have me stay the night rather than take me home. Until this point, he and I had been such close friends and I enjoyed having a brother rather than a boyfriend but I had never been to Jack's place before. I was kind of curious to see where he lived.

"I'll come stay with you!" I said thoughtfully considering what I would do to get ready in the morning and what I would wear to work the next day. I whipped around and bent over my front seat to rifle through the clothes and the shoes that I always kept in my vehicle. I got a change of clothes for the next day and I grabbed a few makeup items and threw them into my purse. I popped out of my truck and slammed the door behind me while trying to manage my filled-to-the-brim purse. Jack let out a laugh and said, "You're prepared. Got a kitchen sink back there too?" He directed me to his truck and we set off for his home in Mentone which was only ten minutes from the bar.

Sooner rather than later we arrived at a cute little trailer. I expected "white trash" style to be the decor within so I was pleasantly surprised when I walked into his trailer and found extremely clean surroundings. It was too clean, OCD clean. I could tell that various women had attempted to put their touch on the place with various throw pillows and some country antique vibes but it was clear that a man lived there. Every surface was clean and clear with nothing on it. To the right of the front door was a comfortable, oversized couch with little throw pillows. Jack disappeared into the back room and emerged with a blanket, a sheet, and a pillow.

"I'll make up the couch for you." My eyebrows raised in

surprise to which Jack replied, "What? You thought you'd be in the bed with me? What do you think I am? I'm no cradle robber!" he chuckled as he spoke.

"I know!" I lied to cover my embarrassment at my assumption.

"I would give you my bed if I didn't have a bad back so you're on the couch. I'm an old man."

"You're only forty." I reminded him in a teasing voice to redeem myself.

"Well, yes I am. Too old for you."

"Ewwww." I feigned disgust at the thought of Jack and I together but the truth was that I was very happy that he would not be chasing me around the trailer tonight because I was used to my trust being broken and I really trusted Jack. The fact was that God was using him to melt away my bitterness toward men.

"Want a beer? What am I thinking? Of course you want a beer. You're an alcoholic. So don't drink all of my beer." He said, softening the sarcastic blow with a huge smile.

"I'm not an alcoholic! I can quit any time, I just don't want to." I grabbed the beer from his hand. "Where's your beer?"

"You know I don't drink."

"Yeah. Why's that?"

"Hey, you don't want to see all of this drunk." he said with two thumbs pointing toward himself. "Then we would both be in a lot of trouble. The last time I was drunk I got arrested so I don't drink anymore."

That was a fantastic opener to a deeper conversation. I plopped down onto my nicely made couch-bed and I drank beer and smoked cigarettes. Jack smoked cigarettes with me one after the other. I think he was lonely and just wanted someone to talk to. He knew, from our conversations at the bar while we both took our smoke breaks that were usually promptly interrupted by some drunk guy needing more beer, that when we had time to just sit and talk that we would have plenty to discuss.

We were friends and we talked about things that we could never say to other people. Layla was my friend but she was someone I did things with and not someone who I could really discuss life with. Jack was an interesting person to talk to. He had stories from every kind of situation and I found him to be a fascinating conversationalist. From trying to help helpless women escape domestic violence to run-ins with the law, he had no shortage of exciting tales from the life of an outlaw. I listened and asked him questions and added my comments from my own brief experiences with life but, mostly, I listened to Jack share and share he did. We talked for hours.

Although there are several stories and life lessons I remember from that night, there were none that impacted my life so dramatically as Jack's story of seeing a fallen angel. This experience that had happened over five years back had changed his life too. I often wonder what change would have been brought into his life had he known someone who could have given him a good Bible study on the topic. I found myself, for the first time since childhood, wishing that I could answer Jack's questions about the Bible. "Through influences seen and unseen, our Saviour is constantly at work to attract the minds of men from the unsatisfying pleasures of sin to the infinite blessings that may be theirs in Him. To all these souls, who are vainly seeking to drink from the broken cisterns of this world, the divine message is addressed, 'Let him that is athirst come. And whoever will, let him take the water of life freely.'" *Steps to Christ* 28.

At the time in Jack's story, he was up to no good. Well, usually he was up to no good but, as far as criminals go, Jack was a Robin Hood of sorts. Back in the story, he was extremely evil and doing things that went against even his hardened conscience. He was down in the Palm Springs area and, according to him, "doing very bad things." What that meant I do not know nor do I want to know. Knowing Jack, it could have been anything.

The dark of night covered the desert landscape. He described it as darker than most nights. My first instinct was to ask him if he was sober as anyone would after hearing his account. He was in his same truck that he had at the time. Traveling down highway 111, coming from Palm Springs back to the Inland Empire, he saw a dark winged creature. It was not a bird, not a bat, but a creature changing in size from the size of a man to something smaller.

The creature came down from the sky and landed on his back window right where he could look it in the eye in his rearview mirror. He could barely keep his eyes on the road. He swerved in traffic as he tried to fling the dark "thing" off his back window but the "thing" stayed firmly attached. As he described the creature's eyes and body, I knew from my experience at church and my limited knowledge of the Bible exactly what it was and the hairs on the back of my neck raised up as he went into extreme detail. I inwardly shivered which was illogical seeing as I denied the Lord in every area of my life. But, then again, sin is not logical and cannot be very well explained other than that it is sin.

"You saw a demon!" I exclaimed.

"That's exactly what I knew it was." He leaned forward as if proclaiming a great truth. He was grateful for my affirmation and I knew that I was likely the only person he had told this story to. "Do you believe in that kind of stuff?" He asked me very cautiously.

"Yes, I do." Enthusiasm marked my reply.

"But aren't you into that witchy stuff?" His eyes narrowed in suspicion as I tried to explain how I knew the Bible but I just didn't follow it and how I chose evil.

"Girl, I saw evil and it changed me. I never saw something more terrifying in my life." He put a hand to his forehead and rubbed his high brow in remembrance of the sheer panic he experienced. It was extremely difficult to explain myself while the hairs on the back of my neck were still standing and I felt a little afraid as he continued with his story. I had no explanation for what I believed and I felt slightly humiliated by the lack of thought I had put into this.

Although I do not believe in ghost stories nor do I think that it is wise to habitually discuss the power of Satan, Christ used Jack's story in a very powerful way that night. He described evil and the workers of evil in such a way that I was ashamed to be promoting such a thing. After that evening, I never practiced witchcraft again, though this was not a conscious decision.

The last time I went to a concert with Layla, I did make a conscious decision to have no more to do with satanism and the calling upon of evil. Layla and I decided to go to an occult, black metal band concert in Hollywood. It was at a more obscure venue but, once inside the concert arena, the place opened wide and the stage was huge. It was black as night inside the venue and there were pentagrams and occult symbols everywhere. There were contortionists extending from the ceiling and women and men dancing in cages.

The room was completely dark and people were biting each other like vampires and cutting each other in the audience and even having sexual interactions all around me. I was in the den of every unclean bird. Even though I was there, and had paid good money to be there, suddenly I started feeling the deep and heavy consequences of evil. I was getting a heavy dose of the actual darkness that accompanies the evil one.

There will be a day when Christ returns to the earth and, thereafter, Satan will be left to roam the earth with nothing to do until those that are the evil lost will be raised and attempt to overtake the Holy City. I looked around the concert and every kind of evil could be found around me. I could see that this is what this evil day will look like. The armies of evil will cause every kind of dark and disgusting urge of lust and haughty pride to be fulfilled. The fallen angels will be frenzied by selfishness, evil, bloodshed, and the threat of loss.

One would think that, even here, where sex, violence, satanism, bloodshed, and abuse are taking place, God could not be in a place like this. This is His earth and God is still the Sovereign of it. Even in evil, God is still able to use it as a force for good. The Bible says in Psalms, "even when I make my bed in hell, You are there." I had made my life a withered flower in the valley of death but God is still in the valley with us. I had made my bed in the bowels of hell but God was there. Even though I had no profession of faith in God, only in darkness, I looked around that night and, in my mind's eye, I could see the ranks of demons swelled in that place and I decided to never return to satanism.

The day after I spent the night at Jack's place, he helped me get my truck started at the bar and I followed him to a biker "run" that was being held at the Diablos' clubhouse. Not everyone gets an invite to visit the clubhouse and I felt nervous and excited to see this place that I had heard so much about.

When I arrived and parked my truck in the yard, I looked around at the grand scale of the property on which the clubhouse sat. It was a massive place to me. There was a larger barn or warehouse building where the men were congregated. What I most remember was the flow of people coming and going on their bikes. It was an intense and disorienting sound. The sound was incredibly loud like a large thunderstorm hanging overhead. You could feel the roar of the bikes throughout your body. The entire earth vibrated as some one hundred or more bikes were running at once.

I particularly noted that there were quite a few women on the back of the bikes doing acrobatic tricks and moves on the back of the bike. It made me nervous to watch these ladies standing on the back. Jack had given me a healthy fear of being a passenger. He did not let me just hop on the back of anyone's bike.

Several nights before, Jack had been privy to my flirtatious conversations with another Diablo member named Crash. Crash had just been released from prison after serving a six year sentence for attempted murder. He was tall and an extremely handsome man. He was clean cut and his job in construction made him very muscular but he had a drug and a drinking problem. He liked to drink until he hit the floor. He too, like Jack, was in his forties. They were "brothers" belonging to the same club and, in any typical situation, Crash and Jack would stick together but Jack defied the traditional code to warn me off of Crash.

Jack had seen the way Crash looked at me and watched me work. It was all too true that Crash was always in my face and flirting with me. He called me names like "sugar" and "sweetheart." I was exactly his type and I knew exactly what his type was because I saw his "old lady" almost every night at the bar. She was a blonder and older version of me. She, too, was in her forties. Half the time she looked at me with daggers in her eyes but I tried so hard to be respectful and kind to her so the other half of the time she looked at me with a look that said, "how do I compete with someone so much younger than I."

It was true that I had youth on my side but I was not interested in Crash. Married men were never my thing. I found it revolting to see married men at the bar pull their wedding rings off just before they crossed the threshold of the bar. On occasion, I would see men party and drink with their wives and the very next night with their girlfriends. I always lost respect for these men and I would spit in their drink or even make sure they got hardly any alcohol in their drinks.

Jack saw the growing tension between Crash's "old lady" and I. He saw the way Crash followed me around and tried to talk to me so Jack warned me, "stay away from Crash! That is just big trouble."

"I know!" I complained in exasperation to Jack while we both shared a smoke on our break together. "I can't get him to leave me alone."

"I'll talk to him." He put out the cigarette and walked back inside the bar. That day we had some serious VIPs in the bar. The president of the Hells Angels chapter was there that day. Everyone was on their best behavior. Jack approached Crash and softly made some gestures toward me and then some gestures toward Crash's "old lady" who was off in the distance dancing on the dance floor. I stood back nervously watching to see what would happen. Crash gave Jack a look of annoyance and I could see him mouth the words, "I don't know what you're talking about."

With that, Crash folded his hands in a dismissive manner as he leaned with his elbows on the bar. He looked straight ahead to focus his attention on anything else and to completely ignore Jack's warnings. Jack made a motion of finality and walked off in a hough and rounded the bar to where I was standing. "He better leave you alone!" He declared in passing annoyance.

I followed Jack's fast and large footsteps back outside to share another cigarette.

"What did he say?" I questioned.

"He didn't say anything but he had better leave you alone because he's asking for trouble. And you, you don't encourage him. I know his old lady and she is a nice woman but don't make her mad!" I was quiet and I listened to Jack's irritated rant regarding a list of Crash's bad choices. I could tell that Jack and Crash had been close friends and that he cared about what Crash chose to do especially being fresh out of the "big house."

That afternoon, I got off my shift and decided to stick around Crossroads and drink some beers. Those beers turned into shots and I found myself very much under the influence of alcohol. At some point, as the sun began to set, Crash sat himself next to me after his "old lady" had left the bar. I watched Jack raise an eyebrow and shake his head at Crash's bad behavior. I tried to ignore Crash but he was the most incredible and charming sweet-talker I had ever sat next to and have yet had the bad fortune of sitting next to again.

He nudged my shoulder with his shoulder in a flirtatious gesture to make me familiar with his touch. He leaned into my personal space and I could smell the smell of a man who doused himself in aftershave and was covered in the smell of the road. At that moment, I could not ignore that he was a good-looking man. Then he broke my frigid iciness like a pickaxe splitting me in two with his sense of humor. I had tried so hard to resist him but after the warmth of the alcohol set in, doing its dastardly work, I found myself unable to stop myself from laughing at his jokes toward the other ladies at the bar. This was Crash's talent. He was an expert at getting people to like him and trust him, no, love him. He was the complete epitome of a lady's man. How would I resist? I kept reminding myself that he was pretty much as good as married in biker culture. I knew that, if I were to sleep with Crash, I would become a liability to Crossroads and the Diablos and that Jack would never forgive me. It felt like a test for me.

As I kept drinking, my ability to resist weakened more and more and my resolve to honor the girl code also became easier and easier to rationalize away. Time and time again, I utterly and completely proved that "wine is a mocker and strong drink is raging; and whosoever is deceived thereby is not wise." Proverbs 20:1.

The president of the Hells Angels had made an offer to Crash and I that we could come to the Hells Angels Clubhouse in San Bernardino. When the head of the Hells Angels makes an offer to come and see the inside of the clubhouse, you go. But, you do not want to ride in a car down to such a place. You want to show up on a hog. In going, I would deepen my involvement in such activities. Also, Crash and I could spend some time together without the watchful eyes of other Diablos.

Crash and I headed out to the parking lot together to mount up and roll out. Crash casually handed me a helmet and I could see the stray blonde hairs in it. "Ewwww." That made my stomach turn. It was his "old lady's" helmet. Was I willing to be the other woman? Not really. But how do I turn down such an illustrious invite to the Hells Angels Clubhouse? It was my desire to go to the clubhouse. I knew in my heart that very few get an invite such as this and that it would only help to totally assimilate me into the biker culture. I was going to go. I put the helmet on, stray hairs and all. I slid onto the back of the bike behind Crash. I wrapped my arms around him and I held on for dear life.

The bike rumbled and thundered underneath me and we started to go. I saw Jack running out of the bar toward us. "Oh no, he's going to stop us." I dared to think of it. "Really, Jack?" I thought. In that moment, I thought of Jack as a wet blanket on the fires of lust. What a drag he was. Jack was indeed running out of the bar to stop us. When he was able to stand in the middle of the road and flag us down, I looked into Jack's face and I saw his earnest concern. He was out of breath and his face looked as if he was out to save the world. He was as serious as one could be when trying to stop your friends from making terrible decisions. He knew that Crash was drunk as a skunk and he knew that I was Crash's passenger. In a motorcycle accident, it is always the passenger that gets hurt the most or dies.

Jack yelled over the rumble of the bike, "you can't take her! I won't let you take her! I warned you man! I'm willing to fight you on this if I have to, brother!" Jack was sober-minded and strong. He was willing to do whatever was necessary to save me from myself. I felt not a little embarrassed. Maybe it was the cold air suddenly sobering me up or maybe it was knowing that a parking lot fight was only a moment away if I did not listen to Jack. I willingly and obediently slid off Crash's bike though I was terribly disappointed that I would not make the Hells Angels party. As my feet hit the ground, Jack pulled on my arm so that I would be standing protected behind him away from Crash.

"Man! Why are treating me like this?" Crash protested.

"You have an 'old lady,' leave her alone, I said!" Jack's eyes and voice flashed an anger that even I feared.

"Whatever!" Crash tried to reclaim some manner of pride after his prey had been snatched clean away from him. He let out the clutch and opened up the engine and let his bike do the talking for him as he drove out of the bar's driveway. I stood there listening to the sound of my fun and exciting party ride away and I felt very left out. I sighed deeply and Jack heard me but he was too mad at me to care that I was disappointed.

"Come inside!" He barked at me. "I still have to close up." I obliged his order though I was now in a bad mood and visibly pouting. I followed Jack into the bar and sat on a bar stool with my arms crossed. The bartender got me a drink, as if I needed another, as a consolation prize for doing the right thing, biker style. I sat and watched Jack stack the stools on top of the tables and turn out the lights. Maybe ten minutes went by when we heard a pounding on the door.

Jack darted a loud whisper in my and the bartender's direction, "everybody to the back!" No one pounds on a bar door after two o'clock for a good reason. Jack went to the door and shouted in his most intimidating voice, "who is it?"

"It's Crash! Man, open the door! I'm hurt!" Jack made quick work of the door and opened it up to let Crash fall in the door. Crash was now lying on the bar floor laughing and so drunk that he collapsed.

"What happened?" Jack still did not know if he should

be angry at Crash or help him up. But it was hard to be angry at Crash who was laughing on the ground declaring through gasps and loud bursts of laughter, "Jack, I'm such an idiot!"

"Yeah," Jack's lips started to quiver in an effort not to crack a smile. "You are." Finally a smile passed over Jack's face and we all breathed easier. Jack craned his neck to look out the door that he was still holding open with his arm. His eyes did a quick scan of the parking lot and he asked with a questioning voice, "uh, Crash? Where's your bike?" Crash was inhaling a deep breath until he heard Jack's question and let out a huge "I CRASHED IT!" In that moment, I was hit with the sudden realization of why Crash was named Crash but Crash again roared with uncontrollable drunken laughter at the fact that he was fulfilling, in every respect, his nickname.

I shuddered, thinking of the fate that Jack had saved me from. Maybe I would have died or maybe I would been paralyzed for the rest of my life. Crash had been in a crash and his bike had gone flying through the air. Crash had injured himself and wrecked his bike because he was so drunk that he could not drive. I knew that Jack had, yet again, saved me from myself.

Chapter 25

T-R-O-U-B-L-E

Walking into the Diablos clubhouse, I was struck with the beauty of the black and red color scheme. They modeled their decor, unfortunately, after the Nazis. It was truly awesome to the eye and had the desired effect upon me though I had no fondness for the Nazi party and the crimes they were guilty of. As I looked around at the positively intimidating setting, I remembered when Jack stood in my apartment and said, "And another thing, this life isn't for you. You are going to be offered anything you want but, you say no, okay?" He had been right up until this moment and I had found myself better off for following him.

I was called over by the Diablos' chapter president. He waved me over and offered me a drink. I had no idea of the gravity of the next few minutes until I was older and understood who I was standing in front of and what he was offering. After we had exchanged some pleasantries and small talk, he leaned in and I will never forget his face as he said, "whatever you want, I can get it for you." I casually replied, "okay," obviously not understanding what he meant so he said it again to make me understand that he was offering me a chance to maybe deal again, be a courier, work for them, whatever I wanted. I did not know what to say at the time. What does one say when offered anything by the king? In my simplemindedness, I could only think of how I wanted another beer so I replied, "can I have another beer?"

The Diablos' president leaned back in his chair, satisfied that I knew of what he was speaking, and he let out a cheerful laugh like a Viking king on his throne. All around me, I was surrounded by the din of motorcycle culture and perhaps some of the most notorious criminals on this side of the country. I felt at home with them, safe with them, and I wanted to be one of them in that moment. This was one of the largest parties that I had ever seen and it certainly was the loudest party that I had ever heard.

I continued to work at Crossroads for some months until I met Hawken. One night, I was working for a Diablos event that had hired a band to play. There was some low-level buzz and gossip about the band that was playing that evening. The girls were all excited because the band members were good looking, younger guys. Typically, the bands that played were old and salty, blown out by the 80s rock scene with leathered and worn skin, toxic livers, and ready to bestow upon anyone who would listen the stories from times when they rubbed elbows with the legendaries of the rock and roll world.

But these guys were younger and better looking than the older guys and they had some local notoriety and perhaps even a little fame on a national level. However impressed the other girls were with these guys, I was unimpressed. I had been there and done that as far as dating the band went and I was trying, oh so trying, to date a better class of men, whatever that meant.

At least, that is what Jack wanted me to do. He had introduced me to a biker guy out of the Boozefighters named Rob who was clean cut as far as bikers went. Rob was extremely good looking. Most importantly, he had no criminal record, a stable job, and a motorcycle patch to a biker club. As far as Jack was concerned, that was all a girl could ever want or need in a man.

I was standing at the bar as I usually did when drink and food orders were slow when one of the band members approached me and said, "Hey, you look like my next girlfriend." Clearly, he was a touch intoxicated and this was not the first time I had heard this line. Sometimes when the guys got really drunk, they would get a little touchy-feely and I always put up with more than I should.

Comments like, "you look like my next ex-wife," were common and, on occasion, they would grab me and not let me go. I played nicely although some of these old timers were hairy and sweaty and I hated being pulled up against them for some cheap feel while they breathed their stinky beer-breath down my blouse. It always made me feel like a piece of meat. I had been trained by my mother to just "do it" and be nice. I was nice but I ran to Jack and complained. Then he would "take care of it." I would love to know, someday, how much Jack saved me from.

Typically, biker chicks were "passed around" and

quickly got on drugs. If you were lucky, you became someone's "old lady." I was somehow not fit for such "passings." It makes me wonder exactly what Jack said to Crash and the chapter president to get all of these old guys to keep away from me like they did. I am eternally grateful to Jack for being God's instrument of protection.

To me, this band guy calling me his "next girlfriend" was just another in the sea of bikers that I needed to fend off to do my job. I said, "oh, okay," as I rolled my eyes and walked away. I walked back to where my cubby was, a brief respite from the day's work. Back there, my coworkers and I could laugh and giggle at the foolishness of the drunk people knowing full well that we were just as foolish when we were drunk. That particular shift a new girl was starting. She had worked there before so she needed no introduction to the place like I did. I shared my annoyance to her. "What's up?" she smacked her lips as she chewed her bubble gum while simultaneously fixing her lipstick in a handheld mirror.

"Nothing, just a guy out there wanting to make me his next girlfriend." I replied in a self-pitying tone.

"Who?" she put down her mirror and motioned for me to point out who it was from behind our back-of-the-bar vantage point.

"That one." I pointed to the band member taking shots with his band mates. He was shorter than most men but he had a presence about him. He was the lead singer, a guitarist, a drummer, a jack-of-all-trades in anything musical. He had dark, curly hair, blue eyes, and a round pudgy face. He was stocky with big muscles and lots of tattoos. He looked like the very symbol of biker or rockabilly subculture. He was reasonably good looking but not the most handsome guy in the room. I had a rule that I did not date guys who could not tower over me when I wore heels. He did not fit the bill because of his short stature. That's when the new girl spoke up.

"Him? That's Hawken Jones. You don't want to date him! He is T-R-O-U-B-L-E with a capital T. You'll stay away from him if you know what's good for you." Trouble, she said. Trouble indeed. I filed that comment away in my mind to process at a later date. We were expecting a large crowd that day. We both tightened our aprons and checked our faces one last time as we darted onto the floor to try to make as much money in tips as we could. I did my best to ignore Hawken and not give him any more reason to bother me that night especially because I had gone to Jack and asked him about Hawken and he said, "NO!" with a capital N-O followed by, "he is a womanizer."

I had been working at Crossroads for a while and my typical restlessness, better described as depression, was setting in. Instead of looking to myself for the reason of my unhappiness, I considered all of the external reasons for it. This usually led me to drink but Jack's words about me being an alcoholic had stuck with me. "I'm not an alcoholic," I thought to myself.

It was a rainy day and I was feeling particularly blue. I missed all the men in my life that had come and gone. I missed my mother. I missed my family. I missed things that I had no name for. I wanted to down that large bottle of vodka in my freezer. I carried on a conversation of inner dialog, "I want something to fill the void. What is the void? Hmmmm? What is it? Do I need a boyfriend?" I thought, "a nice boyfriend this time."

I went through my phone which served as my little black book of men. I was so lonely. My son was at his father's and I was all alone. As the rain fell, I sat on my porch and smoked a cigarette and watched the droplets fall. It was a grey day indeed. I looked through my phone thinking of this man and that man which only led me to feel darker. Just several weeks before, I had been with a few men that I had met at the bar. I was embarrassed of this fact. The Johnny Cash song, "Hurt," came to mind, "what have I become? Everyone I know goes away in the end."

Layla and I hardly hung out anymore. In fact, we were starting to hate each other. Living with a friend does tend to sour the relationship when both are as selfish as we were. She had let one of her close friends come and live with us, rent free. This friend hated me and she was a huge fan of a band that promotes committing acts of murder and mayhem as their gimmick. I did not want my son around these people. It went beyond the occult to actual criminal activity by way of torture and murder.

To be honest, I was afraid of the effect this music was having on Layla. I was afraid that she would kill me in my sleep. I started to sleep with one eye open and never wanted to be home especially since we were now bickering with each other about who ate what food and who took what garment of clothing from each other's closet. A true friend no more. Again, I was looking for any reason to not be home. I started going home with anyone from the bar so I could just have a place to hang out other than my house which had become a haven for every kind of drug-addicted, criminal lowlife. I wanted a semblance of peace in my life.

I sighed and flicked my cigarette to the ground. "I need to lose weight." I continued my inner dialog. One thing about working at a bar is that you have constant access to alcohol while simultaneously having your appearance scrutinized by every customer. I was gaining weight because of my alcohol intake. Drinking a beer was like eating a sandwich. I was eating a lot of sandwiches.

My next thought was, "I'll go for a run." I put some exercise clothes on and decided to "run" around the block. I ran a few steps and found myself out of breath and gasping for air. "Wow, that can't be it." I attempted to keep stumbling along to try to finish the block but I was out of shape and my lungs were filled with tar from my pack-and-a-half-a-day smoking habit. I was so very pleased when my cell phone rang in my pocket.

I stopped and could barely breath out a, "Hello."

"Hello?" the unfamiliar voice said on the other line.

"Who is this?" I sputtered and coughed.

"What are you doing?" The voice exclaimed in curiosity.

"I'm going for a run." Lie. I was stumbling along while trying to breath oxygen. Before even knowing who it was, I was on the defensive and explaining myself. I was so very gullible and trusting. Just let me tell a complete stranger where I am and what I am doing.

"Oh. Well, this is Hawken Jones and I was wondering if you remember me?" Of course I remembered him. He said I was going to be his next girlfriend and that is not easily forgotten. Then, as circumstances would have it, I had seen him around town multiple times after that. I stopped the struggle to "run" since I was being pleasantly distracted from such a terrible struggle. I thought out loud, "How did you get my number?" I quickly filed through all the times I had been super drunk and had lost consciousness. If Hawken had told me that I was drunk and gave it to him, I would have believed him.

What a horrific possibility to lose faith in yourself because of alcohol. I had no faith that there were things that I would not do because I knew that there were things that I simply do not remember because I was so viciously intoxicated. Had I given Hawken my number? I felt so embarrassed until he quietly and shyly stated, "I got your number from Geneva."

"Oh, it all made sense. Wait, is that legal?" I wondered. Hawken continued in a much louder voice, "but don't get mad or tell anyone that she gave me your number because she isn't supposed to do that." I was irritated that my number had been given out but what was I supposed to do now, Geneva was my boss. I can get mad at her but what can I do about it? Nothing.

"So, do you want to go out with me? I live in Hollywood but I can come get you if you want?" He dropped the word Hollywood as if he were throwing out hundred dollar bills like a flower girl at a wedding throws petals for the bride. He knew that he sounded big and bad saying that he worked as an entertainment promoter in Hollywood. At first, I was reluctant but he was a fast talker. I finally got home from my attempted exercise and saw Layla pull up in her car. A load of unsavory people filed out and into our apartment.

"Yes! Yes, I will go with you! Come and get me!" And that was that. Every word that was spoken to warn me would come true. He was T-R-O-U-B-L-E but, in the moment, I wanted escape.

Chapter 26

Fake

The best way to describe the period of our dating is to use the visual imagery of explosives and gasoline or Bonnie and Clyde. At some point, we actually were lighting explosives together. We were explosive on others and to each other which, by this point, should come as no surprise. Our relationship was even more intense than the typical dysfunctional relationships that I had kept up until now. In Hollywood, he would work and I would play and drink. Then, he would get off work and catch up to my drinking and then the "fun" would start and one or both of us would almost get to the point of being arrested. Then we would pass out and go to bed and do the same thing the next day. We were hanging out with all kinds of people in all kinds of places. Living fast was an understatement. I never drank so much or so frequently as when Hawken and I were dating. It was alcoholism on steroids. This part of my life is like a big blur on the timeline of my life.

During this time, my mother and I had started talking on the phone again. Jack had encouraged me to do this. "You need your mother in your life," he said. But when Hawken and I started dating, I was too drunk all the time to really talk to my mother. Everyone was concerned because you could see the effect the alcohol was taking on my body. My skin was showing signs of premature aging. I was now twenty-two with crow's feet around my eyes and my skin looked weathered and worn. I stank of cigarettes all the time and I had little time to do laundry so the smell of body odor mixed with the strong smell of body spray and perfume surrounded me.

I look back on some of these pictures and cringe at what I had become. I had previously been living life on the edge but dating Hawken was like taking a flying leap off the edge. I still had major legal troubles that I had not addressed. I was now regularly driving without a license or insurance. I still had warrants out for my arrest and the man that I had hit had sued me personally. The city had also sued me for damages. The debt I owed was mounting and I knew that it was just a matter of time before law enforcement arrested me and threw me in jail. Everywhere I went, I was terrified of police officers because I knew that, wherever or whatever I was up to, I was in trouble. No one can quite understand this kind of anxiety unless you have gone through it. It makes you feel like panicking whenever you see a squad car or police officer near you and it caused me great paranoia.

Hawken and I are both blessed that we were never arrested during these times of wild nights and drunken days. Hawken often drove intoxicated. We jumped into display fountains and lakes at concerts. At certain venues, we started fights, we punched people, and, on one occasion, we stole a cop's transportation car and then talked our way out of getting arrested. It was insane. I never saw so many fights in my life. I would wake up in the morning with injuries and I was often unsure of how they got there. What a crazy life.

Now I was back and forth to Hollywood and doing my best to postpone and skip my shifts at Crossroads. Hawken was renting a house in the Hollywood Hills across the street from Marlon Brando and almost every other house on Wonderland Avenue had some sort of famous movie star or rock star living in it. Hawken would take me down to shop on Rodeo Drive. This is where he learned that I was not a Gucci or a Christian Dior kind of girl because we found the nearest punk-rock hole-in-the-wall and, there, I did my shopping. I was not used to a man showering me with gifts and whatever I wanted. It was a nice change of pace.

After missing so many shifts at Crossroads, they started to schedule me less and less. Then one day Hawken said, "I don't want you to work there anymore." Just like that, I quit my job and left the biker world. I did not even say goodbye to Jack. I was a professional at walking away. I was very good at leaving friends behind me. This was especially because I knew that Jack was mad at me for dating Hawken and he wanted no part in the alcoholic chaos that was now my life. I quit Crossroads knowing that, eventually, I would have money coming in. It was about that time of the year again when the check from my father's estate would be coming. However, it was not a good idea for me to have nothing to do but drink.

My drinking had gone from bad to worse. One morning, I woke up and I decided that I was done with the partying and the crazy binge drinking. Just like that, I broke it off with Hawken. My mother had called and shared with me how, since I had been gone, she had experienced great anxiety and depression because of my absence. She gave me an opportunity to come home for a month or two. I was so very happy to be going home to my mother that I would have given up anything for it and I failed to consider my mother's ulterior motives since my check was about to arrive. I cleaned myself up to go home to her and I promised I would not smoke in the house or have people over. I desired a change and I felt that it was time to grow up.

Quitting drinking was not as easy as I thought it would be. I would buy beer and drink it at home which was not any big deal because my mother and Dre were wine drinkers and Dre kept a huge bottle of tequila in the back of his closest which he would break out for margaritas from time to time. Growing up, drinking was considered to be wrong but, now, since my mother was no longer attending church, the alcohol flowed freely. I was just happy to be welcomed home again. There were parts of me that were finally at peace. But peace in others, whether it be family, husband, friends, pastor, or children, does not last long. Only peace in Christ is forever and my peace in the acceptance of my family would again only serve as a temporary patch.

During this time, I had also struck up a relationship

with Alec, the man that had raised me. I had not spoken to him in years since my mother and he divorced. It was so hard to balance the love I had for my mother and the hatred and bitterness she held for Alec. Any time I went out with my mother, she would spend the entire time hating on Alec and, any time I went out with Alec, he would spend the entire time hating on my mother. Between my mother and Alec, neither one loved me enough to let go of their bitterness to truly love their daughter.

Whatever peace I had gained by being back home was quickly shattered by a dreaded enemy, the love of money. My mother presented me with a list of debts I owed her, knowing that my check was coming. I owed Alec money for helping me too, I was told. I had picked up a night job as a bartender at a pool hall deep in the heart of San Bernardino. When Alec could not reach me because I was working nights, he thought I was skipping out on my debt because he thought that I had received my check. He decided that my mother had persuaded me not to pay him.

This was not true. I had not received my check and I had no idea that Alec had asked my little brother to spy on the mail I was receiving so he would know when I received my check. Saddened and very confused about what was going on, I told my mother that I had received a nasty voicemail from Alec and I played it for her. "Well, I guess you're in cahoots with your mother now. I guess I should've always known that you would pick your mother's side." Alec declared in the voicemail.

I did not want to pick sides. I loved them both. I was grateful for both of them and I was just getting my life back together again after the pain of their divorce and now things were falling apart again. Perhaps I should have called Alec and told him that I had not received my check yet but I was afraid of him and the terrible, hateful backlash I would receive if he thought I had sided with my mother. My mother, upon hearing this voicemail, whipped herself up into a rage. She frightened me too. I was literally between a rock and a hard place. What to do? I had no check yet to solve the matter.

My mother took her anger to Dre and, consequently, Dre and my mom kicked my little brother out of the house for being a spy. This made me really upset and it still upsets me to this day. My little brother blamed me for the decision to kick him out but I had no idea that this would be the outcome of showing my mother the voicemail. My little brother was only eighteen years old and had never lived on his own. I did not know how to stop the chain of events. It was not my house and I was afraid that I would be kicked out too.

Before my check had even arrived, I got a letter from Judge Judy (yes, the television show). Their producers scavenge the local courts looking for cases that are salacious and a stepdad suing his stepdaughter is indeed salacious.

"Wait, what? My dad was suing me? Yes. I read that right." I said out loud while holding the letter. The pain in my chest nearly knocked me over. It hurt so badly to have a parent and a little brother hate me so much. "Had all the help everyone was offering me only been offered because they knew I had money coming?" I bemoaned. I felt that it was. My check had still not arrived. I took the letter from Judge Judy to my mother and to Dre. It was almost too outrageous to be believable had I not had a piece of paper in my hand to say so.

I tried not to get too upset. I was trying so hard not to drink, not to do drugs, not to sleep around but having the man you call, "dad," try to sue you on the Judge Judy show was a hard thing to bear. It was even harder for my mom and for Dre. I knew that Alec was hurting too but it was still wrong for him to sue me. This was a group of hurting people hurting each other and I was just their daughter in the middle of it all.

Finally, my check arrived. I could hardly celebrate cashing a check that had caused me to lose my family, again. It was an awful feeling to have money instead of love. At last, the relationship between Alec and I would be completely severed when, one day, Dre came to my room and held out a piece of paper.

"What's this?" I asked.

"Read it." He stated with numbness but with a bit of ire in his eye.

I read the letter and I was quietly aghast at it. Dre had a really awful anger problem. No, he never hit me or physically harmed me but a six foot seven man who says about himself, "I'm not angry, I'm just passionate," is rather intimidating. Who wants to live next to a volcano that only erupts once in a while? That was Dre when he erupted. On many occasions, he would release a torrent of angry, verbal abuse at me. On one occasion, he erupted over a few toys being left out and chased me from one end of my childhood home to the other while screaming obscenities and other derogatory names at me. It was terrible and mean and my mother said, "I would've called the cops if you hadn't had so many warrants."

Back to the letter. It was a letter to Alec that Dre had written. Though my mother had asked me not to pay Alec back the debts I owed him, I could not do that. Alec was pretty much living in poverty and whatever help he gave me was because he sacrificed all he could to help me knowing that I would pay him back. I had always planned on paying Alec back so the fact that he was suing me now was devastating. I would pay him $5,000 though I owed him much less. Then my mom took twice that much for what I owed her.

This was always what happened when I got any money. Going to school and doing much of anything else was out of the question after I paid my parents what I owed them. Some people will not have a problem with this. People should pay their debts but I do not treat my children this way. It is so easy in life to live selfishly. Before we go to heaven, I must learn what self-sacrifice means and, if I cannot sacrifice for my kids, what am I? I do not ever put my adult son in debt to his mother. He owes me nothing. We should do whatever we possibly can to encourage our children to live debt-free.

This shows my son the gospel message and how God feels toward him. The Bible speaks of this many times, "a debtor is slave to the lender," Proverbs 22:7 and, "for the children ought not to lay up for the parents, but the parents for the children." 2 Corinthians 12:14. As a parent, I should do everything possible to give my children a good, debt-free start in life.

Back to that letter. Dre towered over me and told me to sign it. He did not ask but told me to. I read it again. It was a letter of total divorce from Alec. It read that I never wanted him to call me again, to write me, and, as far as I was concerned, he was no longer my father and I was no longer his daughter and I wanted nothing to do with him for the rest of my life. It was an awful letter and my heart sank. The thought of my little brother being kicked out of the house shook me to my core. I could not get kicked out now. I had just moved back in here. All of this drama had happened in only the two months since I had arrived and I felt like it was all my fault.

I took the pen from Dre's outstretched fingers and, with what felt like signing away my soul, I signed the letter and gave Dre the $5,000 check to be sent in the letter. My heart ached for Alec who would open the letter to find such a message of disconnection. I was mad at Alec but I did not hate him. I felt that Dre and my mom hated him for the two of us. My next thought was how I needed to get away from this house, away from Dre, away from my mom and her incessant broken record of bitter angst because of her divorce. In those months, I learned the poison that bitterness causes in families. I also learned that I must not be bitter and talk bitterness to my child of his father and I am grateful for that lesson.

Because I had a little money, I was able to move out. I was thrilled because my older brother and I would once again live together in a little rental in Redlands. I had some hope again. I was going to "get it together." I was going to shake off the past like a bad dream and be young and free. I still had no shortage of legal troubles so I was even more ecstatic that the rental would not be in my name and I would be another county over where I was not so well known to the cops. I also made a deal with myself that, for a time, I would leave off driving so that I would not be driving around without a license and insurance.

I had been skateboarding for a while but in the hills, where my childhood home was, it just was not practical to skate around. However, I could skate around Redlands just fine and, in fact, it became my number one love. I would skateboard everywhere I went and the warm summer breeze on my face would wash away all my sadness and depression. I did not even care when people hurled stuff out their window at me. I was just so happy to be alive, getting exercise, and even losing a little weight.

As for drying out as in not drinking? Well, I was trying hard to dry out. As hard as a girl could try. I was even trying to leave off men. I would occasionally slip up and go out with someone but then I would quickly back out as quickly as I could. My identity was becoming wrapped up in being a punk-rock skater chick and I loved skating more than anything. If I had to go to the grocery store, I skated there. If I had an appointment, I would skate there. I had my own money and my own way of getting around. I needed nothing and no one. Well, almost nothing.

It was nearly impossible for me to skate by a bar without going in. Once I was inside, well, I had a little drink of a beer. Once I had a little drink of beer, then I was drinking shots. Once I had shots, then I was drunk on the floor and trying to skate back on my skateboard without falling down in the street and getting hit by a car. I was trying hard not to go into bars but this was really hard so I finally took myself to an Alcoholics Anonymous (AA) meeting. Plus, eventually, when I got around to taking myself to court, it might look better for me if I had some AA meetings under my belt, right? Sure! Two birds with one stone, right? I skated around to different AA meetings, even sometimes four to five AA meetings in one day, and even Narcotics Anonymous (NA) meetings too. I thought I was doing well. I even met some friends there that said I might need a co-dependency group too so, as long as I was doing meetings back to back all day long, every day, I might as well go to one of those too.

Still, once I got out of those meetings after all the talk of alcohol and drugs, I was craving alcohol more than ever. I would begin to skate home and I would see a bar on my way home and, now, I had to sneak inside and make sure no one from the meetings saw me. This made feel very guilty which made me crave alcohol even more to drown out my guilt. Then I would skate home drunk and hope no one I knew from all those AA meetings saw me bobbing and weaving in the streets trying to stand upright on my board. From time to time, I would take a huge fall and wake up with wounds and abrasions and I did not know how the injuries got there.

I desperately tried to hide my drinking from my older brother. I did not want him to disapprove of me. I loved him and I looked at him like a father and even more so because he was my one brother who shared a mother and father with me. I knew that I could look him in the face and possibly see what my father may have looked like and I would often try to see my father's image in him. However much he may have been like a father in my eyes, his behavior, like my own, was very much like my mother's. This made me anxious and worried that, if my drinking got too out of control again, maybe he would find it all too easy to cease to be my brother and I never wanted to lose him.

I told him what I thought he wanted to hear for a while, that I was going to meetings and that I was getting "clean" all while I was drinking and smoking lots of weed. But, eventually, like all sin, he found out. It was impossible to hide my drinking from him since we now lived together. He was angry at me for my alcoholic ways at first but, eventually, his anger turned into acceptance. It was his lot in life to accept that his little sister was an alcoholic. Somewhere along the way, he decided that, "if you can't beat them, join them." I am sure he came to realize that fighting against my drinking was futile. On my twenty second birthday, my brother surprised me by going along with plans to throw me a big birthday party at the Falconer British Pub. There, I went hog wild, jumping and dancing on the bar, and racking up a bar tab of well over fifteen hundred dollars in one night.

Now, everyone knew that I was not in "recovery." I felt very relieved to be out in the open. It was killing me to be a closet drinker. I was always worrying about what other people knew because I knew they must know. It was always awkward trying to hide my breath and wondering how much I was betraying my secret drinking. In addition, I drank more when I was trying to hide it and that was also due to fear. I was fearful that I would not have another opportunity to take a drink so I downed as much as I could in secret instead of leisurely consuming the drink in the cool, calm, comfort of open and socially acceptable alcohol use. Then came the shame that I had been too buzzed in front of my brother and my family. I would drink that anxiety away later that night all alone. I was tired of being a fraud and a hypocrite. This was I, a drinker. I was a problem drinker to boot. I was a drunk, period.

Though I had openly claimed to be an alcoholic, I still secretly thought that I had a handle on my alcohol use and that I could will my alcoholism away. I could be like everyone else and be a social drinker. I was very good at convincing myself and those around me that I could drink and it would not be a problem. I was an addict but I could prove to myself and everyone else that I could be a functioning addict and have a "normal" relationship with drugs and alcohol. It was no big deal. I could drink a little one night and nothing the next so I appeared to be as everyone else. I wanted to be like everyone else and play "normal." In my mind, I could make myself healthy. I could make myself not hurt or be damaged. Everything was getting slowly and systematically swept under the rug. With every AA meeting, I was able to tell myself, "that was it. I am better now. I am doing well." I was slapping temporary bandaids on a huge wound and calling it a day. I was grinning and bearing it. I was a pretender. I was a fraud. I was fake.

I no longer wanted to be the gothic, punk-rock, rebel girl with all those problems. I was trying so hard to be the kind of girl that had her head on straight. I tried hard to hide the scars on my arms with jewelry. I was going to tanning beds and now I was whitening my teeth after my mother had told me that my teeth were the same color as my yellow hair due to smoking. All at once, I looked in the mirror and I saw an old, rugged, road-hardened hag looking back at me. I put myself on a twisted road to self-improvement. My flawed motto was, in order to get better, I had to be better and, if I could get a better kind of boyfriend, then I could wrap a bow on it and call me a finished project.

We were living in a cute little house in Redlands, California. It was built in the 1960s and was a four-bedroom quaint little blast from the past with a front lawn and backyard patio where we could have barbecues and parties. Not only was it a dream come true to get away from my hometown but it was an escape, all together, from everything ugly I had heretofore experienced due to the cheerful middle-America quixotic appeal of living in an area of the one-percent or at least two. Environment really can have an effect on one's psyche.

The house was clean and comfortable even without central air. My room was all my own and in the back of the house just where I wanted it. I bought new beds for my son and I. I made an effort to decorate my room unlike any other room I had previously decorated. Gone was the blood on the walls, the obsession with death, the black, the pentagrams drawn everywhere, and my love for evil. I traded all of this in for some nice green and blue flowered bedding with a few punk-rock posters remaining and skating memorabilia.

I was not so lonely having roommates and it was an all-new experience to live in a house with three other roommates, two of them complete strangers to me. I was not used to the casual coming and going of roommates without wanting to know who they were and how they ticked. I wanted to be best friends with everyone and it was a hard reality to learn that not everyone wants to be best friends with me. I wanted to create the dreamy, sitcom fantasy of a TV episode within our new house. I had visions of my brother, roommates, and I all sitting down at the end of the day to discuss our day together. To me, it would be uncouth to be a room away from a stranger.

It did not take long for me to befriend the new girl that was one room away from me, Mimi. Mimi worked at Trader Joe's (a local grocery store chain). She had graduated from high school a few cities over and she had lots of friends. She was outgoing and funny and kind of a tough, t-shirt and jeans, kind of girl. I really enjoyed her company and this was my first female friendship outside of the worship of evil. She seemed very mid-America and, although she had her own hurts and pains from a family which was touched by divorce, she was basically as normal as anyone can be and I really thought the world of her.

My other roommates were my brother and Chuck. Chuck was a friend of my brother and here, with him, I learned that others were as promiscuous as I was and there was an outstanding and intolerable double-standard regarding men and sex versus girls and sex.

Chuck could have as much sex as he wanted and bring any kind of girl home. It was not unusual for me to wake up in the morning to a strange girl in my shower, using my expensive shampoo, because Chuck had another one-night stand. On one occasion, I was standing in the kitchen and I observed Chuck ejecting a sad, overweight young lady from his room and out the front door. As he escorted her out the front door and closed and locked the door, he exclaimed with a dark chuckle, "wow! I guess I had no idea how fat she was when I brought her home last night! Beer goggles!" My brother and Chuck would then laugh and high five each other over their conquests.

I was quite shocked by their bold and blunt way of speaking about sex. Had I been openly escorting men out the door, I would be called a slut and my brother and Chuck would shake their disapproving heads at me. Although I occasionally slipped in this area thinking that I was meeting "the one," I was trying my hardest to mimic the life of one who was doing "better" and "okay." I was the epitome of the phrase "fake it until you make it!"

Chapter 27

Rag Doll

My brother and Chuck decided to throw a little party at our house for some fellow Trader Joe's employees since that was where Chuck and Mimi worked. They were all inviting a few of their friends over and that would end up being quite the number of people to supply with food and drink. They set up a little barbecue outside and they were putting on a full-scale hospitality spread. I was helping my brother put some beers in an ice chest, just happy to be spending some quality time with my brother in the confines of a happy California day.

There is nothing more good-natured than an American barbecue. My brother's friends would be there and, these days, I was working hard to sip my alcohol slowly during the day so I was not tossed by evening and standing on tables and acting the fool while embarrassing my brother. I really liked our living situation and I did not want to ruin it. "I will carefully manage myself," was my constant inner dialogue. However, I was usually "mismanaged" completely before bed. I would sit all alone at night, listen to sad music that reminded me of old boyfriends, get drunk, and cry. Sometimes, I would "drunk dial" any one of my old boyfriends, hang up on them, and cry some more. Around my brother, I was more careful and measured.

456

The lovely summer afternoon wore on and I had cautiously and judiciously managed to sip my alcohol with discretion. Every time I managed to do this and spend a nice day with my brother, I felt very proud of myself. It was like I had managed to win some points with him for pulling off the "good and normal" girl routine. I was now filtering the all black wardrobe choices out of my closet and opting for a little color in my selection. I donned a more punk and skater girl look now versus the gothic mistress of death look. I was evolving, or trying to. I knew the goth look embarrassed my family so changing how I dressed was my effort to be more socially acceptable but, every now and again, I liked to wear the darkest hues my closet provided.

As the sun set in the beautiful Redlands sky over the A-framed church that was across the street from our idyllic house, the guests started to filter out and a few lagged behind for more festivities. Chuck brought out a bottle of vodka from the freezer and I knew the night was just starting for them but I was opting to go to bed. I really did not know the people that Chuck partied with from work and they were always very snobby toward me. They were used to the pretty surfer-girl types and I was an altogether different type of girl.

I announced, "I'm tired, guys, so I'm going to finish my drink and go to bed." No one responded or cared. "O-kay, wow. These are some really friendly people, not." I said under my breath. The group of guys hanging out in the back yard with Chuck and my brother were clearly not my crowd.

I thought that the party was going to die down when some people left but more people were getting off work and pouring through the door. No one introduced these new guys to me. I felt a weird sense of anxiety come over me, the kind of anxiety that I had only felt before when I was in a large crowd of people in a huge city that I did not know. I did not know these people and nothing I could do would make them really be friendly to me either. They were not interested in talking to me. I did not know how to fly through these skies. These guys were the very definition of stuck-up. I was ready to retreat to the safety of my room where I could lock the door and drink alone.

I finished the beer that I had been nursing for a little while. It was warm and I had lost track of it a few times as I answered the door to let other guests in. I found it again. It was my pride and joy because, in the past, this little baby would only be one among many as I chugged down an entire twelve pack myself. I have always had a high tolerance for drugs and alcohol. Even for surgical procedures, I have required more medication and anesthesia than most people. One time, I even asked the anesthesiologist if he had ever had as many problems as he had with me and he agreed that I was an unusual case and quite a frustration.

The last few gulps of the warm beer went down my throat. I was not one to waste a beer. I was not one to throw any amount of that golden delight to the trash. It was my drug and I relished it as precious. I had only had a few that day so I was only a little buzzed and more sober than I had been in days. I lit a cigarette. I could never drink very well without smoking a cigarette because they went together like peanut butter and jelly.

I felt a little lonely in this crowd that was so visibly shunning me for not being "one of them" and I consoled myself with the drags off my cigarette. Smoking is such a creature comfort to smokers. I lit another off the back of the previous cigarette. Yes, I was a chain smoker, too, just like my biological father, I was told. Daddy's little girl in so many ways, I suppose. I flicked my second cigarette to the ground and I felt more than a little dizzy all at once like I had just taken about six shots only I had not taken any shots.

"Oh no! Am I drunk? I hardly had anything to drink!" I thought in confusion. The backyard seemed to be spinning and I was positively concerned by the state of my brain. "Am I having a drug flashback?" I had been told of such things before but was it happening now? I did not know. I felt like my limbs would give way underneath me. To my brother, Chuck, and the partygoers, it simply looked like I was falling down drunk which would not be out of the ordinary. I had to get to my room and get to bed which was exactly what I did.

How was I to know that cunning and deceitful eyes were watching me? How was I to know that one who so coolly ignored me and acted like I was out of his league was planning my demise? How smooth and wicked of him to act as if I did not exist all day long and diabolically and methodically construct the ways in which he would violate my body while I lay unaware. But would I stay unaware? One thing he did not plan on was my body's ability to tolerate the drug that he spiked my drink with.

I hardly remember that last cigarette and I have vague memories of what it felt like to be drugged. I hardly remember getting myself to bed but I vividly remember waking up and seeing Carver on top of me and attacking me. Carver was a friend of Chuck and Mimi from work. I had met him briefly in passing. He stank of alcohol and the workday and giant beads of sweat were forming on his forehead. We did not have central air in our house and, if I did not turn my floor fan on, I would swelter in the hot, California summers. Of course, since I was barely conscious when I hit my mattress that evening, I had not turned on the fan. When I came to, it was the fact that he smelled dirty and that he was so sweaty that disturbed me. I screamed at him, hoping that someone would hear me screaming. "Get off of me! Go to the couch!" In my trained-to-please female mind, I felt that I needed to provide him an alternative to my bed.

His face looked positively and utterly shocked that I had awakened and, as soon as I screamed, he jumped off of me so fast that the words "couch" hardly rolled off of my slurring tongue before he was out of my room. He ran back to the couch which I later found out was offered to him by Chuck because Carver said that he was too drunk to drive that night. I could not believe what was happening to me but

I hardly had the time to process this information when the horror hit me that I could not move my legs and that I was naked from the waist down. I did not remember taking off my clothes at all. I only had a few lucid moments to recognize my nakedness before I felt a wave of dizziness hit me like a truck and I passed out again.

Promiscuous sex was one thing but, this was not sex, this was rape. He had total power over my body. I was like a rag doll and almost appeared dead if I had not had such a drug tolerance. There was no flirting earlier in the night, no introductions, no acting like he was interested in getting to know me, he was simply a face in the crowd that was partying at my house that day. I had not taken any particular notice of him until he was on top of me.

There is a long-held belief that a promiscuous girl is already having sex so what is the big deal if someone takes what she is already giving away? Promiscuity is a counterfeit pleasure in the search for intimacy but rape is the thieving of a person's personhood. It is power over another in the place of love. It is force and subjugation. It is taking what is not yours and what has not been freely given. Rape is the ultimate opposite of the gospel message in that it is condemnation through shame. The result of rape looks like me. A girl who then recreates the rape, time and time again in casual sexual relationships trying either to stop it, change it, understand it, or heal it, but never getting any results.

It is a cruel type of purgatory, wandering the earth

doing over and over again that which wounded you to begin with. It can take a lifetime to recover from and some never fully recover. I cannot fully understand that which is illogical. What makes a person want to harm another person? What makes a man want power over a limp and lifeless body that can offer no love in return? What makes adults who are created for sexual intimacy look to a child who is incapable of sexual intimacy for its fulfillment? It is evil. It is evil. It is evil. It cannot be understood, only forsaken. To understand evil is to parlay with it.

I woke up a second time to see Carver back on top of me, again. I had managed to go through so many different stages of life but I had thought that I was somehow safe now. I was with "good people" and "clean cut" people now, people that had jobs and went to school. It was supposed to be the criminals and the druggies who were dangerous, not these people. I was horrified and, in that moment, I thought of Jack. If Jack had been around, this would not be happening. The scariest part was being totally incapacitated and unable to move my body. It felt like I had giant-sized arms and legs the size of big boulders. How could I move these things? Being paralyzed was alarming if I could focus on it but I really could not focus on anything.

The heat in the room was stifling and I felt like the air I was drawing into my lungs was too thick to get down my airways. I heard the heavy breathing of Carver raping me. I was thankful that I could barely feel anything. By the way he was breathing, it sounded like he would tear me in two. He was looking away from my face at the wall directly above me and hardly concerned that I would wake up at all. He was brazen and bold. He knew, he was sure, that he could get away with this.

"I must wake up! I must move! I am awake! I am awake," I loudly thought in my head. But he could not hear my thoughts. "I can will myself out of this stupor." I managed to push out a "Stop!" He suddenly looked down at me and somehow, from somewhere inside of me, there was a place that was strong. There was a place inside of me that knew that this was all wrong. This place, where I knew that a God up above never intended for such things as this to happen, fought and fought hard. I managed to pull up a scream from deep inside myself.

"Get off of me!" I hollered with a hoarse voice that had been pulled up from deep inside all the evil that I had been through all these years and I screamed again, "No!" Carver pulled back, sat back on his heels, and looked at me. I knew my eyes appeared wild and brave, I just knew it! Sitting back, he looked at me with a quizzical look as if to wonder, "did my drugs lose their potency? Why isn't she knocked out?" I stayed alert long enough to see Carver run back to the couch. With that, I was out again.

The terrible thing about rape is that, most times, you do not die from it. I have no idea what happened next. For me, my "next" was the sound of cheerful morning birds singing the day's song. The sunniness of the day insulted my sense of reality. My room was still hot and I awoke from my fight in the night late the next morning. I must have slept for hours upon hours because I felt like I had slept for years. I stood up on my feet and I felt like I had to get my land legs. "Was it true? Did I dream it?" I knew that I had been raped by the way my body felt. I was so sore and I was in pain. It was no dream. I collected my pants that had been torn off of me and flung across the room and I got dressed.

I felt hungover but I knew that I had not had that much alcohol to be hungover. I flung open my door and I went tearing down the hallway toward the living room and stopped short in the entryway just at the mouth of the living room. I saw my white leather couch that I had purchased myself. An imprint of a body that had slept there the night before was still leaving its mark on my couch. A blanket was messily flung across the other end of the couch and a pillow was there. He had been here. He had slept here. I stood there gazing upon the evidence that my rape was, in fact, very real. I had expected to run out there and see the police, see the ambulances, see news trucks, see something. I had been devastatingly violated and I wanted time to stop and for the world to recognize what had happened. There was no fanfare for my pain. The house was quiet and still like most homes in the late summer morning.

A voice from the kitchen made me jump as it inquired, "what's wrong with you?" It was my brother sitting at the kitchen table with a hot cup of coffee staring at me as if I were an alien from the mother ship. I might as well have been. I stood there stammering and trying to find a way to make the words come out of my mouth and sound intelligible.

"You're such a lush!" He declared with annoyance at my disheveled state and, with that, he stood up and walked to his room with his coffee while shaking his head in disgust. I wondered if he had heard my screams in the night.

I went back to my room and got ready for a shower. I would stand in the shower for the longest I had ever taken a shower to try to wash off the filth of the night before. Here is where I wish that I could write that I went to the ER, that I had a rape kit done, that I called the police. But, I cannot write that because, in the shower, I decided to not only wash away the evidence of the night before, but I decided to wash away the memory of it too. I decided to bury it in a growing mental and emotional graveyard where all the other rapes were buried. I decided to never tell anyone. Not my closest friend. Not my mother. Not my brother. Only Carver and I know the truth. It has been almost two decades since that event and I wonder how many other women have been raped by Carver. How many women has he affected?

I never told a soul for several reasons. I was ashamed and I thought that no one would believe me. I thought I was a slut. I thought that, in some way, I deserved this and that I had caused it. Yes, I had done things to open myself up to it.

Alcohol is a huge contributor to rape but, even if I had been drinking water, I know Carver would have found a way to do what he did. And tragically, as with many victims, I had been re-victimized so many times that I was now accepting sexual assault and abuse as merely part of the way life is lived.

In this instance, like it is in most rapes, the prevention was in the bystanders. The cure for rape is in the men that surround the possible victims. The prevention for rape is our grandfathers, fathers, brothers, uncles, and friends to take a protective role for the men, women, and children in their lives, to stand when you see something going on, and, if something does happen, to believe them. Believe them! So many people are concerned with false accusations but believe them until evidence proves, beyond a shadow of a doubt, otherwise. But, believe them! I am glad that, though I cannot now gain earthly justice, "vengeance is mine; I will repay, saith the Lord." Romans 12:19. In the following verse, God directly curses the rapist in Scripture. One day, these people that have raped will meet the face of God. Until that day, the Bible says, "Woe to him who gives his neighbors drink, pouring out your wrath and even making them drunk, in order to look at their nakedness! You will be filled with disgrace instead of glory. You also expose yourself! The cup of the Lord's right hand will come around to you, and utter disgrace will cover your glory." Habakkuk 2:15-16.

That day went on. Time kept ticking by. I grabbed my skateboard and I took myself to the bar. Whatever efforts I had made not to drink and to manage myself for my brother's sake had ceased. I took up drinking with greater gusto, enthusiasm, and dedication than ever before. I disappointed many with my return to my old ways but I no longer cared what they thought. I was on my own as I had always been and I refused to pretend otherwise.

Like most roommate situations, the living situation started to shift and Chuck got a job somewhere out of town. The cost of living in Redlands was higher than other areas so Mimi, too, was struggling with the higher rent rates in Redlands compared to surrounding Southern California cities. My brother and I could see the writing on the wall and we did not want to carry the entire rent of the Redlands house with just the two of us staying there. My brother started to look for another place to live and I, too, had to search for a new home and had but a few weeks to find it. I had no pay stub to prove my nonexistent employment, I had terrible debt with civil judgments against me, I had warrants out for my arrest, no valid license, and now I was going to have no place to live again.

The stress was mounting and the pressure to be a success at life was again upon me. With the amount of stress, anger, and trauma that I carried, I was very incapable of dealing with the day-to-day stressors that others are able to handle. I smoked marijuana and drank away my stresses. I was the very definition of slothfulness, putting off today's problems until tomorrow. Avoidance is a curse brought upon one's self and the consequence, the hammer of reality. I got hammered hard.

Chapter 28

Steps Back

I did not want to move yet. I was "happy" right where I was. It was terrifying to think of change. So, what did I do? I did what all professional procrastinators do, I made my own distractions. Just like my mother, my favorite distraction was retail therapy. Impulsive decisions and purchases were my reaction to the trauma. On a walk, I had come across a gorgeous 1979 Lincoln Mark III in merlot red. It was the exact model that Elvis had when he lived in Palm Springs. It was in pristine condition and I could just see myself behind the wheel and driving this vintage beauty. I had never before considered that one could love a car like one loves a man but here my heart skipped a beat looking at this replica of perhaps a happier time. "Wow! Jeepers creepers," was all I could say to the owner who had fallen on hard times. He was sad to be selling his pride and joy.

I skated back home and went to my secret hiding place in the closet where I kept my cash due to the fact that, because of all my legal troubles, I could not have a bank account. I still had some cash left from my check that I had received from my father's settlement. Did I have enough to purchase the car? I went to my brother's room and I found him sitting at his computer. I announced that I was going to buy a car. His response dampened my excitement.

"Well, you don't have a license. It's an old car that you don't know how to work on." The voice of reason was irritating to me. He was right. I did not have a license. Driving the car around would be like calling out to the police to arrest me. It was risky but I could care less about the future risk. I was living life for immediate gratification. Whatever would serve as a temporary solution to my permanent heartache was what I would choose.

I purchased the car and I drove it with pride. All at once, I found myself back at biker bars with my beautiful new car. At one particular hole-in-the-wall bar with a rampant biker culture, I ran into Hawken Jones again. He was playing a show at the bar. I knew he would be there but I also knew that his band drew all the bikers out of their clubhouses and into whatever bar Hawken's band was playing at and I wanted to see some old faces again.

Hawken was gob-smacked by the blonde who had spent an entire summer in the sun on a skateboard and now she was cruising around town in the very symbol of rockabilly culture. I was driving Elvis' car and appeared to be the epitome of "cool." Then and there, Hawken decided that he was going to get me back no matter what. He called his friends and family and announced that he was on a mission to tame the shrew in the merlot red Lincoln Mark III.

However illustrious I appeared in my new car, I was on my own in life, treading water and barely able to keep my head out of the mire. The day came when all the roommates were moving out and I was not sure where I would go and what I would do. I was packing up boxes, not knowing where or if I would unpack them. I could not return to my mother's house. That had already been made clear. When I had stayed at my mother's house at the beginning of the summer, it was because I had the promise of a coming check. Now, I had lost my job and I was running out of money. The fear of being homeless and couch surfing was again a reality and I was sickened by the thought of not having my son with me.

I had two lives: the life I lived when I had my son as a dutiful mother and the crazy party life that I lived when I did not have my son. I tried hard not to let the two lives converge but that was an impossibility. I would be standing at the stove in the kitchen, cooking my toddler's macaroni and cheese, while downing a newly purchased bottle of vodka. We would watch a movie together and I would put him to bed and stay up at night, listening to music, packing boxes, and getting drunk while crying my eyes out at the failure that I was.

One of these nights of self-deprecating pity and sadness while I was drowning my sorrows in a bottle, I got a call from Hawken. I carefully toyed with the phone considering the repercussions of answering the call which would open the Pandora's box of the ex-boyfriend. I had successfully ignored his phone calls for months now. "Do I? Don't I?" I drew in a deep breath and answered the call.

On the other end of the line, Hawken was astonished

that he had managed to get me to answer his call. We managed some small talk for a few minutes when Hawken asked, "so, how are you really? What's been up?" It was so rare for anyone to ask me how I was really doing that the question caught me off guard. No one had inquired how I really was and everyone could see that I was a mess. Whether it was the caring concern of the question or the fact that he was the only one to have asked me how I was doing in months, I began to pour out my heartache. I told Hawken how Alec had sued me, how my little brother had been kicked out of the house and I did not even know where he was, and how I was losing a place to live and I did not know where to go now. However, I made no mention of Carver because I was trying my best to convince myself that it never happened. I knew that, if I told anyone about what had happened, telling it would make it real and I was determined to avoid that reality. Life was collapsing in on me and I had no soft place to fall now.

"Come live with me?" he treaded carefully.

"What?" It can't be as easy as that, I thought. Or can it be? "You're not serious." I quickly dismissed his offer.

"I mean it! Come live with me. You said you had no place to go."

"I can't do that." I tried to play hard to get but the reality was that this was my only offer and I was seriously running through the different scenarios in my head if I were to take him up on it. I had really enjoyed not being dependent on a man during the summer months of skateboarding and freedom. I could come and go as I pleased without caring who cared. Did I want to chain myself down to a guy again? But I felt I had no other options. I had nowhere to live and my money was running out. Maybe I could work with Hawken, I reasoned. I could help him promote the local punk rock scene and the venues that Hawken worked for in Hollywood.

I was quiet on the phone. I did not want to eagerly jump at the offer. A part of me knew that this was a bad idea. I sat silent on the phone as I considered all the crazy things that Hawken and I had done in the past. I did not think that my liver could handle another run at this but what other choice did I have? I was quiet, too quiet. Hawken came up with a plan.

"Tell you what, we don't have to drink," he cheerfully picked up on my inner concerns. "How about I pick you and your son up and we go to Bob's Big Boy in Calimesa for breakfast and then we will see where it goes from there?"

"Okay. I can do that." I was happy to agree. The next morning, Hawken arrived and whisked my son and I away for a day filled with fun and shopping. Hawken had lost his house in the Hollywood Hills and now lived in a back add-on at his mother's house in Beaumont. I loved Hawken's family and I was more excited to go and live with him at His mother's house than I would have been to go live in Hollywood. I was so excited to live in a family-like setting that was warm and loving. But, I was worried that Hawken's family would not accept me. How would they react to me moving in right away? I expressed my concerns to Hawken and he quickly snapped back, "they won't care! They want you to come stay." It was hard for me to believe that they really wanted me to come stay but I was trying to buy into the fantasy so I did not question it any further.

With that, Hawken brought his truck and started to help me move my things into a storage facility in Beaumont and only a few things to his parents' house. At his parent's house, we had our own little wing in the back of the house. The back wing was about 1000 square feet of wide open space. It had a little kitchenette, a sitting area, and we used a long white book case to divide the sitting area from the bedroom. It was like sharing a little studio apartment together. The house was an older home but sat on some property where the family would gather and have bonfires, backyard parties, barbecues, and even hold mini music festivals.

Hawken's mother and father had quite the love story. They had married as teenagers and they were still in love. I looked at them as the ultimate success in love and marriage so I settled into life with Hawken in the hopes of finding a little security in the warm glowing love of this little family. I had never met anyone like Hawken's mother before. She was kind and hospitable. I looked for the traces of resentment or contempt on her face as I arrived and subsequently moved in. I did not find any reproach or unkindness in this sweet woman.

She was the real deal as far as love and kindness went. She was hospitable toward my son and I. She loved everyone she met and they loved her. It was not unusual to find a crowd gathering in her living room toward the end of the day. People would simply drop by unannounced and stay for a visit and they would find a warm reception and be offered whatever she had. In the morning, I would find myself in her kitchen, getting coffee, and staying to chat with her for hours. It was hard to know who I was falling in love with more, Hawken or his family.

I am not quite sure why Hawken had such an issue with alcohol since he had grown up in love and security but he struggled as I struggled and therefore we struggled together. It was the blind leading the blind. When we first started living together we got off to a middle-of-the-road start. We drank every other night but did not go hog wild and we were certainly not causing the havoc that we had caused in the past. Slowly, we started drinking more and more until we were drinking every night and we often found ourselves so sick and hungover the next day that we felt the need to drink again in the morning due to the whole "hair of the dog that bit you" theory.

Even while we struggled with chronic hangovers, we managed to make a good to moderate living working as band promoters. I helped Hawken with booking. For some time, he also managed the entertainment one or two nights a week for the B.B. King Blues Club at Universal Studios City Walk in Los Angeles.

Hawken made a good living making connections with various venue owners and he served as the middle man, much to many band member's consternation because he took home the fees from the door for our earnings. We would work on behalf of the venue owner to supply a large crowd so they made money on alcoholic beverages and food orders and the band gained the benefit of appearing before a large crowd. Hawken would book anywhere from three to twelve bands in a night.

At its very nature, it was almost a scam. The band would invite their family and friends so they could be charged at the door for what they could see anywhere else for free. When we worked hard on the marketing end of things and turned out a large crowd for these venues, we could make thousands of dollars in one night of work.

This was before social media had fully caught on and, thus, Hawken and I served as something of an early version of social media since we were being paid to get the word out, create the advertisements, and provide connections. Myspace was in its infancy and, frankly, I could already see the writing on the wall in regard to the growing popularity of social media. It was a threat to our current way of life.

Hawken had little technology experience and he could hardly navigate a Word document. With the advent of social media, promoters like Hawken would become an archaic thing of the past. He would need to reinvent but, for now, it was how we earned a living. Over the space of a few months we saw that social media was growing and greatly cutting into our earnings month after month.

We operated as if we had a night shift. We slept during the day and worked at night. As soon as the bands went on stage and the flood of people coming through the doors turned into a trickle of stragglers, it was our time to hit the bar and celebrate our earnings. We would watch and judge the bands and make mental notes for the next time we booked another venue. We would try to book the bands we really liked as often as possible. Sometimes we would stay at the venue and drink and sometimes we would go somewhere else. The days were flying by since we were at a live music event every other night. Even among the fast times, these were some of the fastest.

The problem with drinking as much as we drank is that, when we fought, we fought hard. For months we worked on promoting but, the more and more we drank, the more we lost the drive to do what needed to be done for marketing during the day. We were sleeping off our hangovers, smoking weed for the same reason, and we had no desire to get any work done. Hawken would take up some weird backyard project at his mother's house. Occasionally these projects would yield something useful like a stage for the mini music festivals but, mostly, they were pure stoner arts and crafts with no purpose.

This would frustrate me and I could not appreciate the creative genius that Hawken prided himself as being. As soon as I became irritated, Hawken failed to manifest any kind of patience toward me so we would argue all day and he would take off to go drink with his buddies. I would stay home and complain to Hawken's mother. She would dutifully listen to my consternation and angry rants. Then Hawken would come home and redeem himself by announcing that he had booked a gig for his band. I was always surprised by what a good musician he was and how people would enjoy having Hawken play at their events. He could play the drums, the guitar, the bass, the piano, and sing. Whatever irritations I held against him would be washed away by the sound of rock and roll and the taste of Jack and Coke and our fight would be forgotten.

Occasionally, we would run into Jack, the security from Crossroads, and I would proudly walk hand-in-hand with Hawken as if to say, "you were wrong." Jack would nod and smile in my direction as if to say, "just you wait, missy. You are in for it." This alarmed me. I thought Hawken and I had created a good little life. We had made a little family of our own in the back wing of his mother's house. It did not bother me at all that we lived at his mother's house. I could tolerate that as long as they could tolerate me but, as the months wore on, I started to feel the chill of being shut out.

I had always known that Hawken was a womanizer but I figured that when he had decided that, "I was the one," it was his decision to settle down with me. I thought that I had changed him. After all, we were creating a family together. I really believed that I had the power to change him and his womanizing ways. Little did I know that Hawken had "settled down" with many women. I was merely a number among many that he professed to love and promised to marry.

Our money situation was directly impacted by our drinking situation and the promoting jobs were becoming few and far between. Hawken started looking for work anywhere he could find it. I knew that this would not be difficult because Hawken had friends everywhere. He always seemed to "know a guy" who "knew a guy." One of his friends was opening a skate shop and Hawken would temporarily help manage it until something better came along.

The skate shop was down the street from us and Hawken started working there most days. He was happy to be working and I was happy to have him working. But, more and more, Hawken would end up going to get a drink with someone he met at the skate shop and be gone all night or he would get a gig and take off without me. It was all well and good to drink as much as we did as long as we did it together. It was a totally different thing for him to be going off with his friends without me. I was outraged and, the more I demanded that Hawken not leave me to go party, the more he left me.

Soon, I found myself stopping by the skate shop to observe Hawken flirting with some girl that had stopped by to see him. Hawken would always declare, "you're crazy! We're just friends!" But, in the back of mind, I knew his reputation.

I could hear the voice of Jack warning me and it chilled me to the bone and gave me a deep anxiety that I might be hanging all of my hopes on the wrong person. All these boldly flirtatious girls knew his reputation too and they did not care for my vision of the future. All I had to do was to open my eyes and see that this relationship was doomed and would not last. I was trying to make a womanizer an honorable family man and it simply does not work like that. I could not make him what I wanted him to be.

Hawken had friends who were married but carried on affairs they kept secret from their wives. One particular friend boldly carried on an affair with a woman that lived behind the bar that Hawken and I frequented. We would often see his friend's car parked outside the house of this woman and we knew that he was in there cheating on his wife. What did I expect? When you surround yourself with cheaters who boldly and openly cheat on their wives, it makes it easier to cheat too.

This was my ultimate fear. I tried hard to tell myself that our relationship was different and that we had a stronger relationship than he had with all of those other women that he dated, even when I walked into the skate shop and found him leaning over the glass display case and conversing with his "closest female friend" named Lizzy.

"What is she doing here alone with you?" I said in alarm. "I really don't want you two alone here together!" Lizzy turned bright red and went running out of the skate shop. I tried to believe him when he said that she and he were "just friends" but something inside me did not feel right about this. I yelled and screamed at the top of my lungs that he must give her up as a friend. I had learned very well that men and women cannot just "be friends" without someone developing romantic feelings. I was horrified when Hawken refused to give her up.

Later, I secretly overheard him talking on the phone and saying that he was thinking of starting a band with Lizzy. "What? You mean, when you go to band practice, *she* is there?" I screamed as I threw open the door and barged into the room. It all made sense now. This was why he had been ditching me to run off to band practice. He was hanging out with Lizzy and then lying to me about it. I felt like a fool that had returned to her vomit. How could I have been so foolish? My chest hurt so badly and I started to demand that Hawken change or else. But, what could I do? I was living with him.

Hawken's brother had recently married and, before the wedding, Hawken had no money to rent a tuxedo so I sold my beautiful Cadillac so he could have the money for the wedding. I felt that it was a gesture to demonstrate that I was willing to pull my own weight but now I regretted it because I had nothing and no way of escape. I had registered in school and I was taking a few law classes at the local college in the evening but now I was dependent on Hawken for my transportation. I found my situation was made even worse when I tried to borrow Hawken's truck to go to school. He would quiz me when I got home from class about the boys that I saw while I was at school. He immediately suspected me of cheating the moment I arrived through the door and it hurt me deeply because I knew that this level of blame and control only comes from a guilty conscience.

One evening, after a final at school, I drove to a girlfriend's house who I had met at school to celebrate the end of the semester. As soon as I arrived, my cell phone went off and Hawken demanded that I come home immediately. With this type of behavior going on, going to school became nearly impossible with Hawken so angry and suspicious of me. Consequently, I opted to drop out of school to please Hawken. Hawken tried to convince me that, "the only reason why you would go to school is to meet boys." I relented that I needed him and him alone but I was secretly devastated that I could no longer attend school. As seemed to be my life's pattern, every time I made one step forward, I took ten steps back.

Chapter 29

Crying Out

Hawken's birthday was coming up and I made a plan to have a surprise birthday party. Hawken loved parties and he was the party man. So, of course, he would love to have a party. I smuggled his cell phone away from him while he was sleeping and I went through his phone so I could invite all of his friends to the party. Yes, he was a promoter so I expected male and female business contacts but I did not expect to see all the recent phone calls to ex-girlfriends. I was inconsolable but I knew that our relationship was to the point where, if I complained, he might kick me out and I was terrified to lose my place to live even if I was often sleeping on the couch because Hawken and I were fighting. In any case, the party must go on. I wrote down all the names and numbers of his friends and called them to invite them to a birthday party. It was a very long list of people.

What I did not plan on was Hawken waking up the next morning and being in the very worst mood I had ever seen him in.

"I am just getting old and I have nothing to show for it," he grumbled with a sneer.

"You are still in your twenties," I laughed in return at his fatalistic sense of self but this only made matters much worse.

"Shut up!" he snapped in response to my light sarcasm. This started a back and forth between us. We chided each other and said hurtful things. I hoped to make him feel a sense of shame for the way he was treating me by telling him that I had planned a surprise birthday party for him but this only escalated our argument to another level. This was not what I was expecting to happen on his birthday. I was hoping it would be a happy day and that, by throwing this huge party, I could prove my devotion to him.

"You need to call everyone and tell them not to come," he demanded.

"No way! I can't tell everyone not to come." Soon, we were yelling and screaming at each other.

His mother became concerned and cracked the door to our wing of the house to peek in on us just as Hawken picked up a laundry basket that was full of CDs, promotional material, and other odds and ends and lobbed it, full force, at my head. Thankfully, it did not hit me but it came close. This outraged Hawken's mother and she burst in on our argument with a bang.

"Now Hawken, you just stop that now!" Hawken looked ashamed and greatly affected by what his mother had just witnessed. He hung his head for only a moment but then his irritation again flared to anger. He marched past his mother as we followed behind him, urging him to cease his childlike behavior. Hawken walked out the front door, slammed it behind him, and jumped into his truck. He then peeled rubber out of the driveway which kicked up a large cloud of dust.

His mother and I stood in the kitchen watching him out the window. We quietly poured our coffee and lit our cigarettes. We sat and licked our wounds while deeply concerned and shaking our heads at Hawken's self-made bad day. I knew that it was possible that he had just picked this fight with me so that he could take off and go party without me. It was an excuse to leave the house and go do whatever he wanted because we were fighting. I felt happy that I had Hawken's mother to back me in my outrage at his behavior but, ultimately, that was his mother and I knew that the support would only go so far.

Hawken never came back that day so, when evening came around, I started drinking vodka while doing the very unpleasant task of calling everyone on Hawken's party list and uninviting them. I told everyone how badly he had behaved and how he stormed out. I received little sympathy because Hawken's behavior was usually outrageous. After all the calls had been made, I found myself all alone and drinking. Where was he and what was he doing on his birthday? I felt chaotic inside and so angry. I was having little panic attacks thinking of Hawken out there partying it up on his birthday and knowing that he was with his friends who had no qualms about cheating. I knew, deep down, that he was out with other women on his birthday. I felt betrayed.

Maybe it was all the pain of the many years of failed

relationships or knowing that I was on the precipice of yet another failing relationship but I started crying great tears of emotional pain. I was not crying specifically for Hawken but for all the boyfriends that had come and gone and left me alone. Would I never find love? I was greatly tempted to cut myself to feel better. I wanted my physical pain to outweigh my emotional pain. I quietly retrieved a knife from the kitchen and sat in the bathroom with the door locked trying to get up enough nerve to cut myself so I could feel better.

I nicked my arm only a few times with light scratches but both of my arms were covered with the scars from years of cutting and I felt like a poor, pitiful mess trying to cut over old scars. I cursed myself for not having enough courage to really draw blood and I collapsed to the floor, trembling with sadness. I sat there against the dryer pulling my knees up to my face. I cradled and rocked myself while I cried and cried until I could cry no more. I occasionally drew long swigs of vodka from the bottle until I realized that I was completely out of vodka. I had downed the entire large bottle.

I was tired and drunk and I had cried so many tears of pain. I was exhausted. I unlocked the door and dragged my poor tired bones to bed. I flung myself on the bed around eight o'clock in the evening and passed out, cherishing the peace of a deep sleep. Maybe I would wake up to the hope of the newness of another day and Hawken would come home and everything would be okay.

But I would cherish no peace, no peace at all. Around

486

two o'clock in the morning I was roused from my deep stupor by my cell phone ringing. "It's Hawken!" I instantly surmised. "He is drunk and he cannot drive. He needs me to get his mom and we can go and get him together. Things will be so much better now." I thought. I was so happy at the possibility of everything going back to "normal" that all my fears of him out with other women seemed to be a thing of the past. I sat up on the edge of my bed for a few seconds, making sure I was awake enough. Not wanting to miss the call, I picked up my cell phone and was confused by the unknown number on the caller ID. "Maybe it is Hawken calling from a bar," I assumed.

"Hello?" It was a female voice. I was immediately thrown into suspicion and my hopes were dashed that it might be Hawken. My heart physically hurt that my vision of Hawken repentantly asking me to come and get him from his awful ways would never be realized. He was still out there doing whatever with whoever and he was not the one calling me.

"Is this Susanne?"

"Yes!" I hissed at the female voice with ready-made bitter contempt for this woman that was not Hawken.

"This is Kristen. Are you still Hawken's girlfriend?" Kristen? I knew Kristen. I had partied with her and her boyfriend a few times and she and I got along really well. She was a very sweet girl. I immediately softened knowing that it was a friendly call not an antagonistic call but why was she calling? Immediately, I wondered if Hawken had been in some terrible accident or a fight at the bar?

"Yes. I am still with Hawken. We live together. I am at his house right now." I trembled as I uttered those words. Whatever she had to say, I knew that a call at two o'clock in the morning was not a good thing. It usually meant trouble.

"Well, I don't know what to say other than I am at Crossroads right now and Hawken is here," she said loudly. I knew that she loved Strawberry Daiquiris and I could tell that she had ingested a few of them by the way she was yelling her words into the phone and slightly slurring.

"Tell me, what's happening?" I stood to my feet in desperation to know what Hawken was doing. I would have fallen at Kristen's feet to beg her to tell me everything she had seen had she been in front of me. I waited with bated breath listening to her hesitation on the phone. "No, really I need to know." I added after a long pause.

"He's been here at Crossroads for hours and now it's closing time and it looks like he's going home with her."

"Who!?!" I instantly thought, "Who is this other woman who is interfering?" But I knew that it had little to do with her and more to do with him.

"Lizzy! He has been here all night and they have been kissing each other and drinking shots," she said, confirming all of my fears.

Wow. I did not expect that. I could have dropped the phone if I did not need to hear her reassurance of exactly what she saw. Kristen described the female and described the kissing in blow-by-blow detail and then she said they were getting ready to leave together. Oh, how terrible this was. The pain in my heart was extreme. I rubbed my heart through my chest to ease the discomfort inside but that did not help.

I reassured Kristen that she had done the right thing and, with that, Kristen hung up which left me in a frozen state of silence. I fell back on the bed, thinking of my boyfriend with another woman. I was in shock. I was lying there in the dark for ten minutes just staring at the ceiling not knowing what to do or what my next step would be. Was I going to accept this as I had many other things? I was tired of my life being in constant crisis.

I went from shock immediately into anger and wanted to push myself straight into denial but that would take some serious drinking. I got up and walked over to the vodka bottle and lifted it to drink but remembered that I was out. I threw the bottle against the wall and it made a huge thump as it bounced off. I knew there was alcohol somewhere in this room.

I rifled through the fridge and then the freezer frantically looking for alcohol. There was nothing that I could find and I knew that walking to the store at two o'clock in the morning was futile. Most stores would not sell to anyone past two o'clock. I made my way into Hawken's mother's kitchen where I found a bottle of moonshine. This was real moonshine straight from Hawken's grandmother's distillery in Alaska and it was potent stuff that would put hair on anyone's chest if not turn them into a werewolf. It was incredibly strong stuff and I took it out to the front porch and started drawing from the bottle the liquid numbing agent that I hoped would numb my soul.

I sat in the quiet dark of the night, smoking cigarette after cigarette, feeling betrayed and completely alone. The neighborhood in the night was unusually quiet. All I could hear was the creaky porch and creaky chair where I was sitting. Tears streamed down my quiet and still face and a loneliness I had never quite felt before came over me. I had nothing but regrets to comfort me and years of pain and hurt bubbling up which threatened to overtake me. I took another swig of the moonshine and thought back on my life. The men in my life seemed to do nothing but hurt me, betray me, and leave me not to mention abuse me and assault me. When was the last time I had known peace? I could think back to Alec's singing from family worships and the sound of his bass voice broke in on my mind, "they shall obtain gladness and joy and sorrow and mourning shall flee away." Isaiah 51:11. It had been so long since I had thought of a sacred song. The melody of victory had not graced the halls of my thought life for many years.

The Holy Spirit was wrapping me in a blanket of gold from the very walkway of heaven. The value of one child's name was sung in heaven and, though I was a liar, an adulterer, a thief, and almost a murderer, I was loved by the

Son of God who was enthroned there in the beauty of that place where time knows no limits and the sea of glass is still with the Peace of God. I can only imagine the interest of other beings and worlds when one child thinks to return to the place to which they are destined. Heaven is home and it is where we belong. It is where love resides and we are called to a better life. I felt the Holy Spirit speaking to my heart and wooing me with the songs of heaven. It lifted me to my feet but, alas, I was still drunk on moonshine.

It could have been the moonshine but I know that it was so much more than that. My soul cried out after that Man, that Man of sorrows who knew my darkened heart and "could make me whole," that Man that could fill my soul with true love, the Man that died to save me. The One who would never see me as the dirty prostitute would look sadly but sweetly upon my shame and rejoice over my repentance. He was the One all along always with me and I had missed Him, spurned Him, turned away from Him, and cursed His name. "Oh, How I love Jesus," was the Sabbath School song that came to mind. Could it be that simple?

I dared not think that it could be this simple to turn away from a life of darkness and sin. I knew for so many years that I had been running with the demons of hell. All along my runnings I had felt a force always saving me from evil and trying to pull me out. It was like a force field and constant presence that I was actively pushing away. I always knew that God was there but I hated Him as much I hated men.

This thought called me out from underneath the porch so I could see the sky. I wanted to shake my fist at the Man who had let me suffer under the yoke of men's lusty urges and assaults. Though I had willingly put myself in circumstances, time and time again, to suffer the consequences of sin, no one deserves sexual assault even though, without Christ's atonement, we deserve so much worse. I could not imagine a God who had allowed that.

I stumbled out to the front yard where I could look directly up into the starry sky. I raised my hands high up to God and screamed at the top of my lungs, half in absolute humility expecting no answer back at all and half in defiance to all the suffering I had endured, "If you want me back from Satan, come and get me! You hear me God! If you want me, come and get me! I'll be yours but you have to get me out of here! I'll stop but get me out of here!" Seven hours later my life would completely change.

The Bible talks of a difference between prayer and crying out. David, time and time again, in the Psalms, refers to crying out. David says in Psalm 36, "In my distress I called upon the Lord, and cried out to my God; He heard my voice from His temple, and my cry came before Him, even unto His ears." Here in this passage, the Hebrew for the word cry out is *shava*, meaning a cry for help. Crying out loud to God at the top of our lungs not only demonstrates repentance and humility but it can be a battle cry, the cry of a child to a father, and a cry to break the hold of darkness.

Spoken words have power, "Death and life are in the power of the tongue," Proverbs 18:21. So many times I had cried out to Satan to take my soul and, every time I did this, I was plunged into more and more wretched darkness. I needed to cry unto my God who spoke you and I into existence. With His audible voice as the sound that we now know as still and small, God's voice was deep and covered the universe when He commanded the light to shine out of darkness. With His voice, God created the world. With our voices, we proclaim our love for one another and, with our cry, we can break the bond of iniquity. In fact, it is in 1 Samuel where God declares that it was the continual cry (the Hebrew word for shriek from anguish and danger) of the fathers that caused God to pull them out of slavery.

"True, we have no power to free ourselves from Satan's control; but when we desire to be set free from sin, and in our great need cry out for a power out of and above ourselves, the powers of the soul are imbued with the divine energy of the Holy Spirit, and they obey the dictates of the will in fulfilling the will of God." *The Desire of Ages* 466.

Time and time again, the children of Israel had plunged themselves into trouble by turning away from God but, in Judges, we see them cry aloud and God raised up Othniel to save them. He does this over and over in Scripture. I am like Israel. Time and time again, I am falling into sin and trouble of my own making but the Lord hears my cry and He rescues me from myself to call me to God's best in obedience. It takes humility to cry out to God. It can be embarrassing to scream to the sky, especially if you have neighbors, but "God resists the proud and gives grace to the humble." James 4:6. Being humble before our God might just cause a miracle or two or three and save us in our hour of need. "Singing, I saw, often drove away the enemy, and shouting would beat him back." *21 Manuscript Releases* 238.

After I had completed screaming into the sky, I was tired and my legs carried me inside the house. I went back to the little room where I had been living and I had a sense that I would not be here much longer. I had no idea how I would get out of the relationship with Hawken but I knew the end was near.

I looked at the clock and it was nearly four o'clock in the morning. It was still dark outside and there was a chill in the air. I shivered even under the warm effects of the moonshine. I grabbed a blanket and curled up on the green and white checkered couch. I did not want to go to bed in case Hawken came home. The thoughts of where he was still filled my mind.

I knew that every bar in California was closed at two o'clock and that he was at someone's house. I knew that he was likely sleeping in the bed of another woman. "How could he do this to us?" I bemoaned. "Everything that Jack warned me about is coming true."

I must have fallen asleep. The next thing I was consciously aware of was that an hour had gone by. I heard a

494

rustling of keys and the door was opening. I jumped to my feet, ran to the door as it was opening, and hid behind the door. I grabbed a wooden sword, one of my son's homemade toys, that was the size and thickness of a baseball bat. As Hawken crossed the threshold of the doorway, I raised the sword like a warrior princess and brought it down on Hawken's head with great might and ferocious precision. I heard a "crack!" And with that, I welcomed Hawken home with one last birthday gift, a huge goose egg on the back of his head.

"What the [expletive]?" He screamed in pain and anguish. "Are you trying to kill me?" I am not even sure if my words in turn were intelligible. I accused him of cheating which, of course, he denied.

"Are you trying to kill me?" he shrieked again at the top of his lungs.

"Yes! I am going to kill you." I loudly announced with sarcasm. Maybe it was the look in my eye since I had, after all, been screaming in the yard to God and had been drinking moonshine all night. Whatever it was, Hawken believed that I was going to kill him. Like a little girl being chased by a great big dog, Hawken ran away with fear and trembling. I heard his truck skid out of the driveway for a second time in two days. He went to stay at his grandmother's house and announced to all of his family that his girlfriend was trying to kill him. I was the big bad wolf and, thankfully, because Hawken had cried wolf so many times about his girlfriends trying to kill him (maybe it was all the cheating he did), no one really cared to call the cops on me.

With the crack of a wooden sword, I knew that my time was up. Trying to kill each other was what we had come to. I was alone again in the back room and I started to pack my things. But, what to do? It had become so bad that I was desperate. "Maybe my mother will allow me to come home if I beg." I needed out of this place. Heretofore I had only hoped that someday I could go home again and have a peaceful relationship with my mother. It was forever an impossibility, I knew, if I were drinking. "What if I quit drinking? What if I offered that?" I hoped.

I called my mother and I cried out the story of Hawken's womanizing and drinking and I told her, "I promise, if I can come home, I will stop drinking and go to school." There was only one person I knew who hated men more than I did and that was my mother. She was horrified by the things I told her that Hawken had done to me. I failed to tell her that I had cracked him over the head with a giant wooden sword. That part I could leave out. I think that, at any other time if I had not cried out to God, she would have said, "no." Dre and my mom were not known for their mercy in situations like these.

I was always in trouble and it was their belief that I should face those consequences alone. "I had made my bed and, now, I deserved to lie in it," was a phrase I had heard my mother say often. She was somewhat correct. Dre had, after all, lived in his car when he was young and he believed others should suffer as much as he had. So many times before I had hinted about the conditions under which I was living but the offer of coming home was never extended to me. But now, with the commitment of not drinking alcohol or smoking, this daughter could come home. I was thrilled and so happy that my mother had agreed to allow me back home. I was leaving.

Seven hours after I cried out to the Lord, I was gone from Hawken's house. My mother picked me up from his house at about eleven o'clock in the morning. I had endured a rough night but my mother was sweet and kind to me. If she had said an unkind word, I was quickly learning that God has grace-filled earmuffs and I ask Him daily to cover my ears so that the hurtful comments of others do not even register in my mind.

I was weary from a life lived in debauchery and pain. "No more," was my mindset. I was walking away from everything and everyone. I was leaving behind all my friends and associations. Yes, I could call Layla, who had expressed an interested in renewing our friendship, or anyone to come get me and I could have shifted my existence to another person and another scene but I needed real change. I needed to hit the reset button and I knew that, for me at that time, the quickest way to hit the reset button was to go home to my mother.

It was not easy arriving home. I had lived a life free

from rules and authority and now I had made a commitment to my mother to not drink or smoke after drinking alcohol nearly every night for almost five years. Now I was to not only quit a huge drinking habit but also a well established smoking habit. I was back in my old room again and the ghosts of the past threatened to overtake me. I could still see the remnants of demonic writing on the walls of my room from drunken nights years and years ago. My mother had attempted to paint over these harrowing messages but to no avail. The words, "I need help," "Take me Satan," and "I want to die," were a written reminder of the girl who was crying out for help.

As I stood in my room looking at the message that would not be hidden even by a fresh coat of paint, I was tempted to be angry at my mother for not heeding the cry of those written messages from long ago. Some of them were even written above the laundry machines just so she would see my cries for help. She ignored them and painted over them. I was still that same girl with a fresh new coat of paint. How was I going to chip away the paint and get down to the real me and really get better? I did not know. I did not have the first clue on how to change myself.

I "white knuckled" not drinking. I sat in my mother's garage again. For some reason, my room brought back too many memories and it was too dark so I often gravitated to the garage. Occasionally, I would find an old cigarette in the yard and take it out to the street but, for the most part, I was not drinking or smoking. I had the shakes and the sweats at night. It was a rough two weeks but I was able to get clean. The worst part was being alone all the time.

Here I would sit alone and not drink and not smoke and I would cry. I think the crying was an important step. Though most people think it is a sign of weakness, I think crying shows a softening of the heart. Up until this point, I only cried when I was drunk and then it was uncontrollable but now I was weeping for myself and all the pain I had caused my son and I.

I was single again and I planned to stay this way for some time. I did not know what was causing me to drift to a certain kind of man. It was in my DNA to find men who were abusive and drug-addicted like me. I knew that, if I were going to change at all, I needed to be single for now and that was not easy. I had enrolled at the local college immediately after I left Hawken's house and I was attending classes.

Thankfully, Dre was giving me a ride to school three days out of the week. At school, I knew that it would be easy to fall into the wrong kind of associations and it was difficult to abstain from men, drinking, and smoking. I would backslide again and again in these areas. Though I had not made any profession of faith at this point, I could feel a certain kind of power sustaining me and keeping me from getting so discouraged that I gave up and plunged back into darkness. There were times that I failed and fell. Whether it was drinking a couple of beers at a neighbor's house or smoking at school, as soon as I did it I knew that I was on dangerous ground and thus I would climb back out of my hole and try to keep going. I would hang out with the wrong people at school and end up at parties and immediately know that I had done wrong and walk away again and again. This was not a perfect time in my life by any means. I made many, many more mistakes that I am not proud of but I was on a road heading toward repentance.

Chapter 30

My Desire

I had Hawken trying to call me very frequently. He would beg me to come back but I refused. Living with my mother was not easy. I had to face all the same feelings and the same betrayals again and this was the biggest driver to drink. I tried to be loyal and loving to her because she allowed me to come back home but she often brought up all the same feelings of anger and mistrust that had driven me away. I would run away from home and find myself drinking again and then carry myself back home to sit in the garage and cry, starting from square one with being sober-minded.

I got a job as a secretary for a tax accountant in January and it was a very slow time of the year. I was taking classes at the local college so, after I did my schoolwork, I would have hours and hours on my hands to read. I picked up a Max Lucado book from my mother's library and read it and I found a peace come to my heart that I had never known before. I had never had personal devotions in my life and I started to sense that this benefited me in a way that nothing else could. I was literally lost as to what to read next so I picked up a few Christian books written by various authors and gleaned a few things here and there.

The Holy Spirit can use anything and anyone to bring a person to repentance. I could feel a tug-of-war going on around me for my life. The next few years of my life would be exactly that, a tug-of-war. Now, instead of sitting in the garage and listening to rock music which brought the bar experience to me instead of me to the bar, I chose to turn off the music and sit in the calm quiet of the night. This started a regular discourse between something I did not know and I. Now, I can call it prayer but I did not dare to call it that back then.

I was not a Christian yet. I did not identify as any faith but I was talking to something greater than myself and, one night, I prayed out loud for help. I hung my head in shame and dared not even utter the words but I found myself speaking out loud to It. "You know I need help. You know I need out of all of this. Please, please help me?" With that I went on about my business thinking that nothing and no one cared enough about me to help me. I had to help me. I had to pull myself out of the mess I had created. I had made myself a whore, a vagabond, a liar, and a thief and no one could change that. I was a rebel of the highest order and no one could take away all the things that I had done, right?

I was becoming very curious about spiritual things, namely this person called Jesus Christ. I had been curious about religion before but now I was becoming curious about Christ. Religion and Christ can be two very different things. I had grown up as a Seventh-day Adventist and I often heard that Jesus died for me but I knew very little about His life and the details on a personal level. I had taken baptismal courses

502

and even been baptized at twelve years old but, only a year after that, my family situation disintegrated and I thereafter became bitter, angry, and rebellious. I had never really understood the Bible very well. These days I certainly could not understand the Bible. It was hard to read and my mind was still very cloudy from substance abuse. I needed something simpler and more elementary to start reading because I had not read anything in a long while.

I would often sit and talk with Dre about all the things that I was thinking and feeling at the time. These conversations would often go deep and I would tell him about the hard times that I was having not going back to Hawken. In fact, I confided in him more than I ever did to my mother or Alec. He had an easiness about him that could make anyone talk to him about anything and he was a good listener. Even though I confided in him, I still held back many, many secrets of my former life. Even though I started to cautiously view him as a sort of brother or father figure, I feared that, if anyone knew of all the things that I had done, they would no longer love me.

Dre had some idea of just the kind of life I was formerly living because, one day, a woman showed up at our door. Her son, a huge six foot five and three hundred pound Mexican with gang connections, used to hang out with me until he abruptly left town when he stole some drug money from me when I was a dealer. Oddly enough, rumors had circulated that I had put a hit out on his life or that I was planning on killing this man myself. This poor mother stood at the door and begged Dre to ask me to let her son come back to Beaumont without any trouble. Dre knew I was home and both he and I were positively shocked by the fear I had caused this family. This man had been away from Beaumont for years and would not return for fear of my reprisal.

I was grateful for the amount of time Dre was investing in taking me to school and helping me get around. Grateful is not the word, I felt indebted to him for all his help. He sacrificed his time to transport me to school and to work and, for that, I am eternally thankful. Without this sacrifice, I would have had a much harder time sitting at home all day with nothing to do. Boredom is the devil's workshop and I had not yet learned how to manage my free time without filling it with drugs and alcohol.

But, all this time and heart-felt conversation came at a cost. Though I am grateful to Dre for the sacrifice of his time, one of my life's greatest hurts came from this time, a hurt that often is used by the enemy and the father of lies to wound me to this day if I let it. Praise God for victory over bitterness but it has not always been so.

One morning, Dre sat in the kitchen in his big dark robe at the sunny kitchen table. If anyone has ever been in my mother's kitchen, you will know that it is covered in sunflowers. I think it may be my mother's external way of making herself happy because she suffers with great bouts of bitterness and I think it helps her feel better. The kitchen is bright and cheery and I pulled up a chair to have some coffee too. He had been back in his room playing computer games due to the fact that his job at the time did not start until later in the day. We were talking about various topics and having one of our conversations about life when the conversation segued into the topic of my mother. "You know she is suspicious of us being together like we are having an affair," he said it so matter of fact that I could hardly believe my ears.

"What?" I thought for sure that this was just a joke or that I had not correctly heard him.

"That's what she said. I mean she calls me all morning to make sure that I'm not doing anything that I shouldn't be. I think that she resents the fact that I can go into work whenever I want and she can't." He added more details with an irritated tone in the slow and low style in which he speaks but I was still back on the phrase, "You know she is suspicious of us being together..." My mind raced! I felt a hot knife hit my chest and all the old feelings of my mother's betrayal hit me like a wall of emotion. She was the same. Even though I was trying my best to love her and she, in turn, was being sweet, there was an entirely whole other thing going on behind closed doors just like had happened in the past.

My mother's niceness and sweetness toward letting me stay there felt like a facade and she was accusing Dre and I of the same old thing she suspected with Alec. How could she do this again? It was so far from the truth but the fact that

Dre had brought it up made me feel dirty. I remembered a comment he had made to me repeating what one of his employees had said, "I am a lucky man because I get to live with two sexy women." Suddenly, I looked at all of his help as having ulterior motives. I have no idea what my mother really said to Dre. All I know is what Dre said and it hurt so badly at the time that I could not bear it.

"How could my mother think so low of me?" It was so twisted and obscene in my mind that I immediately excused myself from the table with some plausible excuse. In my mind, I had thought that these insinuations were a thing of the past.

I went to my room and closed the door and immediately dropped to the floor and could not breathe. I was panting, trying to catch my breath, and trying to keep my heart from exploding all at once. "How could she? Why does this happen everywhere I go? It must be me. It's me! I cause this everywhere I go! I am the reason I never have wholesome and pure relationships with men." I thought these thoughts and they were so injurious to my soul, let alone total lies from the enemy, but exactly what we, as victims of abuse, tell ourselves.

I grabbed my coat and barely had it on before I was out the door and running down the street. I was crying so hard that I could barely breathe and run at the same time but I was running as fast as my legs could carry me away from my childhood home. I was running so fast that the tears falling from my face were trailing behind me. I had to get away. I was running and wailing, "why?" That's all I could say. "Why? Why is it that, every time I get close to a man, this happens. Why can't I just have a father?" I wanted a father. I needed a father in my life. Who could I depend on to be my father?

I had run down my street and further down other streets until I had come to a vacant field with a ditch where I could drop down into the dirt and be unseen. I flopped myself down into the dirt and sat in the ditch and wailed and wept for all the years I had to go it all alone. All my life, I was always in search of a man to find me and save me. I wept and wept and wept for the little girl that craved a father and was denied. I wept for all the men that I had chained myself to in hopes that they would fill that role of father and they never did. I wept for all the times I had been sexually assaulted and had no one to stand in the gap for me. I cried out to the One I had cried to before, "Why can't I have a Father? Why?" I was angry, I was sad, and I mourned the loss of my earthly father who I had never even met. I wanted a father more than anything else in the world. Without a father, I was alone and felt worthless and without an anchor, a guide, and without any purpose or identity in my life. For the first time in my life, I grieved over the void where there was supposed to be a father and I grieved over all the pain I had heretofore experienced as a consequence of others' and my own sin.

I soon ran out of tears to cry and I grew emotionally exhausted. At that time, I had no idea what crying out meant in Scripture. All I knew was that my life was in continual crisis and I was desperate for change. I was totally helpless and hopeless. I would do anything. I knew not that I had just laid my case bare in front of the King of Heaven. I had little faith that God even heard me or took an interest in me so I picked myself up out of the dirt and brushed some of it off. I had mascara all over my face. My eyes were red and puffy and I had stickers and dirt in my hair.

I was a wreck. "What should I do?" I thought out loud. I cannot go home or, better put, I did not want to go home and deal with the words said and the emotions felt. I wanted to avoid confrontation at all costs. I wanted to avoid the inevitable words that my mother usually said to excuse the inappropriate behavior of herself or her husband, "why are you so sensitive," or "that's not what I said," or, my personal favorite, "he's just joking." I could not take that, not today. I knew that it was neither a joke nor was I being too sensitive.

Most of the time my mother was somehow able to convince me that I had not heard correctly. Because of her, nearly all of my life, the enemy had been able to lie to me and keep me silent. I could always hear, "no one will ever believe you," playing in my head. But those are lies made by the father of lies to destroy me and to destroy you too. We must understand that most of the destructive behavior that we do and the bitter feelings we feel is because we are believing the lies of the enemy.

I knew that I could not talk to my mother about what I

was feeling. I had to figure out a way to stuff my feelings or release them. But how? I was walking back to my house, not quite sure of what to do when I got there. Satan shot a fiery dart to my thinking as I saw a neighbor kid named TJ standing outside his house. TJ was a good-looking blonde kid that was only a few years younger than I. He was a very jovial character and he was not embarrassed at all to share with me that, "I was his dream girl." This made me a little shy around him. It is a lot of pressure to be someone's dream girl.

I self-consciously wiped my face again and checked my fingers to see how much black mascara was really there on my face. I seemed to be getting it all off just fine. It was not but a few years ago that I used to stop by TJ's house and sell him drugs. I sold him ecstasy, mushrooms, and chronic quite frequently. He saw me coming and I could tell he was waiting for me.

"Hey girl!" he said with an illustrious smile full of his usual character and mirth. TJ was raised by his grandparents because his mother was in and out of prison due to drug addiction and the subsequent crime that comes with that lifestyle. I thought, "How apropos. Of course I'm his dream girl. I'm probably exactly like his mother." I sighed with the reality of a ruined life and I felt hopeless and alone. Whatever hopes I had possessed before of cleaning up my life and staying at my mom's house were now replaced with an undeniable feeling that I had to figure out a way to get out. It was a pattern. As soon as I got home, I remembered why I left in the first place and I could not wait to get away again.

"Wanna party?" TJ asked with a gleeful grin.

I hesitated. I was not sure if that was the answer. I had not drank or used any kind of drugs for weeks and weeks. What I really wanted was a cigarette. Cigarettes were the hardest thing of all to quit. It was like giving up the number one, very best thing that relieved stress and made everything just a tad bit better than prior to that cigarette. How could I give up the thing that I needed just to manage my day?

"You got a cigarette?" I asked, hoping to stall a little so I could think about this decision I was about to make. I knew that TJ had massive drugs at his house and an agreement to party with him was indeed agreeing to sully my sobriety in every way. I was not sure. The thing about temptation is that we cannot be tempted to do things that we really do not want to do or else it would not be temptation at all. I wanted to get high and wash away my troubles. That was how I always did it. I would drink until I could not feel any emotional or physical pain at all and this was how I learned to deal with every kind of problem.

Here I had made a nearly deadly error. What I had not overcome had overcome me. The victory I had failed to claim claimed victory over me. I chose, against my convictions, to put off sobriety for another day. But, another day, I almost had not. Please, if Christ is calling you to conviction, if my story has affected you even a little, if you see how dirty I was and yet God came after me while fighting off all the hounds of hell to wrap His bloodstained arms around me, even as I wounded Him with my continual sinning, take His hand now and do not wait as I did. It is Christ you feel now bringing to mind that thing standing between you and He. Repent of it and tell Him you have no power to win the victory on your own. Then, choose to leave it behind. Ask Him for the hatred we all need for sin. Do not wait.

The instant I chose to walk in the way of sin and chose not to follow the forward moving path of constant humility, I let the fact that someone hurt me serve as my reason to hurt myself. This was always my practice. Others would hurt me, I became bitter and angry, and I made a way to hurt myself and take out my anger on myself. I usually consoled myself with the fact that I was not hurting anyone else but I was only hurting myself. This is a lie that the enemy wants us to believe. We are hurting Christ when we injure ourselves.

By no means did God give me up the moment I turned away from Him but I surely plunged into a state of hopelessness. Here I must warn you. After an individual maintains some sobriety and then chooses to dabble again in mind-altering substances, this is the most dangerous time because one does not have the same tolerance as they did before and many people overdose and lose their lives at this point. Only by the grace of God did I survive this night.

The longer I spent with TJ, the more discouraged I became. The more I dwelled on the hurts of my mother, the more I drank and, the more I drank, the more uninhibited I became. I allowed myself to plunge deeper and deeper into discouragement that night and I rebelled against my promises to my mother to be drug and alcohol free. Discouragement and rebellion is a very dangerous sin. It is why the Children of Israel roamed the desert for forty years instead of moving forward to the Promised Land right away. If I wanted to move forward, I would have to forgive my mother...for everything.

But, this night, I drank and drank more than a little. As I drank, TJ brought out some cocaine and I said, "sure." As the effects of cocaine hit me, TJ and I went to his shed where we practiced tagging (spray paint art) on the wall of his shed. We laughed and snorted more lines of cocaine. Cocaine and alcohol go together like eggs and toast. I soon realized that I felt no care for tomorrow and the familiar spirit of a longing for death returned to me. It had been some time since I had felt the strong urge to cut myself. I was dancing with the devil again and it was an all too familiar feeling.

I felt no hope and I could not pierce the dark shroud of my inner turmoil and discouragement. I have never since allowed my mind to travel in these channels of hopelessness for, once these thoughts are allowed to stay in my mind, it is a road easily traveled. Discouragement is a choice and I take up my shield of faith when trials come and choose to rejoice. Instead, this night, I chose death. TJ soon presented something that he was hiding. He had a meth pipe on him.

"Wanna meet my little friend, shabu?" He laughed and laughed. I was so very high and wondered if all the combinations of drugs would kill me and I was hoping they would. Sadly, I took the glass pipe and, after years of being clean from my old friend Crystal, I got high. Immediately, my brain was washed clean of the effects of the alcohol. Meth does that. I was high on cocaine and meth and now we were smoking weed and, later, I found myself huffing paint too. It was a toxic combination.

If TJ had asked me to do anything else, I probably would have done that too. To be honest, my death wish was nothing more than Satan's security blanket that I liked to cuddle myself with. With any kind of emotional pain or life stress that I experienced, I would tell myself, "it doesn't matter because I'll be dead soon anyway." I used to think that suicide was brave but I soon learned that the brave ones are living life.

I could feel my heart fluttering in my chest from all the substances. At a certain point in the evening, I drank so much and did so many drugs that I lost huge chunks of memory from that night. I am thankful that TJ was too afraid of me (due to my violent reputation) to do anything awful to me while I was passed out but that is always the danger whenever you do drugs with another person and lose your cognitive abilities. The goal was to die and I was doing my best to take as much cocaine mixed with meth as I could to make my heart stop.

The next thing I remember was waking up in my bed. I was somehow home and in my bed and was not sure how I got there. I felt terrible. I was disappointed I was alive. Without moving a sore and tired muscle, I glanced to the side at the clock above my bedroom door and I knew that I had been asleep for some time. In the newness of day and without being under the influence of alcohol, I had a new perspective on life. Just like that the pendulum swung and I was angry at myself for being so foolish and risking my life.

I cannot understate the fact at how angry I was at myself. I had relapsed back into my old life again and, not only that, I had tried to kill myself and I could have been successful at it. I was wondering if it was still possible to drop dead because my heart had failed to keep a normal rhythm since the night before and I was still having weird palpitations in my chest. I knew that one more bender like this one and I might not be so lucky. The shame of going back hung over me like a curse and I rolled over in bed and wrapped myself around a pillow. With no human person to console me, I talked aloud to the pillow, "why did I do that?" Yes, I was lamenting the pounding headache and the weird chest pains and the flu-like symptoms of a terrific hangover but I also had a sorrow in my soul and not just for the consequences of sin.

I felt the pure, unadulterated fact that I was resisting the Holy Spirit. "The wrath of God is not declared against the unrepentant sinners merely because of the sins they have committed, but because, when called to repent, they choose to continue in resistance, repeating the sins of the past in defiance of the light given them." *Acts of the Apostles* 62. I knew in my heart that I was resisting and fighting against something, something that wanted something better. I was clueless as to why. I felt I had no value at all beyond what I could offer men and even my mother felt the same way.

All the lies of Satan hit me like arrows of burning tar being fired at the castle of the heart. It was a total onslaught, "You're a failure, you're a looser, you're a slut, no one will ever love you, you're better off dead." As I was lying there, defeated again and lost with no hope and feeling like I will never get better, I felt the Spirit of God come to me. Without an explanation or a reason why, I walked straight out of my room, which was where I had planned on hiding until I could get the smell of the night before off of me, to my mother's bookshelf in the living room and my eyes fell right on a book called *The Desire of Ages*. It was as if a voice spoke to me, "this, this is who you need." I grabbed it out of the bookcase and held it for a second. I had a sense that the history of my life depended on the opening of that one book. I had heard the title mentioned before when I was growing up but I did not actually know what was in it.

Chapter 31

Worst Case

It was a process to eliminate the undesirable things from my life but, as far as meth and cocaine go, that night was the last time I ever tried those things because I found another way. Just because you find Jesus does not mean that life gets perfect. In fact, we get a new struggle, the struggle with the flesh. We are now no longer resisting the Spirit of God and we are never alone anymore. "The same divine mind that is working upon the things of nature is speaking to the hearts of men and creating an inexpressible craving for something they have not. The things of the world cannot satisfy their longings. The Spirit of God is pleading with them to seek for those things that alone can give peace and rest—the grace of Christ, the joy of holiness." *Steps to Christ* 28.

My thought was, "I can't read this right now, I was just drunk and high the night before. Any kind of God isn't going to want me after I just did all that." I felt dirty not knowing that the reason any of us ever feel exceedingly sinful is because we are looking into the mirror of the law of life. It is God's law and His holiness that causes us to feel sinful, very sinful indeed, and that is the voice of God to our soul. If you feel sinful, rejoice! That is God's voice speaking to your heart. "The heart of God yearns over His earthly children with a love stronger than death. In giving up His Son, He has poured out to us all heaven in one gift. The Savior's life and death and intercession, the ministry of angels, the pleading of the Spirit, the Father working above and through all, the unceasing interest of heavenly being,—all are enlisted in behalf of man's redemption." *Steps to Christ* 21.

How could I, in my shame, resist this power that was wooing me? The chief of sinners, the daughter that is the lost coin, the lost sheep, and the prodigal, standing in her mother's living room with alcohol on her breath, her blood tainted with narcotics and a long list of sexual immoralities, was being called home to her Father.

I opened *The Desire of Ages* and, for a week, I devoured its contents. Almost instantly, whenever I opened the book, Hawken would call me. My heart would sorrow and hurt with the pain of all my broken relationships and I wanted to go running back to Hawken to have even a taste of the intimacy I lacked. Then I would open the book and I found that the pages were giving me the intimacy I needed and I was stronger and more resolute than ever, not in myself but in the Man I found in those pages who was healing the wounds of the broken girl who came to Him.

Up until this point, I had suffered every day with the feeling of a broken heart. I lived in a constant state of being wounded and traumatized. I had raging post-traumatic stress disorder and nightmares. I looked for anything or anyone to get rid of this feeling. I had a constant feeling that I was missing out on something, something big, and, whenever I got to where I was going, I was immediately struck by another feeling that I did not belong there. Now, for the first time, I was able to look those feelings in the face and realize that God was using those emotions to bring me back to Him all along. Now, I was not just feeling but actually knowing peace.

Let me tell you who I met on those pages. I met the Man of my dreams in Christ. He came to me, a sinner, and He has become my closest confidant. You may ask how can an unseen person be real and alive? He is real and He changed me, the worst of the worst. Try Him and see. The number of men I have been with is so numerous that I do not actually know the number.

The reason why this book is not solely about substance abuse and sobriety is because my real problem or addiction was men. I craved an intimacy I lacked in an earthly or Heavenly Father. I was essentially living the life of an unpaid prostitute. I craved deep emotional connections and that is how hard I searched for intimacy and love. No one ever told me that love, true love, is the absence of selfishness. Love is not merely an emotion. Emotions are what we experience as a reaction but it is not the root cause. Love is the ability to serve others without motive or pride. Love never condemns and it never gives up.

One of my favorite stories in *The Desire of Ages* and one I clung to was the man by the pool of Bethesda. The waters of this pool would move and, when that happened, whoever was the first to dive into the waters was said to be healed. Many people crowded the area for the chance of divine healing. Trust me, I would lay there too for a chance to be healed. Suffering is a terrible thing. I can imagine all the people with cancer, ALS, and other maladies surrounding the area and fighting each other for the chance to be the first in the pool. It must have been a mad rush like that of wildebeests crowding a single water source. The aged slapping down the young and the stronger shoving back the weaker.

There is one man lying far back because he cannot get past the impatient throng of people. At this point, the man had given up hope of ever making it to the pool. He must have positioned himself on his bed or one of his family members set up his bed for him. They may have questioned him as to whether this was really what he wanted to do. "Can't this man just suffer in his bed at home like everyone else?" they might have said.

This man's suffering and shame were self-made. He had brought it on himself. The book calls it a "case of supreme wretchedness." A young man who was only thirty-eight. "His disease was in a great degree the result of his own sin, and looked upon as a judgment of God."

"Alone and friendless, feeling that he was shut out from God's mercy, the sufferer had passed long years of misery." Whatever disease this man had, it was a disease of the order that comes from rough living and sin that shows the world your shame. It would cause people to point and immediately know that he deserved what he had received.

Perhaps it was a wretched, crippling case of syphilis or the like. Whatever it was, we know he could not walk.

The man was completely and totally helpless and completely dependent on the mercy and unselfishness of friends and family to lift him and carry him to the pool when the waters were agitated but to no avail. His helplessness made him completely unable to reach the edge of the water and, when he did have someone who could lift him and help him, he would get shoved out of the way and someone would make it in first. Daily he suffered with the fear that he would never make it. He would die in his misery.

His life was now a life of shame. I can only imagine his fear to even lift his eyes to heaven and pray knowing that he deserved everything that was happening. He had caused it. The regrets at thirty-eight must have filled his soul. He was old enough to know better and young enough to know he had wasted it all. How does one cope with shame? Not only this but he was plagued with the daily battle of illness and suffering and it all seemed too much to bear.

Discouragement, disappointment, and the abuse of others stronger than he, this was his life. But still he had one tiny shred of hope. Though he had caused the fate that had befallen him by his sin, he believed that there was something out there that could heal him. He could not figure out how he would get it and, most of the time, he believed he was not worthy of it but, to the pool of Bethesda, he came just in case.

The book said he was the worst case possible. This

meant that, out of everyone there, he was the sickest. Daily he was humbled by the limits of his own body, his ill appearance, and by his total dependence on others. He had no ability to help himself in any way. He was poor, wretched, miserable, blind, and naked. He could, of himself, do nothing.

On the Sabbath day, "the sick man was lying on his mat, and occasionally lifting his head to gaze at the pool, when a tender, compassionate face bent over him, and the words, 'Will you be made whole?' arrested his attention. Hope came to his heart. He felt that in some way he was to have help. But the glow of encouragement soon faded. He remembered how often he had tried to reach the pool and now he had little prospect of living till it should again be troubled. He turned away wearily, saying, 'Sir, I have no man, when the water is troubled, to put me into the pool: but while I am coming, another steps down before me.'" *The Desire of Ages* 202.

Christ could read between the lines and He heard, "I have no one on earth who I can lean on. I am all alone. When others should see how wretched I really am, no one will help me and I have no earthly idea how to help myself either. I need everyone and I am in need of everything and, yet, I have nothing and no one and I am so discouraged that I am on the brink of despair and death. I have no hope. I am but an ant on this earth among many and I matter little and I am only a blight on society. I will die soon."

When I read that Jesus chose the worst case, I knew

that this case was I. "I am too awful and too messed up to save, I should just curl up and die." This was my thinking. I could never have a normal life after all the havoc I had caused and the sins I had committed. I dared not even hope but the book said, "Jesus does not ask this sufferer to exercise faith in Him" (as Jesus had done many times before with others). Christ could see this man had no faith at all. He simply says, "Get up, get your stuff, and walk."

"But the man's faith takes hold upon that word. Every nerve and muscle thrills with new life, and healthful action comes to his crippled limbs. Without question he sets his will to obey the command of Christ, and all his muscles respond to his will. Springing to his feet, he finds himself an active man. Through the same faith we may receive spiritual healing. By sin we have been severed from the life of God. Our souls are sick. Of ourselves we are no more capable of living a holy life than was the impotent man capable of walking. There are many who realize their helplessness, and who long for that spiritual life which will bring them into harmony with God; they are vainly striving to obtain it....Let these desponding, struggling ones look up." *The Desire of Ages* 202-203.

When I read this, my heart melted. When I read the part, "he sets his will," I knew I had never exercised my will before but to will to do evil. I thought, if I were paralyzed, and I am paralyzed of my own self and can do nothing, and someone told me they had just healed me, I would decide to stand up. This is the will, making a decision and putting your efforts into standing up into what God says. The will is like a muscle. It wants to be flexed.

If you can understand your weakness, you are on your way to spiritual wholeness. The reason why Christ required no faith from this man was because he was already aware of his weakness and this had prepared him for the Son of God to give him His total and complete life-changing power. How do we know this? Paul wrote, "My strength is made perfect in weakness." 2 Corinthians 12:9. If you are like me and see how dirty you are, how many times you have messed up, the pain you have experienced and caused, your powerlessness to forgive, your hatred for others, your awful thoughts, your inability to do the right thing, and you hardly even have the desire to do the right thing, then you are right where Christ wants you so He can change your life. You cannot come to God strong and expect God to do anything for you. How can a doctor help a terminal patient who thinks they are healthy?

There is a psalm that has become my theme. It is a psalm written by David. When we feel too dirty and disappointed in ourselves, when we feel unsure that we will make it to heaven, or when we are experiencing disappointment and heartache, we need to hold onto this, "The Lord is merciful and gracious, slow to anger, and abounding in mercy. He will not always strive with us nor will He keep his anger forever. He has not dealt with us according to our sins, nor punished us according to our iniquities. For as the heavens are high above the earth, so great is His mercy toward those that fear Him; as far as the east is from the west, so far has he removed our transgressions from us. As a father pities his children, so the Lord pities those who fear Him. For He knows our frame; He remembers that we are dust. As for man, his days are like grass; as a flower of the field, so he flourishes. For the wind passes over it, and it is gone, and its place remembers it no more. But the mercy of the Lord is from everlasting to everlasting on those who fear Him, and His righteousness to children's children, to such as keep his covenant, and to those who remember His commandments to do them." Psalm 103:8-18.

The book says that the man did not stand alone. As he tried, "in acting upon it he received strength." "I do nothing alone?" I questioned. "Yes!" The Holy Spirit was beginning to converse with me like with a friend. It was beautiful and encouraging to me that Christ wanted to change the entire Jewish religion's view of Sabbath from that of rules and a day of oppression to a day of joy, communion with Him, and relief for the suffering. He picked the worst, most pathetic case in all of Israel to do this. Christ wanted to exclaim from every corner of the city of Jerusalem to every hovel that, "God had given no commandment which cannot be obeyed by all. His law sanctions no unreasonable or selfish restrictions." Jesus spoke of God "not as an avenging judge, but as a tender father." *The Desire of Ages* 204.

The messenger of this gospel was the most hopeless of

them all but, once healed, he was the most effective in publishing the news far and wide of Jesus' work on the Sabbath day. Jesus used the most sinful, faithless, and crippled case in all of Jerusalem to awaken an entire city that day. This formerly weak, suffering, and hopeless man was more effective than any news agency could be. After the healing, Jesus suffered himself to be taken to the Sanhedrin to answer why He had healed on the Sabbath. There He gives the entire gospel message to all the officials of the city. Jesus handpicked this wicked, wayward, and ailing man to answer to the most pious and "holy" Jews with courage, gratefulness, and love for the One that had healed him.

Every day I worked at the tax accountant's office was another day I had to read this book. I sat at a large desk while answering phones, making appointments, filing paperwork, and, in between those tasks, God arranged it so that I was literally being paid to sit and read *The Desire of Ages*. I had four to six hours of downtime every day to sit and read. With every page, I started to see how I was "kicking against the pricks" and running from the One I needed. I knew that I had driven my life far off into a ditch. I wondered if it were possible to ever be saved. I was filled with a sense of dread and shame for all the evil that I had done. All the men, all the drugs, all the fights, the violence, and the crime. I was helpless and useless.

Who would ever believe that I was thinking of becoming a Christian? The shame of all the wicked things I had done to my family, friends, and to myself haunted me. I was convicted of my need for Christ and I was being brought to repentance but I was filled with an awesome sense of my own evil. I failed to recognize this as the power of the Holy One. Next to Him, we are all covered in the filth of sin. We need our lives washed and put straight and He will do this for us but, as of yet, I did not understand this. I could not imagine how I would get out of all the legal trouble I was in. I had to make sure that, in every job I was able to get and everything I did, they did not find out about my warrants. I was living with secret shame. My story from this point on is not new. It is found in first and second Samuel in the Bible. It goes like this.

The story unfolds under a king who was regularly filled with rage and who was violent, abusive, proud, and told his son, Jonathan, that he was worthless if he could not take the throne after him. Yes, this was King Saul. The people in Ancient Israel had cried out for a king and they had rejected the direct rulership of God over Israel. "Give us a king," they shouted. In all the years of Israel's history, it was understood that God would one day choose Israel's first king but, now, the people chose a king, not for wisdom or character like Christ, but for his height, his handsome appearance (the most handsome in all Israel), and his abilities in battle. He was from a wealthy family and he had a proud way of carrying himself that drew much attention from the people. But, he had an anger problem and he excused his anger as being "passionate." In fact, Saul excused away everything he did and that ended up killing him in the end.

Saul was crowned king but soon he thought to prove himself higher than God. He had a vile temper and he became abusive to all of his household. When David, a young shepherd boy who was loved by all of Israel for slaying Goliath (a Philistine giant and warrior that oppressed the people), played soothing music for Saul, Saul hated David and tried to kill him.

Saul's son, Jonathan, saw his father as unjust. Jonathan loved David and this enraged Saul to no end. Jonathan lived with an angry and abusive father. There was domestic violence in the home and Saul even tried to kill Jonathan, his own son. Jonathan suffered greatly because of his father's anger but he never sought vengeance against his father but willingly served his father, the King. Jonathan and David suffered the wrath of King Saul together. They made an oath to care for each other and each other's children on a night when Jonathan was helping David escape a death warrant from Saul.

Fast forward to after Jonathan was slain in battle and Saul had killed himself in that same battle. Saul had trained his children to hate and fear David who was now King. When Saul died, all of Saul's family fled from the supposed danger of King David. David's enemies and the father of lies screamed their hatefulness toward David into the ears of Saul's family and they believed a lie. "Surely David will kill us all now." They did not know that David had taken an oath to care for his best friend's family. David was no danger at all.

Saul's family only took what they could carry out of the city and fled for their lives. The rush to leave the city must have been a chaotic scene. No mother, brother, or sister grabbed Mephibosheth. He only had his nurse to care for him. He was just a baby, just barely walking. The nurse was busy and in such a hurry that she dropped this sweet and innocent baby boy. Can you imagine? The fall was so terrible and so extreme that his two feet were completely mangled in the fall. Bleeding and with broken limbs, she rescues the boy and takes not the time to set the limbs straight but continues on her journey. We do not even know if she stayed with the little injured boy who was in pain.

He had lost all of his family in one day. He lost his identity, his heritage, and he lost his legs and the ability to walk. The only kind faces he knew were replaced by the faces of strangers. He was a sick little boy and likely unloved. We know that they told him he was worthless and a burden to them. They told him he was a hunted man and that he had better be careful because his days were numbered. "If David ever finds you, he'll kill you like the dog you are."

In the Near East culture, a dog was the lowest of the low. The pig and the dog were two unclean meats that were detested by all men and women. In fact, when David went out to fight Goliath, Goliath cursed Israel and compared himself to the "dog." It was a terrible thing to consider yourself a dog and of no worth to anyone. Mephibosheth's mind was trained to think of himself as dirty and a failure. I definitely know how he feels. This was my experience. As I thought over all the things that I had done, I started to see myself like Mephibosheth, no more as the big, bad, drug dealer rebel girl but as full of mistakes, failures, and a huge waste of life.

So David, who represents Christ in this story, calls his servant Ziba to the palace to stand in front of him and asks Ziba, "Is there yet any that is left of the house of Saul, that I may show him kindness for Jonathan's sake?" Ziba answers in the Hebrew language, "yes, there is Mephibosheth. He is a crippled young man, living in the house of an unsuccessful and impoverished salesman in the driest and poorest land in all of Israel." The meaning of the name Mephibosheth in the Hebrew is "shame." Mephibosheth is the picture of shame in the Bible. He had inherited a lineage of defeat and failure. Every good thing seemed to be robbed from him. He lived in a desert of despair with a salesman who had nothing to sell but poverty. The Hebrew says that the family with which Mephibosheth lived traded in slavery but he, a cripple, was not even worth selling into slavery. Shame and slavery are bedfellows.

Mephibosheth is terrified as Ziba brings him before King David. Mephibosheth has already been assured by Ziba that David is offering kindness but this is too good to be true for him. He has never known kindness before. He is sure that the day he sees David's face is the day he shall surely die. He passes through the beauty of the city and the former kingdom of his father. He is a former prince and now he is a crippled vagabond whose life is covered in the dark shroud of shame. When he raises his eyes to see the throne room, he is filled with fear and, though he has no legs, he falls on his face. Though he has only known the unkindness of this earth, he feels the awesome sense of the power of the king and falls in reverent pleas for mercy.

The king says first, "fear not: for I will show you kindness for Jonathan your father's sake, and will restore you all the land of Saul your grandfather; and you shall eat bread at my table continually. I am not a tyrant or a bloodthirsty king. I want to be kind to you. Do not be afraid of me. I want to give you all the blessings of the earth and give you a new family. You will find everything you need in me." The thing about shame is that it believes the lies and says, "I cannot lift my eyes from myself and circumstances to believe in the love and forgiveness of God." Mephibosheth exclaims, "What am I but a slave, that you should be so kind to a dead dog like me?" He did not believe he was worth saving. Everything in his entire life had been pain and suffering. He had known no battles or victory. He had not seen the Hand of God in his life. He was a loser, a statistic, a rebel in the camp of Israel and told that, if Israel's king should find him, he would be killed. He spent his life hiding and, thus, he is the Biblical depiction of shame.

So the king said, "if you do not believe me, I will show

you." He called for servants to serve Mephibosheth. To him it was as though he were a servant being served and it was awkward to think of himself as anything but a slave. The king called for food which he had never seen. The king gave Mephibosheth the vision of his future: "You are not fatherless, I am your family now. You will eat at My table for the rest of your life. You are My son now and a prince. I will take care of you. Come, servants, serve your master." King David gave Mephibosheth back everything that had been lost and more.

This is the picture of coming to Jesus Christ. Shame and bitterness keeps us hiding and in rebellion but Christ our King pulls us close and gives us our identity, a vision for the future, and a family. We are tempted to keep our eyes on ourselves and circumstances, that this is too good to be true. But Christ says, "I will show you." He blesses us and the entire world though we deny our heritage and blessings through Him. But that is not the end of the story of Mephibosheth.

Mephibosheth, crippled in infancy by a bitter experience and living with the slave trader in secrets, shame, denial, and hatred for the king, is the pre-Christian experience. The Mephibosheth who came to the palace and for the rest of his life dined with the king is the Christian life after being baptized into the family of Christ. But, it is a picture of one who still has many struggles as an overcomer. Later, he still failed to see himself as anything better than a cripple. No more a dog, he still sees himself as left behind.

He knew that he was now living a better life and had an inheritance but, when King David ran for his life because of civil war, Mephibosheth tried to go out of the city of Jerusalem with his servant Ziba. He was dependent on Ziba for transportation out of the city of Jerusalem to join King David but, sadly, Ziba leaves him behind to rescue David. When David returns, David says, "Why didn't you come with me?" Mephibosheth, thinking of his king as a tyrant and one who means to strike him down for his failure to flee the city in his hurt, accuses Ziba of betrayal and again he falls down and, in his defense, he is again ashamed.

"My Lord the King, my servant Ziba betrayed me....My Lord the King is like the Angel of God, so do whatever you think best. For my grandfather's entire family deserves death from my lord the king, but you set your servant among those who eat at your table. So what further right do I have to keep on making appeals to the King?"

The king is saddened that Mephibosheth still does not understand. He is an adopted son of David from a royal line and, still, he is crippled physically and emotionally. He expects to suffer death at the hands of his king who only loves him and wants him to suffer no more with shame. The king then bequeaths Mephibosheth an equal share with Ziba as if Mephibosheth had gone with David. Thus, this Mephibosheth is a type of the post-Christian battle. He struggles to understand and conceptualize how he gains the reward of salvation without doing a thing to earn it and in his shame, Mephibosheth declares, "Instead, since my Lord the King has come to his palace safely, let Ziba take it all." Mephibosheth thinks to please the king with works that are not required of him. What would please the king is for Mephibosheth to walk in his rightful and noble place, obey the king, and live the birthright he was given. Though Mephibosheth tries to give away his birthright, nothing can undo the oath that was given by David for love to Jonathan just like we inherit everlasting life through the unmerited blood of Christ.

The king protects Mephibosheth all the days of his long life. When armies come to invade and ask for the death of all the house of Saul, because of the oath that the king made to adopt the children of Jonathan, all of the house of Saul are destroyed except for Mephibosheth. He is forever a son of the Most High and his place is not dependent on how he feels about himself but on King David's claim on him.

Whoever you are reading this book, know that, even in the worst days and deeds of your life, you cannot undo what has already been done for you. You have been delivered! You are already a child of the King, your enemy has already lost, you are already loved, and your shame is taken from you. Your spiritual walk is already paved. Though you may feel crippled, you have been adopted and you are not worthless. You have a family and a Father. Christ already won on your behalf and He claims you as His own from the shame of sin.

Walk in the path of your royalty. Say these words: "Lord, I know that the war has already been won. I choose to claim my rightful place in victory. Don't let me be a Mephibosheth, a cripple for life and thinking to please you with things you don't want from me, but give me a clean heart free from shame. I know that all You want is all of me and I am helpless to change. Help my unbelief."

Chapter 32

Touched

I was finishing the last chapters of *The Desire of Ages*. It took me about two weeks to read it and I was captivated by this man, Jesus Christ, who seemed so unlike the cartoonish character I had always imagined. He was peaceful, calm, balanced, the most loving, the most kind, manly in his bearing, merciful, a server, a teacher, an encourager, a friend, a guide, and a reprover of sins. But He was gentle in His reproof. I had been feeling a nagging on my soul ever since I had picked up the book. I knew that the very topic it dealt with would, by its nature, point to the wrongs I had committed. I knew that I had broken man's law but now the understanding of breaking God's law seemed all the more awful and terrible.

My conscience, that so easily excused sin or blamed others, was quickening and I had seen how easily I had jumped to blame my mother, Alec, my brothers, or anyone else in my life for the things I had done. But, standing before a loving father and friend, I knew the sin was all mine. The things I had done, I had chosen to do. Despite being raped, despite abuse, despite the emotional pain, I had the choice to let it destroy me in bitter rebellion or let it change me for the better and I had chosen bitter rebellion.

My life passed before me, all the main events. More

than anything, I could see my own hypocrisy. I had hated my mother for not being a mother but was I being a good mother? I was a worse mother than she was. My son was four years old and he had known only a mother who abandons him for drugs and alcohol. I had been a rebel girl of the highest order. Of the sinners, "I was chief." These were all things that I had not even thought of or considered in years. Jesus Christ was taking me through spiritual counseling and giving me insight into myself that I had never had before. He was indeed my Father, leading me and guiding me through my rough areas to heal me.

I had buried every secret and every hurt so deep so that I would never have to consider my shame. But, it's a fact that the more I hide, the more shame I will feel. I developed a wall of pride around my shame to protect myself. Pride causes us to hide. Pride is an insidious monster that takes many forms. Pride can cause so many symptoms too.

As a victim of sex crimes, I became self-righteous in my suffering. I would look at my mother and think, "she just doesn't understand me. If she only knew all the awful things I've done and been through, she wouldn't treat me this way." Anyone who was happy or joyful around me I looked at with contempt and, in my bitter pride, I would say to myself, "They don't know my life. If they only knew and suffered the things I have suffered they wouldn't be so happy anymore." Toward men I thought, "they are idiotically driven by their sex drive which makes them incapable of love and I hate them all." But, I needed men to validate me.

Pride was also motivating my fears. The problem is, "God resists the proud and gives grace to the humble." James 4:6. I read over and over in *The Desire of Ages* that "No one was so exalted as Christ, and yet He stooped to the humblest duty. That His people might not be misled by the selfishness which dwells in the natural heart, and which strengthens by self-serving, Christ Himself set the example of humility." *The Desire of Ages* 649. I knew that my shame had caused me to live a life of self-preservation. But how do I become humble? "Those who have not humbled their souls before God in acknowledging their guilt, have not yet fulfilled the first condition of acceptance." *Steps to Christ* 37. Acceptance! That was all that I had ever desired. "If we confess our sins, He is faithful and just to forgive us our sins, and to cleanse us from all unrighteousness." 1 John 1:9.

My sense of morality was changing. "When sin has deadened the moral perceptions, the wrongdoer does not discern the defects of his character nor realize the enormity of the evil he has committed." *Steps to Christ* 40. I was now more awake to my guilt than ever. I literally felt sick as the scenes of different men passed before me. The scars on my arms also served as a continual reminder, a physical manifestation of my satanic ways, and I was oppressed. Here is where many Christians and non-Christians alike think to run from this feeling or stifle it. If, before now, I had ever felt a pain of guilt, I gave myself some excuse to ignore it or I shut it out with music. I never listened to it as the voice of God to my being. God's penetrating eye on sin is not enjoyable. When a father catches a child doing wrong, the child's first instinct is to run but, when the child matures in age, they should, if raised with love and justice, want to bring their wrongs to the Father so He can help them through it and overcome it.

This is God's maturation process with us. The instinct of non-believers and Christians, new in their understanding of God, is to run away or hide sin from Him. As we grow and understand God's Father-likeness toward us, we will know, beyond a shadow of a doubt, that God is safe and a soft place to lay our troubles. He will not be harsh when we make a mistake. He wants to offer us an escape but we cannot see it until we see that we are in trouble instead of closing our eyes to our danger. He is more loving than any earthly father can be and, yet, I had failed to see Him there all along. He had been searching for me night after night. I could feel Him looking for me. I could feel Him all along. And He had been saving me out of more trouble than I could ever have imagined.

In the Bible, Mary Magdalene was a prostitute. She had been ensnared into prostitution by some of the religious leaders who professed great holiness. Through the eyes of Mary, we can feel the hypocrisy of the surrounding religions. Much like Christianity today, she was struck with the terrible feeling that all religion is a farce. She was pushed further from God by the hurt and betrayal of her religious leaders. If she looked to them as an example, she was sorely disappointed. The very ones that were anointed to protect and serve her had led her into sexual sin. When all the other Israelites gathered by the thousands to give offerings and praise at the temple, she felt unworthy of joining the throng. She felt very angry, bitter, and ashamed. I know how she felt because I am she.

She had met Jesus and, time and time again, He defended her. So many times we hear in our day the words "don't judge me." This was Mary's anthem too. "Don't judge me. You don't know my pain." Oh how we should desire the judgment of Jesus Christ. When Mary was arrested for prostitution by the very same officials who were using her services for sex, she was sentenced to a very painful execution by stoning. What hypocrites. She is dragged on the ground and pulled into the presence of Jesus. She is bound and a helpless sex worker who the religious leaders are using as bait to catch Jesus in a violation of the Jewish laws. Mary awaits the stones to start hitting her body and she can only hope for a large stone to strike her head to give her a quick death. A stoning could take hours of painful blows to the body before the death blow came. Mary was condemned to die a slow and painful death. She was terrified and ashamed.

No stones are thrown and she is unaware that a quiet and righteous judge is standing strong to defend her and judge righteously on her behalf. Ever so dignified, Jesus stoops to write in the sand and all become quiet except for the soft sobs of Mary. In the Jewish law, it was the husband that was supposed to bring action against an adulterous woman and both the guilty man and the guilty woman are to suffer the consequences. But Christ steps in as Mary's husband. Contrary to popular culture, Christ was perfect in every way and did not use Mary sexually at all. He was honorable and kind with her and showed her how she should be treated after a life of abuse.

"The law specified that in the punishment of stoning, the witness (of the adultery) in the case should be the first to cast a stone. Now rising and fixing His eyes upon the plotting elders, Jesus said, 'He that is without sin among you, let him first cast a stone at her.'" When all of Mary's would-be executioners had quickly run away, "Jesus arose, and looking at the woman said, 'Woman (which was a term of respect in the ancient custom), where are your accusers?'" The accused is set free because of a righteous Judge who reads our heart, knows our character, and our life history. While the world judged Mary for death, Jesus Christ judged her with a life of freedom!

"The woman had stood before Jesus, cowering with fear. His words, 'He that is without sin among you, let him cast a stone,' had come to her as a death sentence. She dared not lift her eyes to the Savior's face but silently awaited her doom. In astonishment she saw her accusers depart speechless and confounded; then those words of hope fell upon her ear, 'Neither do I condemn thee: go, and sin no more.' Her heart was melted and she cast herself at the feet of Jesus, sobbing out her grateful love, and with bitter tears confessing her sins. This was the beginning of her new life, a life of purity and peace, devoted to the service of God. In the uplifting of this fallen soul, Jesus performed a greater miracle than in healing the most grievous physical disease; He cured the spiritual malady which is unto death everlasting. This penitent woman became one of His most steadfast followers." *The Desire of Ages* 462.

I easily understood the gore of the cross with its bloody victim. I knew from all my years involved in the occult that the blood had meaning but now I read that Christ's blood had power to save me from death. It is Satan that accuses men and women of sin, not God. It is Satan who pointed to us and said that sin deserves death. And it was Satan who was silenced by the death of Jesus Christ on the cross. So many things took place on the cross that we will learn more and more about in heaven.

I was waiting to get a ride home from work. No clients had come in all day at the tax accountant's office. There were very few phone calls so I read the chapters on the upper room and the crucifixion of Christ and I was humbled. I knew I was coming to a time of choice. Was I going to ignore what I was feeling and try to keep doing things my own way or was I going to be a Mary and fall at the feet of Jesus? Was I going to lay my case open to Him? Was I going to let Jesus judge me and chase away all my accusers? I sat quietly staring out the truck window. Dre could tell that I was in a quiet mood and he let me marinate in my thoughts. I was a million miles away. Every turn in the road and landmark on my way home served as a reminder of my years with men and being drunk and high.

When we arrived home, I quietly went to my room and closed the door behind me. I was thinking of my failures as a mother, the child that would never be, all the men, all the sexual abuse and assaults, all my legal troubles, and so much more. I locked the door to my room so I could not be disturbed. I knew what I needed to do. I fell to my knees in total surrender and wept and wept for the sorrow of my sins. I confessed out loud as many sins as could be brought to my mind. I had started on my knees but, weighed down by all the sin of my youth, I was brought to my face. I rocked back and forth from my knees to my face, remembering every terrible deed I had done. Every time I fell to my face I remembered something else of which I was guilty and sat back up to my knees to speak it to heaven.

I felt totally emotionally drained and so very small in the grand significance of the universe. I felt that I had wasted so much of my life and God's original purpose for me had been destroyed. My mother often played Handel's *Messiah* in the home. Music is a message to our soul. I cannot stress enough the importance of the kind of music we play in the home for our children. It is either a message of lifting them up when they become discouraged or it will destroy them.

The verse from the *Messiah* broke in on my mind, "Comfort her! And cry unto her, that her warfare is accomplished, that her iniquity is pardoned: for she has received of the Lord's hand double for all her sins!" Isaiah 40. At that moment, a hand laid upon my right shoulder. All heaven reached out to "comfort her."

After all the evil works I had seen and the power of Satan, God, in His mercy, had given this doubting Thomas a sign between He and I that His blood and His power is the greatest power in the world. Though I had given my blood in an oath to Satan, I was assured that the power of Christ can break all sin, all bondage, and all evil. The war is already won, our warfare is accomplished for us in Christ, we have already won, and now I was bidden "to go and sin no more."

Immediately, I jumped when I knew an angelic hand had been permitted to touch me. Even though I knew in my heart that this was given because I had so little faith to believe in my forgiveness, I jumped and startled. I fell back a little and looked around the room with a start and with fearful reverence. I was not alone in the room as I had thought. Angels draw close with interest to the repenting sinner. Angels in heaven shout and sing for joy for just one sinner who turns from sin and I was turning from sin.

Here I must warn readers to be cautious. We should not look for signs and the supernatural in making decisions. Satan knows that these signs are impressive to frail humans so he uses them to direct us and steer us away from Christ.

Even when shown a sign such as this, it is difficult for the human mind to take it in. Almost immediately, my mind tried to make "scientific sense" of a world we, as humans, have no explanation for. The spirit realm is mercifully held back from us. If we could see it, we would, like me, shrink back in fear. When praying for a sign, God always works through His Word, the Bible, and God-given authority to give us the answers to life's questions and decisions. I can assure the reader here that every time we pray, all heaven draws close to us. Christ feels such deep emotions for us when we are hurting and the absolute strongest and supreme assurance we have of the touch of Christ in our lives is a change of heart and a turning away from sin. The only way to see God in this life is to look at Christ in His life and on the cross. The only way to hear the voice of God is to open the Bible. And the only way to talk to God is in prayer. God has given us His method for communication. Anything else we get is an added bonus to assure us that God is in the business of miracles forever and always.

I debated whether to put this supernatural occurrence in this book but, alas, I decided to do so. Unfortunately, because of my experience with the occult, I have opened a door into the supernatural. It is not easily closed once opened and I often warn my children of the danger of curiously wandering into witchcraft. The Lord, in His great mercy, gave me this "touch" to ease my suffering and distress over my sins. He knew that I would need this because the battle with the enemy would only intensify as I took up the Christian life. I was once a soldier in the army of Satan and now I had switched sides, making Satan very angry. My "wrestling with principalities and powers" had just begun and I would need the assurance of God's ministering angels by my side.

When Moses came again to Egypt to free the Children of Israel, working miracles, Satan had his counterfeit too. How do we know the difference? "By their fruits you will know them." I arose that day and I knew that I was forgiven but I had to make some changes. These changes needed to be sure and solid changes but, on my own, I knew I was totally incapable and helpless to make these changes. I needed Christ to create solid change in my life so He took me through a process of cleansing. "Think it not strange when trials come." 1 Peter 4:12. I was being called to God's very best in living and I needed a new life that was free from fear and shame.

Christ was calling me to the Bible every day. My Christian walk was growing but I was still much like Mephibosheth. In fact, there would be many times when I would fall back into my old walk of shame but, through trial, suffering, and the surrendering of myself in giving up my pride, Christ has brought me forth as victorious from shame and the accusations of the enemy. And, soon enough, I came upon Romans 13:1-4, "Let every soul be subject unto the higher powers. For there is no power but of God: the powers that be are ordained of God. So then, the one who resits the authority is opposing God's command, and those who oppose it will bring damnation to themselves. For rulers are not a terror to good works, but to evil. Do you want to be unafraid of the authority? Do that which is good, and you will have its approval. For government is God's servant for your good. But if you do wrong, be afraid..."

I will never forget sitting at my computer desk in my room and reading the Bible. I read these words, "Therefore, you must submit, not only because of wrath, but also because of your conscience." My conscience was being slain by the Spirit of God and I went to war against my flesh. I continually lived with a guilty conscience. Every time I felt like carrying my Bible openly at school, I carefully concealed it so no one would question me about it. I was afraid that, if I told anyone of my newfound faith in Jesus Christ, they would discover my past and my criminal record and call me a liar and a hypocrite. I was so ashamed of my criminal record.

Chapter 33

Advocate

No sooner had I become a Christian than I was filled with excitement for my newfound treasure and I wanted to share it so I pushed aside my guilt and shame over my legal troubles. I had started getting involved with some wonderful people from my local church and a church in Loma Linda, California. I was regularly going out, day after day, to pass out *The Desire of Ages* and *The Great Controversy* in local neighborhoods but I had not yet passed out any material in the city of Beaumont. I was afraid to. I was afraid that I would either run into cops who knew me or run into friends who knew me. Alas, the small group of us interested in sharing the gospel decided that we should pass out gospel tracts in the city of Beaumont and I was terrified.

The apartment complex they chose was across the street from the satanist's house and where I had lived with Draven. Everyone in this particular apartment complex knew who I was because, one night while I was drunk, I started a riot by knocking on a door and pulling the occupant who answered out into the street while punching her in the face. Soon, it turned into a huge fight and everyone involved ran when the police arrived from every direction.

My new friends in Christ had picked me up from my house and I was eager to help pass out tracts until they said where we were headed. Immediately I felt overcome with shame. My style of dress had changed to a classier and wholesome appearance. I was slimmer and healthier looking. The glow of womanhood was returning to me and I looked altogether different. This was a fact I was depending on to disguise me. Would they recognize me? If they did recognize me, what would they say? This must have been the very same feeling Paul had. I had chased known Christians off my property at one point with weapons during my time in the occult. How could I now stand in front of those I had formally worshiped Satan with?

When we pulled up to the apartment complex, I mercifully saw no one that I recognized for, if I had, I would have surely stayed in the car. I got out and went through the motions of organizing gospel materials and taking mental stock of which ones were on which topics. My favorite was always *The Desire of Ages* and now I was reading *The Great Controversy*. I knew that this book, *The Great Controversy*, would appeal to my punk rock and gothic friends more than the rest so I arranged my book bag, an Army surplus satchel filled with books, and headed out to knock on the apartment doors.

I wanted to wait in the car but I also did not want to explain to my new group of friends all the things I had done and where I had been but months earlier. I was afraid they would bar me from their church. I put one foot in front of the other and kept walking. I let the other lady I was with do most of the talking as I stood behind her, shamefaced and filled with trepidation. I knew every door and every apartment in that complex. I had lived here with my new little baby as a teen pregnancy. I had sold drugs here as a drug dealer. I had raged here as an alcoholic. I had lived here with a boyfriend. I had worshiped evil here involved in the occult. I had almost died here on overdoses and, around the corner, I got my DUI. Now I was back and was face-to-face with my former self and I would do anything to hide the ugly truth from the past.

When we knocked on one door, a young mother opened the door. I was more than a little used to having the doors slammed in my face while passing out these gospel tracts and books but I "took it for the team" knowing that I owed Christ my life and more. This young mother was curious about us and interested. The lady I was with urged me to share my experience with her and, with the spotlight suddenly turned on me, I got the courage to speak without hiding behind my mentor.

I told her I was a young mother too and how this book, *The Desire of Ages*, had changed my life. She took the book with interest and excitement and I could see that a power greater than myself was working on the hearts and minds of the people that I encountered. I knew that the fear and shame I was feeling came from the fact that I had not dealt with my crimes and I was keeping all those secrets from everyone. The fact that I was keeping secrets was causing me to be weak in my faith. Though, once you get the sweet little taste of sharing hope in Jesus Christ with others, it will make you want more.

As we left the little two-bedroom apartment with the young mother waving sweetly and thanking me for the book that I had given her, I saw my entire old group of friends standing out on a porch directly in front of the car that we had come in. There was absolutely no way of avoiding the crowd. They were drinking beer and being loud and flicking their cigarette ash to the ground down below them. I could hear the voice of Draven and Layla's brother laughing loudly at the Christian group walking by. I could see the pentagram tattoos of the satanist and all of my friends from before.

They were mocking and jeering at the group of Christians passing out material. The lady I was with exclaimed, "oh my, Satan is trying to discourage us now." Yes, she was right. Maybe only months ago I would have been in that crowd and causing the Christian saints grief. I was quiet. I knew what God was calling me to do and my stomach churned with the butterflies of doubt. My palms grew sweaty and I thought that I might slip in my shoes because my feet were sweating so much. I inhaled deeply and silently prayed for the strength to not now deny my Lord when things were getting a little heated.

I grabbed the stack of *The Great Controversy* books that I had in my Army satchel and I walked right up to the porch where my former friends were standing. Their faces were red with alcohol and they were having great fun teasing the group I was with until they saw me. Their faces dropped in astonishment and I will never forget their shocked expressions. This is how I knew that God was really changing me. Those that knew me before could scarcely believe their eyes. I heard hushed whispers, "is that Susanne? It's Susanne!" Layla's brother, after closing his mouth said, "Wow! Is that you?" And I answered, "it is I. Hey guys, I want to give you the book that has changed my life."

The satanist came forward and his eyes looked me up from top to bottom, taking in every detail. He said with a sharp sneer of contempt, "you're not a Christian now, are you?" I said, "yes, I am." He let out a loud laugh of ridicule and hatred. "I don't want your [expletive] book!" I looked around to see who would take my book. They all stood there staring at me in total silence. That is when I saw Draven standing inside looking at me with pain in his eyes. He had seen me approaching and he had quickly darted inside to avoid me.

I handed the book to Layla's brother who I trusted to not destroy the book. "Please, give this to Draven for me," I said as kindly as I possibly could under the abuse of the assorted names that were being cast my way. I stood there holding out the books over the gated porch and Layla's brother finally leaned forward to accept them. "Yeah, whatever." He took the books and I turned and walked away. I had publicly declared my faith and faced my fears with my Lord. I had suffered some abuse but it was humbling and exhilarating all at the same time because I knew that I was not alone and, whatever they did to me, it was not to me but to Christ. On any other day they would have invited me to join them but, now, I was on the other side. There is a dividing line between the armies of hell and those of heaven. Good and evil cannot coexist for "can a man serve two masters?"

This was one little trial among many. Although just at the beginning of my walk of faith, I had been strengthened. In the past, name calling and hatred from this group would have wounded me deeply. It did me no harm to face abuse and hatred. I had thought that the embarrassment alone would cause me great injury and hurt to my heart but, in Jesus Christ, I was given supernatural strength. I was able to stand in front of all my former associations, a group that I had been terrified to run into, and get the word out to an entire town that I was not the old person anymore but a new person had been born. I decided that, if God can give me this supernatural strength to face former associations, I could submit myself to the law of the land. I would not face my worst fears alone. If I would take a step in faith to follow God's word, He would take control and clean up my life for me.

My stomach was in my throat because I thought that I would likely go to jail upon turning myself in. I made up my mind that I can no longer call myself a Christian and hide my criminal record from those that act as my authority. I was hiding my criminal record from bosses and even my mother did not know about all the charges against me. Freedom from fear and shame meant living an open life. The first step to freedom from sin is to expose it and bring it the light.

I knew that the possibility of losing my son, my job, and my school would have to be laid upon the altar because the likelihood of being sent to jail was high. I decided that, should this happen, I would be a light in whatever facility I was sent to. I clung to the verse, "The king's heart is in the hand of the Lord, as the rivers of water: he turneth it whithersoever he will." Proverbs 21:1. I had to do the right thing and come clean. I had fears and shame because I had secrets. I had to do whatever I could to take my secrets out of the darkness and bring them to the light.

I went to my mother and slowly, over a period of a few months, started to tell her some of the things I had seen and done that she was not aware of and I asked her forgiveness for all the heartache I had put her through. Her reaction was not always good but I was grateful for her love, acceptance, and her forgiveness. I held on to the fact that even her reactions to my crimes were controlled by God. God used the difficult and even painful relationship with my God-given mother to help release me from shameful secrets and guilt. God will always directly bless us through our parents even if our parents are unbelievers. In the past, I would grow weary of my mother and leave home for freedom only to find that I ended up living with even less "freedom" and a more exacting and cruel taskmaster.

I asked my mother and Dre for help in getting my criminal record taken care of and I explained to them how the last judge I had seen had declared that, if he ever saw me in his courtroom again, "you will go to jail!" I needed to prepare myself for the worst-case scenario.

I was no longer angry at my legal situation and offering excuses. These officers of the law had given me a second chance so many times. Often, we view the authorities of this world as hardened and harsh but I know that God had, so many times, worked through them to show me mercy. From judges all the way down to the work-release probation officers, I experienced the love of God from the men and women enforcing the law of our land. So many times, the judges would grant me mercy. Often, they would attempt to show me the futility of my actions, plead with me to change my reckless ways, and tell me that, for my own good, they wished to never see me in their courtroom again. It was God seeing my worth and using the mouth of a judge to speak great truth to me.

As time went on and I increasingly deserved the harsh hand of justice, I was dumbfounded by the forgiveness of the judges. The mercy extended to me started to make me feel as though I did not want to disappoint them. Throughout my life, I wanted to live up to the expectations others had of me. If I knew others expected me to fail, I would fail with great gusto in an attempt to prove how low I could go. On the other hand, if I knew they expected greatness from me, I would be inspired to rise even higher than they expected.

So many miracles occurred when I gave my life over to the Lord. One of them was that my entire attitude toward the law and those that enforce it changed dramatically. I felt the Lord calling me to live a clean life with a clean conscience and cease my running from the law. Yes, I would have to account for my transgressions but I took great comfort in the fact I would not do it alone. I was so thankful when Dre suggested a criminal lawyer that he knew from his days of being a local Ranger.

That afternoon we loaded up into his truck and made the journey down to the heart of San Bernardino. I sat in the waiting room of the lawyer's office rehearsing in my mind the things that I would say in my defense but I knew that a defense was really the last thing to offer. Nevertheless, I thought of everything that I could say to give as a reason for my behavior in avoiding every opportunity to make things right. My legs shook with anticipatory anxiety. I was wearing my nicest outfit because one wears the best thing when one's life is on the line. Dre sat quietly allowing me to feel the full weight of the consequences that I had called down upon myself by running away from the law.

At last, my name was called and we stood up to file into the office of Mr. Victor Esmond. You have to understand that he is an imposing man. He is a cowboy and a gun enthusiast to say the very least and his office is an impressive collection of both cowboy and gun memorabilia and quite intimidating. Sitting across the desk from Mr. Esmond makes one feel small in the little chairs provided. Mr. Esmond, who seemed to be a rather large man compared to myself, had a western mustache placed above his lip. His eyes reflected a man who had seen many murderers and criminals before me and I was grateful I was not coming to him accused of the typical crimes he was used to dealing with.

Mr. Esmond examined me with the seasoned eye of an experienced judge of character and I was very happy that I had worn my best and was able to hide the telltale cuts on both of my arms that revealed an undesirable past condition. As he peered at this helpless young girl over his hardwood desk in his ornately decorated office, I felt his gaze as penetrating as an x-ray machine. It was as though he could see down to my very soul. I quaked inside with the thought that maybe he would not believe my story. He freely shared the fact that he was expensive and that someone like me could not begin to pay the attorney's fees. He was right. He cost at least ten thousand dollars to retain. I wondered how in the world I would pay for this top-dollar defense attorney that I desperately wanted on my side to face the judge. I knew that, if I simply turned myself in to go into court alone, I would surely cause my subsequent incarceration. Once those handcuffs snapped over my wrists, I would be at the mercy of the justice system with no adequate defense.

Mr. Esmond went through an itemized list of the necessary steps and cost of all the things that would need to be done to face my criminal record and turn myself in. His level of expertise was the crème-de-la-crème of legal defense and I was stunned at the cost. My heart sank because I knew that I was unable to pay the retainer to secure his services. I could of mine own self do nothing. I gave the brief version of my "coming to Jesus" story and humbly said, "I have no money at all right now." I hung my head in shame and I knew that this likely meant that he would be standing up to show us out of his office now.

In a firm and decided voice Mr. Esmond said, "look me in the eye and tell me you're done getting in trouble." My hands started shaking. I suddenly felt more poor and naked than I ever had. I knew he would not believe me but I raised my head and gave the man a sturdy look in the eye and mustered up the strongest answer I could, "yes sir, I am done getting in trouble." I must have been a little convincing or maybe Mr. Esmond was more soft-hearted than he appeared. For the first time ever, I uttered out loud all the charges against me while Mr. Esmond looked up my record on his computer.

Suddenly, Mr. Esmond sat back in his chair again then gave me one of the most serious faces I had ever seen. This man was not accustomed to offering polite smiles or trivial kindnesses. He was all business all the time and his stern affect let me know that this was a matter of life and death. With that being said, he asked in a very firm and almost scary voice, "do you have a penny?" This man had years and years of courtroom practice in commanding attention much like a seasoned general operates in battle and commands his troops. I swallowed hard noting the sudden dryness of my mouth and throat. My hands were quivering as I lifted my bag to rummage through the change that might be hiding at the bottom. This change was all I had.

"Please have a penny!" I thought to myself while digging through the old lollipops, mints, and pieces of makeup that sat at the bottom of my bulging bag. Mr. Esmond leaned back in his giant, executive chair waiting with his hands folded across his center like a king at his desk. He waited for me to rifle through my disorganized junk in obedience to his command. "Oh, thank you!" At the bottom of my bag I had found an old and dirty penny and I slapped it victoriously on the desk and breathed a sigh of relief. "Hallelujah, I found it!" I thought.

He leaned forward and reached for the penny, examining it as he brushed off the bits of whatever my filthy purse had placed on it, before placing the penny in his pocket. The silence was deafening. "Now," he said, "I'm only going to charge you a penny for what it's going to take to get you out of this mess but, if you ever get in trouble again and waste my time, I'm going to come after you for every cent you will owe me!" My heart was pounding as I imagined Mr. Esmond and his posse on horseback with gun in hand chasing me down my street demanding blood from a stone. My answer was swift. "Yes, sir." I stammered while nodding my head emphatically to demonstrate just how well I understood him.

I knew, leaving Mr. Esmond's office that day, that I had been given a gift. My desire was to live up to his high expectations. I had felt shame and guilt when arriving at his office. I sat sheepishly before him as I was forced to list my offenses. Mr. Esmond saw something worthy in me that I did not even see in myself. I was a wanted girl running from retribution. I was a rebel girl meeting the consequences of my rebellion. But, at the same time, I was meeting the mercy and justice of God in His love. God was giving me a living example of *The Great Controversy*. This is the thing with Scripture, it is alive! It is supernatural and, whatever you read, you experience in the living of life. For thousands of years, men and women have tried to kill the Bible but to no avail. The Word of God cannot be exterminated from the face of the earth.

In fact, I was reminded of when the satanist and I were involved in some occult activity. He had a particular book that was, in his words, "dangerous." It was a book that, upon being opened, caused supernatural activity to take place because of the evil within its pages. It was said to be the book of the dead and, when I curiously asked if I could see it, he snapped back at me in harsh rebuke, "do not open books unless you are prepared for the consequences!" Even an avowed satanist understood that what we take in will make us or break us and there are consequences for what we allow to shape our thinking. The Spirit of God is in the pages of

Scripture and it will change our lives. As I read Revelation and *The Great Controversy*, my life was taking a course, heading into uncharted waters, into storms, but into amazing peace. I would see a living gospel right before my eyes. I would feel the terror of standing before the righteous judgment of God in all my sin and I would know His effort to save me until the end.

I still had to face the consequences of my actions in court. This meant that I had to surrender myself or turn myself in. Mr. Esmond got my case on the court docket and he called me to tell me that I would have to surrender myself to law enforcement. Once I did this, with the warrants out for my arrest, I was casting my poor wretched soul on the mercy of the court. But I was not alone. I had the embodiment of "God with us" in the form of an Advocate, my lawyer.

The night before I went to court, I could not sleep. I felt that I was eating my last free meal, sleeping my last free night in my own bed, and kissing my son goodbye for the last time without metal bars separating us. I was surrendering the next day and it was a total death to self to do the right thing and not run. That morning I awoke and tried to do my makeup but my hands were shaking and I could not steady them. I put on my best shirt and my best skirt and I looked as business and professional as possible but nothing would take away the look of pale anxiety from my face. The hardest thing was kissing my son goodbye. The words of the last judge were ringing loudly in my mind, "if I ever see you in my courtroom again, you will go to jail!" When I thought of those words, my stomach tightened and I felt like I would vomit. I was facing the music and there was no going back.

For years, every morning when I arose from my bed, I would think about my warrants and my stomach would tighten with fear, anxiety, and then shame. Every time I saw a police officer, I was reminded of my past sins and terrified of the law. In turning myself in, I would no longer be a slave under the law of fear but be reborn and consecrated to walk in a life of freedom. In my rebel years, I would think that being free meant that I could break the law whenever I so desired but I learned the hard way that true freedom is obeying the law of God and man and being freed from the burden of my sins. The life of a rebel was bondage and pain but God's way was peaceful and free.

I seated myself into Dre's truck and buckled my seatbelt. We drove the longer than usual drive down to the local county courthouse which was two towns over and pulled right into a parking space on the back side of the courthouse building. I walked the long sidewalk and I could see the long line of people at the courthouse for various reasons. They all had the faces of annoyance and disinterest. No one enjoyed coming to court so I was not alone in my sentiments. Mr. Esmond was standing at the top of the courthouse steps waiting for me. "You're here!" he said in a voice that told me that he might be a morning person or maybe he had already had his cup of morning coffee or both. "I'm really nervous." I freely admitted. "Well, Good! Maybe you'll think twice before getting in trouble again," he said curtly with a cheerful smile. I was surprised by how alive Mr. Esmond became when at the courthouse. It was like he was brought into this world for the justice system.

Mr. Esmond opened the door of the courthouse for me and walked up to the clerk's window and stated matter of fact my guilt, "Susanne is here to surrender herself." Once those words were said, I felt the air taken right out of me and I tried not to hyperventilate so I held my breath. I looked around to see if anyone else had heard what he said. Once the clerk marked me as present, I was in the custody of the Riverside County Sheriff's Department. I was now in custody and I felt the full weight of the law. I was no longer free. How wrong I was to think that there is freedom in breaking the law of God and man. I was humbled by my choices and decisions and I dared not think that I could ask for mercy.

Mr. Esmond waited with me until the bailiff opened the door of the courtroom. This bailiff knew me by name and, when he saw me standing there, he looked at me with the disappointment he might offer a naughty dog and rolled his eyes and said, "C'mon in Susanne." I indeed had my tail between my legs as I shuffled through the courtroom doors. I was just waiting for the judge to recognize me too and get carted off to the slammer. We took our places in the row of seats in the courtroom and had to watch a short video on the courtroom rules. After that was done, I heard the "all rise" and we stood. Here it comes, the look of recognition that I was dreading.

The door to the judge's chambers opened and I watched the judge take his place on his judgment seat but it was a new judge. The typical judge that rules this courtroom was out sick that day. I was elated but also worried, all at the same time. "Better the devil you know than the devil you don't," as the old saying goes. For all I know this judge could be harsher. My mind was moving through my thoughts at a rapid pace as the bailiff instructed us to take our seats. I was praying that this was a good thing. All the cases with legal representation went first so my case was up and I could barely recognize my name or case number when it was called. "We're up!" Mr. Esmond said as he stood and indicated with his hand that I was to follow behind him. This was it. Time to stand and be judged.

I cannot convey how close I was to fainting at that moment. I felt dizzy, shaky, and my stomach was a mess. The next few minutes would decide the course of my life. If I could have hidden behind Mr. Esmond, I would have. But, as Mr. Esmond took the podium and lifted his head to look at the judge, the judge and Mr. Esmond erupted in cheerful greeting. "Mr. Esmond! How are you? How was your weekend? It's been a little while."

Mr. Esmond smiled and returned the friendly greeting, "Hello! It has been a while. How often do you serve as a pro tem judge?" They carried on a friendly conversation that told me that, not only were they acquaintances, they were close friends. I was shocked as I stared at Mr. Esmond and the ease at which he was conversing with the judge. They were buddies.

You cannot imagine the relief I felt as I observed the camaraderie between my advocate and the judge. But, I had little time to think about this before I was back down to business and the bailiff read the charges out loud for the entire courtroom to hear. I heard a few big guys behind me whisper, "whew, you just never can tell can you." I was so embarrassed and ashamed of myself. I gripped the table in front of me to steady myself. I thought for sure that I could see the bailiff tapping his handcuffs on his belt in readiness to clap on my wrists. For me, the worst part was over. It was the reading of my crimes that nearly made me want to run with shame but that was over and now on to the next worst part.

But, that never came. Although Mr. Esmond had been harsh and stoic with me up until this moment, what flowed from his mouth made me stare in astonishment at this man even more. If I had spoken for myself what I would have said would have been shameful admissions of my guilt void of hope and a purpose. I could not have said what Mr. Esmond said about me because I had no faith in myself but Mr. Esmond had faith in me. He was full of surprises and, to me, he represents Christ, our Friend and Advocate. Mr. Esmond said, "Your Honor, this young lady is guilty of a lot and she ran away for a time. But she is turning her life around now.

She plans to go to school and she is here to account for the things that she has done in the past. She wishes to make restitution and honor her commitment. I have taken her case because I see someone with potential, a future, and I know that she will not waste any mercy that the court may be willing to give her in this matter." Wow, I could hardly believe my ears! He thought all that of me?

This was not flattery. These were the kindest and most faith-filled words anyone had ever spoken to me. They gave me a vision for my future that I had not really had before. My shame was turned to praise in front of all who heard and those present who condemned me ceased to speak. The judge looked over my paperwork and said, "Sure Victor, I can do that for you today. Would Susanne prefer a shorter jail sentence or we can defer her to the work-release program?" Of course I would not prefer jail! I was sentenced to three hundred and sixty-four days in a work-release program but I was expecting so much more aggressive sentencing than just that and I viewed this judgment as extreme mercy to me. With that, I followed Mr. Esmond to sit by the bailiff and wait for my new paperwork to be signed by the court and its witness. I watched in amazement as all my paperwork was processed and the warrants were voided from my record. I was a rebel girl no more! I was no longer under the condemnation of the law but my Advocate and my Judge had worked together with amazing mercy and judgment for my release to walk in freedom and newness of life. I would not now go forward to break any more laws but to, by faith, let Jesus Christ keep me in the way of life.

When we were handed my paperwork, Mr. Esmond and I left the courtroom. Now I was the one leading us out. I no longer shrank with shame but I stood tall. The burden was light. I cannot even describe the feeling I felt of being free of those warrants as I exited the courtroom and walked out of the courthouse doors. As soon as I exited the building under the clear and beautiful blue morning sky, I raised my hands up and let out a cry of celebration and joy, "WHOO HOO!" My mourning had been turned into happy shouts for joy as I was released from rebellion against the law. Mr. Esmond, my Advocate, turned to me and gave me a "go and sin no more" speech and I agreed wholeheartedly. Once I had experienced the freedom from condemnation, I knew better than anyone that sin came with a high price. Obedience is not a burden, rebellion is. Thus, I learned firsthand the great work of the gospel message in clearing us from our guilt through Jesus Christ our Lord and Advocate.

Now for the sentence. I still had consequences for the crimes I had committed but I knew that I deserved far worse than I had been given. I happily and with gratefulness accepted the consequences. This gave me a cheerful attitude when I would be put on a sort of chain gang work-release program. I had to be present every morning at eight o'clock in the city of Calimesa to help with the city works program. I was to keep the city clean. I cleaned parks and public restrooms, helped with landscaping, and helped maintain the roads in a variety of ways. It was not easy but I never complained.

Bill was the man in charge. He was considered to be tough and exacting. He stood about five foot ten but he had a tough, no-nonsense exterior. He never failed to remind me that I was "in one of the toughest programs in the area." When he gave orders, he expected it to get done immediately. On my first day, he sought to show me how tough this program could be on a little girl and literally had me breaking rocks in the hot sun with a pickaxe. He did not think that I would last through the first day, let alone an entire year. But, unlike in the past and by God's grace, I did not give into the temptation of discouragement, hatred, and bitterness for my taskmaster.

I was surrounded by men who had committed crimes and, sometimes, I was worried to be alone with some of them but, after a time because of the hard work I did and my unwillingness to cut corners, I became the most trusted one out of the group. It was a violation of the program to be caught listening to an iPod. Once found in violation, we had to go back to court and possibly serve the rest of our sentence in jail. For me that would be a year or more in jail if I were found in violation. I appealed to Bill and showed him that I wanted to spend my time listening to the Bible, *The Desire of Ages*, and sermons and he allowed me to be the only one allowed to use an iPod in the group.

I walked the entire border of the city of Calimesa picking up trash in the hot sun with a bright orange vest on that I had to wear at all times. Every time I was tempted to be proud, I would experience humility and brokenness of spirit in putting that vest on again and again and remembering that I deserved so much more punishment but I had been shown mercy. It was usually a sweltering ninety degrees or more. I was picking up loads of trash, cleaning parks and public restrooms, and expected to cover the entire city in a day. Then the next day I would do the same again. The entire time I was fortifying my mind with the Word of God. This was the work of cleansing me from my former life. This was the work of restoring me from the thief I used to be, "Let him that stole steal no more: but rather let him labour, working with his hands the thing which is good, that he may have to give to him that needs." Ephesians 4:28.

Often, I would see former associations driving by and they would laugh and holler at me as they passed by. I would often feel like hiding because I was so embarrassed. I told myself that, at least, I could go home at the end of the day and that was better than jail. At the end of an eight-hour work day like this, I would fall into bed with great exhaustion. During my time being gothic and partying at night, I rarely saw the light of day. Now, I was in the sunshine all day long. The drugs and drinking alcohol had been replaced with drinking water. I was sweating out all of the impurities and getting lots of exercise. I felt the best I had ever felt.

Though I was no longer a rebel in the eyes of the law of the land, I still held rebellion in my heart. The root of all fear, anger, and rebellion is bitterness. I held great bitterness in my heart and God was trying to root it out of my spirit. After all, I had been sexually assaulted numerous times and I had experienced great violence as the giver and the taker. I had experienced the turning away and the abandonment of my mother time and time again. Though she was in my life now, I knew that circumstances dictated her love and loyalty toward me. True love, the kind that never fails, the kind that we can rest in as our shelter is the kind of love that only our heavenly Father can offer. I had repented to God and confessed my sins "one to another" and now that same Father desired to restore me and heal me.

My mother and I had a strained relationship and I lived in constant fear of her angry spirit. How does one just get over that? One does not simply just get over it all on their own. I knew that if I ever wanted to get married and have a family that I had to break the cycle of abuse and be different. But how? I knew that I had to forgive my mother and try to live with her in a Christ-like and humble way that pleased the Lord. I needed to take her counsel on the men that would try to date me. I knew that the future peace of my marriage depended on the peace I had with my only living parent.

It was not easy. It was an immense struggle and I failed over and over. This is what I was up against. My mother did not just have an angry spirit, she played many kinds of mind games on me. She was angry and bitter and I was the only one she could take it out on because she cared little how I reacted. For instance, one Sabbath morning I had on a pair of boots. The moment I walked out into the kitchen I could tell she was fuming. This is how it was from day to day. My mother would be angry and I would not know why. Somehow, she seemed to blame me and I believed the lie that "everything was my fault."

If men were inappropriate with me, I believed that I deserved it and that it was my fault too. My mother never believed me when I tried to tell her about some of the sexual assaults in my life. Concerns I had she disregarded as my "being too sensitive." I learned quickly that to try to fight my mother on any issue was futile because she would always win. If she felt I had a valid point, she would, with great disdain for my truth, deliver a hurtful comment with skill and precision and I would be so hurt that I would ignore her for days and days. The more I ignored her, the angrier she got at me until we blew up in a huge torrent of emotion and anger.

In my new Christian walk, I was trying to navigate these waters with new love and devotion for my mother. This was the hardest struggle with the flesh in my life. I wanted to tell her how wrong she was. I had an attitude of superiority toward her. This Sabbath morning was no different. I was proud of my new pair of boots that I had bought myself. Buying myself things was a new phenomenon in my life. I had always depended on men buying me things for the sake of survival but now I was working and earning my own money.

"You look like a prostitute!" She looked me up and down with angry hatred. All I could hear were the word, prostitute, and every shameful emotion returned to me.

"What?" I said in return.

"You're going to wear *that* to church?" She retorted.

I looked in her eyes and I saw darkness. What I should have done was change my boots because I am pretty sure that she was right on the money and that I did look like a prostitute. I have always struggled with knowing what is appropriate and what is not in the area of dress. I am glad that sanctification "is the work of a lifetime" because God has dealt long and mercifully with me. But, at that moment, all I could see was my mother's anger toward me and I immediately grew proud to protect myself from the painful blows she could deliver in a moment. Her words from her tongue had delivered the worst curses of my life.

As a parent, this fact makes me tremble and very cautious before I speak to my children. An angry parent will cause a child to rebel. But, I was no longer a child. I had the assurance of the Lord with me and I was being called to His very best. He was calling me to forgive my past as He had but I could not do that without forgiving my mother. She stood as a symbol of everything that had gone wrong in my life.

I rolled my eyes and walked out the door in a huff to church with my "prostitute boots" on, leaving my mother standing in the kitchen, still angry at me. God speaks through even ungodly parents with the worst kind of motives. My mother was not motivated by a sense of loving protection for a daughter but by competition toward me. The very next week my mother went out and bought a bigger and more provocative pair of "prostitute boots" like my own and wore them to church.

No, my mother did not violently abuse me with her fists but her angry spirit broke my heart and fueled the rebel girl. Evenings before she came home from work I would watch everyone in the house run off to their rooms to hide from her. I would stay in the kitchen as she walked through the back door and attempt to talk to her and her anger would bubble over at me as she would tick off a list of ways I had failed her. I was her outlet. How do I forgive this angry woman in my life? She is the only parental authority in my life that God has given me.

The only way I was ever able to effectively hurt her back for the hurts she caused was to leave her. Nothing I could ever say or do would hurt her more than my absence and I was aware of this. To leave her now would be to plunge back into darkness even worse than my teen years of rebellion. How do I live a Christian life when I am filled with so much hateful anger for my mother and men in general for the pain they have caused me?

I can say now, today, that I love my mother and my heart is broken for her. She has been hurt in the worst ways a woman can be hurt and I cry out on her behalf that my Father will deliver her and her husband from the enemy of souls. My Heavenly Father loves her and wishes to save her but my mother has been totally unwilling to follow Him in this regard. She now goes to church regularly but she has not been changed by the love of the Lord. She has had five stepchildren come into her life and has had four of her own children. My mother and her husband have ceased contact, at the time I write this, with seven of those children. I pray that, by God's grace, restoration comes for all the children that love their parents and have been rejected by them. Until that day, God says, "though your parents forget you, I will never forget you." Isaiah 49:15.

My story of dysfunctional family is not alone. We all have dysfunctional families and we are all given the work of overcoming the inherited sin and our own sin. It is the curse of sin and the enemy that causes our families to be destroyed. The only thing that can heal our families is a personal walk with Christ. The Bible is full of stories of families that have experienced every kind of failure known to man so that we have hope that God forgives and is mercifully patient with all of us. We have been given a blueprint and a plan on how to redeem our families even when we have been guilty of destroying them. I have inherited a terrible anger problem and my mother inherited her anger also. Let us, together, walk through the process of forgiving our parents, our siblings, those that have abused us, and the men and women that have hurt us.

Chapter 34

Soul Suicide

The story is found in 2 Samuel 16 and 17 and the story is of Ahithophel. Ahithophel's story is not well known and, for many years, I failed to learn who Ahithophel really was even though it is plain to see in *Patriarchs and Prophets*. I always knew that Ahithophel was one of King David's wise counselors but I had no idea of the awesome picture of unresolved bitterness that would emerge and, more specifically, the bitterness that comes from sexual assault. Ahithophel is every one of us who have been abused and becomes bitter at our abuser and anyone else who has offended us. We can be successful as far as worldly standards go but, if we are bitter, we will never have any peace. Ahithophel was famous for his wisdom. As far as wisdom goes, Ahithophel rivaled the wisdom of Balaam but the bitterness of sexual assault destroyed his life.

It is amazing how quickly bitterness can come into the human heart. In fact, every one of us will wrestle with bitterness many times throughout our lives. It is important to know what it looks like and how to solve it. In Exodus 15 we see the children of Israel miraculously led out of slavery with the amazing parting of the Red Sea and the first song of praise offered to God. They are at a high point in their walk with God and then quickly, so very quickly, bitterness enters their ranks.

The Bible says, "So Moses brought Israel from the Red Sea, and they went out into the wilderness of Shur; and they went three days in the wilderness, and found no water. And when they came to Marah, they could not drink of the waters of Marah, for they were bitter; therefore the name of it was called Marah." The Hebrew word Marah means bitter and it is the very first time the word is mentioned in the Bible. This is very important because, often when something is mentioned for the first time in the Bible, you will find its best illustration, its best description, and, most of the time, you will find its best definition. This is the case for bitterness. When I am tempted to be bitter, this is the passage that I turn to. I believe that everything I will ever need to know about bitterness is right here in Exodus 15.

So the Bible says, "when they came to bitter, they could not drink of the waters of bitter, for they were bitter." Finding no water is a big deal. With no water, death is looming. The children of Israel are thinking that they were brought through the Red Sea and now they will die with no water to drink. This is a legitimate concern as with many of the trials that we will face. It is concerning, worrisome, and, for many of us, frightening. There will be problems in life when we say, "God, something has to be done about this." They felt that God had done a great wrong to bring them so far and leave them without water.

"But for three days, as they journeyed, they could find

no water. The supply which they had taken with them was exhausted. There was nothing to quench their burning thirst as they dragged wearily over the sun-burnt plains. Moses, who was familiar with this region, knew what the others did not, that at Marah, the nearest station where springs were to be found, the water was unfit for use. With intense anxiety he watched the guiding cloud (God's leading). With a sinking heart he heard the glad shout. 'Water! water!' echoed along the line. Men, women, and children in joyous haste crowded to the fountain, when, lo, a cry of anguish burst forth from the host—the water was bitter."

"In their horror and despair they reproached Moses for having led them in such a way, not remembering that the divine presence in that mysterious cloud had been leading him as well as them. In his grief at their distress Moses did what they had forgotten to do; he cried earnestly to God for help." *Patriarchs and Prophets* 291.

"And the people murmured against Moses," Exodus 15:24. Murmuring is verbally doubting God. Whenever I verbally doubt God, I am murmuring. After all the miracles that the children of Israel saw God do, they are, right now, struggling with who God is and what He can do. I can say that after all the many miracles in my life that the biggest struggle has been to overcome bitterness and, in particular, bitterness over sexual assault and my mother not protecting me from it. This is why, when Jesus Christ was here on earth, He did not work a miracle to show the Pharisees who He was. No amount of miracles will make us believe when we doubt God and what He can do in our lives.

This was not the way to handle the lack of water. The way to handle the lack of water was to go to God and ask God for help. But instead, they verbally doubted God by going against Moses. The number one sin of Israel was murmuring. It is my number one sin too. I have an amazing testimony and, yet, I can doubt God's power in my life.

"And the people murmured against Moses saying, What shall we drink?" Exodus 15:24. This is so important to understand about bitterness and why we doubt God's power in our lives. Are you ready for it? Bitterness is an unresolved violation of our justice system. I am going to write this again so it sinks in for you and for me: bitterness is an unresolved violation of my justice system.

So here is what the children of Israel were saying: "God, what are doing? You save us from Pharaoh, You free us from slavery, we see the ten plagues, You get us through the Red Sea then You leave us out here to die. THAT IS NOT RIGHT! THAT IS NOT FAIR! GOD, THIS IS NOT A RIGHT THING THAT YOU HAVE DONE!" This goes against the justice system of the children of Israel and they begin to doubt God's power in their lives.

Many people will dislike what I am going to write next but, in everything I have seen and read in the Bible, I believe it to be truth: the strongest emotion in man is the emotion of justice, even stronger than love. Love will rarely get a rally cry going in a society but you get a group of people together that believe that something is not right and you have a revolution or a rebellion. God's emotion of justice, unlike humanity's, is love. "God's mercy and justice are the foundation of the law and government of God." *The Great Controversy* 503. It was God's mercy and justice that Satan sought to change. God's character is mercy and justice combined equally which is a serving and protecting love. Justice meaning He will never wrong you or me because His nature is trustworthy and mercy meaning, when we have wronged Him, He has died to save us because His mercy is loving kindness to us. He is the ultimate picture of a Father that will never harm us and seeks to save us because that is the bedrock of who He is.

"In the opening of the great controversy, Satan had declared that the law of God could not be obeyed, that justice was inconsistent with mercy, and that, should the law be broken, it would be impossible for the sinner to be pardoned. Every sin must meet its punishment, urged Satan; and if God should remit the punishment of sin, He would not be a God of truth and justice?...Understanding the character of God, knowing His goodness, Satan chose to follow his own selfish, independent will. This choice was final. There was no more that God could do to save him. But man was deceived; his mind was darkened by Satan's sophistry. The height and depth of the love of God he did not know. For him there was hope in a knowledge of God's love. By beholding His character we might be drawn back to God." *The Desire of Ages*

761.

"Through Jesus, God's mercy was manifested to men; but mercy does not set aside justice. The law reveals the attributes of God's character, and not a jot or tittle of it could be changed to meet man in his fallen condition. God did not change His law, but He sacrificed Himself, in Christ, for man's redemption. 'God was in Christ, reconciling the world unto Himself.' 2 Corinthians 5:19. The law requires righteousness,—a righteous life, a perfect character; and this man has not to give. He cannot meet the claims of God's holy law. But Christ, coming to the earth as man, lived a holy life, and developed a perfect character. These He offers as a free gift to all who will receive them. His life stands for the life of men. Thus they have remission of sins that are past, through the forbearance of God. More than this, Christ imbues men with the attributes of God. He builds up the human character after the similitude of the divine character, a goodly fabric of spiritual strength and beauty. Thus the very righteousness of the law is fulfilled in the believer in Christ. God can 'be just, and the justifier of him which believeth in Jesus.' Romans 3:26." *The Desire of Ages* 762.

"In the temple in heaven, the dwelling place of God, His throne is established in righteousness and judgment. In the most holy place is His law, the great rule of right by which all mankind are tested. The ark that enshrines the tables of the law is covered with the mercy seat, before which Christ pleads His blood in the sinner's behalf. Thus is represented the union of justice and mercy in the plan of human redemption. This union infinite wisdom alone could devise and infinite power accomplish; it is a union that fills all heaven with wonder and adoration. The cherubim of the earthly sanctuary, looking reverently down upon the mercy seat, represent the interest with which the heavenly host contemplate the work of redemption. This is the mystery of mercy into which angels desire to look—that God can be just while He justifies the repenting sinner and renews His intercourse with the fallen race; that Christ could stoop to raise unnumbered multitudes from the abyss of ruin and clothe them with the spotless garments of His own righteousness to unite with angels who have never fallen and to dwell forever in the presence of God." *The Great Controversy* 415. Love is God's united justice and mercy together. For how could God say He loves me if He did not fight to save me from the enemy of souls or forgive me when I fail?

When things are done wrong and I say, "that's not right! That's not fair!" Then I, a frail human, will start to consider revenge and this is wrath born out of anger. We all have a justice system in us and it is incredibly and amazingly strong. Teenagers have a superb ability to detect things that are unjust or hypocritical. In my life as a rebel girl, my number one sin was bitterness at the injustices I suffered. Additionally, we live in a culture that, if life is not fair, we struggle to resolve this in our own justice system. The relationship between my parents and my relationship toward

God was diseased with bitterness. I had a continual unresolved violation of my justice system and, like most teenagers, I noticed how unfair life was. But our God is not a fair God, He is a just God. When I fail to understand the difference between the fairness of man and the justice of God, I am doomed to become bitter.

The children of Israel spat the bitter water out and turned on Moses saying, "Moses! This isn't right! God should have given us the right kind of water! We have a violation of our justice system!" But God is just and we as humans are very unjust toward ourselves, each other, and toward God. Our justice system is flawed. We have two major problems with our justice system. One, our justice system is subjective: we only live in the moment. We cannot see the beginning from the end like God can thus, when we experience something happening in our life, we immediately fail to realize what God is trying to do in our life.

The attribute of God that gave Job the strength to endure hardship, discouragement, and suffering was the justice of God. "The LORD gave, and the LORD hath taken away; blessed be the name of the LORD." Job 1:21. When Job talked to his wife he said, "Thou speakest as one of the foolish women speaketh. What? shall we receive good at the hand of God, and shall we not receive evil? In all this Job sinned not with his lips." This means that Job may not have understood what was going on and he may have observed how unfair things were but He knew that God is just. My God will not do wrong. Justice is so important in our lives but we humans see things from the circumstances where we live and we will often find ourselves struggling to understand why God is allowing unfair things to happen to us. This is when we need to cry out to God to lead us "in the paths of righteousness for His name sake" so we can be like Job and declare "blessed be the name of the Lord."

Our second problem is that our human justice system is flawed. Put another way, what you think is right and what I think is right may not be what God thinks is right because the human condition is, "Every man did that which was right in his own eyes." Judges 21:25.

Bitterness, an unresolved violation of my justice system, can flow two ways. I can be bitter at God or I can be bitter at others around me. Being bitter at God may sound like this, "God, you gave me messed up parents that hurt me! God, you put me in the wrong body! God, I can't accept the way I look! God, I hate my siblings! God, why did You allow my business to fail?" Being bitter at others may sound like this, "What they did to me was wrong! What they said to me was wrong and it hurt me!"

After the children of Israel spat out the water and cried unto Moses saying, "what will we drink?" And Moses, "cried unto the Lord; and the Lord showed Moses a Tree." This tree is a picture of Calvary and Christ Jesus our Lord on the cross. Then the Lord had Moses, "cast into the waters, the waters were made sweet: there he made for them a statute and an ordinance, and there he proved them." When we have unresolved violations of our justice system, we need to go to the Tree of Calvary and see Jesus giving us His sacrifice of justice and mercy for us. If I go to Calvary and I look at the Tree that Jesus died upon and I remember what Jesus Christ did for me on that Tree no matter how bitter I may be, the Tree will make the situation sweet again.

Or maybe I have a problem with God, "God, I don't understand why You have allowed me to suffer through all of this. Why have You made me like this? Why did You give me my mother to deal with?" If I am questioning God, doubting His love, and verbally doubting God, I need to go to the Tree and watch Jesus Christ suffer and die for me to save me from the enemy and death. "Since he did not spare even his own Son but gave him up for us all, won't he also give us everything else?" Romans 8:32. I may struggle but I need to see Jesus Christ crying out in anguish for my personal sin, "My God, My God! Why have You forsaken Me?" Matthew 27:46.

"His flesh lacerated with stripes; those hands so often reached out in blessing, nailed to the wooden bars; those feet so tireless on ministries of love, spiked to the tree; that royal head pierced by the crown of thorns; those quivering lips shaped to the cry of woe. And all that He endured—the blood drops that flowed from His head, His hands, His feet, the agony that racked His frame, and the unutterable anguish that filled His soul at the hiding of His Father's face—speaks to each child of humanity, declaring, It is for me that the Son of God consents to bear this burden of guilt; for me He spoils the domain of death, and the gates of Paradise. He who stilled the angry waves and walked the foam-capped billows, who made devils tremble and disease flee, who opened the eyes and called forth the dead to life,—offers Himself upon the cross as a sacrifice, and this from love to me. He, the Sin Bearer, endures the wrath of divine justice, and for my sake becomes sin itself." *The Desire of Ages* 755. If you are struggling with something that God has allowed in your life or something someone else has done to you, go to the Tree of Calvary and say, "God, I don't understand why You allowed this but I know Your love for me. You loved me so much that You gave Your Son to suffer and die on that Tree of Calvary." When we realize what we have done to our Lord then we can forgive anyone what they have done to us. Go to the Tree!

I have done worse to God than what anyone has done to me. If we are struggling with a violation of our justice system then we need to realize the truth in Ephesians 4:32, "And be ye kind one to another, tenderhearted (compassionate), forgiving one another, even as God for Christ's sake hath forgiven you." Whenever we put the Cross of Calvary into a situation, the bitter water will be made sweet.

How does all of this relate to Ahithophel? That was a huge detour but a necessary one. Now this is all starting to come together. King David up to 2 Samuel is now the king of

Israel and wants to build a house for God and God says, "it's not going to be you but I will make a covenant with you that the temple will come from you." David has incredible victory over the enemies of Israel and then David brings Mephibosheth home. These are all incredible high points in the life of David and his kingdom is growing and expanding. Then we come upon David's sin with Bathsheba.

He sees Bathsheba bathing upon a rooftop and he sees that she is very beautiful to look upon, "And David sent and enquired after the woman. And one said, Is not this Bathsheba, the daughter of Eliam, the wife of Uriah the Hittite? And David sent messengers, and took her; and she came in unto him, and he lay with her;" 2 Samuel 11:3-4. Bathsheba conceived a child. We all know the story from there. David sent to Joab, his army general, to send for Uriah thinking that Uriah will come home and be with his wife so that this pregnancy could be played off as Uriah's offspring.

But Uriah will not rest and go home while his men are struggling though the hot violence of battle so Uriah stays near the palace expecting to go back to battle. David must cover his sin so he gives Uriah his own sealed death warrant to carry to Joab. Joab is ordered to send Uriah into the most violent sections of warfare with the Ammonites and then abandon him there. I can picture Uriah's shock and awe. He is a warrior fighting the enemy and his fellow comrades leave him to die. I am sure that he went down with a fight, swinging his sword, and feeling the sharpest wounds of betrayal.

David believes that his problem has now been solved. He takes Bathsheba, who is mourning her husband, and he marries her as she is carrying his child. Many people use David's story to excuse their own sexual impurity. "If David was a man after God's own heart then God forgives." Yes, God forgives and is always willing to save us to the uttermost but, David was by no means a man after God's own heart when he did this to Bathsheba. This was rape and murder and it should serve as a warning to all of us how close we can be to God yet still vulnerable to committing heinous acts.

"It was when David was pure, and walking in the counsel of God, that God called him a man after His own heart. When David departed from God, and stained his virtuous character by his crimes, he was no longer a man after God's own heart. God did not in the least degree justify him in his sins, but sent Nathan, His prophet, with dreadful denunciations to David because he had transgressed the commandment of the Lord." *Testimonies on Sexual Behavior, Adultery, and Divorce* 94. God never sanctions rape and murder.

Nathan is sent by God to David to carry out justice. All Israel was talking of the crimes committed against Bathsheba and Uriah. Nathan said, "There were two men in a certain town, one rich and the other poor. The rich man had a very large number of sheep and cattle, but the poor man had nothing except one little ewe lamb he had bought. He raised it, and it grew up with him and his children. It shared his food, drank from his cup and even slept in his arms. It was like a daughter to him. Now a traveler came to the rich man, but the rich man refrained from taking one of his own sheep or cattle to prepare a meal for the traveler who had come to him. Instead, he took the ewe lamb that belonged to the poor man and prepared it for the one who had come to him. David burned with anger against the man and said to Nathan, 'As surely as the Lord lives, the man who did this must die! He must pay for that lamb four times over, because he did such a thing and had no pity.'"

"Then Nathan said to David, 'You are the man! This is what the Lord, the God of Israel, says: 'I anointed you king over Israel, and I delivered you from the hand of Saul. I gave your master's house to you, and your master's wives into your arms. I gave you all Israel and Judah. And if all this had been too little, I would have given you even more. Why did you despise the word of the Lord by doing what is evil in his eyes? You struck down Uriah the Hittite with the sword and took his wife to be your own. You killed him with the sword of the Ammonites. Now, therefore, the sword will never depart from your house, because you despised me and took the wife of Uriah the Hittite to be your own.' This is what the Lord says: 'Out of your own household I am going to bring calamity on you. Before your very eyes I will take your wives and give them to one who is close to you, and he will sleep with your wives in broad daylight. You did it in secret, but I will do this thing in broad daylight before all Israel.' Then

David said to Nathan, 'I have sinned against the Lord.' And Nathan replied, 'The Lord has taken away your sin. You are not going to die. But because by doing this you have shown utter contempt for the Lord, the son born to you will die.'"

"After Nathan had gone home, the Lord struck the child that Uriah's wife had borne to David, and he became ill." 2 Samuel 12:1-15. The firstborn child born from David and Bathsheba died. We can choose our sin but we cannot choose our consequences and God will mercifully use consequences for sin to turn us from our evil course and to cure us from rebellion. God's forgiveness is not the absence of consequences but a restoration of the relationship with God that we have severed by our sin. David was forgiven by God for his terrible sin but the consequences of his sin would mar his life story. As the leader of his family, he was weak in this area and this led his family to suffer greatly and started a cycle of inherited tendencies toward evil.

David's family turns from peace and the knowledge of God to a soap opera. Whatever we do in moderation, our children will do in excess. "To the third and fourth generation of them that hate Me, says the Lord." Exodus 20:5. So the consequences of David's sin flow through the line when Amnon viciously rapes his beautiful and virgin half-sister Tamar which is Absalom's cherished and beloved sister too. Consequently, Absalom becomes bitter and he seeks out justice through vengeance and kills his half-brother and plots to overthrow King David, his father. All this started out because Absalom saw that his father, King David, never dealt justly with the rape of his sister, Tamar. Absalom is a bitter son and someone who has an unresolved violation of his justice system due to rape and abuse. But he is not alone. There are others in Israel and in David's court who also saw the unjust way that King David dealt with rape and abuse. It started with Bathsheba and now Tamar. Bitterness never improves on its own but, instead, insidiously grows.

We come to 2 Samuel 15 and Absalom is handsome and witty and he has stolen the hearts of the men of Israel. He is successful in taking the city of Jerusalem from his father, King David, and sets his father on the run. Absalom, now sitting on the thrown of his father, is still in the middle of this turbulent coup so he seeks the counsel of the wise men in the land. He starts to assemble his cabinet. "And Absalom sent for Ahithophel the Gilonite, David's counselor." Here enters the first mention of Ahithophel in the Bible. If you were Absalom and leading a coup, why would you go to the previous king's counselor to get him on your side? This would make no sense unless you knew something about him and his bitterness. Ahithophel will join you in this coup because Ahithophel, too, has an unresolved violation of his justice system like you do.

Thus, the story goes that Absalom finds Ahithophel and both are bitter. In my life, as you have read, bitter people find bitter people to hang out with. The peace and joy of others would rankle in my spirit and I sought out the company of those who matched or rivaled my spirit of rebellion. In other words, birds of a feather flock together. This is more than a saying but a Biblical principle, "can two walk together lest they be agreed?" When in rebellion this rebel girl needed other rebels to be with. If you have a son or daughter who seems okay but they have rebellious friends, then they may be hiding their rebellion for "no one can serve two masters. They will either love the one and hate the other." Matthew 6:24. There is no other sin that will attract more people together than bitterness because we have to find other people who will support our legal view of the injustice of God.

What has occurred in Ahithophel's life to cause him to be so bitter at David? Why would Absalom, in the middle of a coup, seek his counsel? We will soon find out. "And one told David, saying, Ahithophel is among the conspirators with Absalom. And David said, O Lord, I pray thee, turn the counsel of Ahithophel into foolishness." 2 Samuel 15:31. Hushai now enters the scene. He is also one of king David's counselors and is a blessing to the king. So David bid Hushai to return to Jerusalem and say to Absalom, "I will be your servant, O king; as I have been thy father's servant until now, then you may defeat the counsel of Ahithophel." 2 Samuel 15:34. Whatever Ahithophel counseled Absalom to do, King David told Hushai to counsel Absalom the exact opposite. Hushai goes back to Jerusalem as a secret agent and spy in the court of Absalom.

Now Absalom is in the full swing of his reign over Jerusalem. He has won. Absalom calls for his counselors and says, "Give counsel among you what we shall do. And Ahithophel said unto Absalom, Go in unto thy father's concubines, which he has left to keep the house; and all Israel will hear that you are abhorred of your father: then will the hands of all that are with you be strong. So they spread Absalom a tent upon the top of the house; and Absalom went in unto his father's concubines in the sight of all Israel." 2 Samuel 16:20-22.

Now Ahithophel is revealed. What happened upon that same rooftop? When King David was supposed to be out battling with his men and checking the borders, he instead stayed home because of pride. His conscience started to cause him great guilt so King David went out on the rooftop and saw Bathsheba from the same roof that Ahithophel builds a tent upon. What David tried to do in secret with Bathsheba will be done in front of all Israel. Absalom, so embittered by the rape of his sweet and innocent sister Tamar by Amnon, has now become an even worse rapist than his father and brother. We know that David repented for his sin to Bathsheba but now Absalom rapes ten women, the concubines of David, openly and in front of all Israel. Now Absalom has sanctioned rape as his first act as the king of Jerusalem. Why? Absalom is bitter and bitterness will always lead to the embittered stealing of what is rightfully God's, His vengeance.

What were the consequences brought upon King David by Nathan? We know that King David was to lose his life but he repented so God saved his life but the firstborn child from Bathsheba would die. The next consequence for his sin was that David's concubines would be shamed in front of all Israel. I think David was likely wondering, "what in the world does that mean?" He likely thought very little of it because, in his mind, what could be worse than losing a child? There is something worse than losing a child: losing another child to rebellion.

There was someone in the court that day when Nathan uttered his words of woe to King David. One among them heard the consequences that were to fall upon King David because of his crime against Bathsheba and Uriah and that was King David's counselor, Ahithophel. Ahithophel heard the consequences from the mouth of Nathan of what would happen. But, this was not why he was bitter and why he had an unresolved violation of his justice system.

There is nothing a bitter person craves more than justice. They want to see the wrongs done to them put right. This motivation is not wrong. God puts in us a craving for justice. This is so we will report and not keep secret what was done to us. We cannot carry burdens alone. Merely telling friends or brothers and sisters is not enough. Telling an equal is not reporting sexual assault. It must be reported to law enforcement. If you are reading this and you have not reported a sexual assault, everything else will be meaningless unless you come forward and report the wrong. You cannot fully forgive until you have brought the wrong to the light. It is our place to forgive but it is only God and the authority he has established that can pardon. Sexual assault is a life-changing event. We cannot fully recover from this trauma if we are keeping it a secret.

On the other end of the spectrum is continuing to hate our abuser or rapist for the rest of our lives. It is exacting out revenge meant for them on ourselves for eternity. We must be willing to surrender our hatred and forgive for our own sake and for Christ's sake. This has nothing to do with the abuser or rapist deserving forgiveness because they most likely do not and, in most cases, offenders will never repent for what they have done to us. This is not about them, this is about us.

Ahithophel craved justice. Ahithophel desired so badly to get back at David that he devised a way to get justice for Bathsheba and Uriah through more rape and more shame on the same rooftop.

Ahithophel was a very old man and, after having a lifetime of giving wise counsel, he says to Absalom in bitter foolishness, "Let me now choose out twelve thousand men, and I will arise and pursue after David this night: And I will come upon him while he is weary and weak handed, and will make him afraid and all the people that are with him shall flee; and I will strike down only the King and bring back all the people back to you...then everyone will be at peace." 2

Samuel 17:1-3. Absalom looks at this old man filled with bitter revenge who is volunteering to go against the mighty warrior king and David's mighty men and kill him. Though they share bitter hatred for King David, Ahithophel's bitterness has turned all his wisdom to foolish hatred and he can no longer give good direction to anyone. But why is Ahithophel still so bitter to want to kill David?

Hushai comes in and masterfully handles Absalom's pride and bitterness. Absalom goes to Hushai and says, "Ahithophel thinks that I ought to go and kill David now. Attack him now when he is vulnerable but the old man is so bitter that I don't know if I can trust him. What do you think I should do?" Hushai, as the secret and loyal agent of David says, "You don't want to do what Ahithophel says to do. You want to wait a while and that will bring more attention to you." Hushai plays Absalom like a harp. Absalom listens to Hushai instead of Ahithophel.

"And when Ahithophel saw that his counsel was not followed, he saddled his ass, and arose, and took himself home to his house, to his city, and put his household in order, and hung himself, and died, and was buried in the sepulcher of his father." 2 Samuel 17:23. This is an amazing perspective on bitterness. Ahithophel realizes that Absalom did not take his counsel and he goes back to his house and he commits suicide. Most suicide, but not all, is caused by bitterness. I know because I tried to kill myself so many times. It is the ultimate way to get perceived justice and say,

"God! You allowed all these things to happen in my life and now I am going to take my own life!" This is not only a Biblical picture of literal suicide but this is also the Biblical picture of spiritual suicide. The ultimate consequence of bitterness is spiritual and literal death by suicide. Many of us are spiritually dead. If we want revival, we must deal with the bitterness in our hearts.

Ahithophel had a son who was a loyal follower of King David and one of David's mighty men, a warrior, and his name was "Eliam the son of Ahithophel the Gilonite." 2 Samuel 23:34. Whatever bitterness Ahithophel had for King David we know that Eliam did not have bitterness or else he could not have been one of David's mighty men. When Absalom took Jerusalem and King David fled, Eliam went with David. Ahithophel was disloyal to David and stayed to exact revenge and get himself justice. Everything in our life will either make us bitter or we will get better in our walk with Christ. Ahithophel got bitter but his son got better. Ahithophel is a bitter man but Eliam decided to break the cycle of generational sin and stop the bitterness.

The question remains, why was Ahithophel so bitter? What happened to the family of Ahithophel that caused this unresolved violation of their justice system? In 2 Samuel 11:3 we find out that Bathsheba is Ahithophel's granddaughter and the daughter of Eliam. Wow! Ahithophel is Bathsheba's Grandpa. When all Israel is singing King David's praises, Ahithophel knows the truth and hatred starts to destroy his heart. The people say, "David has slain his ten thousands and he has defeated Goliath and he is great!" Ahithophel says, "No, he is not! If you only knew what has happened to me and what he did to my granddaughter! What David did to my family was wrong and I think King David is a wicked king and an immoral man." When all Jerusalem started to whisper about the soap opera going on between the King and Bathsheba, Ahithophel felt betrayed and he looked at King David and felt that justice had not been done. Even after Nathan exacted the justice of God on David, still Ahithophel would not surrender his bitterness and forgive because he wanted to have the justice of man over the justice of God.

Ahithophel became bitter over the crimes committed against Bathsheba and Uriah but Eliam did not. Why? Eliam took the same crime committed against Bathsheba and Uriah to the Tree and the promised Messiah to come. He understood the prophecies and the sacrificial system as a picture of Christ to come and he forgave King David for his sin.

If we have been victimized, the first step we will need to take is to call the proper authorities and report the crime to law enforcement. I reported crimes against me five to ten years later. It does not matter how long it has been. The proper authority to tell is usually your local law enforcement. You may not be guaranteed human justice but this is the first step to resolving a violation of your justice system the way God intended. Even if the statute of limitations has expired, the crime must still be reported because it establishes a pattern that can help other victims that come forward.

Forgiveness does not always mean restoration of a relationship, especially in cases of abuse. In most cases, abuse is generational and the very best thing you can do for someone is to stop the cycle and get away. Do not keep secrets. Forgiveness and restoration of a relationship are completely separate. In cases of abuse and assault, restoration is often impossible. Forgiveness does not mean a lack of consequences or a lack of justice but the opposite. Forgiveness means healing to our own souls. It is taking our own vengeance in the form of hatred and forgiving so that God can truly give His just consequences for sin to the offender. As long as we are bitter, we tie the hands of God to give out the just consequences for sin because God will not violate his word in knowing that we will rejoice in the torment of others.

If we have unresolved violations of our justice system, we can either be like Ahithophel or Eliam. We need to go to the Tree of Christ and say, "it's not right what they did. It's not right what happened in my life. But Lord, I know that you love me and what I did to You was much worse than what they did to me. God, I forgive them and I lay on You what happened to me. Please forgive me for the bitterness that I have held toward others and toward You." We are never so much like God or as Christ-like as when we forgive "the trespasses of others." If we want to see the impossible miracles take place in our lives, we need to forgive.

Ahithophel killed himself because of bitterness and he lost everything. If only he had forgiven King David, God would have given Ahithophel the greatest joy of his life. In many cases, the lives of the wise are prolonged and, had Ahithophel not cut short his own life, he would have been the counselor to his great-grandson and the fruit of the line of King David and Bathsheba: King Solomon the wisest and greatest counselor there has ever been besides Jesus Christ. He missed watching the little child grow in wisdom and stature and he missed seeing his great-grandson become the king. He missed what would have been the greatest joy of his life because he could not forgive.

John 3:16 says, "For God so loved the world that He gave His only begotten Son that whosoever believeth in Him will not perish but have everlasting life." The Greek word for perish means "suicide." By not accepting the gift of Jesus Christ, we are rejecting the Tree of Life and committing spiritual suicide. The result is the sad life of Ahithophel, missing our greatest joys and richest rewards to hang onto the burdens that we were never meant to carry.

What was done to me was not right. All these many things I did and were done to me are certainly wrong. For many years I was bitter at men and bitter at God but, today, I am walking in the light of forgiveness for those that have sinned against me and I choose to forgive. Some days forgiveness is a battle against my flesh and I must choose to go to the Tree every day. It is not always easy because hanging on to bitterness is easier and more natural to the human heart and it is the way that I have known for so many years but I have seen the blessings and miracles of letting go of bitterness.

"The Lord our God is merciful and forgiving, even though we have rebelled against him; For he has rescued us from the dominion of darkness and brought us into the kingdom of the Son He loves, in whom we have redemption, the forgiveness of sins. So forgive us our sins as we forgive those that sin against us and deliver us from the evils of bitter rebellion." Daniel 9:9, Colossians 1:13-14, Matthew 6:12. May God continue to make this once rebel girl's waters sweet again through the Tree of Christ and may He do the same for you too.

Chapter 35

Forked Tongue

As I walk with Christ, my life is now filled with so many more profound and meaningful events that I will continue to write about. There are so many more things I want to write in this book but I must end it here or a thousand pages will surely be in this one volume.

I had spent a great deal of time in the hot California sun picking up trash and doing road work for the work-release program until it was, at last, completed. I was, at the very end, somewhat sad that I would move on from this time in the sun walking with God and drenching myself in His word and His messages of eternal love. Soon, another check from my father's estate would be arriving in the mail and, this time, I had decided to use the money to allow my Lord to reclaim the years that the locusts had eaten and also, this time, to pay tithe.

I had spent many years destroying an already weakened body since birth. I knew that any job as a waitress would put me in the awful position of serving alcohol and I could not make any more provisions for the flesh so I worked to earn a phlebotomist license which was very easy to obtain and this put me in a more professional medical setting rather than bars.

At this time, I did not know how weak my immune

system had become. My chronic, congenital illness, unbeknown to me, was ripening and evolving as my immune system was failing. Putting myself in an environment where I was constantly around the kind of viruses and bacteria that can be fatal was not the wisest thing to do. But I did not know how sick I was and I had, as most victims of sexual assault do, spent a lifetime minimizing trauma and disbelieving myself. No matter how much I tried, I could not avoid or ignore the course that nature was taking. Whether I liked it or not or believed my own symptoms or not, I was sick and I was rapidly getting more and more sick.

With every day that I worked in a hospital setting, I was coming down with almost nightly fevers and my lymph glands were constantly swollen. My tonsils had been so infected for so long that they had developed ulcers. They were "kissing tonsils" and needed to be removed. I kept much of my daily struggle and symptoms quiet. I did not want anyone to know how bad things were getting for me. I was intent on working and earning money. I had grown to love working in a hospital setting so much that I was planning on going to nursing school. I never put two and two together that I was, in fact, the sickest I had ever been while working in a hospital. As the months went by, I was often fighting multiple infections at once on a monthly basis and my heart felt weak with each new infection. I was soon getting large injections of antibiotics to fight what I seemed unable to overcome.

I prayed for help and I felt impressed to register for a two-week cleanse at a lifestyle center located in the high desert of Southern California. Here they followed the health principles detailed in the Bible and the Spirit of Prophecy. This was just what I was looking for. It was somewhat expensive for a young girl such as I but the check from my father's estate would soon arrive and make it possible for me to stay at such a place and receive the kind of life-saving health principles that I continue to follow to this day.

Sometime before I was to attend the health facility, it was made very evident that I had opened a door into the occult that was not easily closed. I was often, and sometimes daily, the focus of Satan's fiery darts especially as I walked the blood-stained path of my Redeemer toward eternity. It had become my practice to fill my backpack with the very books that had changed my life, *The Desire of Ages* and *The Great Controversy*, and go into the places where the homeless, the addicts, the poor, and the suffering congregated to pass these out. I would share brief snippets of my testimony and tell how the Lord had saved me from the bondage of sin and suffering. I would and do still tell how these books comforted me through so much heartache and lifted up my eyes from the darkness of evil to the light of Christ. Often the Holy Spirit would embolden me as I felt no fear to approach gang members and dangerous persons to share the truth of my testimony and the words of life.

On many occasions, I would be surrounded by the

ghetto, fights, and danger on all sides but I felt my steps secured by a Mighty Hand and I walked through the danger unharmed and unafraid. This is the life and part of the fruits of the Christian faith. A submission, which is faith, to obey God's directive despite the fear for one's life and limb, threat of harm, or threat of loss in order to share life-giving water to the thirst-filled sufferers in the earth. Often, I would have the privilege of taking my son with me on these errands to give to the homeless and he delighted in the joy of giving. Doing these acts of kindness with my son began to restore our relationship and give my son a restored joy of salvation.

This particular time, before I headed off to the lifestyle center, I was sitting at a little table outside a cafe prepping my large book supply of *The Great Controversy*. This cafe was in the busy center of Redlands, California during the late summer morning to eat some breakfast before a long day. There were many people passing by on the brick sidewalk as I was struggling with my book bag. I needed to shove as many books into my Army-green backpack as I could. I was about to embark on the adventure of passing out these books to a neighboring homeless community and I did not like running out of the books prematurely.

If I could not find someone who was willing to go with me on my frequent errands of mercy, I would often go alone which was not wise. It was my practice to carry on my person a small stash of cash that I would save for such a time as this. I felt it un-Christian to merely pass out the books without offering some sort of relief for physical needs as well. This was Christ's way and I was working to align my ways with His as much as possible. This homeless community was a growing community in the park right in the middle of the wealthy and privileged historic district.

I had all my books arranged in such a fashion that my backpack was awkwardly bulging. It would be a heavy load to carry all on my own but I was used to my work-release program and the hot sun. This had strengthened me in untold ways and I could carry the heavy load of about fifteen to twenty very large books on my back. I sat back in my chair to eat before I set off. In my mind and spirit, I remembered the words spoken by Roger Morneau in *A Trip Into The Supernatural*. He, a former member of the Church of Satan, became a Seventh-day Adventist after the demons that he regularly conversed with warned him to stay away from these types of Seventh-day Adventist Christians because they had so much Biblical truth that defeats the deceptions of Satan. I also recalled the words of Ellen White who said that one of the most important books out of her vast collection was *The Great Controversy*. This book outlines the entire history of Christendom from the destruction of Jerusalem to the appearing of Christ, our eternal bliss shared there in heaven, and explains the mystery of Daniel and Revelation. It is most assuredly a weapon to strike a mighty blow against the enemy of souls.

As I sat at my little table to collect my thoughts and eat

the rest of my food, I felt a strange sense come over me. It was a sense that I was in danger. I have learned to listen to these senses of the still small voice and take care to pray and read my Bible to discern what these messages of warning may be. I have consistently been saved much grief by listening to these warnings. This day I had failed to pray and should not have been so ready to go it alone. Christians need other Christians to pray, share fellowship, and labor with. I was becoming isolated and unbalanced in my theology. Because of my all-or-nothing style of being in the world, I was in danger of becoming unnaturally extreme. I had heretofore cut my hair short and dyed it a very dark hue.

I had begun to, once again, hate my appearance and the attention it attracted. I was still blonde and more fresh-faced than ever and I felt that men and women could not see past my appearance to hear the message I was fervently trying to share. I was also feeling that much of the male attention I received was my own fault and it caused me great shame when a man stared at me with lust in his eyes. Though I was now walking with Christ, there were many times and still are when I wish I were invisible. There is a sad belief that any woman who is attractive has an easier life. Being attractive can be a curse as is any blessing from God that is not properly guided.

I would writhe under the cruel and hate-filled envy that women would thrust upon me. I would be filled with shame if men's eyes latched on to me like an unwanted pest that cannot be shaken off. To combat this, I would begin to fashion my style of dress and appearance after the style of the 1800s as was the custom of the church I was now attending. Even with skirts that reached down to my ankles and my hair shorn off and darkened, the problem of men's lust did not improve. I thought maybe the problem was deeper than my appearance but I failed to discern this as a problem with the lust of other men and nothing to do with me.

I was ever on a swinging pendulum of extremism and Christ wanted to bring me into the joy of reason, balance, and wisdom in seeing life through His eyes. He had made me to look this way. My Father loves color and variety in humans as much as in the flowers of the field and I was as I am, a bright yellow flower in my Father's world of color. The more we isolate ourselves, the stronger the tendency to become unbalanced. "It is not good that man should be alone." Genesis 2:18. I was determined to go it alone and ignore the Scripture in the sending out of the twelve that we should do the work of God in twos and not alone. I had come back from the dark side and the enemy will take any opportunity to cause us grief.

I sat back in my chair while enjoying the warm breeze and watched the people as they passed as I tried to understand why I now had a strange sense of anxiety. My eyes fastened on a man in the midst of the people passing by. He was a short distance off and walking on the sidewalk toward the cafe where I was seated. There was nothing particularly unusual about his appearance other than that he seemed to have a strange miasma around him. His eyes were darker than most. He wore a white t-shirt with shorts and, to most, would appear as any other skater dude in California. He tightly held my gaze as we unusually maintained eye contact with each other. I closely watched him as he began to approach my table. Just as he began to take steps so that he was directly across from me, he turned his head, let out a snarl in my direction, and a dark black forked snake's tongue fell out of his mouth. The tongue was too long to be a human's tongue and reached far past his chin. This was no human but a demon in human form.

I jumped in horror! I immediately looked around to see if any of the other people around us had seen this supernatural event and I saw that I was alone in my experience. I leaned forward to see where this being was headed and the man had vanished from the sidewalk. My hands went to my head as I immediately tried to make human sense of this totally bizarre and impossible occurrence. Even for someone who had a great deal of experience in the occult, it is still the human condition to disbelieve the supernatural realm. But, it is there. There is a war for our hearts and we cannot deny the existence of a loving Creator God who desires nothing more than to be our Father and an enemy who desires nothing more than to kill, rape, and destroy us.

Immediately, I knew that my practice of going it alone in this walk was putting me at risk in the very real fight with

Satan. I quickly grabbed my cell phone and, with shaking hands, dialed my mother's phone number to share with her that I was in hand-to-hand combat with the evil one and I asked her for prayer on the phone to which she, of course, freely and eloquently gave. When I hung up the phone, I called a few other Christian friends that I had recently met to ask for their prayers also. I am certain they assumed that I was mentally ill but, regardless of their assumptions about me, I desperately wanted prayer. I had never asked for prayer like this before but I was sure that, if I did not, I was risking my safety and the success of my mission to pass out books.

Perhaps I should have postponed my mission until I was not alone but accompanied by another but I was not willing, this time, to let Satan intimidate me into giving up. I knew that I was passing out the kind of material that made all of evil tremble with the fear of Christ. Indeed, Satan was trying to stop me from meeting the people I met that day. I will never forget the recently homeless couple that I met in the park. I gave them money to help their situation and I gave them the books. They were precious to me as they lapped up the words of life like it was everything to them. I hope and pray that the next time I see them will be in heaven.

I had delved into the dark arts and Satan was not simply willing to let this rebel girl slip from his grasp without a fight and I would need the prayers of my Christian brothers and sisters to aid me in the daily battles with evil. Yes, we have the power of Christ in every situation to rebuke and command our adversary, but we also have the added benefit and weapon of our warfare to the pulling down of strongholds in the combined prayers of the faithful. If you are fighting a battle with sin and Satan, you need the prayers of your parents, your pastor, your spouse, your children, and/or your church to aid you in the battle. By associating with other Christians, I was brought to the last story I will tell in this book and a critical step in my new walk with Christ.

Chapter 36

Down to the Jacuzzi

In a Christian community of church, I was now able to steadily grow in the natural order of things. There were now others around me to put a check on my tendencies to become very extreme. The very best person to help me stay on the perfect path of peace at the time was my mother. She, too, had strayed from Christianity and, with my new-found faith, she and her husband were encouraged to return to church. This was encouraging to me though I was learning that simply returning to church does not change well-established sinful traits of character. In fact, church is often a cover for the worst and most detestable secret sin. There has to be a true heart change which is acquired by the humbling of one's self to those we have wronged.

The wheat must grow with the tares so one cannot avoid church simply because there are sinful people there. We must not look at the flawed and sinful people that comprise the Christian church and let it discourage us from Christianity because, if we only look at the people, we will become disillusioned. We must look to Christ and ask Him to lead us into that sweet communion with other Christ-loving Christians.

I especially want to point out that, at this time in my life and around the time of my marriage, I was desiring to have true peace with my mother and maintain a state of forgiveness toward her. I knew that, at this time in my life, this was the right thing to do. Now, I do not have a relationship with my mother although I hold a daily attitude of humility and forgiveness toward her. I forgive her because of Christ. She will likely never be repentant for the pain she has caused in my life. I pray that she one day will be repentant as I am toward her for the rebellion I demonstrated toward her. In most, if not all, cases of abuse and assault, we will have to maintain forgiveness for our offender from afar while they proudly maintain their innocence. The instances where a victim can maintain any kind of contact are rare and I do not suggest it. In the rare case that one's abuser is repentant, one must carefully observe the life to look for the fruit of repentance that comes with time before jumping into contact.

In the story of Joseph and his brothers, Joseph carefully watched his brothers' behavior and waited to see if, under pressure, they would return to their old ways. Joseph would only restore the relationship when, "he had seen in his brothers the fruits of true repentance." *Patriarchs and Prophets* 230. His brothers had demonstrated a true willingness to lay down self for the damage they had caused. They truly mourned the evil they had caused and were not just mourning the consequences of their sin. True repentance will look like an abuser willingly telling authorities and law enforcement all that they have done. They will not minimize the pain they have caused their victims. They will not look for opportunities to be around the kind of population wherein lies their temptation but run from the kind of temptation that tempts them.

Ellen White writes in *Testimonies on Sexual Behavior, Adultery, and Divorce*, a book that every victim should read to realign the compass that gets so skewed by sexual offenses, that the truly repentant will not seek to lessen their guilt nor excuse it. "But David makes no excuse. Justice points to the broken tablets of the law and draws her sword against the transgressor. All apologies or excuses for sin are of no value with God...David utters no complaint...(he says) I will not murmur. I deserve His judgments and will submit to it all." *Testimonies on Sexual Behavior, Adultery, and Divorce* 176 and 180.

David was not a man after God's own heart after he raped Bathsheba, murdered Uriah, and consequently became a weak and iniquitous father. But, through repentance, the blood of Christ and His righteousness, David can become a man after God's own heart again. This fact, that we know that King David will be in heaven, should encourage all of us that Christ's sacrifice can save and change anyone.

Sadly, this true repentance is rarely seen in abusers. It must be noted that, even though Joseph and his father, Jacob, noted true repentance in the brothers, this did not remove the terrible consequences of their crimes. Reuben, who demonstrated a spirit of repentance toward Joseph, was also guilty of sexual sin with his father's concubine in his younger years. Even though repentant, this did not lessen the consequences of his sin. I have had many heart-breaking consequences for my earlier sins and, though I am repentant, this has only given me the grace to willingly accept these consequences as blessings rather than expecting them to be completely removed. We can choose our sin but we cannot choose our consequences. We cannot lessen the necessary consequences leading others to repentance and we cannot keep secrets to hold off the consequences of justice.

Here I would like to add another sidebar. I in no way underestimate the difficulty one will face when forgiving an offender nor am I writing that this will be an easy thing to do. Sometimes, especially around the time of year when certain offenses occurred, I have to pray daily for my offenders and pray for the grace to forgive. If we really desire our offender to "get what is coming to them" and for our offenders to experience the consequences of their crime, we must forgive them.

This is for two reasons. In forgiving our offender, we lose the hatred we hold for them. When a victim is hateful they can appear less credible to authorities, juries, and others in positions of leadership. This is because bitterness can cause us to be blind and blind rage is rarely believable. Sex crimes are most often a "he said, she said" situation. Most sex crimes also lack physical evidence. The authorities usually have to rely solely on victim and witness statements. A victim that is purposing to be forgiving is more sympathetic to the authorities and to juries and, thus, more easily believed in general.

The second reason is because, when we forgive, we free the hands of God to enact justice. Again, this comes from the story of Joseph who was a type of Christ. God wants to bring good out of evil. God in no way brings abuse and assaults into our lives. It is Satan and sinful humans that bring this kind of evil into the world.

"Fear not, he said; for am I in the place of God? But as for you, ye thought evil against me; but God meant it unto good, to bring to pass, as it is this day, to save much people alive....Joseph, through his bondage in Egypt, became a saviour to his father's family; yet this fact did not lessen the guilt of his brothers. So the crucifixion of Christ by His enemies made Him the Redeemer of mankind, the Saviour of the fallen race, and Ruler over the whole world; but the crime of His murderers was just as heinous as though God's providential hand had not controlled events for His own glory and the good of man." *Patriarchs and Prophets* 238-239. Why did God look upon Christ's murderers as though nothing good had come out of the situation? It was because Christ had forgiven them as evidenced by His prayer, "Father, forgive them, for they know not what they do." Luke 23:34.

Some victims are afraid to say that good was brought out of evil because it might somehow lessen the wrong that was done to us. We feel that we need to vigilantly hold our place as accuser or no one will know how exceedingly evil were the acts done to us. If we do not hold on to the details, it will be forgotten and it might happen again. But this is not right. When we forgive offenders and choose to see the blessing and purpose in the evil done to us, this allows God to see the evil that was done to us with the eyes of justice as if no good was present at all. God is freed by our forgiveness and mercy to give out justice. When we purpose to find the good in a situation and we refuse to get bitter, we are giving God the freedom to deal with evil.

My mother started to sexualize my two-year-old daughter by watching sexually explicit movies with full frontal nudity in her presence. When my husband protested this, she publicly mocked my husband for being "immature" when sexually explicit material was being viewed in their home. At that moment, as a new mother of my own daughter, I was called to stop the cycle and not repeat it. I knew it was my solemn responsibility to protect my own children from the same harmful things that terribly wounded my life and to flee from lust.

I decided to establish some well thought out and reasonable rules for my mother to follow. These rules were to protect my children from abuse. Because these rules brought up painful things in my mother's marriage and her own childhood, she used these rules as a reason to disown me. Later, I would report her husband to my church conference and the police for inappropriate conduct and sexual harassment while I was in her home to truly come to a place where I would love and forgive both my mother and her husband and hold no bitterness toward them. I daily pray and cry out for them. I am called to forgive those who offend against me so that I may obtain forgiveness but we are never called to condone and participate in sin. Never.

Being rejected, yet again, by my mother has caused me pain as I experienced becoming parentless in an earthly sense. This is the one singular situation where I have been called to suffer for righteousness sake. In essentially all other situations, I was suffering because of my own unwilling attitude to be humble and obey the Lord which is my tendency. I have to be careful that old habits of rebellion do not rear their ugly head again. I do this by holding careful and thoughtful communion with the Lord every single day. Yet, I am despised by my family for protecting my children from the same abuse that nearly destroyed my life. I am willing to suffer this to stop the cycle and I hope that you, too, are willing to stop the cycles that are destroying our families today.

Though parentless in an earthly sense, I have experienced a greater fathering from my Heavenly Father as never before. He has become my physical, emotional, and spiritual parent in every way possible and I see the fact that my mother has disowned me and reviled me as a huge blessing because it means that my God has taken me up as His own daughter and I have experienced greater blessings because of it. As I have reiterated over and over, forgiveness does not equal restoration. Forgiveness should never mean condoning abuse or sexual assault. We forgive our enemies and offenders because of God's goodness and mercy toward us. I reiterate this often because some victims rationalize contact with their abuser as some sort of twisted gesture of forgiveness and then continue to put themselves in situations where they continue to receive abuse and make provision for the flesh. It becomes the norm and comfortable to be abused. Victims take the blame on their shoulders when it is not their burden of blame to carry at all.

The day came when I was to go to the lifestyle center. I was excited but a bit nervous as I knew that I would be sharing with a few the details and specifics of my past drug use and past promiscuous lifestyle. I felt sure that this would secure me a greater portion of whatever detox methods they used. I was dirty and, like Peter, my soul's cry was, "clean all of me Lord!" I drove myself and arrived at this beautiful desert oasis outside Yucca Valley. I noted that I was the youngest participant and most had been longtime Adventists. Admittedly, I was a bit disappointed when I saw that there would be no other young people like me but providence had prepared the way for my arrival.

Maybe the lifestyle center is accustomed to incredibly profound and meaningful sessions of bliss. At that time, I was not used to every meal and every moment of the day being clear-minded and full of Christ like it is in my life today. Attending the lifestyle center at the same time was the evangelist and missionary, Bill Liversidge. Bill was this short and stocky fireball from Australia. He had bright blonde hair and the largest winning grin that a man can have. He was not happy unless he was sharing the gospel with someone. Anyone that knew him will know that his stories are rousing stories of faith and a call to action. He has many stories of hand-to-hand combat with the supernatural in the witchcraft-filled land of New Guinea and he filled my heart with stories of victory over evil in Christ.

Through long walks and raw and vegan dinners with Bill, the participants at the lifestyle center received the gospel message as it is in an already-won victory in Christ for over two weeks. This was more than chance. The hand of God had led this former rebel girl to the lifestyle center where this colorful and outgoing storyteller, Bill Liversidge, shared his many experiences of defeating evil through the Word of God and by the blood of Christ. I was more than encouraged. I was equipped with what I would need to go forward in the already-won victory of Jesus Christ and, once and for all, lead a life of victory over evil.

It was the last Sabbath at the lifestyle center. The next day we were all to leave this place of peace, healing, and cleansing. I was feeling better than I had ever felt. I had sweated and eliminated all the toxins out of my body. At one point when I was in the sauna, I could actually smell the smell of methamphetamine coming off of me and, when I looked down into the bowl of ice and water I was using to ring out my sweat rag, it had turned dark brown from my toxic sweat. When God wants to change us, He does not do it half way. I felt like a new person. Still, something was nagging at me.

I had spent all this time with Bill and he was constantly dropping the suggestion of baptism to which I would reply, "Bill, I was baptized when I was twelve." He knew from the hints that I kept dropping that there had been a drastic and extreme falling away after my baptism.

In his thick Aussie accent he said, "but you need to be re-baptized, my dear, and commissioned."

"Commissioned?" I inquired as we walked the track behind the lifestyle center.

He smiled with delight and said, "I will be baptizing someone else on Sabbath. Why don't you get re-baptized and, when you come out of that water all cleansed of your sins and past life, then I'll commission you to go forward and share it."

"I'll think about it, Bill." Think about it, I did. That evening at dinner I told the proprietors of the lifestyle center, Mike Casey and his wife Tanya, that I was going to get re-baptized too. They responded with a loud cheer of celebration as I am sure is a mere taste of what the angels do when one sinner repents.

Baptism is a public declaration, a marriage ceremony of sorts, and afterward begins the work of living for Christ. After the baptism begins the work of redemption which is the work of a lifetime. "Our Redeemer has opened the way so that the most sinful, the most needy, the most oppressed and despised, may find access to the Father." *The Desire of Ages* 113. Baptism is a rebirth and our public declaration and acceptance of His redemption. "It is an outward sign, showing that they are sensible that they should be children of God by acknowledging that they believe in Jesus Christ as their Saviour and will henceforth live for Christ." *Child Guidance* 499.

I sat in my room, trembling with the solemnity that was lacking at my first baptism when I was twelve. I knew that the baptismal pool water could possibly turn black from the gross amount of sin that I needed cleansing from but I felt the Holy Spirit leading me to disregard those thoughts that were tempting me to deem myself too tainted and too dirty to come to Jesus. I knew now that those were lies and I wanted to go down into that watery death to rise again as a new person.

Tanya knocked on my bedroom door and offered me just what I needed. She gave a white robe to wear over my black bathing suit and I was glad to not be going to my own baptism in scant clothing but covered in pure white. I put the robe on and walked out the sliding glass door to the jacuzzi just as Bill was wading into waste deep water. He lifted his hands to pray and about ten people surrounded that little jacuzzi appropriately singing the hymn, "I Surrender All."

I waded into the water. I knew not to expect any supernatural sign of acceptance from God but to take the ordinance of baptism in the pure and simple faith of a child. I knew just what I wanted to envision as I went down into the water and came back out again. God had already given it to me. I imagined myself standing in the courts of heaven with the words, "Rebel Girl," over me. My Father and my friend standing next to me and my Father and my judge in front me with a gavel in His hand. As I was submerged down into the water, I pictured all the men that had failed me and abused me, my mother, the rapes, the drugs, the partying, the sin and rebellion, and my brokenness. As I was coming up out of that cleansing water, I envisioned my Father bringing the gavel down and the word, "Pardoned," now in place of, "Rebel Girl." I was forgiven and I would never be fatherless again.

Made in the USA
Columbia, SC
16 May 2019